Emptiness Yoga
The Middle Way Consequence School

Emptiness Yoga
The Middle Way Consequence School

Jeffrey Hopkins

Edited by Joe B. Wilson

Snow Lion Publications
Ithaca, New York USA

Snow Lion Publications
P.O.Box 6483
Ithaca, New York 14851
USA

Printed in USA

Library of Congress Catalogue Number 86-6484

ISBN 0-937938-31-9 Paper
ISBN 0-937938-36-X Cloth

Library of Congress Cataloging-in-Publication Data

Hopkins, Jeffrey.
  Emptiness yoga.

  Bibliography: p.
  Includes index.
  1. Prāsaṅgika. 2. Buddhism — China — Tibet — Doctrines.
I. Title.
BQ7477.H67 1987   294.3'42   86-6484
ISBN 0-937938-31-9 Paper
ISBN 0-937938-36-X Cloth

Contents

Preface

In 1973, when I was finishing my doctoral dissertation, *Meditation on Emptiness*, I also was meeting with a small number of fellow graduate students in the University of Wisconsin Buddhist Studies program to give commentary on a similar text on emptiness. My intent was to open up the topic — to make it accessible — both by supplying necessary doctrinal points and by making suggestions on how to enter into this world-view in a personal, confrontational sense. Although alive to culture-bound dimensions of religious teachings, I by no means consider that all religious teachings are so culture bound that they have no applicability to persons of another culture. Rather, I hold that religious and philosophical teachings must be confronted in a personal way, within knowledge of a culture, gradually constructing the world-view of a system and allowing it to resonate with one's inner being. I hope, therefore, that when I present perspectives of Tibetan Buddhists, no one will make the mistake of thinking that I am putting these forward as necessarily *the* preferable world-view.

Fascinated and challenged by Tibetan Buddhist teachings, I try in this book to bring the doctrine of emptiness down from the clouds of abstract discourse to everyday relevance. This relevance, however, is by no means easy to absorb; rather, the system takes meaning within an extensive, intricate, highly developed architecture of religious doctrine and practice. Thus, the book not only speaks to nitty-gritty problems but also simultaneously stimulates the grand metaphysical imagination, the latter for me being reminiscent of a story of an imaginary land. My studies with the tantric abbot Ngawang Lekden and several other lamas have molded the style of my presentation of this imaginary land of metaphysical insight; he could tell any story, whether historical or philosophical, as if he knew every detail from intimate experience. Thus, some sections of my commentary may sound as if I am speaking from profound realization, standing at the gates of the city of emptiness beckoning the reader to enter. Actually, as should be clear from the more mundane examples found in my commentary, I am an enthusiastic story-teller who has struggled to bring what many pass off as abstract prattle down to a level of personal relevance.

To do this, I take much that is presented in the system for granted and thus do not probe claims of historical accuracy, etc. The focus, therefore, is on intimate encounter with a world-view that questions the basic appearance of objects — their appearance as if they exist in their own right — and thus challenges emotions built on the presumed correct appearance of persons and other objects. It is at once a beautiful vision and a harrowing emotional challenge.

The two threads of my commentary on the Tibetan text — once scattered pieces of background information setting the scene have been explained in the first several chapters — are to draw the reader into playful but serious consideration of the implications of emptiness and to consider typical objections, sometimes seemingly bizarre but quite understandable such as "You're not trying to say that I wouldn't feel it if someone cut off my ear, are you?" I hope that the approach — externalized as advice to others on how to probe the meaning of the doctrine of emptiness but actually a reminder of my own attempts to internalize these doctrines — is of use to those who consider religion and philosophy as something more than abstract formalism or idle speculation.

The lectures were edited into book form by Professor Joe B. Wilson of the University of North Carolina at Wilmington. After his laborious and painstaking work, I again edited the text twice, adding an initial chapter on the biography of Jang-gya, the author of the Tibetan text that serves as the basis for commentary and adding footnotes. Without Joe Wilson's attention, the work never would have been brought to completion.

The book could not have been attempted without the kind teaching that I have received on an almost day to day basis from many Tibetan lamas over the last twenty-three years. Close dialogue with them has brought these doctrines, which otherwise would have seem to be mere public stances, to life.

I would like to thank Dr. Elizabeth S. Napper for making copious editorial suggestions and both Gareth Sparham and Guy M. Newland for typing several chapters. As usual, Professor Richard B. Martin of Alderman Library at the University of Virginia has been of immense bibliographical assistance.

Charlottesville   Jeffrey Hopkins
Virginia

Technical Note

The names of Tibetan authors and orders are given in "essay phonetics" for the sake of easy pronunciation; for a discussion of the system used, see the Technical Note at the beginning of *Meditation on Emptiness*, pp. 19-22. The marks for high tones are given in only the first chapter and the notes. Transliteration of Tibetan in parentheses and in the glossary is done in accordance with a system devised by Turrell Wylie; see "A Standard System of Tibetan Transcription", *Harvard Journal of Asiatic Studies*, Vol. 22, 1959, pp. 261-7. For the names of Indian scholars and systems used in the body of the text, *ch*, *sh*, and *ṣh* are used instead of the more usual *c*, *ś*, and *ṣ* for the sake of easy pronunciation by non-specialists.

In the translation portion, with the first occurrence of each title, the Tibetan and, if appropriate, Sanskrit are given in a note. The full Tibetan and Sanskrit titles are to be found in the bibliography, which is arranged alphabetically according to the English titles of sūtras and tantras and according to the authors of other works. Often Jang-ḡya refers only to the title or the author of a work, whereas both are given in translation to obviate the need for checking back and forth. Jang-ḡya's text, without commentary, is given in a separate section in the back of the book; six chapter headings have been added to facilitate understanding. In order to aid in finding the material in the Tibetan text corresponding to the translation, an outline of Jang-g̱ya's text is given at the beginning of the translation section with corresponding page numbers in the commentary, translation, and Tibetan text, and a list of page numbers going from the Tibetan to the English is provided in an appendix. For a glossary of English, Sanskrit, and Tibetan terms, see *Meditation on Emptiness*, pp. 737-753.

The footnotes often identify where corresponding topics are discussed in *Meditation on Emptiness* for those who want more elaboration.

1 Jang-gya's Biography

We shall be considering a text on schools of tenets written in Tibetan by the great Mongolian scholar and adept Jang-gya Rol-bay-dor-jay,[1] also known as Ye-shay-den-bay-drön-may,[2] 1717-1786.[3] Jang-gya was born on the tenth day of the first month[4] of the Fire Female Bird year in the north-easternmost region of Tibet — in the western Lotus district[5] of the four districts of Lang-dru[6] in the Am-do[7] province north of Dzong-ka.[8] His father, Gu-ru-den-dzin,[9] was of nomadic Mongolian stock; he was a village priest and a subject of Chi-gya-bon-bo[10] and thus was known as Chi-gya-tsang-ba,[11] the priest of Chi-gya. His mother was called Bu-gyi.[12] Around the time of his birth, his parents had unusual dreams such as the mother's dreaming that her body had become golden, and many unusual signs occurred.

Since the officials of the Gön-lung-jam-ba-ling Monastery[13] and the Jang-gya estate were uncertain as to where the former Jang-gya, Jang-gya-nga-wang-lo-sang-chö-den,[14] had taken rebirth, they asked for assistance from the aged scholar and adept Jam-yang-shay-ba, who had been tutored by Jang-gya-nga-wang-lo-sang-chö-den. Jam-yang-shay-ba indicated that Jang-gya had taken rebirth near an area that was high in the north, the entrance to which

15

was from the north through a ravine, and other means of divination were in agreement. Jam-ȳang-shay-ḃa further told them to take articles belonging to the former Ĵang-ḡya, along with others similar to them, to test the candidates and then to advise him on what happened.

When the son of Chi-ḡya-tsang-ḃa and Bu-ḡyi was asked to identify the articles, the boy took the right ones, saying, "This is mine." Jam-ȳang-shay-ḃa was informed of what occurred, and after many qualms were pursued in detail and despite the son of a wealthy Mongol prince being put forward as a candidate, in the end the boy, whose name at that time was Drak-ḃa-sö-nam,[15] was recognized as the reincarnation of Ĵang-ḡya-nga-ŵang-lo-sang-chö-den. The biographer, Tu-ḡen-lo-sang-chö-ḡyi-nyi-ma,[16] criticizes the politicking and corruption that frequently accompany the identification of reincarnations — the import being that this reincarnation, in his opinion, was chosen properly.

At age three, on the first day of the fifth month of the Iron Mouse year (1720), the new Ĵang-ḡya began the trip to his monastery, Gön-lung-jam-ḃa-ling, and on the tenth day of the sixth month arrived to be welcomed, by more than three thousand monks, in the midst of offerings, incense, flowers, the sounds of conch, and music. He was adorned with the saffron robes of one who has left the householder life and conducted to the rooms of his previous incarnation. Receiving the vows of a novice monk from Chu-sang Rin-ḃo-chay,[17] he was given the name Nga-ŵang-chö-ḡyi-drak-ḃa-den-ḃay-gyel-tsen.[18] Conducted to his residential compound within the monastery complex, the boy assumed the cross-legged posture on the fearless lion-throne.

At age six, Ĵang-ḡya received the vows of a full-fledged novice monk from Chu-sang Rin-ḃo-chay. In the same year, 1723, a prince of Kokonor, Ḋen-dzin-ching-wang[19] revolted against China, whereupon a punitive expedition was sent to Am-do province. A number of monasteries in the area were put to the torch, and the monks of those monasteries were slaughtered, presumably because of their aid to

the rebels. Then, in 1724, a Chinese unit approached Gön-
lung-jam-ɓa-ling; a group of panicking monks attempted
resistance but were defeated; the monastery was ordered
burnt to the ground. As Gene Smith's condensation of the
biography says:[20]

> The guardians of the young Jang-ǧya[21] managed to
> flee with their charge into the wilderness. The
> Emperor, in the meantime, had ordered that the
> young incarnation should not be harmed but should
> be conducted to China via Zi-ling as a "guest". The
> Chinese coerced the Jang-ǧya refugees into surren-
> der through threats against the populace of the area.
> The seven year old Jang-ǧya was taken to the tent of
> Yo'u Cang-jun, the joint commander of the expedi-
> tion, who accused him immediately of treason. The
> plucky lad stood up with wit against the great com-
> mander to the amusement of the assembled officers.

In this way, Jang-ǧya came at age seven to begin his monastic studies in Beijing. There he was tutored by renowned
Tibetan scholars including the second Tu-ǧen, Nga-wang-
chö-ǧyi-gya-tso[22] (whose reincarnation was to become Jang-
ǧya's biographer) who, by 1729, obtained permission to
rebuild the Gön-lung-jam-ɓa-ling Monastery, the attack on
which had impelled Jang-ǧya's escape and eventual arrival
in Beijing.

Though the Emperor Yung-cheng (reigning 1722-1735)
was slightly interested in Buddhism, he favored indige-
nous Chinese Buddhism over the Tibetan variety, and even
though the seventeenth son of Emperor K'ang-hsi (the
second Manchu Emperor who died in 1722), Keng-ze Chin-
wang, also known as Yun-li Prince Kuo (1697-1738), was a
great patron of Tibetan Buddhism and a scholar of some
ability, he favored the older sects and was openly hostile to
Jang-ǧya's Ge-luk-ɓa sect. Jang-ǧya understood that for
the Ge-luk-ɓa sect to thrive in China, the teachings of the
founder, Dzong-ka-ɓa, would have to be translated into

Manchu, Chinese, and Mongolian; hence, he began studying these languages. One of his fellow students was the
fourth son of the Yung-cheng Emperor, who became a close
friend and later became the Emperor Ch'ien-lung. This
friendship became the key to Jang-ḡya's tremendous influence in China, Manchuria, Mongolia, and Tibet.

Jang-ḡya studied Chinese Buddhism, coming to the conclusion that the system expounded in Tibet by the Chinese
abbot Hwa-shang Mahāyāna in the famous debate at Sam-
yay around 775[23] no longer existed in China. He found the
most widespread view of Chinese Buddhism to be like that
of the Mind Only School and to have great similarities with
the Tibetan Shi-jay-ba School.[24] Jang-ḡya identified Pa-
dam-ba-sang-gyay,[25] the Indian founder of Shi-jay-ba, as
Bodhidharma.[26]

Jang-ḡya's teachers wanted a Ge-luk-ba appointed as his
tutor, but Prince Keng-ze Chin-wang, the seventeenth son
of the previous Emperor, wanted a Ñying-ma-ba. Eventually, the Ge-luk-ba teachers were able to frustrate the prince's
plans, and Lo-sang-den-bay-nyi-ma,[27] Throne-Holder of
Gan-den, which is the highest position within the Ge-luk-ba
order, was invited to Beijing. The twelfth son (probably of
Emperor K'ang-hsi) became a faithful patron of the Ge-luk-
ba sect, and relations with Keng-ze Chin-wang deteriorated
rapidly. During this period Jang-ḡya was invested with the
same imperial privileges and titles that his previous incarnation had held — Teacher of the Empire. Thus, by age
seventeen he had assumed a considerable role.

In 1734 (or 1735), the Emperor ordered Prince Keng-ze
Chin-wang and Jang-ḡya to accompany the Seventh Dalai
Lama, Ḡel-sang-gya-tso,[28] who had been in exile for seven
years at Gar-tar[29] (which is not far from Li-tang in Kam
Province) back to Hla-sa. The previous Emperor, K'ang-
hsi, had acted as the protector of the Seventh Dalai Lama
who was installed in 1720 after a series of events
including:[30]

1 the murder of the Regent, with the moral support of the

Emperor, in 1706 by Hla-sang[31] Khan — the Mongol
so-called "King of Tibet" — and a small army

2 recognition of Hla-sang as Governor by the Emperor

3 the capture of the wayward Sixth Dalai Lama and his
death (murder?) on the way to China, with the Emperor
ordering his body to be dishonored

4 Hla-sang's attempt to install one of his own protégés as
the Dalai Lama

5 the murder of Hla-sang by the Mongol Dzungars who
had supported the former Regent and wanted to install,
as the Seventh Dalai Lama, a child discovered in Li-
tang[32] and now living at Ḡum-bum[33] Monastery in far
eastern Tibet under Manchu protection due to the political foresight of the Emperor

6 a failed Chinese attempt with 7,000 soldiers to oust the
Dzungars

7 the retreat of the Dzungars due to repeated attacks by a
loyalist of Hla-sang, Po-hla-s̄ö-nam-d̄op-gyay,[34] with
Tibetan supporters

8 the arrival of a new Chinese army which was welcomed as
friend and deliverer from the hated Dzungars who had
plundered widely, the Chinese being seen as restoring the
proper Dalai Lama who was brought from his supervised
stay in Ḡum-bum Monastery.

In 1721, Emperor K'ang Hsi decreed the status of Tibet as
a tributary vassal, but Tibetans have persisted in character-
izing the relationship in terms of "patron and priest". In
any case, this was a period of the establishment of Chinese
influence in Tibet even though, through skillful government, direct Chinese interference was kept to a minimum.
   When K'ang Hsi died in 1722, his son and new Emperor,
Yung-cheng, withdrew the powerful Chinese presence from
Hla-s̄a, after which internal troubles gradually erupted in
civil war but were eventually settled before the Chinese
army arrived. In 1728, imperial representatives called
"ambans" with a strong presence of Chinese troops were
established in Hla-s̄a (this practice continuing until 1911), and

Po-hla-sö-nam-dop-gyay organized a government that ruled for twenty years. About Po-hla-sö-nam-dop-gyay, Snellgrove and Richardson report in their *Cultural History of Tibet:*[35]

> In his relations with China he shrewdly saw that as long as Tibetan policy did not endanger the wider interests of China in Central Asia, Chinese over-lordship in Tibet could be reduced to a mere formality so far as internal affairs and even Tibetan relations with her Himalayan neighbours were concerned. Thus the substance of Tibetan independence was preserved thanks to Chinese protection but without fear of Chinese interference. His success was complete; he won the full confidence of the Emperor by his competence and reliability, and in Lhasa his dealings with the Ambans, as the Chinese representatives were called, were firm but friendly, so that they remained little more than observers and diplomatic agents of their Emperor.

Po-hla appears to have done with the Chinese what the Fifth Dalai Lama did with the Mongols — used their power but controlled their influence.

During the civil war of 1727-1728, the Seventh Dalai Lama and his family were suspected of troublemaking by backing the losing side. Thus, the Dalai Lama was banished to Gar-tar in eastern Tibet despite his original Chinese backing, and the Emperor, before Po-hla was in control of the situation, made the Paṇ-chen Lama sovereign of his region to counterbalance the power of the Dalai Lamas, who, as Snellgrove and Richardson say, "never regarded it as conveying anything more than the subordinate position similar to that of a local hereditary ruler."[36] By 1734, however, with Po-hla in firm control, the Dalai Lama could be brought back to Hla-sa with the Emperor's escort which included Jang-ġya. He met the Dalai Lama at Gar-tar on the twenty-third day of the eleventh month, 1734.

During more than a year (which is called "three years" in Tibetan reckoning because it took place during the years of 1734, 1735, and 1736) in Central Tibet, Jang-gya heard many teachings from the Dalai Lama on the stages of the path, tantric systems, and so forth. Though his previous incarnation had entered the Go-mang College of Dre-bung Monastic University, he did not enter into a particular monastic college; instead, he visited several of the monastic colleges in the Hla-sa area, making vast offerings and hearing teachings from many lamas. At the end of 1735, he took full ordination at Dra-shi-hlun-bo[37] from the aged Pan-chen Lama Lo-sang-ye-shay,[38] at which time he received the name Ye-shay-den-bay-drön-may. However, with the news of the sudden death of the Yung-cheng Emperor on October 8, 1735, Jang-gya returned to Hla-sa and then to Beijing in 1736.

In Beijing, his friend, the fourth son of the late Emperor, now reigned as Emperor Ch'ien-lung, the reign lasting from 1735-1796. The Emperor appointed him the lama of the seal.[39] This highest of positions for a Tibetan lama in the Chinese court had been held by Tu-gen, who by now had passed away, and although the rank had passed to Tri-chen Lo-sang-den-bay-nyi-ma, the latter surrendered it to Jang-gya at the Emperor's request.

The Emperor asked that Jang-gya undertake the project of translating the canon of Indian commentaries[40] from Tibetan into Mongolian. The word of the Buddha[41] had already been translated into Mongolian, but the canonical commentaries had not; in preparation for the project, Jang-gya compiled an extensive bilingual glossary[42] for the sake of introducing consistency in translation equivalents, given the wide variations in Mongolian dialects. With imperial patronage, the dictionary project was undertaken by what must have been a great number of scholars since they completed this monumental task in one year beginning at the end of 1741. The task of translating the canonical commentaries was completed in the first month of summer in 1749, having taken roughly seven years.

In 1744, the Emperor and Jang-ğya established a teaching monastery in Beijing. The first of its kind in the imperial capital, the monastery had four teaching colleges for philosophy, tantra, medicine, and other studies. The monastery had five hundred monks and was called Gan-den-jin-chak-ling.[43] (Eventually it came to be called the "Lama Temple" in accordance with the Chinese policy to brand Tibetan Buddhism "Lamaism" as if it were not Buddhism.) Jang-ğya requested the Seventh Dalai Lama to appoint a high and learned incarnation as abbot of Gan-den-jin-chak-ling; Da-tsak-jay-drung Lo-sang-bel-den[44] was appointed, and Jang-ğya continued his studies with him.

During this period, Jang-ğya taught the Emperor frequently. In 1745 (or 1746), Jang-ğya bestowed the Highest Yoga Tantra initiation of Chakrasaṃvara on the Emperor, who, at that point, had been learning Tibetan for several years. During the initiation, the Emperor observed the convention of taking a seat lower than the guru, prostrating, kneeling, and so forth at the appropriate times. The biographer, Tu-ğen-lo-sang-chö-ğyi-nyi-ma, recalls the Sa-ğya master Pak-ba's[45] initiation of Kublai Khan into the *Hevajra Tantra*[46] and speculates that both Kublai Khan and the Ch'ien-lung Emperor were incarnations of Mañjushrī.[47] Jang-ğya's linguistic abilities had advanced to the point where he was able to preach in Chinese, Manchu, and Mongolian; these skills were undoubtedly keys to his influence and effectiveness.

In 1748, the eleven year old reincarnation of the second Tu-ğen, Tu-ğen-lo-sang-chö-ğyi-nyi-ma (who was to become Jang-ğya's biographer), invited Jang-ğya to visit their monastery, Gön-lung-jam-ba-ling, the burning of which had impelled the subsequent events of his life — his escape, being brought to China, becoming a friend of the Emperor to be, etc. Asking the Emperor for leave, Jang-ğya was told to wait until the next year when he would be authorized by imperial decree to arrange for additional restoration and repairs not only at Gön-lung-jam-ba-ling Monastery but also at Gum-bum[48] and Dzen-bo-gön.[49] This was authorized as promised, and during the visit in 1749, Jang-gya conducted the ceremony of full ordination for the reincarnation of Jam-yang-shay-ba; the latter, it will be remembered, had helped in identifying him as the reincarnation of the previous Jang-gya. Jang-gya named him Gön-chok-jik-may-wang-bo;[50] he also taught him a version of the stages of the path to enlightenment and conferred tantric permissions for meditative cultivation of certain deities. Gön-chok-jik-may-wang-bo was to become Jang-gya's main student.

After only two months at his own monastery, Jang-gya returned to China. The period from 1749-1757 saw a monastery for Manchu monks founded west of the imperial palace, the translation of the liturgy into Manchu, and a school of Tibetan studies established within the beaurocracy. The Emperor wanted to introduce the Highest Yoga Tantra practice of Kālachakra into China and asked Jang-gya to arrange it. Jang-gya requested an expert in the *Kālachakra Tantra* from the Seventh Dalai Lama. He sent Gel-sang-tsay-wang,[51] who had escaped the beatings of his teacher, Rin-chen-hlun-drup,[52] and gone to Hla-sa where he met and impressed the Dalai Lama with his learning in the Kālachakra system, no doubt owed to his teacher. During this period, Jang-gya also figured in political events, pleading with the Emperor to lighten the punishment of the murderers of the ambans (the Emperor's ambassadors), pacifying a rebellion in Khalkha through lama-to-lama influence, and sending a mission to Tibet.

Upon the arrival in Beijing in 1757 of the news of the Seventh Dalai Lama's death, the Emperor sent Jang-gya to Hla-sa to help in searching for and correctly identifying his reincarnation. The Emperor indicated that it was hard for him to let Jang-gya Hu-tok-tu[53] (a title for high Mongolian lamas) go so far away but he was allowing it since it was for a very important purpose of the Tibetan teaching; however, after completing his task, Jang-ǧya must return immediately. Among those who joined the party travelling to Hla-ša at the May-dro-ru-tok[54] hot springs were Gön-chok-jik-may-ẇang-ɓo (the reincarnation of Jam-ȳang-shay-ɓa) and Tu-ǧen-lo-sang-chö-ǧyi-nyi-ma (Jang-ǧya's biographer to be); the company made the trip most pleasant with stimulating conversation.

They arrived in Hla-ša during the twelfth Tibetan month, which would be January of 1758, where they were received by the regent and welcomed by a huge assembly of high and low lamas, etc., with all the typical Tibetan formalities. Jang-ǧya was first taken to the Hla-ša Cathedral where he paid homage to the central image, Jo-wo Rin-ɓo-chay, and then was installed in a government residence, newly prepared for his visit, near the Cathedral. During this period, Jang-ǧya and Tu-ǧen visited all the great monasteries around Hla-ša, making offerings and so forth. At the request of the Tantric College of Lower Hla-ša, Jang-ǧya conferred the Guhyasamāja initiation upon six thousand monks and also was invited to give teachings at the various monastic colleges.

While visiting Pur-bu-jok Jam-ɓa Rin-ɓo-chay[55] (whom he had avoided during his earlier visit to Hla-ša due to that lama's having supported a rival to the Seventh Dalai Lama) for a day, Jang-ǧya, despite his failing sight, noticed an image of Padmasaṃbhava in the lama's chapel that the lama himself had not noticed before, and thus the lama was amazed at his visitor's vision. Jang-ǧya's biographer Tu-ǧen-lo-sang-chö-ǧyi-nyi-ma also describes a period when he was receiving teaching from Jang-ǧya along with Gön-chok-jik-may-ẇang-ɓo and another reincarnation; Jang-ǧya's sight was so poor that he had someone else read his works aloud, but nonetheless Jang-ǧya demonstrated an amazing ability to, without error, keep up with and even keep ahead of the reader. Jang-ǧya also amazed them by being able to identify the quality and origin of statues as well as the type of metal from which they were made merely by passing his hand over them. He was also able to identify the artistic quality of scroll paintings merely by waving his hand in front of them. Awe-struck, one philosopher made the joke that according to his textbook it was contradictory for a Buddha to be able to realize all things with his body consciousness and yet, in fact, not be able to see with his eyes.

In the fourth month of 1758, Jang-gya travelled to Drashi-hlun-bo to meet the young Third Pan-chen Lama, Belden-ye-shay[56] and ask him for help in identifying the reincarnation of the Dalai Lama. After Jang-gya's return to Hla-sa, the Pan-chen Lama also was invited there in connection with identifying the new Dalai Lama. Upon Jang-gya's request, the Pan-chen Lama performed the entire Kālachakra initiation with all the phases of preparation including construction of a mandala of colored sands, the seven initiations in the pattern of childhood, the four high initiations, the four greatly high initiations, and the initiation of a vajra-master great lord.

At that time, there were three strong candidates for recognition as the Dalai Lama, and since the five great oracles could not agree, Jang-gya recommended that the Pan-chen Lama make the recognition. Jang-gya's recommendation was adopted, and the Pan-chen Lama chose the candidate from his own Dzang[57] Province. Jang-gya performed the consecration of the reliquary of the late Dalai Lama and wrote the official biography at the unanimous request of the regent and a great number of officials.[58]

With the reincarnation of the Dalai Lama decided, Jang-gya returned to Beijing in 1760, where he chose a replacement for the abbot of the Beijing monastery who had died in his absence (the replacement also died soon thereafter). During this period, the Emperor called Tu-gen-lo-sang-chö-gyi-nyi-ma to Beijing where teacher and student (Jang-gya and Tu-gen) met again. Also, in accordance with the Emperor's order, Jang-gya ordained the third Jay-dzun-dam-ba[59] of Kalkha, naming him Ye-shay-den-bay-nyi-ma.[60] During this period, he also composed a biography of the Throne-Holder of Gan-den, Tri-chen Nga-wang-chok-den,[61] a tutor of the Seventh Dalai Lama.

In 1763, upon hearing the news of his father's death, Jang-gya immediately performed the rite of Achala for seven days and, in accordance with advice from divination, had the *Liberation Sūtra* and the *Lotus Sūtra* written out in gold ink as a means of purifying his father's karmic obstructions. In connection with his father's death, the Emperor allowed Jang-gya a short vist to Am-do Province and his original monastery, Gön-lung-jam-ba-ling, which Jang-gya visited by way of Mongolia. On the way to the monastery, he was afforded a supreme escort and welcoming by the high and low lamas of the area as well as clergy and others. At the monastery, Jang-gya made offerings of tea and money for the monks and offered a set of fifty scroll paintings of the biography of Shākyamuni Buddha to the monastery in general.

While at Gön-lung-jam-ba-ling Monastery, Jang-gya went into strict retreat, meditating on the deities Vajrabhairava and Mahākāla. His success was such that he had various meditative visions, and an offering of beer boiled in its bowl in front of him, becoming bubbly and giving off a fragrant odor. Also, one day when he was meditating, he asked his attendant to bring an offering bowl to him; he put the bell-metal bowl upside down on top of his head and then meditated for a short time. When he gave it back to the attendant, it was so hot that it was as if it had just come out of fire. Jang-gya smiled, saying, "This is my sign of achievement."

When he left the retreat, he taught for fifteen days the Fifth Dalai Lama's *Sacred Word of Mañjushrī*,[62] instructions on the stages of the path, in great detail to two thousand five hundred persons, clerics and lay, with Gön-chok-jik-may-wang-bo (Jam-yang-shay-ba's reincarnation) as the patron at the head of the assembly of listeners. As Gön-chok-jik-may-wang-bo had just retired as abbot, he asked Jang-gya to assume the post, and upon the repeated urging of the monastery, Jang-gya became the new abbot. In that position, he newly instituted the study of Dharmakīrti's *Commentary on (Dignāga's) "Compendium of [Teachings on] Valid Cognition"*,[63] first using the additional textbook literature of Jam-yang-shay-ba and then that of Jay-dzun Chö-gyi-gyel-tsen[64] of the Še-ra Jay College of Hla-ša. Jang-gya also arranged for a new carving of the textbook literature composed by Jay-dzun Chö-gyi-gyel-tsen, with the carving to be done in Beijing and the blocks to be stored at Gön-lung-jam-ba-ling Monastery. Then, having appointed another lama in his place, in 1764 he returned to Beijing by way of Mongolia.

Gön-chok-jik-may-wang-bo also went to Beijing where he received teachings from Jang-gya on practice of the path according to the oral lineage of En-ša-ba.[65] During this period, Gön-chok-jik-may-wang-bo wrote a commentary on Jang-gya's *Song of the View*,[66] which Jang-gya highly praised. Gön-chok-jik-may-wang-bo could not find the books he needed for the commentary, so he recited the text three times daily and made prayers to Jang-gya, with the result that when he thought about the meaning, it suddenly flashed to mind. Gön-chok-jik-may-wang-bo reported that such was the power of Jang-gya's compassion and blessings. Also during this time in Beijing, Jang-gya gave, at Gön-chok-jik-may-wang-bo's request, the oral transmission and explanation of Dzong-ka-ba's *Lamp Illuminating (Nāgārjuna's) "Five Stages"*[67] on the stages of the path in the *Guhyasamāja Tantra*.

In Tibet, Dra-di-ge-shay[68] was promoting one of the unsuccessful candidates for Dalai Lama as the genuine Dalai Lama and had him installed as such at the Geu-tsang[69] retreat. A number of people became convinced, and reports reached the ambans (the Emperor's ambassadors) who informed Beijing. The Emperor wanted to order both the candidate and Dra-di-ge-shay to Beijing for punishment, but Jang-gya intervened, suggesting that the boy be put into the service of the Paṇ-chen Lama at Dra-shi-hlun-бo, away from his promoter. The Emperor accepted the suggestion, and the schemers were saved. Jang-g̱ya gave similar, timely advice when such a situation arose with respect to the claims of someone vying to replace the Jay-dzun-dam-ба incarnation.

In 1767, Jang-g̱ya began a yearly practice of spending the fourth through eighth months in solitary retreat at Wu-t'ai-shan, the Five Peaked Mountain Range,[70] a place sacred to Mañjushrī. From 1768-1771, his activities include performing potent rituals to help subdue tribes of the Yunnan border area, consecrating in 1770 ten thousand statues of Amitāyus to mark the Emperor's sixtieth birthday, and consecrating a model of the Potala, the Dalai Lama's famous palace at Hla-sa, at Jehol after giving the monastic vows to the Jay-dzun-dam-ба. Between 1772 and 1779, he organized, at the Emperor's request, the translation of the word of Buddha into Manchu, laboriously checking each volume and submitting it to the Emperor for his approval. The Emperor also ordered that Jang-g̱ya translate the *Shū-raṅgama Sūtra* from Chinese into Tibetan. Then, when the Emperor's mother, Empress Hsiao-sheng (born 1693), passed away in 1777, Jang-g̱ya performed the funeral rites for seven days. As Samuel M. Grupper says:[71]

> The fact that her funeral was presided over by Tibe-tan clergy led by the most prominent lama resident in China would seem to indicate that Tibetan Buddhism was an integral matter of faith in Man-chu ruling circles independent of the requirements of showing toleration of the beliefs of the Manchus' Mongol allies.

In many respects, the Ch'ien-lung Emperor appears to have been a devout Tibetan Buddhist.

Upon imperial invitation, the Third Paṇ-chen Lama came to Jehol in 1780 where he was housed in the newly completed model of Dra-shi-hlun-бo that had been special-ly built for his visit. The Paṇ-chen Lama and Jang-g̱ya wintered with the imperial Court in Beijing, but the Paṇ-chen Lama contracted a fatal case of smallpox; Jang-gya conducted the relics to Ch'ing-hai.

In 1781, the Emperor and Jang-gya visited the temple of Tin-ting-phu, a few days west of Beijing, where Jang-gya was asked to perform the consecration rites of an image of the thousand-armed Avalokiteshvara that had recently been repaired by imperial order. Also, between 1781 and 1786, Jang-gya performed rituals propitiating a powerful mountain deity that controlled the headwaters of the Yellow River where the Ch'ien-lung Emperor had ordered dikes to be constructed for flood control. The Emperor expressed his appreciation for his lama by ordering a lavish seventieth birthday celebration; in the Tibeto-Mongolian way of reckoning age, the years in which one has lived are counted, and thus in 1786 Jang-gya was seeing his seventieth year. A throne of red sandalwood adorned with precious metals and stones was provided for him during the celebration which lasted many days.

Though Jang-gya usually went to Wu-t'ai-shan in the fourth month for his annual retreat, the Emperor decided to move there in the third month of 1786 and commanded the lama to be in attendance. Prior to departure from Beijing, Jang-gya made unusual, extensive offerings and prayers at all of the temples. Then, at Wu-t'ai-shan Jang-gya headed an assembly of prayers in front of an image of Mañjushrī; the Emperor joined the prayers, which were conducted like those at the annual great prayer festival at Hla-sa. The biographer comments that their coming together in such a special place for a final great festival of prayer-wishes itself was an effect of their having made such wishes and having had such altruistic intentions over a long period of lives and also served as a means of creating in the future the dependent-arising of similar helpful activity for the sake of sentient beings.

On his way to Wu-t'ai-shan, Jang-gya's health had begun to fail, and at Wu-t'ai-shan, despite the efforts of Chinese and Tibetan doctors, on the second day of the fourth month of 1786 he assumed at sunset the cross-legged posture with hands set in the pose of meditative equipoise. He ceased breathing around dusk, "manifesting the clear light of death as the Truth Body of Buddha".

In his will, Jang-ġya requested that his body not be preserved in a reliquary of gold and silver but that his remains be burned, the ashes being used to make small, impressed images which could be put in a copper reliquary in a temple at Wu-t'ai-shan. However, the Emperor, upon being presented with Jang-ġya's will in Beijing, refused, saying that he had not deviated from his lama's word in anything but would not follow him now on this point since there was no vajra master in that area fit for conducting a cremation rite and since it was unthinkable to cremate such a lama's remains which were like a wish-granting jewel. Instead, he ordered that a gold and silver reliquary be constructed at Wu-t'ai-shan for the remains as an object of veneration for all beings; approximately seven thousand ounces of gold were used. Fearing that with the changes of time the monument, which was also decorated with precious substances, might be disturbed by sinful beings, the Emperor had an extensive room constructed deep in stone under where Jang-ġya had given teachings, and the reliquary was installed there on a throne of precious substances, surrounded by inconceivable articles of offering, with the remains being put inside it on the twenty-fourth day of the sixth month along with precious relics from great beings. Since the monument was intended as an object of veneration for gods and humans until the end of this eon, the Emperor had a temple built on top of it, fit for the eyes of all beings, high and low, with a stone reliquary in it. The blessed salt that was used to dry and preserve Jang-ġya's remains was put in the stone monument.

FAMOUS STUDENTS

The last chapter of Jang-ġya's biography gives a long list of his noteworthy students. These include:

seven who were in a mutual relationship with him as both
   teacher and student,
his chief disciple Gön-chok-jik-may-wang-bo,
twelve incarnations from central Tibet,
eleven incarnations from eastern Tibet,
nineteen incarnations from Mongolia,
seven abbots of Gan-den,
twenty-three abbots of other monasteries in central Tibet,
seventeen abbots and scholars of eastern Tibet,
seven scholars from Beijing,
eight famous scholars from Mongolia,
five translators from Beijing,
twelve meditative ascetics,
three attendants,
and seven advanced students.[72]

No matter how exaggerated this list may be in the sense of
merely including the names of lamas who received tantric
initiation from him, it indicates the far-reaching effects of
Jang-gya Rol-bay-dor-jay's activities throughout the vast
region of Tibetan Buddhism.

   One of his students, having cultivated love and compassion in meditation, attained such great experience that he
remained crying about the plight of sentient beings. One
day, the student, so poor that he had nothing to offer, cut
off his own finger and offered it to Jang-gya in a mandala
offering at Wu-t'ai-shan. Later, when Jang-gya was staying
in a retreat, he repeated the mantra of Achala and burned
the finger in fire, whereupon it gave off just a fragrant odor.
The student also wanted to offer his body as a lamp by
wrapping it in cloth soaked with oil and burning himself in
front of an image of Mañjushrî, but Jang-gya refused him
permission; so, the student went south to Ninghai, where
he made many prayer petitions, finally offering his body to
Avalokiteshvara and ending his life. The biographer reports
that Jang-gya had many students who realized emptiness.

JANG-GYA'S WRITINGS

An early turning point of Jang-ġya's life was the burning of his monastery by the Chinese when he was seven years old. This caused him to flee, whereupon the Emperor commanded him to Beijing where he spent most of the remainder of his life. There, he eventually gained a position of considerable influence, helping to restore his monastery and, through his linguistic abilities and close association with the subsequent Ch'ien-lung Emperor, fostering the Buddhist teaching in general by his translations into Mongolian and Manchurian and also spreading the teachings of Dzong-ka-ba in China, Mongolia, and Manchuria.

Despite his vast travels and activities, it is important to note that Jang-ġya remained in retreat four months each year for most of his last nineteen years and over his life composed approximately two hundred works in eight volumes.[73] His writings include biographies of the Seventh Dalai Lama and of a Throne-Holder of Gan-den, Tri-chen Nga-ŵang-chok-den; a commentary on Dzong-ka-ba's *Praise of Dependent-Arising;* a commentary on the *Prayers of Samantabhadra;* a short grammar;[74] rites of guru yoga; booklets on Wu-t'ai-shan and Kvan-lo-ye; a Tibeto-Mongol dictionary;[75] a history of the Sandalwood Image and inventories of the White Stūpa on the Western Gate at Beijing; many prayers including one in connection with death, intermediate state, and rebirth and another on examining the signs of death; many short tantric texts related with specific deities; texts of instruction on the view of the Middle Way; essays on points of training in altruism; epistolary essays in answer to students' questions; texts on exorcism of self-centeredness; and iconographies of three hundred gods and three hundred sixty gods.[76] A text on the stages of the path was dictated by Jang-ġya after being visited by Mañjushrī in a dream on the first day of the ninth month of 1785 in Po'u-ting-phu'u. He had been in retreat at Wu-t'ai-shan and at night on the seventeenth day of the sixth month had had a profound mystical experience, the dream coming after the period of seclusion was over.[77]

Among the eight volumes of Jang-gya's Collected Works, his longest work and philosophical masterpiece is the *Clear Exposition of the Presentations of Tenets, Beautiful Ornament for the Meru of the Subduer's Teaching*,[78] more commonly known as the *Presentation of Tenets*.[79] Jang-gya wrote it during the period between 1736 and 1746; Gene Smith[80] speculates that "the initial stimulus was perhaps his interest in Vijnanavada [the Mind Only School] preserved by the Chinese Buddhist schools," noting that Jang-gya completed this chapter first.

In the *Presentation of Tenets*, Jang-gya discusses the major tenets of the non-Buddhist schools and the four Buddhist schools of India as well as briefly treating mantra. Though he clearly draws from, and occasionally criticizes, Jam-yang-shay-ba's *Great Exposition of Tenets*,[81] his style is very different. Whereas Jam-yang-shay-ba's work presents a wide-ranging anthology of literature on tenets, often cited in abbreviated form, with commentary that is sometimes cryptic due to its brevity and complexity, Jang-gya gives a more free-flowing discussion of many issues. Also, whereas Jam-yang-shay-ba kept the works of Dzong-ka-ba (the founder of his order, the Ge-luk-ba sect) more in the background, Jang-gya puts Dzong-ka-ba in the foreground, most likely because, with his position of enormous influence in Beijing, he was introducing the doctrines of Dzong-ka-ba to the region as a viable form of Buddhism.

Jang-gya frequently refers to Dzong-ka-ba as the "Foremost" (*rje*), a term commonly used in Tibetan for a great religious leader which takes on special significance here since it is limited in usage almost entirely to Dzong-ka-ba. In the section translated in this book, Jang-gya calls him "Foremost"[82] three times, "Foremost Father"[83] five times, "Foremost Great Being"[84] eleven times, "Foremost Lama"[85] twice, "Foremost Omniscient"[86] nine times, "Foremost Omniscient Father"[87] once, and "Omniscient Father" once.[88] The term "Omniscient" is used rather loosely in Tibet, even sometimes for learned persons whom a scholar is refuting, but in this text its nearly exclusive usage for Dzong-ka-b̄a takes on a sense of promoting and glorifying a central personage who has interpreted Buddha's teaching for a particular age. J̄ang-ḡya definitely is exploring and trying to determine Dzong-ka-b̄a's thought, within the implicit understanding that the great figure's writings, due to his penetration of the teaching, provide access to what otherwise would be impenetrably arcane. It is clear that from J̄ang-ḡya's viewpoint Dzong-ka-b̄a's scholarship and yogic insight have provided access to the profound realizations of the founder, Buddha, as well as the main Indian interpreters of the doctrine of emptiness, Nāgārjuna, Buddhapālita, Chandrakīrti, and Shāntideva.

In the section discussed here, J̄ang-ḡya cites Dzong-ka-b̄a's works twenty-three times[89] whereas Jam-ȳang-shay-b̄a, in the corresponding section in his *Great Exposition of Tenets*, cites Dzong-ka-b̄a only eleven times despite his far greater emphasis on the citation of sources.[90] A reason for the disparity may be that Jam-ȳang-shay-b̄a, while similarly devoted to probing Dzong-ka-b̄a's thought, is more concerned with exploring the founder's sources within an atmosphere of Dzong-ka-b̄a's works being accepted as a high authority for this age whereas J̄ang-ḡya, living and writing in Beijing, is concerned with establishing Dzong-ka-b̄a as just such a figure.

The introductory nature of J̄ang-ḡya's exposition is a reason for its clarity, but J̄ang-ḡya by no means gives a simplistic presentation for the sake of clarity. Rather, he frequently introduces the reader to complex issues but does so within abbreviating many minor points to which Jam-ȳang-shay-b̄a gives major attention, such as the formation of the Sanskrit term for Buddha's cardinal doctrine of dependent-arising, *pratītyasamutpāda*. The two texts — the first by Jam-ȳang-shay-b̄a, who helped in the process of locating the J̄ang-ḡya reincarnation, and the second by that reincarnation, J̄ang-ḡya Rol-b̄ay-dor-jay himself, who became the teacher of Jam-ȳang-shay-ba's reincarnation, Gön-chok-jik-may-w̄ang-bo (who also wrote a short text on the schools of tenets)[91] — complement each other in that Jam-ȳang-shay-ba's attention to detail often makes Jang-ǧya's abbreviations of such points more accessible and Jang-ǧya's generous presentation of the great issues often puts Jam-ȳang-shay-ba's vast array of information in perspective.[92] Jang-ǧya shows his practical orientation not only in his issue-directed exposition but also in his frequent refrains when, as will be seen below, he criticizes both those who attempt to meditate without having studied the great issues and those who rattle on about points of doctrine without applying themselves to meditation.

Let us turn to Jang-ǧya's exposition of what is considered in Tibet to be the highest insight into the nature of phenomena and the means of release from suffering, the view of the emptiness of inherent existence as presented in the Middle Way Consequence School.[93] I will give explanation as gleaned from oral and written traditions of Tibetan Buddhism and, occasionally, from my own attempts over the last twenty-three years to probe and to internalize the meaning. These comments are at the margin, and Jang-ǧya's text is indented. Since much background information must be given before the topics start to take on their own impetus, the first several chapters are primarily concerned with identifying major landmarks within a world-view, after which it becomes feasible to function within that world-view, confronting the harrowing and liberating implications of an emptiness of inherent existence that is in total opposition to ingrained afflictive emotions and is the foundation of transformation into altruistic effectiveness.

2 Consequentialists

The title of this section of Jang-gya's text is:

BRIEF EXPRESSION OF THE SYSTEM OF
THE GLORIOUS MIDDLE WAY
CONSEQUENCE SCHOOL, SUPREME
SUMMIT OF ALL SCHOOLS OF TENETS,
BEARING THE SUBDUER'S OWN SYSTEM

Buddhists are those who, from the depths of the heart, accept the Three Jewels as their sources of refuge within an understanding of what they are. The Three Jewels are: Buddha, who shows where one can go for refuge; his Doctrine, the true cessations and true paths that are the actual refuge; and the Spiritual Community, who aid in achieving refuge. Proponents of Buddhist tenets, in addition to being Buddhists, assert the four seals that testify to a doctrine's being Buddhist:

All products are impermanent.
All contaminated things are miserable.
All phenomena are selfless.
Nirvana is peace.

Jang-gya's text centers on the Middle Way Consequence School's assertion of the four seals.[94]

The Subduer is Shākyamuni Buddha who taught four

schools of tenets — or, more literally, established conclusions[95] — based on the capacities of different trainees. The four are the two Lesser Vehicle[96] schools — the Great Exposition School and the Sūtra School — and two Great Vehicle schools — the Mind Only School and the Middle Way School.[97] Their tenets, no matter how much they may differ, are "established conclusions" in the sense that they are established for the minds of those who hold them and will not, at least for the time being, be forsaken for something else.[98] In Tibet, the Middle Way School of tenets is considered almost universally to be the highest, and when the Middle Way School is divided into the Autonomy School and the Consequence School, the Consequence School is considered to be the higher, representing the actual thought of Buddha.

The presentation of four schools — the first two Lesser Vehicle and the latter two Great Vehicle — is used as a device for ordering the many philosophical positions of Indian forms of Buddhism. Of course, the actual history was not so neat; the presentation of schools of tenets is not primarily intended to be an historically oriented depiction but rather to provide a framework for stimulating the metaphysical imagination with a variety of opposing views so that the nature of phenomena can be more easily penetrated. All desire, hatred, enmity, jealousy, and so forth are seen as relying on a false estimation of the nature of oneself, other persons, and other phenomena; therefore, penetration of reality is at the heart of the practice of purification in that realization of the actual nature of things serves to undermine all afflictive emotions. The aim is to emerge as a source of help and happiness for other beings, who are viewed as close friends wandering in a prison of cyclic repetition of birth, aging, sickness, and death.

The four schools are divided by way of their view of selflessness, the two Lesser Vehicle schools presenting only a selflessness of persons and the two Great Vehicle schools presenting also a selflessness of other phenomena. The supreme of all these views is considered to be that of the Middle Way Consequence School.

[The explanation of the Consequence School] is in two parts: definition and assertions of tenets.

DEFINITION OF A CONSEQUENTIALIST

The means of positing, or definition of, a Consequentialist is:

> a Proponent of the Middle Way School who asserts that it is not necessary to establish the modes of a reason from the viewpoint of the common appearance of the subject [of a debate] to non-mistaken valid cognitions of both disputants through the force of an objective mode of subsistence of things, but rather that an inferential consciousness cognizing selflessness is generated by a reason which has the three modes and which, leading only from the other party's assertions, is approved by that very other party.

"Middle Way School", in terms of the name, refers to one who follows a middle way between the extremes of reification and annihilation. Proponents of the Middle Way School avoid the extreme of reification by rejecting all assertions of any truly existent phenomena and avoid the extreme of annihilation through rejecting all assertions that things do not exist at all, that they do not exist even conventionally. "Things" are conventionally existent phenomena such as people, chairs, mountains, and so forth. No one would assert the existence of the horns of a rabbit or a cloak made of turtle hairs, traditional examples of non-existents.

The two subschools of Middle Way School tenets, the Autonomy School and the Consequence School, are named by the means they use to generate in others an inferring consciousness cognizing emptiness — the former using autonomous syllogisms[99] and the latter, consequences.[100]

An inferring consciousness is crucial in meditation; therefore, it is important to understand how to produce it.

A Consequentialist uses consequences, *prasaṅga*, to produce this crucial consciousness. A consequence is a logical statement in this form:

It follows that the subject, a table, does not inherently exist because of being a dependent-arising.

It is called a consequence because "does not inherently exist" follows as a consequence of "being a dependent-arising", and the statement is worded in the form of "It follows that ... "

In the example, the first part, the subject or basis of debate, is "a table". The second part — the fact that follows from the reason — is called the clarification. In the example, this is "does not inherently exist". The third part is the reason or sign, "dependent-arising".

When a correct consequence that sets forth the Consequence School's own view, as this one does, is stated, there are three ways in which you can draw meaning from it through applying, roughly speaking, the rules of syllogisms: (1) The "presence of the reason in the subject" is a table's being a dependent-arising. (2) The entailment (or pervasion) is that all instances of dependent-arisings are necessarily instances of an absence of inherent existence, or, in other words, whatever is a dependent-arising necessarily does not inherently exist. (3) The counter-entailment is that all instances of inherent existence are necessarily not instances of dependent-arisings, or whatever inherently exists is necessarily not a dependent-arising. These are, roughly speaking, the three aspects of a reason in a valid syllogism — presence of the reason in the subject, entailment, and counter-entailment — here applied to a consequence.

These three are all qualities of a table. They are not just verbiage. That a table itself is a dependent-arising is called the presence of the reason in the subject. The fact that every instance of dependent-arising to which you can point in the

world is an instance of no inherent existence is the entailment. That if you could point to an instance of inherent
existence in the world, it would be a case of non-dependent-
arising is the counter-entailment.

Terms like "entailment" or "pervasion" are technical
ways of referring to qualities that are naturally in phenomena. If a table's being a dependent-arising were not a
part of its nature, an understanding of this could not help to
generate a cognition of its absence of inherent existence.
You would just be producing a cognition of another flower
in the sky, another cloak of turtle hairs. You could never
get to the point of incontrovertible cognition because the
process of thought would not reveal what is actually there.

We have two ways of incontrovertibly discovering what is
true, inferential cognition and direct cognition. When you
understand that there are *two* means — not just direct sense
perception as we tend to feel — you open yourself to inferential cognition, a way of realizing the unseen. Inference
is important; it is a key to the door out of cyclic existence.
You might have the idea that inference always involves
discursiveness; however, an actual inferential cognition is
not talkative. It is not like continually reading passages in a
book, continually mulling over words.

An inferential cognition is what we, in our ignorant way,
might take to be a direct cognition. For, when you arrive at
the point of an actual inferential cognition of emptiness, for
instance, you cognize only an emptiness of inherent existence. At that time you will not be going over the reasons;
you will not even actively take the reasons to mind. The
effect of your reasoning will be your cognizing the absence
of inherent existence of, for example, your body.

For instance, if right now you looked out the window and
saw billows of smoke, you would know that fire is near.
You would not be going over and over in your mind,
"Where there is smoke, there is fire. Here there is smoke.
Therefore, here there is fire. Where there is smoke, there is
fire. Here there is smoke. Therefore, here there is fire ..."

You would stay with your knowledge of fire, and you would do something about it. It is just the same with emptiness. This is very important. It is possible to become so addicted to reasoning that when you arrive at the point where you are about to cognize emptiness, you leave it and return to the reasoning. If you find that one of these diamond instruments of reasoning works, settle down and stay with it, getting used to the result of the reasoning, a cognition of emptiness.

Staying with the cognition that results from reasoning is called stabilizing meditation. First one does analytical meditation and then afterwards stabilizing meditation — again alternating back to analytical meditation when the cognition becomes weaker, and so forth. This is hard. People who get addicted to reading and studying have great difficulty with moving on to and staying with a conclusion and do not want to stay in understanding. An inferential cognition is conceptual, but concepts do not mean, in this case, a whole lot of talk. Rather, you are not seeing the object directly; there is still an image of emptiness as a medium of understanding, but only an image, not a lot of words.

Direct cognition is the other means by which we know incontrovertibly what exists. Both direct and inferential valid cognitions are non-mistaken about their main object; they cognize their main object correctly. They differ in that a direct cognition is of an object itself without the medium of a mental image of that object, whereas inference relies on an image.

The system of the Ge-luk-ba order of Tibetan Buddhism that follows the late fourteenth and early fifteenth century scholar and yogi Dzong-ka-ba[101] implies that for us to know correctly anything at all, our perceptions must have an element of valid cognition. So, abstractly at least, we can talk about valid cognitions in even our ordinary perceptions, not only in perceptions in meditation. But when we talk about valid cognition in our ordinary everyday perception, there is little that we can point to; the mistaken and the non-mistaken are so tightly mixed.

If we take Dzong-ka-ba's teaching about valid cognition as affirming the way we perceive the mode of existence of things, then we are wrong. We usually perceive things as inherently existent, or as being findable if we search for them, whereas in reality all phenomena are empty of inherent existence and are analytically unfindable. Also, if we take the way things appear as the way they exist conventionally, we are wrong. Conventional existence is validly established existence; this is not what appears to our usual perception. We *usually* conceive things to exist inherently, but that does not make inherent existence valid *conventionally;* conventional does not mean "usual"; it implies validity.

If we decide that our present perceptions are completely correct, then we will have many difficulties in trying to practice Great Vehicle Buddhism. For, in Great Vehicle Buddhism it is important to see that an infinity of time and space can fit into a single moment and a single particle, whereas we usually freeze ourselves into a restricted way of seeing time and space. Talk about valid cognition in ordinary perception can just freeze it all the more. However, the teaching of valid cognition in ordinary perception is important because it draws you into differentiating the right and wrong parts of ordinary appearance. Despite Dzong-ka-ba's teaching that ordinary perceptions can be valid, he holds that even a direct valid sense cognition is mistaken with respect to the mode of existence of its object.

For instance, looking at a table, we see something that covers a certain area. However, through applying Middle Way reasonings, we can understand that there is nothing covering the parts; at that point, we have to accept that all valid cognitions we have now are mistaken with respect to this important point even if those cognitions are right about the mere presence or absence of an object. All things appear to our senses and our minds to be inherently existent and findable but are not.

Or, to phrase it differently, all direct valid cognitions that we now have are infected by this appearance of inherent existence. Once the object has appeared wrongly, our minds usually misconceive or hold onto this false mode of existence of things. The mind takes the raw data of the false appearance of inherent existence and reinforces it.

What instrument can get at this misconception of inherent existence? Inference. Inferential cognition can reveal the nature of these objects so that they can be cognized differently. If this proper cognition of the nature of things were always to be conceptual, it would be like superimposing an overlay on reality, but it becomes non-conceptual through meditative habituation and intensified analysis, and, finally, with the attainment of Buddhahood, removes even the error of false appearance.

First, you generate inferential cognition and then become accustomed to it. In conjunction with inferential cognition you develop calm abiding[102] — deep, one-pointed concentration of the mind — and when calm abiding has been achieved, you can enter into particularly forceful analysis, which, when alternated with stabilizing meditation, gradually induces special insight. When stabilizing meditation and analytical meditation are of the same strength and mutually supportive, you attain special insight into emptiness and reach the path of preparation.[103] During the path of preparation, you pass through four levels during which the image of emptiness that is the object of conceptual cognition disappears.

At the beginning of the path of preparation, what appears to your mind is an *image* of utter vacuity — an object's lack of inherent existence. When inferential cognition is taken this far, nothing appears to the mind except this vacuity — a negative, an absence, of inherent existence.

For us, however, since we are so used to seeing inherent existence, when it is no longer there, it seems as if there is nothing. Thus, there are two types of people when it comes to cultivating inferential cognition of emptiness. Some people cannot stand to stay with it and want to go back to the reasons when they should not. They need to engage in stabilizing meditation on the emptiness that is the conclusion of their reasoning. Others get overwhelmed by the vacuity that appears, and they forget what they are doing; there is no longer any sense of a specific negative of inherent existence. It becomes just non-existence. They arrive at an utter vacuity of inherent existence, but it becomes an utter vacuity that is an annihilation of everything. At that point they should refresh the reasonings through analytical meditation. One word or even one phrase may be enough.

When you understand the way in which cognition of emptiness is developed, you can understand why it is so important to generate an inference through the proper means — through consequences and syllogisms. The Consequentialists say that as soon as you state a syllogism, for instance:

The subject, a house, does not inherently exist because of being a dependent-arising,

then you could immediately be frozen into what you think the mode of being of a house is. Since we feel that the consciousness that validates the object that is the subject of the syllogism (here, a house) also validates its inherent existence, we are stuck in our ordinary incorrect perception of the nature of house. This is especially so if you think that the valid cognition that establishes it and certifies its existence for you is the same in this respect as the valid cognition that establishes it and certifies it for a Consequentialist. For instance, if you were a non-Consequentialist, and I were a Consequentialist, then in your system the valid cognition that establishes the existence of this house would also establish its inherent existence, its existence from its own side. However, in the Consequence School, the certifying consciousness establishes the mere existence of the object, not its existence in its own right.

Now, if you, as a non-Consequentialist, were nevertheless a Buddhist and thus a proponent of dependent-arising, I could say:

It follows that the subject, a house, is not a dependent-arising because of inherently existing.

This will cause you to ponder because, being a Buddhist, you definitely want to say that a house is a dependent-arising. But if it inherently exists, it cannot be a dependent-arising.

This gets you to thinking. Probably, at this point, you will not accept it. You will say, "No entailment." This means that you do not accept that whatever is an inherently existent thing is necessarily not a dependent-arising.

If you do say, "No entailment," then I must work with you. To make it clearer I might say:

It follows that the subject, a house, does not depend on its causes because of inherently existing.

Or, I could have a discussion with you about what the word "inherently existing" means, explaining that it implies, by extension, existing in and of itself without depending on causes and so forth.

Or, I could say:

It follows that the subject, a house, does not depend on its parts because of inherently existing.

Indeed, I will probably have to state several different consequences because it is very hard to move someone who is stuck to a position. If it were not difficult, everybody would be a Consequentialist. Everyone would be convinced of the fact that things do not exist in the way they appear.

When meditating, you can fling these same consequences at yourself. You take the way a house is appearing to you, your thoughts about it, "This is really a great house," or maybe, "This house is lousy, why did I move in here in the first place!" You have to notice the way you are conceiving it. You have to identify your own sense of its inherent existence. You have to catch your mind when it is assenting to the appearance of a concrete, findable house. Even if you do not seem to be caught in this feeling at present, remember a moment when you were caught in it and state this consequence to yourself:

It follows that the subject, this house, is not a dependent-arising because of inherently existing.

If you are a Buddhist, you feel anxious because dependent-arising is the foundation of Buddhism — the cornerstone of Buddha's doctrine. You are either forced to give up dependent-arising because the house inherently exists or to give up inherent existence because the house is a dependent-arising.

Another method is to take yourself as the subject. You would say:

It follows that the subject, I, do not depend on parts because of inherently existing.

If you take a look at how you were thinking about yourself walking around town today, feeling important (or feeling lousy), making plans, and so on, you can identify the sense of inherent existence. You, not an external opponent in debate, are "asserting" inherent existence. This "assertion" is implied in your living in a continual sense of existence from your own side. On the other hand, because you have reflected on your dependent nature, you want very much to say that you depend on your parts. So you are running an inner conflict.

The import of this consequence, stated as a syllogism, is: The subject, I, do not inherently exist because of depending on parts. To construct a syllogism from a consequence that implies its opposite, you (1) take the opposite of the reason in the consequence — inherently existing — and make that the predicate of the syllogism — do not inherently exist — and (2) take the opposite of the predicate in the consequence — do not depend on parts — and make this the reason of the syllogism — depending on parts.

A consequence forces you to see that you are in a spot where you do not want to be, whereas a syllogism is trying to *push* you into a spot where you do not, at this moment, want to be. But a consequence is not necessarily going to grab you and force you into seeing that you are in an unwanted position. You have to work first.

You need to remember, take to mind, that you have been feeling just recently that you inherently exist. For instance, if earlier someone kicked you and you got angry, you should examine, "Who is the one who got hurt?" You can point to your sense of self, and then you can state the consequence about that person. From the consequence, you will see that if you hold that you inherently exist, then you must hold that you are not imputed in dependence on a basis of designation — such as mind and body; you must hold that you are not a dependent-arising.

If you do not first have a sense of your own concrete existence, then it is all just talk. You are not striking at anything. You are shooting an arrow but you have no target. You are dispatching the troops but have no sense of where the enemy is. As the Fifth Dalai Lama says:[104]

> If both the self [that is the validly existent person] and [the self that is] the non-existent object of negation are not intimately identified, it is like dispatching an army without knowing where the enemy is or like shooting an arrow without having sought out the target.

If the target of the reasoning is not identified, you are apt to refute either the object itself rather than just its inherent existence or merely some intellectually superimposed idea that is not usually found in our perception of objects.

A consequence is often less abstract than a syllogism, for when you state the reason, "because of inherently existing", you have identified that this is the way you feel about the subject. At that point, you are right inside your own feeling. Then you are forced into something that you do not want to accept. "It follows" here means that an absurdity follows because of the tenets you are currently holding — because of the way you are looking at things. This is called an <u>unwanted consequence.</u> (As we saw above, not all consequences are unwanted, for Consequentialists can use consequences to state their own positions.)

A bone of contention between the Consequentialists and all the other tenet systems is whether or not after stating a consequence you must openly state the corresponding syllogism. All systems use consequences in order to break down the pointedness or vibrance[105] of a person's wrong view. Then, according to the non-Consequentialist systems, you must state a syllogism to that person, turning your original consequence around and stating it in the opposite way. For example, first you state a consequence:

It follows that the subject, a person, is not imputed in dependence on that person's parts because of inherently existing.

Then, once the opponent's resistance has been broken down a little — or, in meditation, once your own resistance has weakened — you state the corresponding syllogism:

The subject, a person, does not inherently exist because of being imputed in dependence on parts.

Consequentialists say that if you have a smart opponent or if you are dealing with yourself and you are not too dull, it is not necessary to reformulate the consequence into a syllogism. If you are smart, you can figure that the meaning of the syllogism is necessarily contained in the consequence that has been stated. Thus, in brief, Consequentialists say that it is not *necessary* to state a syllogism after you have stated a consequence in order to generate an inferential cognition of an absence of inherent existence.

Consequentialists say that when they debate with non-Consequentialists, the three aspects — the presence of the reason in the subject, entailment, and counter-entailment — cannot be established within the context of subject, predicate, and reason being established as existing in the same way in their systems and in the systems of their opponents. Under what conditions would phenomena appear similarly to both in the sense that phenomena would be established similarly in both systems? Only if phenomena had an objective mode of subsistence, a mode of existence intrinsic to the phenomena themselves instead of being posited by the mind. For, in the system of someone who needs to learn the view of the emptiness of inherent existence, the valid cognition that establishes the subject and so forth is believed also to establish their inherent existence.

"Objective mode of subsistence" means a thing's being there, right with its parts. Take, for instance, a cat. Cat is the object, and right with its parts — mind and body — cat would be there, not just designated, but with the body and mind of the cat — in, of, and by itself. The object would be self-existent; it would exist there in itself.

When you recognize that you feel, "Of course, it has to exist by itself" — when you notice that you feel opposite to the way the Consequentialists assert things to be — you are tuning in to this system for the first time. For, it is undeniable that phenomena appear to us as if they exist from their own sides. You are making progress because you are noticing this basic appearance, even if you do not yet realize it to be false.

If phenomena did inherently exist, the valid cognition that correctly establishes their existence would be similar for both a Consequentialist and a non-Consequentialist. However, the Consequentialists assert that phenomena do not inherently exist and that, therefore, it is not necessary and, in fact, is impossible to construct syllogisms in which the three aspects of a reason are established within the context of the subject, predicate, reason, and example all appearing similarly to both parties in the sense that both parties hold similar views on what the valid cognitions that establish these actually establish. Although these phenomena appear similarly to both parties in the sense that these *appear* to both to be inherently existent, a non-Consequentialist *holds* that valid cognition of an object also establishes the inherent existence of the object whereas a Consequentialist does not. In this sense, the Consequence School says that there are no commonly appearing subjects and so forth when debating about the final mode of existence of phenomena.

For Consequentialists, the best methods for helping others begin with their own assertions. They favor a consequence that shows an internal contradiction — something outrageous — in a position. Therefore, Jang-gya says:

> Furthermore, in that way Chandrakīrti's *Clear Words*[106] gives, together with [showing its] correctness, the reason why a thesis is proven by a reason approved by the other party and why autonomous [syllogisms] should not be asserted:
>
>> With regard to an inference for one's own purpose, [even you say that] just what is established for oneself is weightier at all [times], not what is established for both [oneself and an opponent, for in an inference for one's own purpose there is no opponent]. Therefore, expression of the definitions of logic [as they are renowned in the systems of the Autonomists and below][107] is not needed because the Buddhas help beings — trainees who do not know suchness — with reasoning as it is renowned to those [beings].

There are two kinds of inferences: inference for one's own purpose and inference for another's purpose. Inference for one's own purpose is a *consciousness* produced upon stating reasons to yourself as, for instance, in meditation. Inference for another's purpose is comprised by the *sounds* stating a reasoning to an opponent during debate and thus is said not to be actual inference, which necessarily is a consciousness.

In meditation, the reasoning should be applicable to yourself; in debate, it should apply to your opponent. Āryadeva, Nāgārjuna's chief student, says that you cannot teach a barbarian with sophisticated language:[108]

Just as a barbarian cannot be
Approached with another language,
So the world cannot be approached
Except with the worldly.

You have to approach barbarians with their own language. In just the same way, a Buddha helps people on their own terms.

Chandrakīrti also indicates this with a worldly example; his *Clear Words* says:[109]

> It is just by a reason established for oneself, not by one established for the other [disputant], since such is seen in the world. In the world, sometimes [one party] prevails and [the other] is defeated by the word of a judge whom both take to be valid and sometimes by just one's own word, but victory or defeat is not by the other's word. Just as it is in the world, so it is also in logic because only the conventions of the world are appropriate in treatises of logic.

Positing the import of [being] a Consequentialist in that way is the flawless thought of [Chandrakīrti's] text.

Jang-gya's definition of a Consequentialist follows Chandrakīrti's *Clear Words*. Who presented Chandrakīrti's thought in this way?

Dzong-ka-ba's *Great Exposition of the Stages of the*

Path to Enlightenment says:

> Proving a thesis with a reason that is established for both parties with valid cognitions such as were explained previously is called an autonomous reason. One who proves a thesis not that way, but through the three aspects [of a reason] approved by the other party is posited as a Consequentialist. It is very clear that this [explanation of the meaning of a being a Consequentialist] is the thought of the master [Chandrakīrti].

In that case, a Consequentialist may also be defined as a Proponent of the Middle Way School who, without accepting autonomy, asserts that an inferring consciousness cognizing an absence of true existence is generated merely through what is approved by the other [party]. Moreover, it is suitable to give the definition of a Consequentialist as: a Proponent of the Middle Way School who does not accept, even conventionally, phenomena that are established by way of their own character.

It is important to note that Jang-gya defines Consequentialists since some Western interpreters of the Consequence School say that the main tenet of the school is that phenomena are devoid of definitions. They hold that what the Consequence School's presentation of emptiness refutes is that phenomena have essences in the sense of definable characteristics that occur with every instance of that phenomenon. From the viewpoint of Jang-gya and Ge-luk-bas in general, such a position has fallen to an extreme of nihilism; rather, according to them, what is refuted is a reified status of phenomena, and that reified status, inherent existence or establishment of objects by way of their own character, does not exist either conventionally or ultimately.

Furthermore, the final root of the Consequentialists' many uncommon ways of positing the two
truths is this non-assertion of establishment of objects by way of their own character even conventionally.

In the non-Consequentialist systems, if something exists,
then it has to be findable among its bases of designation;
therefore, they say that phenomena are established by way
of their own character, at least conventionally. Even if
proponents of non-Consequentialist systems hold that persons do not substantially exist in the sense of being self-
sufficient and even if Middle Way Autonomists hold that
there are no phenomena that have their own mode of subsistence not posited through the force of appearing to a
non-defective awareness, they hold that you must *equate* a
phenomenon with something among its bases of designation. Otherwise, there would be no difference between an
actual snake and one imputed to a rope.

A snake imputed to a rope cannot perform the functions
of a snake; it cannot bite you; its poison cannot be used for
medicine. The collection of the parts of the rope is not the
snake. The individual strands are not the snake. From
every aspect of it, looking at it in every way, there is no
snake there.

The Consequentialists alone say that in the same way,
when an actual coiled snake is present, the collection of its
parts is from every aspect not a snake. The basis of designation of snake is non-snake. In dependence upon something
that is non-snake, snake is imputed. Thought imputes a
snake in dependence upon what is not a snake — all of the
parts of a snake, separately or together, are not a snake.

It is the same way with ourselves. Mind and body — the
individual parts, the whole, the parts over time — are our
bases of designation but are not us, and we are not them.
Still, if the basis of designation does not have certain qualities such as consciousness, then it does not have the prere-

quisites for being called a person. These qualities make it suitable to be a basis of designation of a person, not to *be* a person. A person is posited by thought in dependence upon these.

The question is, what does it mean to *be* an object? What does it mean to *be*? We mistakenly take it to mean that a phenomenon in some way governs or covers a certain field that is its basis of designation. This is the way we live; this is the way that things appear to us. This is not the way things are.

3 Self

Jang-gya continues:

> Chandrakīrti's *Autocommentary on the "Supplement to (Nāgārjuna's) 'Treatise on the Middle Way*' "[110] says ...

When Nāgārjuna wrote the *Treatise on the Middle Way*,[111] neither the Mind Only nor the Autonomy systems had appeared, but they had by the time Chandrakīrti wrote his *Supplement to (Nāgārjuna's) "Treatise on the Middle Way"*. Thus, Chandrakīrti perceived a need to establish that it was wrong to interpret the *Treatise on the Middle Way* according to the Mind Only or Autonomy systems. He did this by showing that it should not be asserted that phenomena are established from their own side and by showing that the conception that phenomena are established from their own side is an obstruction to liberation from cyclic existence. In this sense, his work is a supplement[112] to Nāgārjuna's *Treatise on the Middle Way* in terms of teaching about the profound emptiness.

Also, based on Nāgārjuna's own works such as the *Precious Garland*[113] and *Compendium of Sūtra*,[114] he supplemented Nāgārjuna's *Treatise on the Middle Way* with the teaching of compassion, explaining its three types. The first has suffering sentient beings as its object of observation. The second observes sentient beings qualified by imperma- nence or by the lack of being substantially existent entities able to stand by themselves. The third observes sentient beings qualified by emptiness.

For instance, think about the way in which things are appearing to the sentient beings in this town — as if in- herently existent, as if existing in and of themselves. Things seem not to depend on thought but rather to be objectively findable. In order to satisfy desire and hatred that are based on accepting this appearance, persons engage in manifold unsuitable activities that only bring them trouble in the future. When, upon realizing this, you observe beings not just as suffering but also as qualified by an emptiness of inherent existence, it is easy to generate even greater com- passion since the root of suffering has been ascertained as an unnecessary error.

People are out of tune with reality — trying to satisfy a falsely conceived self, living in a world where objects seem to exist in their own right. Except for those who have realized emptiness, everyone lives as if objects exist from their own side.

If you understand a little about emptiness, you under- stand that it is possible to overcome suffering. When you see this possibility, then it is also possible to open greater feelings of compassion, feeling how nice it would be if beings could overcome the misconception of the nature of things that is at the root of suffering. For, when you see that there is a way out of suffering, compassion is both possible and sensible. We now feel that torture, for instance, is unnecessary but that the sufferings of birth, aging, sick- ness, and death are unavoidable. What if there were some- thing that you could do about even these sufferings?

In the end, it might be a simple error. When you realize emptiness, it must appear that liberation is simple and that there is a means to bring everybody to that point. A small error produces a big problem, like getting on the wrong airplane.

Besides adding teaching on compassion, Chandrakīrti's *Supplement* sets forth cultivation of the altruistic intention to become enlightened as well as non-dualistic understanding on the level of a common being. Based on Nāgārjuna's *Precious Garland*, he presents the ten Bodhisattva grounds[115] as well as the qualities of Buddhahood. He shows that it is necessary for a student of Nāgārjuna's system to ascend the ten grounds in order to become a Buddha. Thus, not only from the viewpoint of the profound emptiness but also from the viewpoint of the vast method, Chandrakīrti's text supplements Nāgārjuna's *Treatise on the Middle Way*.

Jay-dzun-ba,[116] the textbook author for the Jay[117] college of Se-ra[118] monastery, says that emptiness, called "the profound", is extensively taught in Nāgārjuna's *Treatise on the Middle Way* but that the vast deeds of compassion, the paths, and so forth — "the extensive" — are not. Jam-yang-shay-ba,[119] the textbook author for the Go-mang[120] College of Dre-bung[121] monastery, says that both the profound emptiness and the extensive paths of compassion and so forth are taught explicitly and extensively in Nāgārjuna's *Treatise on the Middle Way*, even though he admits that the extensive paths of compassion and so forth are not taken as a main topic. He says that it is not necessary that a book on a subject be long for it to teach that subject extensively. For example, Maitreya's *Ornament for Clear Realization*,[122] which is the root text for the study of the paths in the Middle Way School, is short but extensive. Conversely, Chandrakīrti's *Supplement* is much longer than Nāgārjuna's *Treatise on the Middle Way*, but the latter presents emptiness from many points of view that Chandrakīrti never mentions, and thus Nāgārjuna's *Treatise* must be considered more extensive in its treatment of emptiness than Chandrakīrti's *Supplement*.

But how, according to Jam-yang-shay-ba, does Nāgārjuna's *Treatise* extensively present the paths? His answer is that not only does Nāgārjuna, in the chapter on the four noble truths, speak about how conventionalities can be posited within an emptiness of inherent existence, but also, for example, when Nāgārjuna talks about the four noble turths, he mentions Foe Destroyers, the eight levels of entering and abiding, and so on. This, according to Jam-yang-shay-ba, is sufficient to say that Nāgārjuna's *Treatise* extensively treats the varieties of paths and so forth.

However, Nāgārjuna's *Treatise* does not explicitly give even such an enumeration for the Great Vehicle. Also, the mention of paths and so forth is mostly within a context of presenting them as bases for refuting that they inherently exist. If such an enumeration in a process of refuting inherent existence were sufficient for it to be decided that a text extensively presents the paths and so forth, then one would have to say that the Perfection of Wisdom Sūtras explicitly present the paths. However, the monastic textbooks are unanimous in agreeing that the Perfection of Wisdom Sūtras present the paths only in a hidden manner, neither explicitly nor implicitly. Therefore, it seems to me that Jay-dzun-ba's position that Chandrakīrti's *Supplement to (Nāgārjuna's) "Treatise on the Middle Way"* supplements Nāgārjuna's text in terms of the vast paths through an extensive presentation of something that Nāgārjuna did not teach in the *Treatise* is better than Jam-yang-shay-ba's position that Chandrakīrti made more extensive what was already explicitly and extensively presented in the *Treatise*.

Chandrakīrti's *Autocommentary on the "Supplement to (Nāgārjuna's) 'Treatise on the Middle Way' "* says:[123]

> May scholars ascertain that, in terms of the doctrine of emptiness, the system which appears in this [treatise] — set out together with objections and answers to any [other] system — does not exist in other treatises.

He is saying that his own [Consequence School] system is not shared with commentaries by other Proponents of the Middle Way School [such as those by Autonomists, including Bhāvaviveka].

In explaining the meaning of that passage, the Foremost Great Being [Dzong-ka-ba] says in his *Essence of the Good Explanations:*[124]

> In the [Consequentialists'] own system, phenomena that are established by way of their own character are not asserted even conventionally, whereas those [Proponents of True Existence] only posit [all phenomena] in the context of that [establishment of objects by way of their own character].

The Consequence School has many uncommon features, or special tenets, that it does not share with other systems due to the fact that it does not assert the establishment of objects by way of their own character in any way. The other systems assert such and, as a result, assert many other phenomena that the Consequentialists do not accept.

For example, in the Consequence School there is no mind-basis-of-all[125] even conventionally. In the Mind Only School a mind-basis-of-all is necessary in order to carry over the karmic seeds and predispositions from the particular time and life when a deed was done. However, the Consequentialists say that when a deed ceases, it does not utterly cease with absolutely no continuation, as an inherently existent cessation would imply. Therefore, nothing extra is needed to carry it over to other lifetimes. In the Consequence School the state of the cessation of an action, being empty of inherent existence and impermanent, is sufficient to cause an effect that might arise eons later.

> Earlier Tibetan scholars also used the term "Thoroughly Non-Abiding Proponents of the Middle Way School" [for the Consequentialists]. This

appears to be based on a statement in the master Shūra's [i.e., Ashvaghoṣha's] *Essay on the Stages of Cultivating the Ultimate Mind of Enlightenment:*[126]

> Through synonyms such as emptiness,
> [suchness, final reality] and so forth,
> Limitless examples such as likeness with a
> magician's illusions, [dreams, mirages]
> and so forth
> And the skillful means of a variety of
> vehicles,
> [Buddha] characterized the meaning of the
> middle way not abiding [in any gross or
> subtle extremes].

Moreover, in reports of statements by the Foremost Elder [Atīsha] this convention [of calling Consequentialists "Thoroughly Non-Abiding Proponents of the Middle Way School"] occurs, and it also does not appear that the Foremost Father [Dzong-ka-ba] and his spiritual sons [Gyel-tsap and Kay-drup][127] refuted it.

Although there are a couple [of scholars] who say that Shūra's text was not written by the master Shūra, such is exhausted as a mere thesis without proof. It appears that all the great chariots [i.e., path-blazing leaders] of the snowy land [Tibet] as well as all of our own [Ge-luk-ba] scholars and adepts who appeared over the years accepted it as valid.

A description of different internal divisions in the Middle Way Consequence School, like those in the Autonomy School, does not appear in other texts, and neither is there seen an explanation of divisions of the Consequence School by the Foremost Father and his spiritual sons. [Hence, there are no significant subschools within the Consequence School.]

ASSERTIONS OF TENETS

This section has four parts: how to settle the view of the bases, the features of how, in dependence on that, a presentation of the two truths is made, how to progress on the path, and the fruits [of the paths]. We shall look only at the first of these in this book.[128]

How to Settle the View of the Bases
This section has two parts: explaining what is negated in relation to what bases and settling the selflessness that is the negative of the object negated.

There are two ways of settling, or delineating, emptiness. The usual way — the way Jang-gya is about to describe here — is to present "a view of the bases". This is an explanation of an emptiness — a negative of inherent existence — as a quality of a basis or object. All phenomena are bases — substrata of the predicate, emptiness.

The other way to describe emptiness is in the context of its realization, how emptiness appears at the time of direct cognition during meditative equipoise. At that time, there is no base, or subject, appearing at all, only emptiness — all elaborations whatsoever have ceased. From this point of view, an emptiness is an absence of the object it qualifies. Within the context of meditative equipoise it is suitable to present emptiness this way, but it is not suitable in general. Emptiness must be understood as a quality of a base, of an object, its final mode of being.

> *What is negated in relation to what.* Proponents of Mind Only and of Autonomy assert that the two selves — through the negation of which in persons and phenomena the [two] selflessnesses are posited — are different and that the modes of conception of them also differ.

The Consequence School, the Autonomy School, and the

Mind Only School comprise the three major divisions of Great Vehicle tenet systems, the first two being subdivisions of the Middle Way School. All three explain emptiness from the viewpoint of a selflessness of persons and of phenomena. A person is any sentient being — you, me, other human beings, animals, bugs, and so on. "Phenomena", as interpreted in the Consequence School, include all phenomena that are not persons — rocks, houses, minds, bodies, chariots, space, emptiness, and all instances of the five mental and physical aggregates save one. The one exception is the person, the mere I, which is considered to be an instance of the fourth aggregate, compositional factors. All impermanent phenomena in all world systems are included within the five aggregates — forms, feelings, discriminations, compositional factors, and consciousnesses.

Within the framework of a self of persons and a self of phenomena, there is also a distinction made between coarse and subtle selves. Subtle self is harder to overcome than a coarse one. Here in our text, Jang-gya is referring to the *subtle* self as well as the *subtle* conception of self, that is to say, a consciousness conceiving subtle self.

In the Consequence School, "subtle self" refers to inherent existence, wrongly predicated to either persons or other phenomena. In the other Great Vehicle systems, however, there are two kinds of subtle self, one with respect to persons and another with respect to phenomena in general, including persons. In the Mind Only School, the subtle self of persons is a person's being a self-sufficient substantial entity, and a subtle self of a phenomenon is that phenomenon's being a different entity from the mind that perceives it. The Proponents of the Mind Only School also posit a second self of phenomena that is an object's being established by way of its own character as a basis of a name, such as "chair".

In the Autonomy School, just as in the Mind Only School, the subtle self of persons is a person's being a self-sufficient substantial entity; the subtle self of phenomena, however, is a phenomenon's true existence — its being established by way of its own uncommon mode of subsistence without being posited through the force of appearing to a non-defective consciousness.[129]

In the Consequence School, the subtle self of both persons and phenomena is inherent existence. Of a person, it is a self of persons, and of a phenomenon other than a person, it is a self of a phenomenon.

In all Great Vehicle tenet systems except the Consequence School, the two subtle selflessnesses are differentiated, not by the object with respect to which self is negated, but by the kind of self that is negated. In the Consequence School, however, a negative of inherent existence as a predicate of a person is a subtle selflessness of a person, and a negative of inherent existence as a predicate of a phenomenon other than a person is a subtle selflessness of a phenomenon. Thus, the Consequentialists differentiate the two selflessnesses by way of the objects with respect to which self, inherent existence, is negated, not by way of what is negated.

In the non-Consequence schools, the subtle selflessness of a person is the negative (lack or absence) of a person's existing as a substantial or self-sufficient entity. According to Jang-gya, earlier in this book but not translated here,[130] this kind of selflessness has only persons as its bases or substrata since it is called a selflessness of *persons*. How could we talk about conceiving a table to be a self of persons? Nevertheless, Jang-gya does show how the selflessness of persons can be related to phenomena because all phenomena are empty of being the objects of use of a substantially existent person. When you realize that a person does not exist as a self-sufficient substantial entity, you can understand that these other phenomena do not exist as the objects of use of such a person. You change the way that you view the objects you use.

Jang-gya's presentation is based on the division of all phenomena into user and used, or enjoyer and enjoyed. The person, yourself, is the user, and all the phenomena in the world that you deal with are the used. It might look as if this distinction of user and used — for instance, the town in which we live is used by us — is just an intellectual fabrication, but do we not sometimes look at things this way? I am the user, and all these stores are the used. This is one way that we experience the world.

If a substantially existent or self-sufficient person does not exist, what would a substantially existent or self-sufficient person be? When I say or think, "My mind," "My body," "My book," and so on, I seem to be first, and then the thing owned appears to depend on me. The I is the owner, controller. It seems that this I does not depend on the mind or body; rather, the mental and physical aggregates seem to depend on the I. Due to the great force with which we conceive this, the I and the mental and physical aggregates appear to be, respectively, the controller and the controlled. The apprehension of the aggregates seems to depend on apprehending the I, whereas the actual fact is that the apprehension of the I depends on apprehending the mental and physical aggregates. This is the way that the innate mind that misconceives self-sufficient existence sees the I. Thus, self-sufficient existence is not just a philosophical concept; it is innate, born with us due to the conditioning of former actions and afflictive emotions. We innately misperceive our own nature.

Though the I and the aggregates are apprehended as being basically different, the difference is not necessarily that of entity, but rather of what depends on what. For example, in a store the salespeople have to do whatever the head salesperson says. He/she orders them about; they do not tell the head salesperson what to do; they have to ask his/her permission, "Should I do this?" and so on. Within this context they are dependent on the head salesperson and not he/she on them. Of course, in other ways, the head salesperson has to depend on them to get things sold and so forth, but that is not the point here. The point is that the head salesperson is a salesperson, not completely different in character from the workers in the store, yet is in a position of controlling the other workers. According to Jam-yang-shay-ba,[131] this is the way in which a person appears to be a substantial or self-sufficient entity. Like a boss within a group, the I seems to control mind and body.

According to most other writers on the subject, the I and the aggregates appear to us, in this coarse innate misconception, in the manner of a lord and his subjects. The lord does not depend on his subjects; they depend on him. The I has a privileged position in relation to the aggregates. However, Jam-yang-shay-ba warns against misinterpreting this example. According to him, exemplifying the I and the aggregates as a master and his subjects could suggest that the I and the aggregates seem to be different entities, for a subject is not a lord and neither is a lord a subject, unlike the head salesperson who is a salesperson too. It is important to keep in mind that in innate misconceptions, whether coarse or subtle, the self and the mental and physical aggregates are not conceived to be different entities.

The Dalai Lama made the point in a lecture that only the person and not other phenomena are misconceived to be self-sufficient in this way. We sometimes have a strong feeling of I located in the center of the chest, a feeling that comes naturally, but we do not naturally have such a feeling of house located in the center of the house. The way in which we see a house as being one thing although it has five rooms is not like the way that we see the person to exist self-sufficiently. When, for instance, you are walking along a cliff and you become afraid of falling off, the I that appears is a self-sufficient I, seeming to have its own character.

When meditating in order to destroy the conception of a substantial or self-sufficient person — to get rid of any possibility of having a consciousness conceiving a substantial or self-sufficient person — first you must ascertain well this appearance of a substantially existent I. Then you analyze to find out whether or not it is sensible for such a person actually to exist. You consider whether or not the I is different from the mental and physical aggregates, or whether or not it depends on those aggregates that seem to be under its control. You should be able to see that such a person is not a different entity from mind and body, that it does not exist in itself but depends on mind and body.

After you have thought and meditated on this, then consider body and mind, mentally rejecting each as a self-sufficient I. Since there is also no person separate from these, wherever you search for such a self-sufficient or substantially existent person, you will not find it.

The place where you are most likely to find a substantially existent I is in your own mental and physical aggregates, not, for instance, among external phenomena. Therefore, look within your own aggregates first; when that search has been completed and you have concluded that a substantially existent I is not there, look among all the other external phenomena that appear to mind; you will see, of course, that such a person does exist there either. This is what Jam-yang-shay-ba may mean when he says that it is sensible to talk about the absence of a self-sufficient person in phenomena other than the person.[132]

In brief, the way to meditate on not being a self-sufficient substantial entity is as follows: First cause the I that seems to be a self-sufficient entity to appear to the mind, and ascertain the appearance of a substantially existent I. Then, consider whether mind and body depend on the I or whether the I depends on them. Having looked among the aggregates and decided that a substantially existent I does not exist there, you might have slight doubt that it may be elsewhere. Why? The conception of a substantially existent I is very persistent. The mind has supported what the I wanted to do for a long time. It has believed in it. So, check all phenomena outside of mind and body — deciding thoroughly and completely that it does not exist anywhere.

This is Jam-yang-shay-ba's system. For Jang-gya, the

second step would be to discover that other phenomena are not the objects of use of a substantially existent I. The two ways are compatible.

4 False Appearance

For Consequentialists, substantial, self-sufficient existence is negated as the *coarse* self of a person. For Proponents of the Great Exposition, Sūtra, Mind Only, and Autonomy Schools, it is negated as the *subtle* self of a person. In the Consequence School the subtle selflessness of a person is a person's absence of inherent existence. Here the selflessness of persons is equally as subtle as the selflessness of other phenomena; persons and other phenomena are merely the different objects with which the meditator is dealing. If you meditate on a person's emptiness of inherent existence, you are meditating on the subtle selflessness of a person. Likewise, if you meditate on some other phenomenon's emptiness of inherent existence, you are meditating on the subtle selflessness of a phenomenon.

In the other Great Vehicle systems, however, any phenomenon is suitable to be a base of a selflessness of phenomena, persons included. For example, in the Mind Only system, the realization that the form of the letter "A" does not exist as a different entity from the eye consciousness that apprehends it takes the letter "A" as the base that is empty and thus is a realization of a subtle selflessness of a phenomenon, the letter "A". The realization that the person apprehending the letter "A" does not exist as a different entity from the letter "A" that he or she apprehends is also a realization of the subtle selflessness of a phenomenon, a person.

Likewise, in the Autonomy School, a person's absence of true existence is a subtle selflessness of a phenomenon, not a subtle selflessness of a person. For them, the subtle self-lessness of phenomena is subtler than the subtle selflessness of persons. Autonomists say that it is not necessary to realize the subtle selflessness of phenomena in order to get out of cyclic existence; realization of and prolonged meditation on the subtle selflessness of persons, which is coarse in relation to that of phenomena, is sufficient. Hearers and Solitary Realizers think about and meditate on the subtle selflessness of persons; Bodhisattvas, on that of phenomena. Within the Autonomy School, that is the position of the Sutra Autonomy School,[133] founded by Bhāvaviveka. In the Yogic Autonomy[134] School, founded by Shāntarak-shita, Hearers meditate on the selflessness of persons whereas Solitary Realizers[135] meditate on the coarse selflessness of phenomena, which is the non-existence of subject and object as different entities — an object not existing as a different entity from the subject which perceives it and the subject not existing as a different entity from that object. Bodhisattvas meditate on the subtle selflessness of phenomena.

Consequentialists say that a person's emptiness of being a self-sufficient or substantially existent entity is the coarse selflessness of persons; therefore, many people wrongly feel not to meditate on this coarser selflessness, meditating only on the subtler. However, it is said to be very helpful first to meditate and understand the coarse selflessness. For if you cannot understand the coarser, how can you hope to understand the subtler?

Even in the books of instruction for meditatively cultivating the view, the coarse selflessness is often what is identified even though it is called subtle. For instance, someone is accused unjustly, and a strong feeling of I arises. It is the "place accused". Also, when someone helps you in an especially significant way, this I is the "place helped". The books of instruction for meditating on the view direct you to think about times when the I appears strongly as if substantially existent or able to stand by itself. This is a coarse sense of self; identifying it serves as a means of gradually identifying the subtler misconception of inherent existence.

In every Buddhist system, it is necessary to overcome the afflictive obstructions in order to be liberated from cyclic existence. For the Consequentialists, a consciousness conceiving inherent existence is the chief affliction; thus, no matter what phenomenon is held to exist inherently — a person or a cup — any consciousness conceiving inherent existence is an affliction and must be removed in order to gain freedom from cyclic existence.

In the Middle Way Autonomy School, however, a consciousness conceiving true existence is an obstruction to omniscience; as such, it has to be removed in order to attain Buddhahood, but not for liberation from cyclic existence. According to Autonomists, the chief among the obstructions to liberation is a consciousness conceiving the person to be a self-sufficient, substantially existent entity. Therefore, they hold that liberation from cyclic existence is achieved through cognizing and becoming accustomed to the person's not being an entity able to stand by itself. Consequentialists disagree, saying that in order to be liberated from cyclic existence it is necessary to cognize both persons and other phenomena as being without inherent or true existence. For them, conceptions of both persons and other phenomena as existing inherently are instances of afflictions binding one in cyclic existence.

Jang-gya presents positions of the Mind Only School and the Autonomy School that are contrary to the Consequence School:

Therefore, although one realized the subtle selflessness of persons [as presented by the Proponents of Mind Only and of Autonomy], it is not necessarily the case that one would also have cognized the subtle selflessness of phenomena. This being so, [the Proponents of Mind Only and Autonomists] assert that it is not necessary to realize the subtle selflessness of phenomena in order merely to attain liberation.

The Consequentialists disagree with this. As was mentioned earlier, there are two kinds of valid cognition, direct and inferential. When the emptiness of a person is realized through direct cognition, then — according to the Consequentialists — you also cognize the emptiness of all phenomena. For, when you realize the emptiness of one thing directly, you realize the emptiness of all things.

When you cognize the emptiness of a person by means of an inferential cognition, you do not *simultaneously* realize the emptiness of other phenomena but can immediately thereafter understand their emptiness too. Suppose you are meditating on an emptiness with the syllogism:

The subject, a person, does not inherently exist because of being a dependent-arising.

By means of the reason — being a dependent-arising — you realize the thesis — that a person does not inherently exist. Then, through the force of the functioning of that reasoning, without needing to state another reason, you can immediately realize the emptiness of a different subject, such as the body.

As long as you remain within the state of not forgetting your realization of the emptiness of the person, you can immediately realize emptiness with regard to any other phenomenon. Āryadeva says in his *Four Hundred Stanzas on the Yogic Deeds of Bodhisattvas:*[136]

That which is the viewer of one thing
Is explained to be the viewer of all.

That which is the emptiness of one
Is the emptiness of all.

This is understood in Ge-luk-ba commentarial traditions as
meaning that a person viewing the emptiness of one phenomenon with even inferential cognition is able immediately to cognize the emptiness of any other phenomenon merely by turning the mind to it.

Based on this stanza, some other scholars hold that the
emptiness of one thing is the emptiness of any other thing.
The emptiness of a person is the negative of its inherent
existence; the emptiness of a house is the negative of its
inherent existence, and so on; how could mere negatives be
different? Many passages suggest this. Ge-luk-ba scholars,
however, say that the emptiness of one thing and the emptiness of another are different despite the fact that the object
to be negated, inherent existence, is not different *in type*.
For them, if all emptinesses were one, then the bases of
these emptinesses — person, house, tree, and so on —
would also be the same.

Let us return to Jang-gya's point. The Proponents of
Mind Only and the Autonomists assert that the subtle
emptiness of persons and the subtle emptiness of other
phenomena are emptinesses of different kinds of misconceived modes of being. For them, persons are empty of
existing as self-sufficient, substantial entities, and — the
Mind Only School position — all phenomena are empty of
being different entities from the consciousnesses that perceive them or — the Autonomist position — all phenomena
are empty of true existence. They also say that once you
have destroyed the conception of a person as a self-
sufficient entity, you are liberated from cyclic existence.
Therefore, for them, a cognition of the selflessness of persons does not necessarily lead immediately to a cognition of
the selflessness of other phenomena, which must be induced by a different kind of reasoning. The reasoning
proving that a person does not exist as a self-sufficient,
substantial entity will not prove that a phenomenon is not a

different entity from a consciousness perceiving it or that it does not truly exist.

Thus, according to the explanations of the Mind Only and the Autonomy Schools, when Hearers meditate on the selflessness of a person, they realize that a person is empty of being a self-sufficient, substantially existent entity. They realize this only as a quality of persons, for self-sufficient existence is a quality that is not innately erroneously predicated of other phenomena.

Similarly, the Low Vehicle philosophers — I am not speaking of Low Vehicle followers of the Consequence School who assert the tenets of that school but have a lower motivation of mainly seeking their own release from cyclic existence rather than the higher motivation of seeking everyone's attainment of Buddhahood, but am speaking of Proponents of the Great Exposition and the Sūtra Schools — say that the person does not exist but the mental and physical aggregates do. If they were actually dealing with the subtle selflessness of persons — the person's lack of inherent existence as taught in the Consequence School — their realization would immediately apply to everything, as Āryadeva has said. However, they differentiate between the status of the person and the status of other phenomena; they apply selflessness only to persons, not to other phenomena. This is a sign that they have not understood the subtle selflessness — the absence of inherent existence — set forth in the Consequence School. They base their system on the rejection of a mistaken conception that involves only the person, that of being a self-sufficient or substantial entity.

This, as various Ge-luk-ba scholars interpret it, is Chandrakīrti's teaching. However, this does not imply that no Low Vehicle yogis realized the most subtle emptiness and that, therefore, none were able to leave cyclic existence. Chandrakīrti's point is that there are Low Vehicle yogis who follow, not the Low Vehicle schools of tenets, but a presentation of emptiness that accords with that of the

Consequence School. For, Ge-luk-ba scholars hold that according to the Consequentialists, when Hearers meditate Vehicle scriptures teach the most subtle emptiness. Hence, according to the Consequentialists, when Hearers meditate on the selflessness of persons, they soon realize emptiness in relation to everything. Because the Consequence School does not make a distinction of subtlety between the objects negated in the subtle selflessness of persons and the subtle selflessness of phenomena, they say that when Hearers realize the selflessness of persons, they cannot help but realize the selflessness of all phenomena.

Perhaps the Low Vehicle philosophers explained the path the way they did out of concern that a teaching that the mental and physical aggregates do not inherently exist might cause people to fall into nihilism. From the viewpoint of the Consequence School, this has to be given as the reason why Buddha taught such systems. Nonetheless, if it is taken at face value, the assertion by those systems that the person does not (ultimately) exist whereas the aggregates do, that the person is merely the collection of the aggregates, shows that their realization of selflessness does not extend to the mental and physical aggregates. Still, it is important to understand that the main force of their argument is against the existence of persons as self-sufficient, substantial entities and that realization of this level of selflessness is valuable.

In any case, according to Dzong-ka-ba and his followers, it is Nāgārjuna's teaching that the conception of a self of phenomena is a cause of the conception of the self of persons. As Nāgārjuna's *Precious Garland* says:[136a]

As long as the aggregates are [mis]conceived,
From that there is [mis]conception of an I.

Thus, even if you could withdraw your mind from conceiving an inherently existent person, once the conception of a self of phenomena remains, at some point the conception of a self of persons will come out again. Mind and body are the bases of designation of a person; without being fully able to realize their emptiness, how could one have realized one's own emptiness? It is, therefore, necessary to destroy the conception of inherent existence with respect to all objects, from its root, in order to overcome cyclic existence.

This [Consequentialist] system asserts that it is necessary to cognize the subtle selflessness in order to achieve any of the three enlightenments [of a Hearer, Solitary Realizer, or Buddha]. For it is said in the Perfection of Wisdom Sūtras[137] that those who discriminate true existence[138] are not liberated. Shāntideva says,[139] "Scripture says that without this path there is no enlightenment."

In order to achieve even the least among the three enlightenments of a Hearer, Solitary Realizer, or Buddha, it is necessary to have destroyed all the afflictions.[140] When the Perfection of Wisdom Sūtras say that someone who still conceives true existence has not yet reached liberation, this implies that the conception of true existence — a consciousness conceiving that phenomena inherently exist — is not an obstruction to omniscience but an afflictive obstruction, obstructing attainment of liberation. The obstructions to omniscience, on the other hand, prevent direct cognition of all phenomena simultaneously — the omniscience of a Buddha — and are more subtle.

Therefore, the two selflessnesses are differentiated by way of the bases that have the attribute [of selflessness], persons and [other] phenomena such as the [mental and physical] aggregates. It is not asserted that they are differentiated from the viewpoint of two different non-existent selves.

About any selflessness, three factors have to be considered. First, there is the *base of the emptiness*,[141] which is the phenomenon that is without such a mistakenly imputed quality. Then, there is the *self*, or mistakenly imputed quality of inherent existence, that is negated in the view of selflessness. Third, there is the *selflessness*, or emptiness, the lack of a false quality such as inherent existence mistakenly imputed to an object.

When Consequentialists divide selflessnesses into those of persons and other phenomena, they are making a division of different kinds of emptinesses in terms not of the object negated but of the bases or phenomena that have the attribute of emptiness. The other Great Vehicle tenet systems, the Autonomy School and the Mind Only School, assert a distinction between different kinds of emptiness in terms of the object negated.

Out of this comes the fact that, in the Consequence School, the term "phenomena"[142] — in the context of the division of all objects of knowledge into persons and other phenomena — does not refer to persons. In general, phenomena include persons, but in the context of the two emptinesses the term "phenomena" refers to phenomena that are not a person, such as a mind, a body, or a house.

> Just as an emptiness of true existence of a phenomenon such as a [mental or physical] aggregate is posited as a selflessness of a phenomenon, so also must an emptiness of true existence of a person be posited as a selflessness of a person. For the reason [to do so in both instances] is the same. That is the thought [of the Consequence School].

It is important to understand that one usually meditates on *an* emptiness — for instance, an emptiness of your body. About a direct cognition of emptiness, we can speak with more cogency of emptiness in general rather than *an* emptiness, since all emptinesses are being realized at that time within the context of their not appearing to be different. However, prior to that level, it is very helpful to orient oneself to *an* emptiness as well as emptiness*es* instead of an amorphous emptiness, for *a* reasoning with a specific subject, predicate, and sign proves *an* emptiness. Even when, in tantric practice, you visualize a deity appearing out of the sphere of emptiness, this is the emptiness or ultimate nature of oneself and the deity; you first contemplate the specific emptiness of inherent existence of yourself and the deity, and then appear out of that emptiness.

Therefore, Chandrakīrti's *Supplement to (Nāgār- juna's) "Treatise on the Middle Way"* says:[143]

> In order to release transmigrators [from the afflictive obstructions and the obstructions to omniscience], this selflessness was set forth in two aspects by way of a division into phenomena and persons.

Sentient beings are called transmigrators because through the force of various virtuous and non-virtuous actions they travel from one birth to another in the six realms of cyclic existence — hell-being, hungry ghost, animal, human, de- migod, and god — moving from one level to another, but always caught within cyclic existence like a fly trapped in a jar.

Persons and other phenomena are the bases for the im- putation of a false predicate — self, or inherent existence. At present, although we know that certain things exist, we do not know *how* these things exist. All persons and phe- nomena appearing to our minds seem to exist inherently. Therefore, although these bases of emptiness are actually the *conventionally existent* person and other *conventionally existent* phenomena, we do not have knowledge of them *as* only conventionally existent. We see them with an overlay that prevents seeing them as they are.

Suppose from always wearing green tinted glasses you saw a white building as green; if you knew merely from repute that the building was white without yourself know- ing what white is, you could not say that you know that the color of the building is white. We are in a similar situation.

For example, when something such as a house is stated as

the subject of a syllogism, it actually is a conventionally or merely nominally existent house, but we do not know what such actually is. A Proponent of the Middle Way does not hold that his or her consciousness certifying the subject of a debate — a house, for instance — also certifies that it exists from its own side. Thus, he or she cannot hold that there are commonly appearing subjects because their opponents assert that the consciousness certifying the subject of the debate also certifies its existing from its own side. It also seems to me that the Consequentialists' preference for consequences over syllogisms reflects a preference for using a form of communication that other persons realize as operating within their own assertions, in order to jar them out of thinking that the consciousness certifying the subject also certifies that it is established from its own side.

The house that is the subject of debate or the subject of meditation appears to exist inherently; the very thing that you are trying to refute is utterly mixed with what is appearing within their own assertions, in order to jar them out your consciousness that certifies the existence of the subject does not also certify its inherent existence.

Nevertheless, although the right and wrong appearances of the subject are utterly mixed, realization of emptiness is not a matter of merely seeing the right appearance of the object. For, most Ge-luk-ba scholars hold that, in the sūtra system, during explicit realization of emptiness by anyone except a Buddha, the object entirely disappears.[144] This is because you are searching to determine whether the object inherently exists or not through examining whether the object can withstand analysis, and finally you cannot come up with anything to posit as the object. You are left with a mere vacuity that is the absence of the object's inherent existence, and you remain in meditative equipoise as vividly and as long as you can without losing the force of the non-finding of the object under ultimate analysis. Then, after dwelling as long as you can in this vacuity of inherent existence, it is helpful, when loosening from meditative equipoise, to watch the reappearance of the object as qualified by an absence of inherent existence.

You might think that this would be the order from the very beginning, that the seemingly inherently existent object would change right in front of you and become something that in itself was qualified by an absence of inherent existence. This, however, is not the way that meditation on emptiness proceeds, at least according to most Ge-luk-ba explanations. When meditating on the final nature of a house, for instance, you search to see whether or not you can find an inherently existent one, such as now appears, by taking as your reason that the house is a dependent-arising, and eventually understand that an inherently existent house cannot be found under such analysis. At that point, appearance of the object, the house, vanishes; a conventionally existent house does not appear when its emptiness is realized.

Although there is nothing at all to be found and the object has completely disappeared, you have not fallen to an extreme of annihilation because you are within ultimate analysis. For, since a house only conventionally exists, if it were to appear upon ultimate analysis, it would have to be ultimately existent.

When the object has disappeared and nothing appears but an utter vacuity, it is important to keep remembering that this vacuity is not a vacuity of nothingness, but is just the absence of a solidly, or concretely, existent house covering its parts, that such a house as presently appears to our minds does not exist.

When an inferential cognition of emptiness is attained, it is through the route of the appearance of an *image* of the negative — the absence — of inherent existence. As one approaches closer to direct cognition, this imagistic appearance slowly disappears, eventually leaving only the utter vacuity, which, however, is still not a nothingness, but a specific absence of concrete or inherent existence. Direct cognition, although without conceptuality, is not contentless; the absence of inherent existence is being *realized*, is being *known*, is being *comprehended*.

After dwelling in that state for some time, let the house reappear. There should be a change in its appearance such that its very appearance means that it is analytically unfindable.

Because now we do not have the benefit of such meditation, the appearance of a house calls forth our agreement that it inherently exists. However, when a meditator has become used to this type of reasoned investigation, the strong adherence to the false appearance of inherent existence lessens. This, in turn, causes a change in the appearance of the object. Technically speaking, you are not yet actually removing the appearance of inherent existence, but the house's appearance as very solid due to adherence to its false appearance will partially disappear. Also, through becoming used to the deep import of the reasoning establishing that a house does not inherently exist, eventually even the appearance of its inherent existence induces understanding of its lack of inherent existence. At that point, the conflict between appearance and reality has been realized to the degree that the false appearance itself induces mindfulness that it is false. The Dalai Lama has compared this to the colors seen when wearing sunglasses; the very appearance of the distorted color induces knowledge that it is not true.

You can only accomplish this through trying to find an inherently existent object, discovering that it cannot be found, and then, within knowledge that it cannot be found, again looking at the object. Initially, there was something at the end of your finger at which you were pointing and which was the house, for inherent existence is pointability. Then, when analyzing, you see that there is really not anything that you can point to; the appearance of such a concrete, massive house is recognized as false. By getting used to investigating things with reasoning, you come to realize that you have been deceived. As Nāgārjuna's *Treatise on the Middle Way* says,[145] "All conditioned phenomena have the attribute of deception; therefore, they are falsities."

5 Own Thing

What is the self to be negated in terms of persons and [other] phenomena? Chandrakīrti's *Commentary on (Āryadeva's) "Four Hundred"* says:

> Here, "self" is an inherent nature[146] of phenomena, that is, a non-dependence on another. The non-existence of this is selflessness. Selflessness is realized as twofold through a division into phenomena and persons — a selflessness of phenomena and a selflessness of persons.

Even though, in general, the term "self" means person or I, here in the context of selflessness, "self" means inherent existence, establishment of objects from their own side. "Self" thus connotes independent existence. An object that has it does not depend on other things such as an imputing consciousness; it just has its own thing.

People often talk about doing your own thing; even objects like oranges are said to have their own thing. Everything does indeed have its own defining characteristics, but it seems that when people speak about objects having their own thing, they include the objects' establishment by way of their own character. This is an artificial conception of inherent existence — artificial in the sense of being intellectually acquired as opposed to innate. We have many such artificial conceptions of inherent existence, relying on world-views and reasons to affirm our assent to the way things appear to be established from their own side. Still, noticing the own-thingness of objects is helpful in that it directs us toward raw sensation without conceptual overlay, even if this experience of everything as having its own independent essence is false.

Based on the view that everything has its own thing, we affirm the way objects appear to us, thereby developing an even stronger sense of an orange or a book as having its own thing. If you base yourself on what undeniably appears, you are practicing reaffirming the own-thingness of objects. Nevertheless, valuing direct experience roots one more in the stuff of appearance and less in thought, and makes it possible to appreciate what the Middle Way Consequence School is getting at — a refutation of the seeming establishment of objects by way of their own character.

When you get down to the level of being able to ascertain the appearance of objects as if they are established from their own side, if you are a Buddhist there may be a struggle, for it may seem that Buddhism is wrong since it refutes this own-thingness of phenomena. However, this step is crucial, for if you do not get into your own experience, into what is appearing to you, you can treat "absence of inherent existence" as merely an abstract topic and feel sure that it is correct without ever understanding its implications, whereupon actual progress on the path is difficult.

In order to cognize or even gain a preliminary understanding of emptiness, it is necessary first to have a somewhat clear feeling of the object negated, inherent existence. If you have this, it is much easier. First, you should affirm this object of negation vividly in experience. Go out and try to experience the own-thingness of a flower, for instance, really feel it. The feeling can be very strong and vivid, but if you do enough of this, you may get a sense that you are being deceived. For instance, feel a chair's thingness, its chairness, the factuality of chair. Then go out of your house and leave the chair behind; it is not there anymore.

Then come back and experience the way you are sitting, with your hands and your body arranged a certain way. Get into it to the extent that you understand that if your posture existed the way it appears, it would not be possible for you to change the position of even your hands. When you see that things do change, you have to create a theory of impermanence, and then you have to convince yourself that things are impermanent. Why do we have to tell ourselves so much? Because things are appearing to us in a false way.

This has to be more than intellectual understanding. You have to feel it, to experience that nobody could ever knock down that table if it existed the way it appears. Take something that you value and imagine that someone has come in and walked all over it, destroyed it so that there is no longer anything there for you to cherish. It is said that if things existed the way they appear to us to exist, they would have to be permanent and thus could never change. You have to notice and feel and experience that things do appear to exist in and of themselves.

We must root ourselves in direct cognition in order to realize emptiness, and yet all of the direct cognition we now have is affected by a false element. Even all direct sense experience is infected with the false appearance of objects as if they exist in their own right. Further, just waiting to come out as soon as we become involved in anything is the heavy force of actively assenting to that false appearance.

So, we cannot just sit around and wait for emptiness to dawn. We have to figure out a way to achieve this internal direct cognition. First, get a vivid sense of inherent existence, and then reflect on a reasoning, discovering from the depths that you cannot find such concrete objects. The appearance of things will change; such reasoning works you right into the stuff of reality. You must really become engaged in this. If you just dryly repeat, "It does not exist the way it appears, it does not exist the way it appears," it will not help. We are not aiming in the end to be thinking or reciting something to ourselves, but to *realize* the truth.

> Thus, whether the base is a person or a phenomenon, the innate mode of conception of self is to conceive that it exists objectively through its own entity and is not posited through the force of conceptuality.

You do not feel that the chair you are sitting on is posited by thought and is not really there in itself. Upon investigation, you will perhaps decide that the name is posited by thought, but if you do not think about it, you will see even the name as if it were fused with the object. Look around, there is a clock, a glass, a table; even the names sometimes seem to appear from the side of the object. This is the way that we learn to identify objects easily. I see you, and your name jumps out at me from your side. We could at least practice making it so that the names of things did not jump out of them, there, at us, here. The name's existing there objectively is a very coarse misapprehension, much easier to recognize than the conception of inherent existence.

> The conceived object of that conception is the self to be negated on this occasion and is the hypothetical measure of true existence.

A consciousness conceiving or apprehending inherent existence is a thought consciousness; the object that appears to it, called the appearing object, is a mental image of inherent existence. The mental image exists, but the object to which it refers — its referent object, or the object being conceived — does not exist. For instance, the image of an inherently existent table appears to a thought consciousness; the conceived object of that thought consciousness, an inherently existent table, does not exist, even though the image as well as a mind apprehending or conceiving it do. A consciousness conceiving inherent existence is destroyed by meditating on emptiness, but self, inherent existence, has never existed and thus can never be and need not be destroyed. The erroneous conception, that is, the erroneous consciousness, is uprooted by seeing the non-existence of its object, inherent existence.

In the terms "true existence" and "absence of true existence" what is the meaning of "true"? Hypothetically (since it does not exist), it is the objective existence of a phenomenon through its own entity without being posited by thought. This mode of existence is the referent object of a consciousness conceiving self; it is the "measure" of true existence, the estimate of self or inherent existence in this system. It is self in the view of selflessness in the Consequence School.

The literal translation of the Tibetan original of "hypothetical" is "holding an extreme for the sake of analysis".[147] True existence is to be sized up even though there is no such thing. The hypothetical synonyms of true existence are inherent existence, existence from the side of the object, objective existence, existence by way of the object's own character, ultimate existence, existence from within the basis of designation, existing as its own suchness, existing as its own reality, existing as its own mode of subsistence, existing by way of its own entity,[148] and so forth. In this context, "existence" and "establishment"[149] mean the same thing; therefore, the hypothetical synonyms include inherent establishment, establishment from the side of the object, objective establishment, establishment by way of the object's own character, ultimate establishment, establishment from within the basis of designation, establishment as its own suchness, establishment as its own reality, establishment as its own mode of subsistence, and so forth.

Jang-gya describes self as objective existence. Therefore, a selflessness is an absence of objective existence, a phenomenon's lack of inherent existence; similarly, a conception or apprehension of self is a conception of objective existence — existence right with the object, integral to the object's basis of designation. For instance, if a table objectively existed, it would subsist from its own side as opposed to being imputed, or designated, from the subject's side. This is called "existence with the basis of designation". The basis of designation of a table is all the parts of that table — four legs, a top, and so forth; on them, with them, right with them, is a table. This is the way "self", inherent existence, appears, and this is how we feel it; this is how we conceive it. But, in fact, it does not exist that way, in its own right.

> The Proponents of the Middle Way Autonomy School make the distinction of refuting the three — true existence, ultimate existence, and existing as its own reality[150] — but not refuting the three — inherent existence, existence by way of its own character, or existence by way of its own entity.[151] However, in this [Consequence] system, true existence, etc., and existence by way of its own character, etc., are asserted as having the same meaning.

The Autonomists refute — both ultimately and conventionally — true existence, ultimate existence, and existence of an object as its own reality. However, they are willing to accept the other category — inherent existence, existence by way of the object's own character, existence from the object's own side, and existence by way of the object's own entity — conventionally, but not ultimately. This means that the Autonomists refute that objects have a mode of subsistence that is not posited through the force of appearing to a non-defective awareness. However, it is admissible in the Autonomy School for an object to have a mode of subsistence that is posited through appearing to a non-defective awareness.

Consequentialists refute all these modes of existence both conventionally and ultimately, saying that all these terms are hypothetical synonyms. Thus, the difference between the two systems in words is obvious, though the difference in meaning is difficult to fathom. Basically, for the Autonomists, a table conventionally can be found as the collection of its parts within the context that its mode of being is posited through the force of its appearing to the mind. The table, therefore, does have its own mode of subsistence, which is posited through the force of its appearing to a non-defective awareness, an unimpaired eye consciousness, for instance. It does not have its own unshared mode of subsistence that is not posited by way of appearing to a non-defective consciousness.

According to the Autonomists, the "non-defective" consciousness that posits objects can be either a sense or mental consciousness, whereas in the Consequence School only a conceptual mental consciousness posits objects. For Autonomists, an object appears to a non-defective consciousness and is thereby posited. "Non-defective" means, for example, that you are not travelling in a car and seeing things as moving or that you do not have so much bile that you see even white objects as yellow. It also means that the consciousness is not affected by the conception of true existence; otherwise, a truly existent table could be posited as existing. Through appearing to such a non-defective consciousness, an object attains its mode of subsistence.

The practical difference between the Autonomy School and the Consequence School rests on whether you as a practitioner work with objects as if they *are* the collections of their parts or whether you work with objects as things that are merely imputed in dependence upon a collection. This makes a great difference in the way you face the world.

> Therefore, Dzong-ka-ba's *Differentiation of the Interpretable and the Definitive* [also called the *Essence of the Good Explanations*] says, "The existence of an objective mode of subsistence [means] a self-powered entity."

"Self-powered entity"[152] could also be translated as "an

entity that is under its own power". In the Autonomy School, an objective mode of subsistence is possible if it is posited by the mind. This may seem contradictory, and to the Consequentialists it is, but not for the Autonomists. Suppose, for instance, that a magician were to create right here for us the appearance of a luscious piece of cake. Even though it has no mode of subsistence that is not posited by our mistaken consciousnesses under the influence of his spell, it does have its own mode of subsistence since it is effective, causing our attraction. Just so, according to the Autonomists, all these other phenomena have their own mode of subsistence, but not one that is not posited by the mind. It falsely seems to us as if objects have an independent, uncommon mode of existence that is not posited by the mind; this is our basic error.

The Autonomists are at once trying to get rid of an objective mode of subsistence and yet hold onto it. One lama said that when Autonomists say that the mental consciousness *is* the person, it is as if they had plunged into a river and were trying to hold onto something. In the Consequence School, you let it go. You cannot point to anything and equate it with the person. Thus, an objective mode of subsistence implies self-powered entities.

> Since it is asserted that autonomous[153] and self-powered[154] are synonyms, when the Middle Way Autonomists maintain that the three modes [of a reason][155] are established from their own side, this has the full meaning of true existence in this system [of the Consequence School]. Āryadeva's *Four Hundred* says,[156] "All these are not self-powered; hence, there is no self [inherent existence]." Also, Chandrakīrti's *Commentary on (Āryadeva's) "Four Hundred"* states these as having the same meaning: "own entity, inherent existence, self-powered, and non-reliance on another".[157]

Independent phenomena and emptiness are incompatible; likewise, phenomena that are dependent on other phenomena and are mere nominalities are incompatible with inherent existence.

> *Question:* Since the self refuted on this occasion is [a thing's] existing by way of a mode of subsistence that is not posited through the force of conceptuality, in "posited through the force of conceptuality" to what does "conceptuality" refer? How are things posited through its force? What is the difference between this and the Autonomy School's assertion that a mode of subsistence not posited through the force of an awareness does not exist?

The Autonomists maintain that existence is posited by an awareness,[158] whereas the Consequentialists say that it is posited by conceptuality.[159] Awareness, or consciousness, is much wider than conceptuality; all instances of awareness — all consciousness — are not necessarily instances of conceptuality, but all instances of conceptuality, conceptual consciousnesses, are necessarily awarenesses, consciousnesses. An eye consciousness is an awareness, but not a conceptual consciousness.

> *Answer:* With regard to the way in which things are posited through the force of conceptuality, Āryadeva's *Four Hundred* says:[160]

>> Without [imputation by] conceptuality [like the imputation of a snake to a rope], there is no [finding of] the existence of desire and so forth. If so, who with intelligence would maintain that a real object is produced [dependent on] conceptuality? [For, being imputed by conceptuality and existing as its own reality are contradictory.]

Chandrakīrti's commentary on this passage says:[161]

>> There is no question that what exists merely due to the existence of conceptuality and

does not exist without the existence of conceptuality is, like a snake imputed to a
coiled rope, to be ascertained as not established by way of its own entity.

If something exists only if conceptuality, that is, the conceptual consciousness imputing it, exists and this thing does
not exist if conceptuality does not exist, then it does not
inherently exist. However, it is undeniable that things do
appear to us as if they inherently exist and that, based on
this, we conceive them to exist inherently.

Some in the West say that if there were no people to see
things, nothing would exist, but even they have the idea
that things are there in and of themselves when there are
people to see them. They have a little understanding of an
object's dependence on conceptuality, but they do not realize that they see things in exactly the opposite way. We see
ourselves, others, and our relationships with others as if
they inherently existed, as if their existence were independent of conceptuality, as if they were objectively there,
certainly not as if they depend on conceptuality. This chair,
for example, appears to exist in its own right. Thus, when
we superficially claim that the existence of everything depends on conceptuality, it is abstract; we are not actually
applying this profundity to the way in which things are
appearing to us right now.

Therefore, conceptuality [here refers to] this ordinary, innate awareness which makes designations of
forms and so forth through having become accustomed again and again since beginningless time to
thinking, "This is a form," "This is a feeling," and
so forth.

A designating or imputing consciousness is not necessarily
wrong. For, even though a conceptual consciousness imputing true existence is wrong, not all conceptual consciousnesses necessarily involve conceiving true existence,

as in the case of a conceptual consciousness apprehending a table. Still, the object of any conceptual consciousness *appears* to exist inherently, but, having appeared thus, only sometimes is it *conceived* or *held* to exist inherently.

Since things always appear to us as if they inherently exist, it may seem a bit abstract to talk about conceptuality as if it were not necessarily wrong. However, Dzong-ka-ba explains that, in general, there are three kinds of conceptuality or conceptual consciousnesses: those that conceive their object to exist inherently, those that conceive that their object does not inherently exist, and those that do neither of these.[162] Since the objects of all three of these *appear* to exist inherently, all three are mistaken with respect to their appearing object but not necessarily so with respect to their conceived object because they do not necessarily conceive, or apprehend, that the object inherently exists.

In order to leave cyclic existence, we must directly cognize emptiness; in order to do that, it is necessary to generate an inference of emptiness, which is a type of conceptual consciousness. This inferential consciousness is not totally flawless since, as some Ge-luk-ba scholars say, even the emptiness appearing to it *appears* to exist inherently, but it does not *conceive* emptiness to exist inherently. It is apprehending the absence of inherent existence of the object.

"Conceptuality" in the context of the consciousness that posits objects refers to an ordinary, innate mind. In general, there are two kinds of innate minds, an innate consciousness conceiving inherent existence and the usual innate mind apprehending this or that without considering inherent existence. The latter is also known as a valid cognition of conventional phenomena, or innate valid cognition, and can be any of the six consciousnesses: eye, ear, nose, tongue, body, or mental consciousness. Here, the usual or ordinary innate mind is a conceptual consciousness that imputes the various phenomena.

It is important to differentiate between the mistaken and

non-mistaken[163] on the one hand and wrong and non-wrong[164] on the other; for instance, minds that conceive I are of both types. One that conceives the I to exist inherently is both mistaken and wrong. The valid cognition — which everyone has at times — is a light cognition of I; it is not wrong, but is still mistaken in that the I *appears* to exist inherently. Even with this non-wrong variety, as soon as we pay strong attention to it, the conception of true existence becomes dominant. The border between these two is difficult to ascertain in experience, since without engendering realization of emptiness we cannot differentiate between existence and inherent existence.

The usual valid cognition of I apprehends the conventionally existent I. However, when the correct view of the middle way has been generated, it is possible to conceive and understand the I *as* only conventionally existent. Even if occasionally we already have a valid cognition of I and even if the I that appears to this valid consciousness only conventionally exists, we do not understand its conventional existence. We understand only I.

For example, remember thinking, "I need to go to the store," without any emphasis on I. This is a valid cognition of I, but this vague feeling of I without an overlay of misconception will not offer opposition to further conceptions that the I inherently exists. That can only be done through penetrative understanding that the I is not established by way of its own character, after which it can be understood that the I only imputedly exists.

Since phenomena require a consciousness to certify their existence, an innate valid cognition of conventional phenomena also serves the purpose of certifying those phenomena. Mañjushrī, the deity who is the physical manifestation of the wisdom of all Buddhas, is said to have told Dzong-ka-ba in a visionary experience that he should value appearances, and thus, in Dzong-ka-ba's system of explaining the Middle Way Consequence School, there are said to be, even in the continuums of us ordinary beings, consciousnesses certifying the existence even of the I. Dzong-ka-ba's presentation of this perception should not, however, be taken as an end in itself, as if we were to take some relief in the fact that we have correct cognitions. For, since we cannot, at this point, differentiate between existence and inherent existence, we cannot use our occasional, already correct perception of I or other phenomena to understand their nature. Still, recognition that these objects are validly established even though we do not properly understand their mode of subsistence will help to keep us from an extreme of nihilism.

6 Validity

There have been many great philosophers and yogis in all four major orders of Tibetan Buddhism, Nying-ma, Ga-gyu, Sa-gya, and Ge-luk.[165] One approach, rather different from Dzong-ka-ba's, interprets the Consequence School such that there is no universally valid consciousness certifying the existence of phenomena, no such valid establishment. In this interpretation, all that appears to our minds as inherently existent is mistaken and, therefore, non-existent except for an ignorant consciousness. The non-existent appears vividly. Why is this not nihilism? Even though, beyond merely allowing for what appears to an ignorant consciousness, they deny any validity in what appears to us now, they teach that underlying these appearances — or, in another way, replacing them once we pass beyond them — is the one great sphere of reality.[166] Teachings such as this prevent a practitioner from falling into nihilism until direct cognition of the great sphere of reality is manifested. Even if only through a lama's telling you about it, you know that there is not nothing.

In this interpretation it is wrong to value present appearances because this would affirm the way things are appearing to us now, reinforcing the ordinary way in which we deal with these things. When it comes down to practice, subtle presentations of a mixture of right and wrong appearances could be misleading. Why? Because, as even Ge-luk-ba scholars themselves admit, we do not know how to differentiate with valid cognition between inherent existence and conventional existence until we have realized the emptiness of inherent existence.

Dzong-ka-ba's teaching on this point is complex. In his interpretation, the correct and wrong appearances are mixed. For instance, an eye consciousness apprehends a rug that appears to be inherently existent. Along with the inherently existent rug, a conventionally or non-inherently existent rug also appears. Since these two appear mixed with one another, our sense of rug is so fused with inherent existence that it is an abstraction to speak of an eye consciousness that certifies the existence of a rug, but Dzong-ka-ba frequently speaks of such. Moreover, in terms of experience, the object that appears to us now would *seem* to be negated in the process of finding the view of the Middle Way.

The ordinary innate mind that is accustomed to thinking thoughts such as, "This is a form," and so forth, is in general said by Dzong-ka-ba's followers to be an innate valid cognition. But, it is extremely difficult in our own experience to draw the line between the valid and the invalid. We have a mind thinking, "This is a rug," and as far as the appearance of the rug as inherently existent goes, the mind is mistaken. How are we to draw the line on the subjective side between the mind that is just thinking, "This is a rug," and another that conceives and assents to the appearance of an inherently existent rug? Phenomena are posited correctly by thought, but their appearance is completely suffused with a mistaken appearance of objective existence.

> [The example of a rope-snake illustrates] how things are posited through the force of [ordinary innate conceptuality]. When darkness has fallen on

a rope, it is thought to be a snake since the
variegated colors of the rope and the way in which it
is coiled are like a snake and it is seen in a dim
place. At that time, neither the color of the rope, its
shape, its other parts, nor the collection of those
parts may be posited as something that is a snake.[167]
The snake of this occasion is only a mere designation by conceptuality in dependence upon the rope.

A rope appears to the mind and, in dependence on that and
other adventitious conditions, "snake" is imputed. However, there is nothing on that spot which is a snake.

Similarly, when the thought "I" arises in terms of
the five [mental and physical] aggregates that are its
bases of designation, neither the individual aggregates, the collection, their continuum, nor their
parts can be posited as something that is I.[168] Furthermore, there is not in the least any phenomenon
that is a separate entity from those [mental and
physical aggregates] and can be apprehended as
something that is I. The I is merely posited by
conceptuality in dependence upon the aggregates.

The thought "I" arises in the context of the five aggregates
of body and mind, but this does not mean that all five
aggregates must appear with each conception. Any one of
them, a collection of them — whatever is appearing at the
time of thinking "I" — is suitable. A collection of the
aggregates would be any group of mental and physical
aggregates appearing at one time. A continuum is a collection of moments over time. This can be the continuum of
the body, mind, or both — whatever is appearing. Usually,
it is feeling, breath, some part of the body, a particular
consciousness, or a combination of these.

Although the way in which all phenomena are imputed by conceptuality is, in this way, like the
imputing of a snake to a rope, a rope-snake and

phenomena such as forms are not the same with respect to whether or not they conventionally exist. For they are dissimilar in terms of whether or not conventional valid cognition damages an assertion [made] in accordance with what is being imputed.

In one case, "snake" is being imputed to a rope, which in no way can perform the functions of a snake. It would not be possible to get its poison to use in medicine. Therefore, a conventional valid cognition of the rope — such as upon aiming your flashlight at it and seeing that it is not a snake — would be able to damage, or invalidate, an assertion such as, "This is a snake," or "It can perform such and such as a function." Although all phenomena are posited by the mind, not everything posited by the mind exists.

Furthermore, with respect to how [phenomena] are mere nominal imputations, one engages in adopting [virtues] and discarding [non-virtues] in dependence on mere nominalities which are conventions designated to these phenomena such as forms, "This is a form," "This is a feeling," and so forth, and through this, desired aims are accomplished. Also, within the context of mere nominality, all affirmations and negations of correctness and incorrectness, etc., as well as all agents, actions, and objects are possible. However, if one is not satisfied with mere nominalities and enters into searching to find the object imputed in the expression "form", [trying to discover] whether it can be taken as color, shape, some other factor, or the collection of all these, and so forth, one will not find anything, and all presentations [of phenomena] will become impossible.

We assume that the objects with which we are involved are objectively fused with their own parts. We never operate on the level of their only being imputed in dependence upon bases of designation. We fuse the two, the basis of designation and the object, together.

If you are satisfied with mere nominalities, then existence, change, and so forth are possible. If you are not satisfied, you have to find something that *is* the phenomenon designated. But upon searching, you cannot come up with anything. For instance, we say that this book is a form, that it is an object of the eye consciousness. Well, what is the form? Is the form the colors black, white, and so on? Or is it the shape? If the book is identical with all the many colors, then is the black color the book? Sure, it is. Is the white color the book? Sure. In that case, there are two books. Or, if you have something that is all one color, you can divide it into this portion and that portion. But, of course, when we say book, we do not mean color. Is it both color and shape? Or is it another quality, such as obstructiveness, or perhaps the collection of all these things. We feel strongly that an object is a whole, but where is this whole? Can you point to it? Is this the whole? Is that the whole?

> Making presentations of what is and is not correct in the context of mere nominalities is most feasible. For example, there were two villagers who went to a city to see the sights. They went into a temple and began to look at the paintings, whereupon one of them said, "That one holding a trident in his hand in Nārāyaṇa; the other holding a wheel in his hand is Maheshvara." The other villager said, "You are mistaken; the one holding a trident is Maheshvara, and the one holding a wheel is Nārāyaṇa." And thus they disputed.
>
> A wandering holy man was nearby. They went up to him, and each spoke his thought. The wanderer thought, "Being murals on a wall, these are neither Maheshvara nor Nārāyaṇa." Although he knew that, still he did not say, "These are not gods, but paintings." Instead, in conformity with the conventions of the world, he told the two villagers that one

of them was right and the other wrong. Through his speaking thus, the wishes of the two villagers were fulfilled, and the wanderer also did not incur the fault of telling a lie.

Likewise, although all phenomena do not have objective establishment, presentations such as, "This is correct, and that is incorrect," are feasible within the context of mere nominalities. Although the Supramundane Victor [Buddha] sees that all phenomena do not truly exist, even he teaches the adopting [of virtues] and discarding [of non-virtues] using terminology as the world does, thereby bringing about the welfare of transmigrators.

Although there are no phenomena that exist in accordance with their appearance to us now, Buddhas teach using our own terminology and through that can lead us out of cyclic existence.

You can see how easily people would think that this example means there is no valid establishment of phenomena. It is, in fact, more difficult to explain certain passages within a context of valid establishment. For example, it is said that Chandrakīrti milked a painting of a cow to overcome in others the idea that things truly exist.[169] Is it not difficult to say, then, that the painting of a cow is validly established as a painting? Moreover, might it not be that when you realize that things do not truly exist they become cross-functional — that a painting of a cow might be able to serve as a cow? Also, it is said that every particle has a Buddha-field in it; is it not then possible for anything to be there? How can you say that this square thing in front of us is validly established as a table?

The Ge-luk-ba answer is that transformations of matter, as in Chandrakīrti's milking a painting of a cow, are due to the special powers of yogis, whereas such a presentation of valid establishment is within the *coarse* conventions of the world, which yogis do not contradict — they merely can operate on a subtler level. In other interpretations, however, it is said that these coarse conventions appear merely through the power of ignorance. I think that it is possible to bring these two interpretations together in such a way that you can practice them in union by recognizing that the Ge-luk-ba emphasis at this point is on ordinary perceptions whereas, for the most part, the other orders of Tibetan Buddhism are emphasizing the extraordinary perceptions of yogis. Still, even in Dzong-ka-ba's system, a Buddha is not limited by the time-space limitations that we now have, despite the fact that ours are validly established within the realm of coarse conventions.

> This way [of presenting nominalities] was taught by Buddhapālita, a great master who had attained yogic feats, in his commentary on the eighteenth chapter of Nāgārjuna's *Treatise on the Middle Way*. The honorable Chandrakīrti and the revered Shāntideva also, through many examples and reasonings, explain still other ways in which agent, object, and action are feasible within the context of mere nominalities. I will not elaborate more on the topic here.

Jang-gya now declares that what he explained above actually is the view of the Consequence School.

> This presentation of conventions is the uncommon way in which the three masters [Buddhapālita, Chandrakīrti, and Shāntideva] comment on the thought of the Superior [Nāgārjuna].

This way of explaining the suitability of conventions or designations is uncommon because other Indian masters explained the Superior Nāgārjuna's philosophy in different ways. In general, a Superior is someone who, from among the five paths — of accumulation, preparation, seeing, meditation, and no more learning — has reached the path of seeing. A Superior, then, has experienced a direct "seeing" or cognition of emptiness.

> The Foremost Omniscient Father [Dzong-ka-ba]

and his spiritual sons [Gyel-tsap and Kay-drup] frequently advised that just this is the final difficult point of the Middle Way School view.

That things validly exist conventionally and yet are not findable under ultimate analysis is hard to fathom.

About this way [of presenting conventionalities], the *Questions of Upāli Sūtra* says:[170]

> These alluring blossoming flowers of
> various colors
> And these fascinating brilliant mansions of
> gold
> Are without any [inherently existent] maker
> here.
> They are posited through the power of
> conceptuality,
> The world is imputed through the power of
> conceptuality.

And the *King of Meditative Stabilizations Sūtra* says:[171]

> Nirvana is not found
> In the way nirvana is taught
> By words to be profound.
> The words also are not found ...

The profound state of nirvana can be, to some extent, described in words; however, nirvana is attained by looking very closely to see whether or not you can find phenomena — such as nirvana or even the words describing it — and thereupon finding a non-finding. This realization cannot be depicted through words in just the way that it is experienced.

And a *Perfection of Wisdom Sūtra* says, "It is this way: this 'Bodhisattva' is only a name. It is this way: this 'enlightenment' is only a name. It is this way: this 'perfection of wisdom' is only a name ..."

The tantric abbot Kensur Ngawang Lekden said that the phrase, "It is this way," using the proximate term "this", is an indication that Buddha sees the truth directly — "This is how it is."

And the Superior Nāgārjuna's *Precious Garland* says that name-only does not exist ultimately:[172]

> Because the phenomena of forms are
> Only names, space too is only a name.
> Without the elements, how could forms
>   [inherently] exist?
> Therefore even "name-only" does not
>   [inherently] exist.

If you can determine that forms are only nominalities, then space also is name-only since space is the absence of the obstructiveness of forms. But, we feel that forms inherently exist; therefore, Nāgārjuna says, "Without the elements, how could forms exist?" Thus, in the end, this line of reasoning rests on a refutation of the true existence of the elements — earth, water, fire, and wind.

To have forms, the earth element — hardness — has to be present. Further, in order for minute particles to form an aggregate, the water element — cohesiveness — must be present also. In order to have one, the other must be present; it is the same also for temperature (fire) and motility (wind). If they were utterly in one spot, they would not be four. Moreover, if one is needed in order to have the others, then there is no first element, no second element; there is no way to separate them from each other.

Nāgārjuna's conclusion is that the elements' very nominality does not exist objectively and findably, that name-only is name-only. Once there are no truly existent phenomena that possess names, then those names also do not truly exist. A name goes with a phenomenon; once you cannot find that phenomenon, how can you possibly have an inherently existent name for it?

This is a key to understanding cause and effect, dependent-arising, how things work. As we are now, we move between holding the extreme of inherent existence and the extreme of total non-existence. We do not know the middle way. Getting to it is not a matter of putting together the ways we already know things — for instance, by mixing a little inherent existence and a little nihilism — but of constructing something entirely new.

Some who call themselves Proponents of the Middle Way School say that phenomena do not exist because they cannot find them upon analyzing. They feel that phenomena perform no functions, that when you cognize emptiness, there is nothing. However, this is not the middle way. When you are unable to find things upon searching, it means that they are not findable in the way in which you are accustomed to thinking. This does not make them utterly non-existent. A distinction has to be made between not finding something and finding it to be non-existent; the inherent existence of a table is both not found under analysis and found to be non-existent, but although a table is not found under such analysis, its non-existence is not found. For, the conventional existence of a table, or anything else, is outside the sphere of competency of ultimate analysis. Ultimate analysis can only determine whether an object *inherently* exists or not.

Moreover, it is hard for us, when we discover that things are unfindable, to engage in any kind of sensible participation in the everyday world. Participation requires attention, and once we pay attention, we lose our "understanding" of emptiness. Again, when we are completely unable to find the thing we are looking for, especially if it is something we intensely want, great discouragement sets in; we then want nothing to do with the object, and the mind goes on to something else. When we find out that people do not inherently exist, we want to have nothing to do with them, we become indifferent to them. However, this is just due to our addiction to the extremes; actually, emptiness is supposed to be the key to compassion. Our addiction to the extremes pollutes even our approach to emptiness.

It is difficult to sustain a mind that cannot find phenomena once you have left meditation. At that time, you need the mind that knows that phenomena are name-only. For example, when you ride in a car, no matter how much you are otherwise engaged in conversation, you remember that you are going along in a car; otherwise, you would be frightened when you looked out the window and saw the world racing by. Just so, it is important to retain an understanding of emptiness while engaging in activities, knowing all along that these things are only nominally imputed and are analytically unfindable. According to the strength of one's realization, one has more or less understanding of this in whatever one is doing.

> And Nāgārjuna's *Precious Garland of Advice*[173] also says that, except for what is merely posited by the power of nominal designations, nothing at all exists:
>
>> Other than as a convention
>> What world is there in fact
>> Which would be "[inherently] existent" or
>> "[inherently] not existent"?
>
> Based on not understanding those reasons, Middle Way Autonomists and below [i.e., Proponents of Mind Only, Proponents of Sūtra, and Proponents of the Great Exposition] maintain that when the expression, "This person did this deed," is imputed, an accumulator of deeds[174] and so forth can be posited [only] if there comes to be something that is posited as the person upon finding it — for instance, a part, the collection [of parts], or the continuum from among the bases of designation [of that person]. If nothing is found, [an accumulator of deeds] cannot be posited.

For the Autonomists and below, there has to be something among the bases of imputation of a phenomenon that is that phenomenon. Thus, in all Buddhist tenet systems except the Consequence School, a phenomenon that is only imputed by conceptuality is one that does not exist *apart* from the bases of its designation, that is not an independent entity.

This is evident in some contemporary Buddhist meditation systems. They say, "The person does not exist; it is just consciousness," or, "The person is nothing; it is just this collection of mind and body." "The person does not exist," means it does not have a separate independent entity; rather, it is one of the aggregates or their collection — "It is just this collection of mind and body." According to such systems, if there is nothing from among the bases of designation of the person that is the person, then there is no person. Indeed, it is very difficult to understand that something can be analytically unfindable and still exist.

In the Consequence system, although all things are effective, they are like a magician's illusions. A magician puts a salve on a pebble and casts a spell, which affects the eye consciousnesses of the audience and also his own, causing all to see the pebble as a cow. You see a cow there and think that it is real, pure-bred, and providing tasty milk. The cow also appears to the eye consciousness of the magician, but he does not conceive it to be a cow. You, the audience, conceive this to be a cow. It appears to him exactly as it appears to you, but he is not deceived. There is nothing to draw him into ruminations about tasty milk; he, without any doubt, knows that it is not a cow.

In just this way, all phenomena appear to exist inherently but do not. Those who remain within the force of realizing emptiness are like the magician; after cognition of emptiness, but still within not forgetting it, they do not conceive phenomena to exist inherently in any way. It is like wearing sunglasses; you usually remember, at least subliminally, that you are wearing them, knowing that the colors of the objects that you see are deceptive. Although they all appear to be green, you are not amazed. Just so, although a concretely existent self does not exist, such appears but is understood as non-existent by those who remain within the force of realizing emptiness.

Ordinary people are like the magician's audience, assuming the inherent existence of what appears. A Buddha is like a passer-by whose eye consciousness was not affected by the spell and who sees only a pebble. Nothing appears to Buddhas to exist inherently; only from their knowledge of what we perceive do inherently existent objects appear to them. Until Buddhahood, all phenomena are like a magician's illusions, appearing one way but existing in another way; nonetheless, there still is validly established effectiveness.

7 Withdrawal Is Not Sufficient

Those who understand the selflessness of persons a little might occasionally think, "It seems that the person does not inherently exist." Nevertheless, they mostly would feel that because an action is performed, there must be an inherently existent agent. "I can do something, can't I? Therefore, I must exist from my own side." Although they have searched for the I and been unable to find it, they think that since persons can act, persons must exist in their own right. Hence, in his *Treatise on the Middle Way*, Nāgārjuna showed various ways to analyze actions, as a part of the analysis of the three — action, agent, and object — that is important for understanding emptiness.

Since actions are a primary reason for feeling there is a truly existent person, they must be analyzed. For instance, does a talker talk? Or does a non-talker talk? The latter is impossible, but the former is just as impossible. If you are already performing that talking by which you are called a talker, of what use is another talking? It is said that by studying the second and eighth chapters in Nāgārjuna's *Treatise on the Middle Way* and meditating over a long period you can understand actions to be unfindable; then, you can understand that agents of actions are also false, appearing to exist inherently but not so. Also, because they do false actions, they are false doers and cannot be found under analysis. The very actions that were signs of inherent existence become signs of emptiness.

Instead, nowadays we think that because these actions appear to our minds, they are inherently existent and that, therefore, the person who does them must also inherently exist. For instance, you may feel, "I may well not be either the same as or different from my mental and physical aggregates, but I was born, was I not?" or, "I have a family," "I have a house," "I have a body, do I not?"

Sometimes when you meditate on the selflessness of the person in this way you are not actually getting at the inherently existent person but at something coarser, the self-sufficient person. In a public lecture in India in 1972, the Dalai Lama explained how to test the subtlety of one's understanding of emptiness: If you think that you have identified the inherently existent person and that you have attacked it, then since, as explained earlier, your cognition of its emptiness should apply effortlessly to other phenomena, switch your focus from yourself to your head or your teeth and see if your understanding of emptiness applies there. If it does not, then the emptiness that has been understood is on a coarser level than the emptiness of inherent existence. If it does apply immediately to the other phenomenon, then you probably are on target. Similarly, if you actually have understood that persons lack inherent existence, then when actions performed by a person who is empty of inherent existence appear to your mind, you should understand those actions immediately as without inherent existence.

One often has to analyze a number of topics — production, ownership, going — wherever your mind moves. Sometimes you should stay just on the topic you are analyzing because you are penetrating it well. Other times you should move on to several other phenomena until arriving at the point of conviction that the same analysis will apply to them. Some people, however, through only analyzing the person, take it so deeply that their understanding is sufficient to apply to everything else.

It is important to remember that Nāgārjuna's *Treatise on the Middle Way* contains twenty-seven chapters of analyses — all concerned with the emptinesses of different kinds of phenomena in the world. Ge-luk-ba scholars rely heavily on Chandrakīrti's commentary on it, the *Clear Words*, one reason being that in objections and answers he illustrates the types of shifts and dodges that the mind makes. Chandrakīrti gives introductions to each chapter and to each development in the argument.

A Bodhisattva uses many different ways to meditate on emptiness in order to loosen the false network of reasons that freeze things into inherent existence. The variety of approaches makes the force of analysis even stronger.

In the end, it comes down to experiencing the inability to find the phenomenon designated either among its bases of designation or separate from them. According to Dzong-ka-ba's interpretation, this sets the Consequentialists above the other schools of tenets. In the lower systems, if nothing that can be pointed to as the object designated can be found, then that object cannot be said to exist.

> It is the same also for the Sūtra School's positing as space the non-affirming negative that is a mere elimination of any obstructive tangibility and is the same also for [the presentations in] higher [systems but not the Consequence School].

According to the lower schools, something within the basis of designation of a particular phenomenon *is* that phenomenon, even in the case of an uncompounded, negative phenomenon such as space.

> In this system [of the Consequence School], it is admissible, without having in that way to search for and find the object designated, to posit all agents and actions, as in the case of a person as an accumu-

lator of deeds *(karma)*. This is a marvelous distinctive feature [of the Consequence School].

The Autonomists maintain that in [the phrase] "a mode of subsistence not posited through the force of an awareness is to be taken as the object negated [in the view of selflessness]", the word "awareness" refers to an unmistaken non-defective consciousness. However, in the Consequentialists' [assertion of phenomena] as being posited through the force of conceptuality, conceptuality is asserted to be a mistaken consciousness. Hence, they differ.

A non-defective consciousness, besides being without the error of the conception of true existence, is also without error arising from a faulty sense faculty such as a jaundiced eye that causes everything to be seen as yellow, or from a place, such as a moving car or ship that results in stationary objects appearing to be moving, etc. For the Autonomists, a non-defective consciousness is also not mistaken about the inherent existence of its object; it perceives as inherently existent what actually inherently exists. However, it can be mistaken in other ways; for example, all schools accept that inferential cognitions are mistaken because, in brief, the mental image of the object appears to be that object. As mentioned two chapters ago, such a non-defective consciousness can be any of the five sense consciousnesses or the mental consciousness.

When the Consequentialists maintain that things are merely posited by conceptuality, they are referring to the designation of phenomena by a consciousness that is mistaken about the mode of existence of objects — in that what does not inherently exist *appears* to do so — but is correct as far as the object in general is concerned. In this way, the two terms, "awareness" (or "consciousness") in the Autonomy School and "conceptuality" (or "conceptual consciousness") in the Consequence School, do not at all refer to the same kind of consciousness.

Therefore, the Consequentialists even posit the

mere I or mere person as the object of observation of the innate [false] view of the transitory collection[175] [as an inherently existent self]; they do not posit the [mental and physical] aggregates, etc., [as its object of observation].

The innate false view of the transitory collection is the main ignorance and thus the chief cause of wandering in cyclic existence. The term "transitory collection" refers to the five aggregates which are impermanent and an aggregation; thus, the object of the false view of the transitory collection, if we were to think about it superficially, would seem to be the mental and physical aggregates since we are speaking about a view *of* the transitory collection. It is indeed the case that first we apprehend the mental and physical aggregates, conceive of them as inherently existent, and then conceive of an inherently existent person; still, in the Consequence School, the object of observation of a false view of the transitory collection — that is to say, of a consciousness misconceiving an inherently existent I — is the mere I, not the mental and physical aggregates. "Mere" excludes inherent existence. The continuum of this mere I or mere person has existed from time without beginning. It is the conventionally existent I, not a universal or collective mind. The continuum of any being's mind has existed from beginningless time, but a human mind has not, because that person has had animal minds and so forth in former lives.

The object of observation by the innate false view of the transitory collection — the conventionally existent I — exists; however, its conceived object, an inherently existent I, does not. Thus, it is a consciousness mistaken about its conceived object, holding it to exist whereas it does not.

Although the mere I is the object of observation of the innate false view of the transitory collection, if the mental and physical aggregates do not appear, then neither will the mere I, for prior to its being conceived to exist inherently, the aggregates appear and are conceived to exist inherently. From this point of view, it is called a false view *of the transitory collection.*

The conception of the aggregates as inherently existent serves as a necessary cause of conceiving the I to exist inherently. Nevertheless, when initially meditating, one does not concentrate on the conception of a self of phenomena, the cause, but on the conception of a self of persons, the effect, because it is easier to get at. Then, because a self of phenomena is similar, the same reasoning can be applied to it.

> The object of observation of an innate [false] view of the transitory collection that [mis]conceives mine is mine itself.

The mine, in general, can be either included in your continuum, like your hand, or not, like your shirt, but here it refers to phenomena included within the continuum. Some say that "mine" refers to the phenomena included within the personal continuum that are considered to be mine, but Jam-yang-shay-ba takes the term more as what I would translate as "my" and is thus a person. In the former interpretation, in order to be included within the category "mine", a phenomenon such as a hand has to be distinguished as mine. It is distinguished as belonging to an I that inherently exists, and this misconception of I as inherently existent, which is necessarily involved in misconceiving my hand, is the false view of the transitory collection as inherently existent mine. Thus, an object has to be distinguished as mine in order for the conception of the I that is the inherently existent owner to qualify as a false view of the transitory conceiving of inherently existent mine.

Jam-yang-shay-ba[176] says that mine (as mentioned just above, according to his interpretation "mine" would be better translated as "my") is a person. For him, the my is the one who makes things into mine. Normally when we say "mine", we think of the object possessed, but you can also look at the mine more as "my" and thus a person, the owner. Even if I and my are both persons, this does not mean that there are two persons; they are one entity.

Why does Jam-yang-shay-ba explain it this way? If "mine" were the objects towards which possession is felt, then this kind of innate misconception of the transitory collection would be a conception of a self of phenomena, not of persons as it must be. However, as explained above, others say that the innate false view of the transitory collection that conceives mine is a special conception of a self of persons. Because the I must be misconceived to exist inherently prior to misconceiving the mine to do so, the latter can indirectly be considered a branch of the former. Whether or not you distinguish the object as being mine, a mind that conceives of your body, for instance, as truly existent is not a false view of the transitory collection, but a conception of a self of phenomena other than the person.

To me, it seems possible to use both of these interpretations. Jam-yang-shay-ba is pointing out that there is a sense of the person that is the owner, my, and another sense that is I. They indeed are different; I is more alone; my, more active. The other interpretation is emphasizing the mistakenly understood I that is involved in considering something to be a belonging of that I. In both of these interpretations, the innate false view of the transitory collection is of two types, misconceptions of I and mine as inherently existent, and both are considered to be misconceptions of a self of persons.

> A consciousness conceiving persons of other continuums to be established by way of their own character is not an innate [false] view of the transitory collection but is an innate conception of a self of persons.

When you conceive yourself to exist inherently, this is both a conception of a self of persons and a false view of the transitory collection conceiving I to be inherently existent. When you conceive someone else to exist inherently, this is a conception of a self of persons, but not an innate false view of the transitory collection conceiving I to be inherently existent.

The objects of the innate conception of a self of phenomena are the aggregates of forms and so forth, either those included in [your own] continuum or not. Although in that way the objects of observation of a consciousness conceiving a self of persons and of a consciousness conceiving a self of phenomena are different, their subjective aspects are the same in that they [both] conceive that the object is established by way of its own character. Hence, there is no fallacy of its [absurdly] following that there are two discordant modes of conception that are roots of cyclic existence.

The way in which these two misconceive their objects is exactly the same — as inherently existent; thus, there are not two roots of cyclic existence but one, the conception of inherent existence.

The way in which an innate consciousness conceiving true existence conceives an inherently existent person in the context of the aggregates of form and so forth is not to conceive such upon having analyzed [whether the person and the mental and physical aggregates] are one or different. Rather, it conceives such through the force of ordinary familiarity, without any reasons at all. [This] innate consciousness has no mode in which it conceives of oneness, difference, and so forth [of the person and the mental and physical aggregates].

A consciousness innately conceiving that a person inherently exists does not analyze whether the person and the mental and physical aggregates, which are its bases of designation, are one thing or different. It conceives the person to be inherently existent out of natural conditioning to do so.

If while walking along a cliff you fear that you may fall off, the appearance of I is together with the appearance of mind and body. Despite there being a solid and tangibly existent I, the mind conceiving it does not differentiate it from mind and body and does not consider it to be the same as mind and body. When someone sticks a pin in your hand, you say that you were stuck. The Fifth Dalai Lama says that the appearances of mind, body, and an inherently existent I are mixed like milk and water.[177]

This is not to say that one could not differentiate the I and the aggregates — only that *this* consciousness does not differentiate them. Thus, we are not looking for a self that is innately conceived to be a different entity from the aggregates, since an innate consciousness misconceiving the nature of the person does not enter into such analysis as to whether the basis of designation and the object designated are one or different. There is no mind that innately conceives of a person as a different entity from the mental and physical aggregates.

This may seem to be contradictory. It is said that the innate mind does not conceive the person and the aggregates to be one and that it does not conceive them to be different. It is also said that the appearance of the aggregates and the person are mixed like milk and water. On top of that, it is said that it is as if the person has its own entity. All of these describe one mode of appearance and conception; within the context of the appearances of mind, body, and I being mixed like milk and water, the I appears to exist in itself, able to set itself up, self-instituting. Even if it and the aggregates appear to be fused, it is essential to identify that part that is the appearance of an inherently existent I. Still, sometimes it seems that it is *almost* impossible to separate the I from the things that are its bases of designation. As Kensur Ngawang Lekden repeatedly said,[178] we see a designated phenomenon as being fused with its basis of designation like water mixed into milk, whether we are dealing with I, aggregates, book, bed, or any phenomenon, but a Buddha does not.

> Therefore, the Foremost Omniscient [Dzong-ka-ba] spoke even of the *non-analytical* innate conception of true existence.

A consciousness conceiving true existence is non-analytical because it does not enter into analyses such as whether the object designated and the basis of designation are one or different.

Previously, we have talked about the subtle conception of a self of persons, that is, of *inherently existent* persons, and about the coarse conception of a self of persons — of a person as a self-sufficient or substantially existent entity. There is a third form of the conception of a self of persons considered by Consequentialists to be the coarsest of all — of a permanent, unitary, and independent person. Dzong-ka-ba describes this mode of conception as merely artificial, due merely to acceptance of false tenets, there being no innate form of it. The Sa-gya scholar Dak-tsang Shay-rap-rin-chen,[179] however, says that then it would absurdly follow that there is no conception of yesterday's person and today's person to be one, for according to Dzong-ka-ba there is no innate conception of a permanent person. Moreover, Dak-tsang says, it would absurdly follow that persons have no innate conception of themselves going to the east and themselves going to the west as the same person. It would also follow from this that there is no innate conception of the mental and physical aggregates as the objects of use of an independent I.

It is clear that we do have these innate conceptions. We automatically feel that this is the book we had yesterday, that we are the same one who went to the store yesterday, and so on. We can easily confirm this; thus, we have to accept that these have innate forms.

Dzong-ka-ba, however, must be referring to the conception of a permanent, unitary, and independent person as the non-Buddhist systems present it. We do not have an innate misconception of the nature of the self as all three of these — permanent in the sense of not changing, unitary in the sense of being partless, and independent in the sense of not depending on the mental and physical aggregates.

Dak-tsang seems to say that when you refute the philosophical monstrosity, the artificial conception, you are always getting at an innate conception. Dak-tsang explains that we have innately a conception of sameness and a conception of difference of the person and the aggregates, saying to Dzong-ka-ba that it would be a waste of time to refute the other systems if there were no innate forms of these misconceptions. The answer from Dzong-ka-ba's tradition is that refutation of the artificial conception is a branch of the refutation of the innate conception; otherwise, it would indeed be senseless — but that we do not naturally conceive the I to be one with or different from the aggregates that are its bases of designation. Nevertheless, if such a solid, inherently existent I existed, it would have to be the same as the aggregates or different from them. Therefore, if you refute the systems that propose sameness and difference, you are also refuting the innate conception of inherent existence, as long as you identify the subtle object of negation and realize that it is the target of the reasoning.

It seems that Dzong-ka-ba and Dak-tsang are almost saying the same thing — that the refutation of the artificial mode of the conception of self extends to the innate form. Their disagreement is over how and why. Dak-tsang holds that the refutation of the artificial form applies to the innate because the innate form itself conceives the I and the aggregates at some times to be one and at other times to be different. Dzong-ka-ba is saying that the innate form conceives the I and the aggregates neither to be the same nor different. This is a difficult point. Does Dzong-ka-ba mean that the subtle innate conception could not conceive someone to be the same person seen yesterday? Certainly you would consider this person be the same person that you saw yesterday, but would such a conception mean that you have to conceive him or her to be *one* with the person that you saw yesterday? It may be that today's person and yesterday's person are conceived to be *as if* undifferentiable but not exactly one.

Dzong-ka-ba's system describes a sense of a concrete person that is not explicitly conceived to be *one* with yesterday's person. If it were one — if it were that obviously misconceived — perhaps we would already have been drawn into analysis. Also, Dzong-ka-ba is speaking here about whether we innately *perceive* something and its basis of designation to be one or different, not whether we innately *conceive* someone seen today to be one with the same person seen yesterday.

When Dak-tsang says that the I and the aggregates are conceived to be one, does he mean that this consciousness is thinking "one"? I doubt it. If not, then Dak-tsang and Dzong-ka-ba are saying the same thing. Thus, when Dzong-ka-ba describes the innate conception of inherent existence as "non-analytical", he means that this consciousness does not conclude, or specifically think, "one" or "different".

We are living within the non-analytical innate mind conceiving inherent existence most of the time; it must be located and watched. In order to get rid of it, it is necessary to find it.

> Although even a consciousness conceiving true existence is posited as an object to be refuted through reasoning, the main [object to be refuted through reasoning] is the conceived object itself [inherent existence].

There are two objects to be refuted through reasoning, one existent and one not. The existent object of refutation is a consciousness conceiving inherent existence, whereas the non-existent is the conceived object of that consciousness — inherent existence.

A consciousness conceiving inherent existence is the root of cyclic existence; therefore, it must be stopped. In order to stop it, we first have to refute its conceived object. Once we no longer believe in the object, inherent existence, the consciousness conceiving inherent existence itself will disappear.

It is possible just to withdraw your mind from the grosser aspects of such a conception; you can do this in meditation. The production of a mistaken consciousness that conceives self, at least in its grosser forms, will temporarily cease; however, this is not very helpful. In order to eradicate the consciousness conceiving inherent existence, you have to cultivate its antidote in meditation; the only antidote is a consciousness that understands the object in a way exactly opposite to the conception of inherent existence. When that is developed, the consciousness conceiving inherent existence will gradually diminish. Otherwise, it is like being angry and then forgetting it. In one sense, you have gotten over your anger of the moment since it is no longer intruding, but you have not gotten over anger, either in general or even with respect to that object, not at all.

This happens in meditation: we find some way to smooth problems out so that as soon as we notice one, we can escape from it into a pretension of spirituality. However, that will not help to overcome the conception of inherent existence. Moreover, it is necessary to find a way to generate a consciousness that believes in inherent existence and to keep it there so that it can be refuted; then, you have to work on an antidote that breaks down that consciousness. When you do not create an antidotal view and merely ignore the object of negation, it is like "reforming" your naughty child by removing it from your sight. Using an antidote is like working with and correcting the child right there while he or she is being naughty.

The object of meditation that helps to destroy the consciousness conceiving inherent existence is not merely something other than inherent existence but a negative, an absence, of inherent existence — emptiness. You have to know that emptiness applies to an inherently existent person, the non-existent object of negation. It has to affect your usual mind that is so completely convinced that a truly established person exists. If you do not feel a bit shattered, it is just abstract. You have to keep figuring out how to make it personal, making up relevant examples, and so forth.

> In order to distinguish the fine points of these presentations, it is necessary to rely on many causal collections — training in detail in the great texts as well as relying for a long time on a wise spiritual guide who has thoroughly penetrated the instructions in the teaching of the Foremost Father [Dzong-ka-ba] and his spiritual sons [Gyel-tsap and Kay-drup], and so forth.

Before you can meditate effectively on emptiness, many subsidiary practices are necessary. Through serving and learning from a spiritual teacher, you acquire an accumulation of merit. This includes such practices as prostration and making offerings, but the main practice is to achieve what the spiritual guide teaches. The altruistic intention to become enlightened — the wish to attain Buddhahood for the sake of others — is especially important as it is a quick way of opening the mind so that emptiness can be understood.

> These topics are not in the province of either those professors of vanity who are biased toward foolish meditations or of those professors of public speaking who meditate on wasting their human life with criticism directed outside as if such were the supreme state.

Jang-gya is scolding both those who are addicted to a simple-minded meditation as if it were the most fantastic thing that ever was and those who are all puffed up with their own accomplishments in criticizing other scholars to the extent that it seems that, for them, debate and criticism of others is the equivalent of meditative cultivation of Buddhahood. The Tibetan word for "professor" (*mkhan po*) is usually used for a high teacher or abbot, and by sarcastically using the term for these two types of ersatz practitioners, Jang-gya indicates the perversion that they bring to the Buddhist teaching. The burden of his message is that practitioners must know the general features of the complete path and make sure to put what is appropriate for their level into practice.

8 Reasoned Refutation

SETTLING THE SELFLESSNESS THAT IS THE NEGATIVE OF THE OBJECT OF NEGATION

This section has two parts: an identification of the main reasonings refuting the object of negation and how those reasonings refute the object of negation, the two selves.

IDENTIFICATION OF THE MAIN REASONINGS REFUTING THE OBJECT OF NEGATION

This section has two parts: the purpose of refuting the object of negation through reasoning and an identification of the main reasonings.

In Buddhist philosophy assertions are supported by reasoning and citation of scripture. In dependence on the teachings of Buddha and the great masters, self — inherent existence — must be refuted *through reasoning* because mere trust and belief have little power with respect to eradicating the root of cyclic existence. Often outsiders view the reasonings establishing emptiness as merely abstract arguments much like establishing that a table is not an elephant. They understand neither the means for cognizing emptiness nor its benefit.

Purpose of Refuting the Object of Negation
Concerning that, the honorable Superior Nāgārjuna made commentary on the thought of the definitive sūtras, and two who made clear commentary on those in exact accordance with [his] meaning are Buddhapālita and Chandrakīrti. Also, the great master Shāntideva expounded in agreement with these two.

Sūtras of definitive meaning[180] are those in which Buddha mainly taught emptiness explicitly. Sūtras whose meaning requires interpretation[181] are those in which Buddha did not mainly teach emptiness explicitly. This explanation of "definitive" and "requiring interpretation" is from the viewpoint of the means of expression, the sūtras themselves. From the viewpoint of the content, emptiness is definitive, and all other phenomena are objects requiring interpretation. For example, table is not the mode of existence of a table; its mode of being has to be interpreted as something else, emptiness. To us, however, table appears to be the final mode of being of a table.

According to the assertions of these three great chariots [i.e. great leaders], it is the thought of the sūtras of the perfection of wisdom class that, without even considering omniscience, in order merely to attain[182] release from cyclic existence, one must necessarily realize the suchness of persons and phenomena. For, passages in Perfection of Wisdom Sūtras say (1) that those who have discrimination of true existence[183] are not liberated, (2) that the completely perfect Buddhas of the past, present, and future as well as even all from Stream Enterers through to Solitary Realizers attain [their respective levels] in dependence upon this perfection of wisdom, and (3) that "even those who wish to train in the grounds of the Hearers should train in this perfection of wisdom," etc. This is also the thought of the Superior Nāgārjuna, for his *Sixty Stanzas of Reasoning*[184] teaches that there is no release for those who have fallen to the extremes of [inherent] existence or [utter] non-existence:

> Through [the view of inherent] existence
> one is not released;
> Through [the view of] no [nominal]
> existence there is nothing but cyclic
> existence.

The extreme of existence is the inherent existence of phenomena. The extreme of non-existence is no conventional existence at all. Once the extremes are identified this way, Nāgārjuna is seen to be implying that you cannot be liberated from cyclic existence through meditating on the coarse selflessness. Since the conception of phenomena as inherently existent is the cause of the conception of the person as inherently existent, how could meditating merely on a person's non-self-sufficiency release you from cyclic existence? Since you would continue to see phenomena as inherently existent, you would also continue to generate the conception of inherent existence with respect to the person that is designated in dependence upon those phenomena.

And then, [Nāgārjuna's *Sixty Stanzas of Reasoning*] says that Superiors are liberated from cyclic existence through unerring knowledge of the suchness of things and non-things:

> Through thorough knowledge of things and
> non-things,
> A great being is liberated.

Things and non-things here are impermanent and permanent phenomena. Thus, Nāgārjuna is saying that Superiors are liberated through knowledge of the emptiness of all phenomena, not just of persons.

And also Nāgārjuna's *Precious Garland of Advice for the King* establishes that the means for achieving high status[185] [as a human or god] is the faith of conviction, and that with such faith as a precursor one becomes a vessel for wisdom, which is the means for achieving the definite goodness[186] [of liberation and omniscience]. He says that wisdom is the knowledge that the two — I and mine — do not ultimately exist. And, based on this [reason], he says that when one knows that the [mental and physical] aggregates do not truly exist, the conception of [a truly existent] I is extinguished.

In order for someone to conceive an inherently existent I, that person's mental and physical aggregates must first appear to the mind and be conceived to inherently exist. Thus, once the conception of inherently existent mental and physical aggregates is destroyed, a consciousness conceiving an inherently existent I cannot arise.

Also, he says that until the conception of the aggregates as truly existent is extinguished, cyclic existence is not overcome and that when [this conception] is extinguished, cyclic existence is overcome.

Thus, according to Nāgārjuna, those propounding that things other than the person are ultimates have not gotten out of cyclic existence, although they are certainly in a more refined state than we are.

Also, he says that through the view of [utter] nonexistence, one cycles in bad transmigrations and that through the view of [inherent] existence, one cycles in happy transmigrations and, therefore, in order to be free from these two [types of transmigrations], one must understand the reality that is not based on the two extremes of [inherent] existence and no [nominal] existence. Nāgārjuna's *Precious Garland* says:[187]

> As long as a [mis]conception of the
>   aggregates exists,
> So long, therefore, does a [mis]conception
>   of I exist.
> Further, when the [mis]conception of I
>   exists,
> There is action, and from that there is birth.

If you analytically search to find the person, you will find the emptiness of the person. But if the analytical mind searches to find the emptiness of the person, it will find not that but the emptiness of the emptiness of the person. What it finds depends on what it is searching for. Based on this, many scholar-yogis from other orders of Tibetan Buddhism say that there actually is no emptiness, that since it cannot be found, it does not exist — the "realization of emptiness" being just this non-finding of what you are seeking. Everyone agrees that you should think that an emptiness is merely a non-finding and should not make a positive identification, "This *is* emptiness," because then you would be realizing the *existence* of an emptiness instead of just the non-affirming negative[188] that is emptiness itself. Though emptiness does exist, you want to cognize merely this elimination of inherent existence, not its existence. For instance, the Dalai Lama says in his *Key to the Middle Way:*[189]

Also, even if the meaning of an emptiness has been ascertained, but the thought, 'This is an emptiness,' appears, then one is apprehending the existence of an emptiness which is a positive thing. Therefore, that consciousness then becomes a conventional valid cogniser and not the ascertainment of an emptiness.

A mind that cognizes the *existence* of an emptiness is a valid cognition of a conventional phenomenon, not one engaged in ultimate analysis.

In order to sustain the assertion that a valid cognition of emptiness realizes only a non-affirming negative, a mere absence of inherent existence, it is said that a mind realizing emptiness does not realize the existence of emptiness but that, still, through the force of the realization of emptiness, the existence of emptiness is understood later upon leaving that realization, without any further cogitation. Thus, a mind realizing emptiness does not cognize the existence of emptiness either explicitly or implicitly, but still the exist-ence of emptiness is understood through the force of that realization. Indeed, if you realized emptiness, that would be enough for you to put it together that emptiness exists. Nonetheless, this hair-splitting distinction has the scent of trying to have your cake and eat it too. For, with phe-nomena such as a rug, different consciousnesses that realize the rug and that realize its existence are not posited, there being no need and no way to do so. Geshe Gedun Lodrö offered the thought-provoking explanation that the certain-ty that emptiness exists is easier to realize than emptiness itself because it can be understood — before generating valid cognition realizing emptiness — that without empti-ness, phenomena would be impossible.

In Dzong-ka-ba's presentation of the Middle Way School, emptiness is a phenomenon, an existent — which, nevertheless, is a non-affirming negative. It is important to remember that an emptiness is merely an absence, an elim-ination, a negative of inherent existence; otherwise, you can become confused by talk about the existence of empti-ness and seek only to realize that. Other presentations avoid this possible pitfall by saying that emptiness is merely a term taught to people who do not know the truth. Since, when you search to find something, you come up with nothing, how can you say, "This is an emptiness"? Indeed, as soon as you think or say, "This is emptiness," you are substituting a positive thing as your object of mind for what is a mere absence. Rather, without putting something posi-tive in its place, we need to realize that the object negated does not exist at all. A consciousness that cognizes a mere negative is needed in order to attack misconception with full force. Thus, to avoid being led into over-reflection on the existence of emptiness, some say that it is only a convention, meaning that it is not an existent, not a phenomenon.

Others say that an emptiness truly exists. For, when you search for the phenomenon designated, you find its emptiness. The consciousness that finds this is fully qualified to investigate whether phenomena truly exist or not, and it finds an emptiness; hence, they conclude that emptiness must truly exist. According to Dzong-ka-ba's system, however, even though the emptiness of a table, for instance, is found when analytically searching to determine whether a table inherently exists or not, this does not necessitate that the emptiness of a table inherently exists. Indeed, if an analytical consciousness searching for a table found a table, then the table would inherently exist, but it does not; it finds, or realizes, the emptiness of the table. Similarly if, when it searched for the *emptiness* of the table, it found the emptiness of the table, that emptiness would inherently exist. But it does not; it finds or realizes the emptiness of the emptiness of the table. Thus, all things, including emptinesses, do not inherently exist. The two types of "finding" are different; the first is the finding of a phenomenon upon searching for it whereas the second is not.

Let us talk a little again about valid cognition. The fact that non-Ge-luk-ba presentations of the Middle Way School do not present what, for Ge-luk-bas, would be full valid cognition means that when we talk about valid cognition in the Ge-luk-ba way, we will probably misunderstand it. Still, let us try, for once you understand this, you can avoid several possible pitfalls.

First of all, it is possible to talk about an element of valid cognition in our ordinary perceptions. Suppose we take as an example an eye consciousness looking at a white bedspread. What appears to this eye consciousness is something white that seems to cover a certain area. Therefore, this white bedspread is appearing differently from how it actually exists; it appears to be a truly existent bedspread that is able to cover its bases of designation, which are the many white threads. Thus, the eye consciousness to which this appears is mistaken from the viewpoint of its appearing object.[190] However, the eye consciousness itself does not mistakenly conceive the white bedspread in that way; it does not take this appearance and affirm it. Thus, from the viewpoint of its object of engagement,[191] which is just the white bedspread, it is non-mistaken. Since the eye consciousness apprehends the bedspread *as a bedspread*, it is said to be non-deceived about its main object and to be, therefore, a valid cognition.

It is also possible for an eye consciousness to apprehend its object wrongly. For example, if you put on red sunglasses, you will apprehend a red bedspread. Or, if you put the bedspread outside in the snow and apprehended it as snow, this also would be a wrong apprehension. These wrong apprehensions are completely non-conceptual; there is no thought involved, but they are wrong, not valid cognitions. In contrast, the majority of our ordinary perceptions have an element of valid cognition in that they are not deceived about the main object they apprehend. The mistaken part of our sense perceptions is the *appearance* of objects as inherently existent. This is our fault, actually, not the fault of the object, although it is not a mistake made *after* an object appears to us. Our own mistaken predispositions cause the object from the very first moment of perception to appear as if it covers its basis of designation. This false appearance of objects is included within the obstructions to omniscience; it is a result of previous misconception of inherent existence.

The eye consciousness apprehends an object such as a bedspread as a bedspread and is thus non-mistaken about its main object of apprehension. Sometimes, however, a mental consciousness takes this seemingly inherently existent bedspread and assents to the false appearance of its mode of being, conceiving it to be an inherently existent bedspread. This conception of true existence is of two types: one based on reasoning and teaching — an artificial misconception — and one that is our ordinary, habitual affirmation of the way things appear to us, an innate misconception. Examples of the first are conceptions of ourselves that we have learned from mistaken psychological and philosophical systems and from teachers.

When we pay strong attention to an object, the conception of true existence comes out. It does not have to be manifest all the time; you can be thinking about other things. According to scripture, we are supposed to have only one mental consciousness at a time, no matter how fast the mental consciousness changes from one object to another.[192] In cases where you are doing many things, your mind is rapidly shifting from object to object. However, when you are meditating and watching your mind with an introspective consciousness, you have to watch at exactly the same time as you meditate; you cannot do it later. The mental consciousness pays attention, for instance, to emptiness, and mindfulness makes sure that you stay on your object. If you cannot allow this simultaneity in your philosophy, it may block generation of mindfulness and introspection in practice. Thus, at minimum, mindfulness and introspection are said to be portions of the mind viewing the general mind at the same time.

This problem appears in discussions on the conception of true existence because any conception is a thought consciousness, a conceptual consciousness, and sūtra seems to say that you can only have one thought consciousness at a time. Thus, if you are thinking about the color of a wall, during that time you cannot have any conception of the true existence of the wall, despite the fact that the wall *appears* to be truly existent all the time. In response to this, Jam-yang-shay-ba's followers[193] explain that it is possible to have a consciousness conceiving true existence as a subliminal thought. For example, when watching a movie, you at least subliminally remember that what is being seen is not real. Thus, could there not always be a mind affirming the way things appear to exist inherently? Is it possible that this affirmation is only sporadic, that you have it only when you mark out a person or thing and pay strong attention to it? When we are paying involved attention, there is no question that we affirm the way things appear to us. There is no question that, for example, when we become angry, we have — prior to the anger — affirmed the way that the object appears to us; this indeed causes us a great deal of trouble. Still, perhaps, we also agree to the way things appear most of the time; when particularly afflicted, such as with anger, it gets even more solid, but it is with us all the time.

The Tibetan word translated here as "subliminal"[194] literally means "hidden". It is, in Jam-yang-shay-ba's system, a halfway point between being completely manifest and being a seed. We have many predispositions towards feelings and so on, carried in our mind as seeds, that, given the right circumstances, become actual consciousnesses. Subliminal minds, on the other hand, are not seeds but actual consciousnesses. However, they are not on the surface of consciousness. For example, when you talk to someone while riding in a car, you do not necessarily keep track of your body every moment, but you are subliminally aware of being in a car.

You come into a room and lock in on the important things in the room; you do not have to keep going over them. You quickly become accustomed to the room. For example, when you dream, do you not lock in an acceptance of whatever scene appears as soon as it appears? You feel that what is appearing is true; there is a continuous, subliminal decision that what is happening is real.

Most instructional texts for cultivating the Middle Way view in meditation say that we have a consciousness conceiving a truly existent I continually; for instance, the Fourth Paṇchen Lama says that even in deep sleep we have a continuous sense of an inherently existent I.[195] Yet, if you can have only one conceptual consciousness at a time, there often is no chance to have a consciousness continually misconceiving the nature of I; it is obvious that we have other thoughts too. It seems to me that we usually first settle that there is an inherently existent I and then stay within this, sealing it, freezing it, and then working from this basis. The continual stream of this conception of I is a subliminal consciousness conceiving true existence. We do not challenge whether we inherently exist or not; we passively and continuously accept it.

All Ge-luk-ba philosophers accept that there is a subliminal conception of true existence, but they differ on what "subliminal" means — whether it is an actual consciousness or is merely in seed form, like a cat ready to spring. To exist in seed form means not to be presently active as a consciousness, but to be ready to come out in full force. A crouching cat already has the potential to jump, which affects the way it stays. I am raising these points because, once a consciousness conceiving inherent existence is the root of inherent existence and once it must be overcome to get out of cyclic existence, it is important to identify its forms.

And Nāgārjuna's *Praise of the Supramundane* says:

> You [Buddha] taught that without realizing
> Signlessness there is no liberation.

Signlessness is one of the three doors of liberation — signlessness, wishlessness, and emptiness. "Sign" in the context of the three doors of liberation means "cause", and thus signlessness refers to a phenomenon's not being inherently produced from causes. Outside of this context, it seems that "sign" refers to signs of inherent existence, in which case a cognition of signlessness is a cognition, for example, of a rug in such a way that it would not contain any signs of inherent existence. In any case, Nāgārjuna is clearly saying that without realizing the emptiness of inherent existence, there is no attainment of liberation.

And so on. [These passages from] the *Precious Garland* and the *Sixty Stanzas* mainly prove that realization of the subtle emptiness is definitely necessary for a path releasing one from cyclic existence.

Why is it said again and again that you have to cognize emptiness in order to be freed from cyclic existence? It is to feed the importance of emptiness into your mind. For, if you come close to cognizing it, you are sometimes so stirred up that you can easily be thrown another way. You will rise from the meditation cushion and go eat or turn on the tv — anything to avoid the anxiety that such probing of the nature of things can bring out. Although you may be improving in meditating on emptiness and it may be appearing more easily, why would you want to stay on it if it were making trouble? However, if you have thought about how cognition of emptiness and familiarization with it will eventually free you from cyclic existence, and if you have a strong wish to get out of cyclic existence, then you will remain with your meditation until facility is developed to the point where it becomes a source of joy.

This is also the reason for so much talk about suffering. You have to be realistic and open yourself up to the suffering of the world, to realize that not just manifest mental and physical pain are suffering, but that ordinary pleasurable and even neutral feelings are suffering — in that ordinary pleasure easily leads to pain and in that all feelings, even the neutral, are caught in a contaminated, uncontrolled process of conditioning. With such stark recognition of suffering and a sense of being caught within it like a prisoner in a prison, you will value meditation on emptiness as a means of overcoming suffering.

This is also why the altruistic mind of enlightenment is emphasized; you continually vow to help people such that when you come to something like emptiness that twists your mind a little, you will not want to give up, since realization of emptiness is so vital to being able to help others in a vast and effective way. If you cannot keep on emptiness at that point, then all you have said and felt about compassion is just words.

We have a lethargy that comes from countless years of looking at ourselves and the rest of the world in wrong ways. When you approach emptiness through reasoning, you are taking your thought, your mind, and trying to make it stronger in order to overcome this lethargy. Thought that has emptiness as its object has a valid foundation and can become very strong.

This does not mean that cognition of emptiness always comes slowly. If you become locked into the idea that it is always developed slowly, you may someday pass up a chance to do it quickly. There are techniques in tantra through which, if you are used to working with emptiness, you can quickly generate a different type of consciousness, a very subtle one, immediately getting over the mental lethargy that blocks cognition.

For, Dzong-ka-ba's *Ocean of Reasoning, Explanation of (Nāgārjuna's) "Treatise on the Middle Way"* says:

> In this [*Praise of the Supramundane*] and also in the former two [the *Sixty Stanzas on Reasoning* and *Precious Garland of Advice for the King*] there are indeed many teachings on the suchness of dependent-arising, which is the negation of inherent existence in persons and phenomena. However, they appear as branches proving the chief [assertion] — that understanding the meaning of the reality that is not based on the two extremes is definitely necessary for a path releasing one from cyclic existence.

The cognition of the emptiness of inherent existence of all

phenomena is not just for Bodhisattvas but for anyone who wants to get out of cyclic existence, Hearers and Solitary Realizers included.

> Moreover, it is necessary to realize suchness with [a mind] that eradicates the mode of apprehension of an innate consciousness conceiving self. Through merely not engaging the mind in the two selves [i.e., the inherent existence of persons and the inherent existence of other phenomena] or merely stopping the mind from moving to other objects, it cannot be posited that one has realized emptiness. For, otherwise, it would [absurdly] follow that even [such minds as] sleep and fainting, etc., would realize suchness.

If the mind is withdrawn from other objects and stabilized, bliss, clarity, and non-conceptuality can be attained. Even a little clairvoyance may be acquired. At that time, because everything is so different, you may assume that you are cognizing emptiness or that you have gotten out of cyclic existence.

Also, if you have a coarse sense of what inherent existence is and know that you are not involved in it, you may think that you have understood emptiness, whereas you have only withdrawn from grosser misconceptions. Though it is necessary to develop the meditative stabilization of calm abiding — alert, one-pointed concentration — so that you have the concentration necessary to destroy a consciousness conceiving inherent existence, the purpose of meditating on emptiness is not merely to withdraw from a consciousness conceiving inherent existence into another state but to weaken that conception. It must be directly opposed. If it were otherwise, then such mental states as dreamless sleep would be cognitions of suchness.

> All the chariots [i.e., great leaders] of the Great Vehicle speak — with one voice and one thought — of [the necessity for analytically refuting inherent

existence]. Āryadeva says:

When selflessness is seen in objects
The seeds of cyclic existence are destroyed.

And the honorable Chandrakīrti says:[196]

[Extreme] conceptions arise with [a
consciousness conceiving inherently
existent] things.
It has been thoroughly analyzed how
phenomena do not [inherently] exist.

And the master Bhāvaviveka says:

With the mind in meditative equipoise
Wisdom analyzes in this way
The entities of these phenomena
That are apprehended conventionally.

And the venerable Shāntideva also says:

When [these things] are sought as realities
Who is attached and to what is there
attachment?

Etc. And the glorious Dharmakīrti also says:

Without disbelieving the object of this
[misconception]
It is impossible to abandon [misconceiving
it].

Etc.

Āryadeva says that once you "see" that objects are selfless,
you destroy the effectiveness of the seeds that produce
cyclic existence. Chandrakīrti talks of thoroughly *analyzing*
the way in which there is no inherent existence. Bhāvaviveka speaks about *analysis* through wisdom; it is necessary to get right down to the object and analyze it — you
cannot just withdraw your mind from it.

Shāntideva says that when you *search* for all the things

that appear to you now to see if they are their own reality, you will find nothing to desire and, indeed, nothing that desires. An implication is that when you can in no way find the object you desire, this same analysis will affect your thought, "*I* want." You will, through the force of the previous realization of the objects of desire, immediately realize that the desirer, I, also does not inherently exist. However, it sometimes happens that you analyze and cannot find the object, but still want it due to a lack of depth and strength to the analysis. Then you have to turn around and identify this one who is thinking, "I want," and purposely analyze the wanter. If your analysis of the desired object were better in the first place — if you had taken it right down to the end and had gotten to emptiness — it would automatically apply at the very moment your mind turned to the I.

Dharmakīrti says that it is impossible to destroy a consciousness falsely conceiving an object without refuting the object of that conception. Though it is helpful to take a vow and hold yourself from doing certain things that harm other people, this does not remove the source of harm. We must stop believing in truly existent objects; we have to take out all of the underpinnings of harmful states of mind such that they cannot get started anymore.

> Therefore, one must analyze well what that which is conceived by consciousnesses erroneously conceiving [persons and phenomena] as the two selves is.

Before we can proceed to refute inherent existence, it is necessary to do thorough analysis just in order to find out what a consciousness conceiving the inherent existence of persons and phenomena is and what it conceives.

> After analyzing that, it is necessary to bring about the collapse of the false edifice of mistake by way of inducing conviction through pure scripture and reasoning that [things] do not exist as they are conceived by this [erroneous consciousness]. That this

is needed is an indispensable excellent essential [of the path]. Hence, it is important to analyze again and again with the wisdom of individual investigation.

First, we need to find out just exactly what is being misconceived; we need a strong sense of the object of negation. Then, through citing scripture and reflecting on reasoning, we must understand that what is being conceived does not exist as it is conceived. We must understand that the inherent existence being conceived is non-existent.

It is important to continue to investigate in this way again and again, to keep rebuilding the analysis. If you get discouraged, in order to reinstate enthusiasm for analysis, look at the consequences of non-analysis — ignorance, cyclic existence, and suffering for yourself and countless others.

An inferential cognition that realizes emptiness is generated through ordinary reasoning — realizing the presence of the reason in the subject and the pervasion of the reason by the predicate[197] — which we are capable of right now. Studying Buddha's scriptures and the commentaries of the great masters supports the reasoning process, letting you know that you are on the right track. This kind of inferential cognition cannot give knowledge about such things as the structure of the universe and the subtle relations of cause and effect; for this, scriptural inference is necessary. Among the three classes of objects of comprehension — the manifest such as objects of the sense consciousnesses, the slightly hidden such as subtle impermanence, and the very hidden such as the minute details of the cause and effect of karma — emptiness, fortunately, is only slightly hidden, not very hidden; thus, we can get at it through reasoning. This is not a dry process; you have to be able to *feel* the object of negation and you have to *feel* the emptiness that is its negative.

In that way the *Superior Sūtra of the Sport of Mañjushrī* also says,[198] " 'O daughter, how is a Bodhisat-

tva victorious in battle?' 'Mañjushrī, when analyzed, all phenomena are unobservable." ' And the
Superior Sūtra of the King of Meditative Stabilizations
says:[199]

> If the selflessness of phenomena is analyzed
> And if this analysis is cultivated in
>   meditation,
> It causes the effect of attaining nirvana.
> Through no other cause does one come to
>   peace.

And the *Superior Sūtra of the Cloud of Jewels* says,[200]
"To analyze with special insight and thereupon
realize the lack of inherent entityness is to enter into
signlessness." And the *Questions of Brahmā Sūtra*
says,[201] "Those who properly investigate phenomena individually are the intelligent."

Therefore, in general, the great chariots have set
forth — through refutations and proofs — many
paths of reasoning that differentiate, among the
word of the Conqueror, what is definitive and what
requires interpretation. In particular, the statements of many forms of reasonings for delineating
suchness were made only for the sake of illuminating for the fortunate the path to liberation. They
were not made for the sake of becoming intent on
debate.

Many think that reasoning is only for explanation and debate, not for meditation; for them, reasoning could
never generate any feeling of emptiness — all it can be is
talk. However, reasoning is the very means by which we
can arrive at the startling and profound emptiness.

> The *Buddhapālita Commentary on (Nāgārjuna's)
> "Treatise on the Middle Way"* ...

Buddhapālita's commentary is called by his own name, the
Buddhapālita Commentary.

... says:[202]

> What purpose is there in teaching depen-
> dent-arising? The master [Nāgārjuna],
> whose nature is compassion, saw that sen-
> tient beings are oppressed by various suffer-
> ings; in order to release them, he assumed
> the task of teaching the reality of things,
> just as it is; hence, he began the teaching of
> dependent-arising.

And Chandrakīrti's *Supplement* says:[203]

> The analyses done in [Nāgārjuna's] *Treatise*
> are not for attachment
> To disputation but for liberation; they teach
> suchness.

And the Foremost Great Being [Dzong-ka-ba] says:

> All of the various, reasoned analyses set
> forth in Nāgārjuna's *Treatise on the Middle
> Way* are only for the sake of sentient beings'
> attaining release.

One must understand well what is excluded by the
words "not for attachment to disputation" in the
former quote and by the word "only" in the latter
quote.

Analysis is taught not merely to construct a beautiful philosophical system but for meditation, for the sake of leaving
cyclic existence. When Dzong-ka-ba says that this teaching
is set forth *only* so that sentient beings might attain liberation, he implicitly excludes that the purpose is external
disputation.

> In general, analysis of individual investigation that
> takes valid scripture and reasoning as the means of
> attestation[204] is important whether you are hearing,
> thinking, or meditating. Moreover, if [your prac-

tice] is conjoined with the special causal and continual motivations that involve directing these analyses as means of yourself and others attaining liberation and omniscience, you come into accord with the meaning of what both the unsurpassed Teacher [Buddha] himself and the great chariots taught with such striving. Therefore, it is right for those who want goodness to strive in this way.

The special motivation of the Great Vehicle is to aim at establishing all sentient beings in Buddhahood. In order to accomplish this, it is necessary to engage in practices that will allow continuation of progress from lifetime to lifetime. It is helpful to realize that if you practice giving, for example, with good motivation, one of the effects will be that you will have good resources in a future life; those resources, in turn, should be dedicated to further practice for the welfare of others. But if giving is practiced merely out of the hope of gaining good resources in a future life, it is not a Bodhisattva's motivation at all. Also, when Bodhisattvas practice virtue within dedicating its fruits to the benefit of all sentient beings, the best possible resources come to them, far more than if they had dedicated the merit for their own ends.

Since both Lesser and Great Vehicle practitioners must realize the same emptiness of inherent existence, motivation and its attendant deeds determine whether you will become a Foe Destroyer or a Buddha. The attainment of Buddhahood is not an automatic result of meditating on emptiness; rather, others' welfare has to be your primary purpose, with Buddhahood seen as the means to that. Altruistic deeds are the attendant requirement.

The direction we give our minds is important. For instance, at our stage it is helpful to determine consciously that if we understand emptiness, we will not have desire, hatred, or ignorance. If your meditation on emptiness does not lead toward a state free from desire and hatred, you have not understood it properly. Explore how the understanding of something could oppose desire and hatred; is there something which, when understood, would make desire and hatred impossible?

Since we are working now with a very weak conceptual mind, we have to bring all these points together, thinking, "How can this lessen desire, how can this make desire impossible?" Even if your meditation on emptiness does not seem to be working against desire, you can pretend it is just to explore the feeling. This will give a hint about the structure and import of cognizing emptiness.

Pretending to have such cognitions and their results might seem objectionable because it might seem that an understanding of emptiness should itself overpower you and get rid of desire on the spot. Indeed, in the end it will; however, we are now far from that. We have many obstructions that prevent us from even having the time to be affected by the implications of emptiness. Thus, it is necessary to set up the mind so that it can be affected by emptiness and so that the process can start. For example, when you read a book that sets forth many reasonings for generating the cognition of emptiness, it is best not to insist that by its own force it immediately make sense, but instead be willing to put some time and energy into unfolding the meaning. We generally do not have the time or the leisure for such profundity to come home. Our minds are usually filled with something else, and the part of the mind that is attracted to it cannot settle on it.

For example, upon discovering a suitable practice, we first need to create a mind aspiring to mindfulness in order to keep the practice going. Just taking an interest in emptiness indicates good predispositions, but even with good predispositions, it is necessary to instill mindfulness since the mind is so accustomed to wandering that distraction is constant and powerful, almost as if it were against the nature of the mind not to wander.

Reflect on reasons for having mindfulness. Slapping his head, the Nying-ma lama Khetsun Sangpo said, "Distraction has gotten me into all this trouble, and here I am doing it again!" Reflect on the faults of what you are doing. For example, suppose you had a blister that you scratched, leading to an infection. Realizing this, later when you get another blister and again scratch it, you automatically feel, "This is just stupid," since you are making it worse. Although you are making an attempt to help other sentient beings, you are ruining yourself with distraction. How can a ruined person help other people? A ruined person usually ruins others; as Nāgārjuna's *Precious Garland* says:[205]

Afraid of the fearless abode,
Ruined, they ruin others.
O King, act in such a way
That the ruined do not ruin you.

We ourselves will someday be Buddhas. Since our minds are empty of inherent existence, sometime, even if not in this lifetime, we will be Buddhas. Buddhas have special characteristics, among which is intense altruism; everything they do is for the sake of other sentient beings. We can become just like that because our minds are empty of their own inherent existence, not frozen into afflictive states as it now seems. Since the emptiness of the mind and the mind cognizing that emptiness have a valid foundation and since mental qualities, unlike physical achievements, have a stable basis, given enough lifetimes we will become Buddhas.[206]

Although the mind can develop into infinite goodness, there is no way in which the mind can become infinitely rotten. Wrong minds — such as a consciousness conceiving inherent existence itself, or desire, hatred, and obscuration — have no valid foundation. There is a natural wrongness in these minds in that they do not at all accord with reality and hence cannot be increased infinitely.

Just as in learning a language, so in developing a motivation to help all sentient beings, we sometimes feel nervous or embarrassed. This is because our minds are ingrained with the pursuit of our own selfish purposes. We would be embarrassed to become a great or superior person; we would not be like our neighbors. This seems undemocratic, and we resist it — but what could be more humble than serving the needs of other beings?

We have to open ourselves to a Buddha's altruistic motivation and accept the consequences of it. One strong incentive to this comes from facing that we are going to die. In that light, except for fixing up our motivation, accumulating virtue, and understanding phenomena, all of what we are doing now is worthless. If we were going to take a trip to Alaska, we would prepare for it; so why not prepare for death and the next rebirth? The only helpful thing that we can do in the long run is to transform our minds, amassing a set of realizations and virtues that will have an effect on death, the intermediate state, and rebirth. It is helpful to work on cognizing emptiness with the motivation to leave cyclic existence, attain Buddhahood, and help all sentient beings. This motivation is causal in the sense that it initially impels actions, and it is continual in the sense that it should operate during those actions.

Most of the hearing,[207] thinking, and meditating as well as explaining, debating, and writing done by those who boast of practicing religion and boast of helping [Buddha's] teaching is not only not helpful to themselves and others, but also pollutes their mental continuums with many ill deeds related with the doctrine. It should be understood that in the end those who think that they are maintaining the teaching through fighting, quarrelling, heaving [stones, etc.][208] and [wielding] weaponry and clubs are, due to impure motivation, only [like] medicine that has become poison and deities who have become demons.

Therefore, Āryadeva says that one makes the suffering of cyclic existence more distant even through having doubt tending to the fact with regard to the profound nature of phenomena:[209]

> Those whose merit is small
> Have no doubts about this doctrine.
> Even through merely having doubt
> Cyclic existence is torn to tatters.

Three types of doubt are described in the basic textbooks on psychology, called Awareness and Knowledge: doubt tending to the non-factual such as the suspicion that phenomena inherently exist, equal doubt such as the suspicion that phenomena might or might not inherently exist, and doubt tending to the fact such as the suspicion that phenomena do not inherently exist. All doubt is a two-mindedness, going in two directions, but in the first and third varieties the mind is predominantly tending in one direction.[210] Āryadeva is interpreted here as speaking about doubt tending to the correct opinion that phenomena do not inherently exist.

As was mentioned earlier, even factually concordant doubt takes to mind to some degree the final mode of subsistence of phenomena — their emptiness of inherent existence. If it is mentally disruptive when we first have doubts about a friend, imagine how disruptive it must be to doubt that phenomena inherently exist, to suspect that oneself, others, and all other phenomena do not exist the way they appear.

> And in particular, the glorious Chandrakīrti says[211] that at this time of the end of [Buddha's] teaching, it is very good fortune merely to take interest — for even a moment — in this very profound topic. He says:

> > In this tumultuous age when Buddhism is deprived of the essential meanings taught by the Omniscient One, anyone who can clear away two-mindedness for even a moment and cognize emptiness is fortunate.

And the *Taming Demons Chapter*[212] and the *Ajātashatru Sūtra*[213] say that since taking an interest in this profound nature of phenomena purifies even the karmic obstructions that lead to immediate rebirth in a hell,[214] what need is there to mention [its purifying] minor [infractions of] rites and ethics?

Having gained conviction well in such, you should strive at means to expand [in your own continuum] the potential of this type of doctrine. For, the Foremost Great Being [Dzong-ka-ba] says:

> Therefore, you should plant wishes for hearing the texts, memorizing them, and thinking and meditating on their meaning, as well as having faithful interest [in the profound emptiness] in all lives within not damaging conviction in the dependent-arising of causes and effects.

Since emptiness negates inherent existence and not phenomena themselves, emptiness is compatible with cause and effect. Furthermore, it is said that a realization of emptiness assists in understanding cause and effect and that an understanding of cause and effect assists in understanding emptiness. The realizations of dependent-arising and emptiness are not only compatible but also mutually assisting. Therefore, one makes wishes to be able to continue to study, contemplate, and meditate on the profound nature of phenomena over a continuum of lives, all within not becoming disoriented with respect to emptiness such that emptiness and dependent-arising seem to be at odds. Wishing can be a form of meditation that has powerful influence on the shape of the future.

9 The Main Reasonings

IDENTIFICATION OF THE MAIN REASONINGS

In general, the countless forms of reasonings for ascertaining selflessness that are set forth in the texts of the Middle Way are included within two types, reasonings for ascertaining the selflessness of persons and reasonings for ascertaining the selflessness of phenomena. This is because the bases of adherence to the two selves — which are the chief of those things that bind one in cyclic existence — are persons and phenomena and, therefore, the main bases with respect to which selflessness is ascertained must also be persons and phenomena.

The bases of our conception of inherent existence are the things that we conceive to exist inherently. They themselves exist but are objects of observation of a consciousness conceiving something that does not exist — inherent existence. Thus, the person who is a base of the conception of a self of persons is the conventionally existent person, mistakenly conceived to exist from the object's own side. The I is not just an illusory figment of the imagination like a

148

rope-snake, but an existent phenomenon; however, we do not now know it as it is, qualified by mere existence.

In that way Dzong-ka-ba's *Differentiation of the Interpretable and the Definitive* says:[215]

> The principal fetters [that bind one in cyclic existence] are adherence to the two selves (1) with regard to the person, which is the object of observation that generates the thought "I", and (2) with regard to the phenomena of that person's continuum. Therefore, these two are also the principal bases with respect to which the conception of self is refuted through reasoning. Consequently, the reasonings also are included in the refutations of the two selves.

Your own person is the conventionally existent phenomenon that is the object of observation of a mind correctly conceiving I. When we then conceive this person and the other phenomena in the same continuum, such as the mental and physical aggregates, to exist inherently, we are bound in cyclic existence. Therefore, among the many different conceptions of inherent existence, that of the inherent existence of one's own person and of one's own mental and physical aggregates are the most virulent. Therefore, these two, the person and the phenomena of your continuum, are the principal objects which are meditated as lacking inherent existence. Furthermore, the reasonings attacking inherent existence are set up in the context of this same division into persons and other phenomena.

Here Dzong-ka-ba is talking about the main fetters that bind us in cyclic existence. In the Consequentialist system, the conception of the true existence of either persons or phenomena other than persons is an affliction — an obstruction to liberation from cyclic existence. Conceiving a house to exist inherently or conceiving things that do not belong to you to exist inherently are similarly afflictions, but not the chief obstructions that bind us in cyclic existence; the conception of what is right here, us and what are included in our own continuums, as inherently existent does the most harm. Therefore, the reasonings are organized around refuting a self of persons and a self of other phenomena.

Furthermore, among them, the main reasoning for settling the selflessness of phenomena is just the reasoning refuting production from the four extremes.

The four extreme types of production are: a thing's being produced from itself, from others, from both self and others, and causelessly. The set of reasonings refuting these will be discussed in detail in the next chapter.

For, when the Superior Nāgārjuna explained the thought of the statement in the *Sūtra on the Ten Grounds*[216] where it says that a Bodhisattva enters onto the sixth ground through the ten samenesses, he considered that through only demonstrating with reasoning that all phenomena are the same in being without [inherently existent] production, the other samenesses would be easily demonstrated.

The ten samenesses are different ways in which all phenomena are identically empty of inherent existence. Nāgārjuna, in the *Treatise on the Middle Way*, chose to explain them through explaining the sameness of non-production of all phenomena since this is the easiest way to understand the others.

And thus, at the beginning of the *Treatise on the Middle Way* Nāgārjuna says:[217]

There is never production
Anywhere, of any thing
From itself, from others,
From both, or causelessly.

And in the glorious Chandrakīrti's *Supplement to*

(*Nāgārjuna's*) *"Treatise on the Middle Way"* the demonstration of the reasoning for settling the selflessness of phenomena is seen to be only the reasoning refuting production of the four extreme types — "It does not arise from itself; how could it arise from others? ... Those who analyze will quickly be released."[218] Therefore, Dzong-ka-ba's *Differentiation of the Interpretable and the Definitive* says,[219] "The principal reasoning proving the selflessness of phenomena is the reasoning refuting production from the four extremes."

The main reasoning for settling the selflessness of persons is the sevenfold reasoning (1) because Chandrakīrti's *Supplement to (Nāgārjuna's) "Treatise on the Middle Way"* says that just as a chariot is not found through searching in the seven ways but is posited as imputedly existent — imputed in dependence upon its own branches [i.e., parts] — so a person also is to be posited that way, and it says that just this is a method for easily finding the profound view:[220]

How could what does not exist in these
    seven ways be said to exist [inherently]?
Yogis do not find the [inherent] existence of
    this [chariot].
Since through that [way yogis] easily enter
    also into suchness,
The establishment of [a chariot] also should
    be accepted in that way.

The sevenfold reasoning is a set of seven central signs that indicate an absence of inherent existence; it is illustrated through the example of a chariot. If you search for a chariot (1) which is one with its parts, (2) which is inherently other than its parts, (3) which inherently depends on its parts, (4) upon which its parts inherently depend, (5) which inherently possesses its parts, (6) which is the mere collection of its parts, or (7) which is the shape of its parts, you will not be able to find it. Though a chariot cannot be found when it is sought in any of these seven ways and hence does not inherently exist, it is posited as designatedly, or imputedly, existent in the sense that it is designated in dependence upon its own parts. Because it is easy to understand the application of the sevenfold reasoning to a chariot, Chandrakīrti teaches it first so that the same analysis can be done with respect to the person and then other phenomena in order to arrive at their final nature. Chandrakīrti recommends the sevenfold analysis as an easy way to enter into, to realize, suchness — the emptiness of inherent existence.

Jang-gya continues showing why the sevenfold reasoning is the principal one for establishing the selflessness of persons:

> And (2) because in that treatise [i.e., Chandrakīrti's *Supplement*] ascertainment of the selflessness of persons is done only through the sevenfold reasoning, and (3) because this reasoning is said also in Dzong-ka-ba's *Differentiation of the Interpretable and the Definitive* to be the principal one.[221]

Now Jang-gya states something that appears to contradict what he just said:

> The reason of dependent-arising is the main of all reasonings in this system. All these former reasonings derive from just that of dependent-arising.

Dependent-arising is the principal reasoning for ascertaining selflessness in the sense that it is the foundation and source of the reasonings establishing the selflessness both of persons and of phenomena other than persons. However, this does not make it the one that yogis principally use — that being the sevenfold reasoning. All of the other reasonings can be traced back to that of dependent-arising, which, however, is so succinct that it is often hard to get at. The sevenfold investigation is more expansive.

It is said that the sevenfold reasoning is for persons, that the other three reasonings are for the ascertainment of the selflessness of phenomena, and that the reasoning of dependent-arising is for both. However, in practice, the sevenfold reasoning is applied to all phenomena, and the other three also can be applied to persons. The sevenfold analysis is set forth particularly to ascertain the selflessness of persons, but even to apply it to persons you first get accustomed to it with respect to a chariot; then, when you have used the sevenfold analysis with regard to the person and some experience has emerged, you apply it to everything else, just as when you did it earlier with the chariot. Thus, the association of these reasonings with either persons or phenomena indicates a predominant usage, not a limitation.

In this way, moreover, the honorable Chandrakīrti says:[222]

> Since things are dependently arisen,
> They cannot sustain these conceptions [of
>   being produced from self, other, and so
>   forth].
> Therefore, this reasoning of
>   dependent-arising
> Cuts through all the nets of bad views.

It is very difficult to realize how all the other reasonings must derive from this [reasoning of dependent-arising] and do not have such an exceptional ability to cut through the nets of bad views as this does. Therefore, the Foremost Father [Dzong-ka-ba] and his spiritual sons [Gyel-tsap and Kay-drup] praise it, saying that the reason of dependent-arising is the king of reasonings.

As beginners, we are at a stage when we may have to do the other reasonings, the ones that derive from dependent-arising; then, when we are skilled in these, we can pour all that understanding into dependent-arising, enhancing our understanding of it.

Dependent-arising itself refutes both extremes at the same time. Things are dependent-arisings; that things are dependent refutes that they inherently exist; that they arise refutes that they are utterly non-existent. Therefore, they do not inherently exist but do imputedly exist.

> The refutation of production of the existent and non-existent and the refutation of production of the four alternatives are reasonings for settling the self-lessness of phenomena.

The three sets of reasonings that are said to be for ascertaining the selflessness of phenomena other than persons are: (1) the refutation of production of the four extreme types — production from self, other, both, and neither; (2) the refutation of production of the four alternatives — one cause producing one effect; many causes, one effect; one cause, many effects; and many causes, many effects; and (3) the refutation of the production of an existent effect, of a non-existent effect, of an effect that is both existent and non-existent, or of an effect which is neither existent nor non-existent.

> The lack of being one or many is applied to both selflessnesses. The extensive teaching of the reasoning that is the lack of being one or many by way of an analysis of four essentials set forth in Dzong-ka-ba's *Small Exposition of the Stages of the Path*[223] is based on the eighteenth chapter of Nāgārjuna's *Treatise on the Middle Way*.

Dzong-ka-ba wrote three expositions of the stages of the paths. The one called "small" is actually the medium length version of those three, the smallest being the *Concise Meaning of the Stages of the Path*, which is in verse. These three expositions of the stages of the path are written from the viewpoint of the paths common to Low and Great Vehicle practitioners; they are not just catalogues of religious practices, but the ways that a person aspiring to the Great

Vehicle practices the Low Vehicle and Great Vehicle paths. It has none of the features that are peculiar and limited to the Low Vehicle. For instance, when you practice the section on the being of middling capacity, you do not develop the motivation *just* to get yourself out of cyclic existence. Rather, you recognize the faults of cyclic existence and so forth in order to form the basis of practice as a being of great capacity. For, without stark recognition of suffering, great compassion and the effort that such stark recognition impels are impossible. Thus, these stages are a coherent series of practices for one person. It is not that since you want to be a being of great capacity, you then disregard the practices of the two lower types of beings. In order to become a being of great capacity, you must have practiced and mastered the stages that are also explained for beings of small and middling capacities.

In the *Small Exposition of the Stages of the Path*, Dzong-ka-ba sets forth meditation on emptiness through an arrangement of the steps in four essentials, four fundamental movements. The first is to ascertain the object of negation, inherent existence; the second is to ascertain that whatever is not inherently one or inherently many does not inherently exist; the third is to establish that a person and the mental and physical aggregates that are the person's basis of designation are not inherently one; and the fourth is to establish that a person and the mental and physical aggregates that are the person's basis of designation are not inherently many, or plural, or different. Then, without further thought, you realize that you do not inherently exist.

> It is said that this [eighteenth] chapter teaches the meanings of all the other twenty-six chapters of Nāgārjuna's *Treatise on the Middle Way*, arranged in stages of practice; hence, [Dzong-ka-ba's teaching of the four essentials] in this way is very important. There are many reasons for this, but I will leave them for the time being.

10 Can Something Give Birth to Itself?

HOW THOSE REASONINGS REFUTE THE OBJECTS OF NEGATION, THE TWO SELVES

This section has three parts: (1) reasonings refuting a self of phenomena, (2) reasoning refuting a self of persons, and (3) the king of reasonings, the reason of dependent-arising, refuting self with respect to both persons and phenomena.[224]

REASONINGS REFUTING A SELF OF PHENOMENA

Explaining the Reasoning of the Diamond Fragments Refuting Production of the Four Extreme Types[225]
Nāgārjuna's *Treatise on the Middle Way* presents four theses of non-production from the four extremes:[226]

> There is never production
> Anywhere of any thing
> From itself, from others,
> From both, or causelessly.

Furthermore, these theses are merely non-affirming negatives, not implying any other positive phenomenon.

156

This is chapter one, stanza one of the *Treatise*. There is never production of anything anywhere from itself, from others, from both self and others, or causelessly. These are the four theses.

Some people feel that because Consequentialists use consequences based on the positions of their opponents, they have no theses of their own. Although it is certainly correct that Consequentialists often use consequences that draw out the absurdity of their opponents' positions, it is not true, at least according to the Ge-luk-ba tradition, that they do not also assert a position of their own. In general, there are two kinds of theses, inclusive and exclusive. According to Jam-yang-shay-ba,[227] Nāgārjuna and Chandrakīrti use both. That Nāgārjuna has inclusive or positive theses is clear from his *Essay on the Mind of Enlightenment* where he says, "I *assert* dependently arisen activities to be like dreams and magicians' illusions." Also, his *Refutation of Objections* says, "We do not set forth a non-assertion of conventionalities." And, his *Sixty Stanzas of Reasoning* says:

Those who assert dependent phenomena
As like moons in water,
As not real and not unreal,
Are not tricked by views.

His *Praise of the Supramundane* says, "You [Buddha] have taught that agent and object are conventionalities. Your assertion is that they are established as mutually dependent."

Also, Chandrakīrti's *Autocommentary on the "Supplement to (Nāgārjuna's) 'Treatise on the Middle Way'"* says, "The wise should think that this position is faultless and beneficial and should definitely assert it." Also: "Therefore, because dependent imputation is asserted in accordance with the assertion that dependent-arisings are just conditional, it does not not follow for our position that all conventionalities are annihilated; it is suitable also for the opponent to assert just this." Thus, it is clear that both Nāgārjuna and

Chandrakīrti have positive theses, as should also be clear from their use of dependent-arising as a reason why phenomena do not inherently exist.

About exclusive or negative theses, the four theses that negate inherently existent production are examples of exclusive theses; they merely exclude or negate without setting any positive assertion in place of what is negated. Nevertheless, when you understand the consequences proving these theses, you will be able to understand further that, therefore, phenomena are without inherently existent production. The four theses serve as four reasons proving that things are not inherently produced. Also, having understood this, you will be able to conclude that things do not inherently exist. Therefore, although non-affirming negatives do not imply any positive phenomenon in their place, they can imply other non-affirming negatives of the same type; the four reasons imply, or prove, an absence of inherently existent production, which in turn implies, or proves, that things do not inherently exist.

> *Question:* Why are only four theses stated?
> *Answer:* If things were inherently produced, then [this production] would necessarily be one of the four extreme types of production. Due to that, if these four theses are established, it is easily established that there is no inherently existent production. Therefore, the reasoning refuting the four extremes is a decisive reasoning.

The possibilities of inherently existent production are determined to be four; hence, if you can negate these four, you can conclude that there is no inherently existent production such as appears to us now. If you could not determine that the possibilities are limited to four, you might think that there were five or more, and you would have to wait for other possibilities to come along; you would be perpetually waiting for new philosophies to refute. This is not the Middle Way School procedure; one is not merely refuting currently accepted theses, but is covering all possibilities and refuting them so that a conclusion of no inherent existence can be made.

> *Objection:* If, when production of the four extreme types is refuted, a negation of inherent production is implicitly established, then it follows that these theses are not non-affirming negatives.
>
> *Answer:* There is no such fallacy. For something to be an affirming negative it must prove or imply another *positive* phenomenon.

The point of this objection is that since the four theses that refute the four extremes are non-affirming negatives, establishing them cannot lead to a cognition of emptiness, for in that case they would be proving something else — an emptiness of inherently existent production — in place of what was negated, production of the four extreme types. However, the answer is that realization of them can lead to such a cognition; although a non-affirming negative cannot affirm, prove, or imply a positive phenomenon, it can affirm, prove, or imply another non-affirming negative. These theses prove a negative of inherent production. This negative of inherent production is itself a non-affirming negative, not a positive phenomenon, but a mere lack of self-existent production. It, in turn, proves an absence of inherent existence, another non-affirming negative.

> The reason why, if there were inherently existent production, it would necessarily be one of the four extreme types of production, is that it is certain that production is either caused or causeless, and if it is caused, it is limited to three types — production of an effect (1) that is the same entity as the causes, (2) that is a different entity from the causes, and (3) that is a composite of being the same entity as and a different entity from the causes. The Foremost Omniscient [Dzong-ka-ba's] saying this in both of his *Great Explanations* — of Nāgārjuna's *Treatise on*

the Middle Way and Chandrakīrti's *Supplement* — is a very important, good explanation of the great texts from his experience. However, it seems that most of those who write on the Middle Way School put this in a category of minor importance. In any case, they discuss it very briefly.

The point of Nāgārjuna's limiting the possibilities of production to four is usually not explained. The four theses are explained, but how they are limited to four is seldom mentioned. However, Dzong-ka-ba emphasizes cutting off the possibilities at four because once it is decided that there are no other possibilities, if you refute these four, then you have refuted inherently existent production and, thereby, the inherent existence of phenomena. Hence, conviction in the limitation to four is important.

The only sensible type of production is from others, so why consider the other alternatives? One reason is that there are other tenet systems that assert production from self, both, and neither, and it is necessary to confront their assertions on their own grounds. But even more so, if you want to meditate on this, you must cover every possibility of production, no matter how airy or inconsequential it may seem. If you are to become convinced that these refutations are comprehensive, you must go through them all.

First you have to see that all these things must be products, that they are all produced from causes and conditions. You have to use your imagination wherever you go and in whatever you do, allowing everything that is appearing to appear within the context of being a product. You have to go around, pointing at things and saying, "This tree is the product of a seed, soil, and air," and so forth. Your imagination is vast; extend this thought as far as you can. Then you will start noticing how things appear to you. Here is a system that says that all these things do not exist the way they appear; this system attacks these appearances by means of reasoning. You have to open your mind to noticing how objects appear.

Even after you have gained facility with the reasonings and have understood a little about emptiness, these products will continue to appear to you as if they are inherently existent, established from their own side. There will still be a mind which, though it is slowly being consumed through meditating on the absence of inherently established production, thinks that there is findable production. Take that mind and direct it into an investigation of whether this production is there or not. You have to become, at least for awhile, confused about how things could be both produced from causes and at the same time be empty of such analytically findable existence.

> *Refutation of production from self.* The refutation of the production [of an effect] from a cause that is the same entity [as that effect] is this: If a sprout that is being produced were produced again from its own entity, that production would be senseless. For, the sprout's own entity would have already attained existence earlier at the time of its causes.

The tantric abbot Kensur Lekden identified a sprout as a shoot about a foot high. Thus, we are considering two things — seed and sprout — that are obviously different. We are not playing with a subtle distinction between two very similar things, a seed and a tiny sprout just coming out of it. Although it is certainly the case that there is a tiny germinal sprout within the seed, the sprout being talked of here is the young plant that has developed roots and is no longer anything resembling a seed.

Superficially, this argument is directed mainly at the Sāṃkhya system, an ancient non-Buddhist Indian school of philosophy which takes this position on production. They say that an effect exists unmanifestly within its cause; a sprout exists in the same entity as its seed but is not manifest at the time of the seed.

Jang-gya applies Buddhist terminology to the Sāṃkhya position. If the sprout is existent at the time of the seed which is its cause, and if the sprout is an impermanent thing, it is, therefore, something that has already been *produced* since production must refer to the gaining of an existent entity. Thus, if the sprout needs to be produced again despite having been produced once already, it is a case of what has already been produced needing to be produced again.

It may seem unfair to the Sāṃkhya position to criticize it by juggling the terminology. Still, in order to decide whether this is fair or not and, therefore, whether it is applicable or not as a reasoning, it is necessary to play along with the game for a while and get to know it; only after having done that can you stand back and criticize it. If you step in right away claiming that this argument is invalid, you will never get beyond first base, will never see how it works. Some people feel that if you throw your mind into something like this, you will become stuck in it and will lose your perspective. If that is the case, it follows that you would not be able to look at anything at all and afterwards be retrieved. If that were so, there would be no hope for us — we would never be able to investigate new topics, and we would be stuck in cyclic existence forever. However, it may be that by learning to play the game well, you are better able to take it apart.

There is entailment because production is for the sake of [an effect's] attaining its own entity.

The reason is pervaded by the predicate: "All instances of sprouts that have already attained their own entity at the time of their causes are necessarily instances of things whose repeated production would be senseless." This pervasion, or entailment, is established because production is for the sake of attaining an entity and if something has attained its own entity, it has been produced and does not need to be produced again. Therefore, every instance of this kind of production is an instance of senselessness. If something exists, it *has* its own entity, and therefore you can say that it has already *attained* its own entity. There is no question about this latter point; the Sāṃkhyas should accept it. If, in addition, production means something's attaining its own entity, then we have refuted the Sāṃkhyas' position.

According to the Sāṃkhyas, however, production is manifestation of what is unmanifest although already existent. However, this may be a mere shift in terminology, for the manifest entity is what is being produced, and something that was previously unmanifest is being manifested — it attains a manifest entity.

> *Objection:* It is not contradictory for something to have already attained its own entity but to be produced again.
>
> *Answer:* If that were the case, then continuations similar to the effects — such as sprouts — would never be produced and the causes' similar continuations — such as seeds — would be produced without interruption until the end of cyclic existence. For, just that which was already produced would have to be produced in duplicate again and again.

The opponent has just said that it is not contradictory for something that has already attained its own entity to be produced again. However, if there were no contradiction for a seed that has already attained its own entity to be produced again, then there would be no chance for the effects of that seed to emerge. For the seed, though produced in the sense of having attained its own entity, would need to be produced yet again and again and again and again, infinitely.

Once you say that what exists must be produced to be made manifest, then since you would be forced to say that what is manifest also exists, it also would require production again and again forever. Indeed, the very same seed and not a later moment of that seed would have to be produced forever.

Chandrakīrti's *Supplement to (Nāgārjuna's) "Treatise*

on the Middle Way" says:[228]

There is no point in the production of
   something from itself.
Also, the production again of what has been
   produced is just not feasible.
If it is thought that the already produced is
   produced again,
One would not find the production of such
   things as sprouts here [in the world],
And a seed would just be produced to the
   end of cyclic existence.

It seems to me that we do not have to be limited to considering this reasoning from the Sāṃkhya viewpoint of an effect
being produced from causes that are of the same entity.
Rather, imagine that an object produces itself again — not a
case of a former moment producing a later moment, but
just producing itself again without any change. There is no
question that this is completely foolish and that such production would go on forever. It is helpful to see the fault in
this way at first.

Despite the evident unfeasibility of this position of production from self, the refutation of it can be astounding
because it raises doubt about this inherent existence that
appears so vividly. Moreover, this refutation attacks the
view that impermanence means the production again and
again of the same object. If you have the coarse sense that
momentary existence means the flashing into existence each
moment of, for instance, this same blade of grass, this
reasoning will get at it.

When going through this reasoning, one needs to feel
pushed. You had four possibilities for inherently existent
production, and now you are being pushed down to three.
Incidentally, it is not necessary to meditate on these four
extreme types of production in the order given in Nāgārjuna's text. In his *Key to the Middle Way*[229] the Dalai Lama
puts causeless production first, probably because it is so

easy to dispose of. Then, he explains the refutations of production from self and production from other, with production from both self and other last because the reasoning that refutes each individually is brought to bear on the two together. We have the strongest attraction for production from other, but production from both self and other is refuted last because the refutation of production from other is needed for refuting the dual assertion. If you then turned to consider causeless production, the force of your thought might be dissipated, for at the time of refuting production from other your interest was at its strongest. This is probably why he considers causeless production first.

Use whichever way works best for you; it is not as if there were only one order and you have to do it that way. When meditating with these reasonings, we have to work with our own minds, and therefore, we can determine the best and easiest way.

> Concerning this, since the Sāṃkhyas assert that seed and sprout are mutually different, they do not assert that a sprout[230] is produced from a sprout; however, they assert that the nature of the sprout and the nature of the seed are one and that their natures are mutually each other. Therefore, the previously explained fallacies apply [to their position].

The Sāṃkhyas themselves maintain that a seed and the sprout which is its effect are mutually different: seed is different from sprout and sprout is different from seed. However, they also say that the nature of the seed and the nature of the sprout are the same. They feel that if the seed and the sprout did not have the same nature, then all causes and effects would become confused. For example, the Sāṃkhyas say that although one sprout has many causes, they produce one effect, thus showing that the many causes have one nature. If you want to grow corn, it is necessary to have one collection of causes; if you want to build a house, you need another. There has to be a binding relation between cause and effect. Otherwise, there would be no certainty that apple seeds would produce apples, pear seeds pears, and peach seeds peaches. Therefore, the Sāṃkhyas say that a particular group of causes has the same nature as its effect. Thus, cause and effect are not one, but different manifest states within one nature — cause state and effect state, seed state and sprout state.

We have to find out what "nature" means to a Sāṃkhya. Does it affirm the way things presently appear? Is it a way to establish inherently existing production? In the Sāṃkhya system, everything is produced from the Nature[231] and dissolves back into the Nature. Also, when something is produced, it is still the same entity as this Nature. For them, production and disintegration are manifestation and dissolution.

If you were doing Sāṃkhya meditation, you would sit down and dissolve the world, going through the process of the evolution and dissolution of the world, out of and into the Nature. At the point of total dissolution, there is no appearance of conventional phenomena at all, just what is called "Self", that is, pure consciousness. Similarly, in the Consequentialist system when you are meditating on and cognizing emptiness directly, the mind is utterly fused with emptiness with no other appearance at all. This is somewhat like the consciousness that is alone after dissolving all manifestations back into the Nature in Sāṃkhya meditation. Moreover, in Buddhism it is said that the Truth Body of a Buddha pervades everywhere, that there is no place where the Truth Body is not.

From where we stand, Buddhist and Sāṃkhya teachings are pointing to almost the same thing; thus, anyone who wants to experience the Buddhist world-view has to be very careful in refuting non-Buddhist systems. For, there are similar evolution and dissolution meditations in Buddhist tantra in which all phenomena appear out of and later dissolve into a single syllable; however, when all things disappear and reappear, they are qualified with analytical non-findability, with emptiness, making the process different from Sāṃkhya unless the Sāṃkhya experience of pure consciousness causes phenomena to be qualified with a sense of radical dependence that negates their seemingly solid appearance.

It is important to know what to refute and what not to refute. For example, Vedāntins speak of a Self pervading all phenomena. The conventional self, subject to suffering and impermanence, has an immediacy; it is vividly right here. In the pursuit of Brahman, ultimate reality, the limited qualities of the self are cancelled, leaving this immediacy. Brahman, for them, is the ultimate truth, the underlying nature of all, which is commonly considered to be distant. In meditation, the sense of distance of Brahman is cancelled and the diseased limited nature of self is cancelled, whereas the sense of Brahman as reality is retained, as is the immediacy of self; these two are then equated. *Tat tvam asi* "You are that." "You" become pure, and "that" becomes immediate, the two being fused.

If you claimed that none of this exists in Buddhism, you would be making a mistake. For, when a direct cognition of emptiness is presented in the Middle Way School, it is said to be like water poured into water — the wisdom consciousness is fused with the emptiness, or final nature, of everything. Rejection of Vedānta out of partisanship to Buddhism might prevent opening up to essential Buddhist practices. For example, making fun of Hindu yogis for seeing God in everything might close the mind to discovering that emptiness is the "substance" of appearance, that phenomena are the sport[232] of emptiness. For practitioners, the line of refutation must be drawn carefully.

> The [Sāṃkhyas] themselves do not assert such, but because the two, seed and sprout, are [for them] one by inherent nature, their being one becomes the mode of subsistence of seed and sprout, whereby they would be undifferentiable. [The Sāṃkhyas] are logically forced [into this position] whereupon

the fallacy is demonstrated.

[When production from self] is refuted in Chandrakīrti's *Supplement* and in his commentary on it, the reasonings used are those that he makes in commentary as well as [other] reasonings [cited] from Nāgārjuna's *Treatise on the Middle Way*. [The first are:]

1. If cause and effect were one entity, it would [absurdly] follow that seed and sprout would not differ with respect to shape, color, taste, and capacity.

What Chandrakīrti is saying in the end is that if two things are one nature, or one entity, *and are inherently existent,* then they are one. You have to face this and decide whether or not it is valid. If their nature is one, then how can there be any difference?

For example, if the hand — fingers, palm, nails, and so on — were inherently one entity, then all these would be one. You can point to all the things that are the basis of the designation "hand". Is there anything else that is the "hand" that at first so forcibly appeared? You cannot point to anything else right there that is the hand. Without mentally spreading a sort of oneness over your hand as you would spread mayonnaise on bread, there is nothing there in itself. The point is that there is no chance for the hand to be an analytically findable one. This is very hard; you have to work a lot on this. Once you have played the game a little by following the reasonings given in the books, you have to internalize it and go into every facet of it.

A seed and the sprout that is its effect are either the same or different. If they are *inherently* the same nature, everything that is true of the seed must also be true of the sprout. If the seed is white, the sprout must be white. If you could make a meal out of the seed, you would be able to make the same meal out of the sprouts. If the seed is bitter, the sprout also must be bitter, and so on and so forth. It is not being said that mere existence entails that two things that are the same entity must be the same in all respects; rather, if things exist the way they appear — if they exist from their own side — then, two things that are the same entity must be the same in all respects.

> 2. It would [absurdly] follow that when its former state [as a seed] was given up, the single nature of seed and sprout would be lost.

The seed state is given up when the sprout state is manifested. However, once the seed is gone, how are you going to say that the nature of the seed and that of the sprout are the same?

This type of problem also appears in Buddhism. Saying that all conventional phenomena are the sport of emptiness, manifestations of emptiness, seems to come down to saying that objects are only different states of emptiness. This view is not just tantric; it appears in the sūtra systems. For instance, the Fourth Panchen Lama speaks of viewing appearances as the sport of emptiness:[233]

Subsequent to meditative equipoise, all phenomena — the I and so forth — should be meditated on as the sport [of emptiness] like a magician's illusions. In other words, rely on developing a strong conviction of truthlessness [the knowledge that phenomena do not inherently exist] during meditative equipoise and afterwards learn to view all that appears, even though appearing [to exist inherently], as the sport [of emptiness] like a magician's illusions, truthless and false.

Since the emptiness of inherent existence makes appearance possible, phenomena are, in a sense, the sport of emptiness. It even may be said that their basic substance is emptiness. However, emptiness is a non-affirming negative, a mere absence or mere elimination of inherent existence, which does not imply anything in place of inherent existence even though it is compatible with dependently arisen phenomena. Hence, emptiness is not a positive substance giving rise to phenomena. Still, emptiness here almost becomes a substance, something out of which everything is made. This is somewhat like the widespread Hindu position that everything is an appearance of a basic substance.

> 3. It would [absurdly] follow that during each of the states of seed and sprout, both seed and sprout would be equally apprehendable or not.

At the time of the manifest seed, the sprout is not there; however, because, according to the Sāṃkhyas, seed and sprout are of the same nature, if the seed is apprehendable, the sprout would have to be apprehendable too. Similarly, at the time of the manifest sprout the seed would also have to be apprehendable. In the same vein, the Buddhist logicians make the point that when a worm who will be born as an elephant in his next lifetime is atop a blade of grass, there is really an elephant on top of that piece of grass. Indeed, the Sāṃkhyas would agree that on that grass is a nonmanifest elephant. This *looks* absurd; it is a case of attacking a theory in debate through making their position appear unattractive in ordinary worldly terms.

> 4. Worldly renown damages [the position] that seed and sprout are of one nature.

Though the world, that is, ordinary uneducated persons, do not even know of such things as the "sameness in entity of seed and sprout," the world knows that you cannot see the sprout when the seed is there. However, if worldly renown were enough to ruin anything, then emptiness would never stand. The Consequentialists report that Buddha said, "I accept what the world accepts," but, indeed, he does not accept the mode of being of phenomena the way the world conceives it.

> In refuting production from self, [Chandrakīrti] also uses the reasonings in Nāgārjuna's *Treatise on the Middle Way* that it would [absurdly] follow that

the producer and the produced would be one and
that the three — action, agent, and object — would
be one.[234]

If the producer — the seed — were the same entity as what
it produces — the sprout — then the agent and the object
would be one. If agent and object could be one, a sword
could cut itself, a finger could touch itself in the same spot,
etc. Because of such absurdities, it cannot be accepted that
a cause and its effect are the same entity, or the same
nature.

Mere words are not sufficient; the refutation must be
contemplated in meditation to the point where deep conviction that this position is impossible is developed and, conse-
quently, the seeming concreteness of objects, their existing
from their own side, begins to be disturbed. You begin
wondering how you could posit these objects; you start to
be shaken.

11 Does a Plant Grow?

Refutation of production from other. "Other" in "production from other" is not merely other; it is other that is established by way of its own character.

This "other" is not a conventionally existent other. It is an other that exists by way of its own character, that exists inherently, an outflow of which is that it would be an analytically findable other.

There are many unwanted consequences stemming from an assertion that effects are produced from causes that are inherently existent others; for instance, a correlation of certain effects with certain causes would be impossible, since all things, including those usually considered not to be causes of a certain thing, would equally be inherently existent others.

You may feel here that a quality of inherent existence is being imposed on this other that is not in your usual conception of causation. The Consequentialists agree; they say that we do not innately conceive cause and effect to be inherently existent others. We innately conceive them to inherently exist, to exist by way of their own character, but we do not innately enter into any thought of whether they are same or other, at least when considering substantial

172

causes and their effects.

When we think about an oak tree's having grown from an acorn, it might seem that we are considering the tree and the acorn to be other. However, Chandrakīrti appears to dispute this, pointing out that we say, "I planted this tree," when we only planted its seed, "I engendered this child," when a male merely planted his seed in the womb:[235]

Worldly beings, from planting only seeds,
Say, "I engendered this child," And think, "I planted [this] tree.'
Therefore, production from other does not exist even in the world.

In this statement, Chandrakīrti is, most likely, referring to those times when we consider the *production* of this from that, since within this context, an otherness would suggest that cause and effect are unrelated.

However, once cause and effect exist, they must be either the same or other, and sometimes we do indeed emphasize the difference of things that are cause and effect — for instance, when we perceive an apple and imagine the apple seed that produces it. If you asked for an apple at a fruit stand and the seller gave you an apple seed, you would certainly know that an apple seed differs from, is other than, an apple. Dzong-ka-ba says that we do not innately conceive cause and effect to be *inherently existent* others and that indeed an otherness of entity of cause and effect is not established in a worldly perspective.[236] Still, I wonder if we actually do conceive them to be inherently existent others in this type of context.

In any case, the Consequentialists' claim is not that we innately perceive cause and effect to be inherently existent others and thus unrelatedly other. Rather, they claim that *if* cause and effect existed the way they appear to (that is, as inherently existent), they would be unrelatedly other.

Moreover, those who propound production from other assert that in the same way that a rice seed is established by way of its own character as other than the sprout of rice that is its own effect, so such things as fire and charcoal also are established by way of their own character as other than the sprout of rice.

If we limit ourselves at this point to considering merely the part of their assertion regarding "other", then, in just the same way that the causes of a book — the trees from which the paper was made, the ink, the printer, and so on — are established by way of their own character as other than the book, so the book and the chair you are sitting on are established by way of their own character as other. With respect to their status of otherness, they are exactly the same.

A clue to this analysis is to zero in on something without considering the other thing to which you usually relate it. For example, here you have an apple seed and an apple. They are other. You could not eat the seed and get the taste of an apple; it is clearly other than an apple. It even seems, from its own side, to be other. Once you have considered the seed, zero in on the apple; it also seems, from its own side, to be just other; that seems to be its nature.

If those two modes of being other are asserted to be similar, then thick darkness which [is supposed to be] cleared away [by light] would [absurdly] arise even from a blazing flame that [is supposed to] clear away [darkness], and anything would come from anything else, whether they are cause and effect or not. For, they would all equally have otherness that is established by way of its own character.

Anything could arise from anything else, whether or not they are usually considered to be cause and effect. For, you have lost all criteria for specifying what is a cause and what is its effect. If you can have cause and effect between two naturally established others, then, since everything is equally other, you can have cause and effect between *any* two others.

In the end, it is a question of what a relation is. Two things are cause and effect; they have to be either the same or different. In which category are you going to put the relation of cause and effect? The Sāṃkhya wants to put the relation in the category of sameness; the Buddhist wants to put the relation into that of otherness. Even for Consequentialists, at least as interpreted by Dzong-ka-ba and his followers, cause and effect are other entities, but they are not inherently existent others, for a relation of causation cannot be sustained within what are inherently existent others.

This is the reasoning taught in the twentieth chapter of Nāgārjuna's *Treatise on the Middle Way:*[237]

> If cause and effect had otherness,
> Cause and non-cause would become equal.

This reasoning is also taught in Buddhapālita's commentary on this point and by the glorious Chandrakīrti who says:[238]

> If, depending on others, another were to
>   arise,
> Then thick darkness would arise even from
>   a tongue of flame
> And all would be produced from all
> Because even all non-producers would
>   equally have otherness. ...

Objection: Things are not posited as cause and effect merely because they are others that are established by way of their own character. Things are posited as cause and effect only because they are a special kind of others — [the cause] having the ability to bring about the effect and so forth. Thus, the determination of causes and non-causes [with respect to a particular effect] is feasible.

Jang-gya said previously that the "others" in the refutation of production from other are not merely "others" but others that are established by way of their own character as others. Here, an objector says that things are not posited as causes and effects *merely* because they are such others; the objector is seeking to eliminate *unrelated* others. For, we do indeed call things "causes" and "effects" not just because they are different from each other, but because they have a certain relationship. In other words, being inherently existent others is acceptable as one criterion for cause and effect, but there is an additional criterion of being related — in the sense that the cause has the ability to produce the effect. That which is other and assists in producing an effect is its cause; that which is other and does not help to produce this particular effect is not its cause. The cause has to help produce the effect; it has to precede the effect, and it has to be other than the effect.

> *Answer:* That also is incorrect, for once things are established by way of their own character as other, being other must be their mode of subsistence. Once that is the case, they must be other factualities that are utterly devoid of any relation with each other. Thus, it would be utterly impossible for a rice seed and a barley seed to differ with regard to having or not having the ability to produce a rice sprout and so forth.

Since naturally existent others are unrelated others, we cannot posit a relationship that ties together a seed and the sprout that is its effect. Therefore, we cannot say that a rice seed has a special ability to produce a rice sprout and that a barley seed is without this special ability. Since they are both equally other than the rice sprout and since this otherness is in their nature, the one cannot somehow be less other than the other. We can at least say that this reasoning will attack the way we sometimes feel when we see a totally distinct other, even if this feeling is artificial and not innate.

Furthermore, if production from other existed by way of its own entity, the effect would have to exist before it was produced. For once production is asserted, the two — the ceasing of the cause and the nearing to production of the effect — must be simultaneous, and in that case the two actions of production and cessation also would have to be simultaneous, whereby cause and effect would also have to be simultaneous.

The sprout that will be a foot high is growing even when you are putting water on the seed. When I grow corn, the cornstalk is growing. No matter how small we make the thing that is in the process of growing, we still have a problem, for the thing that is growing has not quite grown there yet.

When a sprout is growing, an action of growing is present, and this action needs an agent, a grower. The grower is the sprout, the plant; the action of growing depends on it. This may seem very technical; yet, we talk about "growing" as if it existed right there in and of itself, and we should examine whether this thing to which we give the name "growing" is as substantially existent as it seems to be or is only posited by the mind.

The reason for [the consequent simultaneity of cause and effect] is that an action of nearing production has to depend on something, such as a sprout, that is the agent in the expression, "This effect is growing." Therefore, they are supporter and supported.

The supporter is the effect, the sprout, the grower. That which is supported is its activity, growing. The agent, the sprout, is the base of the activity.

If such a supporter and supported were established by way of their own character, then whenever the activity of growing existed, the sprout would have to exist. For, its nature could not possibly change. Therefore, Chandrakīrti's *Supplement to (Nāgārjuna's) "Treatise on the Middle Way"* says,[239] "Without an agent, this growing is also not a feasible entity."

If the supporter, the sprout, and the supported, its growing, exist from their own side, they must exist at the same time. The sprout that is the agent performing the activity of growing must exist at the same time as its growing. For, it is senseless to have an activity without an agent. Once the sprout is inherently established as the agent that is the support of the activity of growth, it is unchangeable. Once something is inherently established, its nature is locked into one thing.

It is important to qualify this refutation as referring to others that are established by way of their own character because in the Consequentialist system conventional production *is* asserted — dependently arisen production that is analytically unfindable.

> In terms of nominally existent production, if things become supporter and supported at some time, it is not necessary that they be so at all times. Therefore, [mere, conventional production] does not have these fallacies. The Foremost Omniscient [Dzongka-ba] maintains that this is a subtle[240] and very meaningful reasoning in this system that refutes production from other.

In conventionally existent growing, you do not make this sort of investigation into growing. Something grows without a grower present; we say that a cornstalk is growing, but it is not there yet. The analysis of whether the grower is there now or not — the same thought that many children have and that bothers us now and then — is ultimate analysis. Moreover, the validity of conventionally existent production does not affirm how we now feel about growing and so forth. The growing that we know now is so utterly mixed with inherent existence and a sense of findability that it is impossible to identify conventionally existent production in our own experience. If you passed by a field and noticed only that the corn was growing without putting strong attention into it, your sense of growing might accord with the fact in the sense that you are not actively superimposing inherent establishment on it. However, such knowledge of growing, even if not wrong about the status of growing, does not provide an understanding of its actual nature. In other words, in order to understand something as only conventionally existent, we must first cognize its emptiness.

> Not only is production from other not asserted even conventionally by this system, but also it is asserted that no innate consciousness conceives causes and effects as others that are different by way of their own character.

Consequentialists do not assert production from other, even conventionally. They do assert conventional production; cause and effect are still other, but they are not analytically findable others.

Innate consciousnesses include both inborn forms of ignorance and also some valid cognitions; the one being discussed here is ignorance. It apprehends cause, effect, and production as established by way of their own character. However, it does not apprehend effects to be *others that are established by way of their own character*. We conceive cause and effect to be inherently existent or findable, but we do not innately, naturally enter into investigation of whether they are one or other.

> Chandrakīrti's *Supplement* says,[241] "There is no production from other even in the world."

The world does not enter into thoughts about whether something is produced from itself or from another. As Nāgārjuna says,[242] "When this is, that arises." When you have a seed, sun, water, and other favorable conditions, a sprout arises. In terms of the nominality, "When this is, that arises," the world is right. However, the world has a very strong feeling in addition that these things inherently exist, even though the ordinary world does not construct false philosophies to reaffirm this innate misapprehension.

Are people who study philosophies such as Sāṃkhya and so forth worse off than others? From the viewpoint of the Consequence School, they are indeed fortifying their innate problems with intellectually acquired encrustation, but, as the tantric abbot Kensur Lekden said, to understand the Middle Way School you need a good mind, and studying a system like Sāṃkhya trains the mind and serves as a good preparation for the study of the Middle Way School. For example, according to certain current popular philosophies, you must have your own individual substantial being. When you create a sense of this, you fortify the problem; however, by setting yourself into this problem even more strongly, an awareness is fostered that makes recognition of the middle way more possible.

Refutation of production from both self and other. That part which is production from self is refuted by the reasoning refuting production from self; that part which is production from other is refuted by the reasoning refuting production from other. Chandrakīrti's *Supplement* says:[243]

> Production from both is also not an
>   admissible entity
> Because the fallacies already explained are
>   incurred.

Some think that they can take the good parts of production from self and production from other and rescue findable production in that way. They want to have their feet in both camps in order to get the good fruit that is in each. However, they also get the bad parts of each: they get eaten by lice in this camp and rats in that camp. Though they might want to make use of the virtues of both positions, they also have to accept the fallacies endemic to both; if you can negate production from self and production from other, you can negate production from both self and other.

Refutation of causeless production

One of the non-Buddhist Indian philosophical groups, the Nihilists or Hedonists,[244] says that at least some things are produced without cause. They propound that since no one sees anyone paint the colors on flowers or carve peas to make them round, these things are without cause; they are just produced this way due to their own nature. I remember having such thoughts as a child. Where did the sharpness of a thorn come from? No one sharpened it. One possible answer is that this is merely its nature, the way it is, that it is not caused.

The Nihilists take a very concrete thing, like the point of a thorn which appears as if established in its own right, and fortify this appearance by saying that it is produced without cause. This *is* a type of production; for, they are talking about impermanent things that were not here yesterday but are here today. They say that such things arise from their own nature.

> If [things] were produced causelessly, there would be no causes for production at a certain place and time and of a certain nature. Therefore, something produced from one thing would be produced from all things, and all work would be just senseless.

If you plant corn seeds in that field over there, they are not going to grow in this field over here. Moreover, they will grow in the summer, not in the winter. Finally, when you plant corn seeds, you can expect production of a specific nature — corn, not apples. Such limitations would be impossible in causeless production.

Again, because there would be no causes to make production specific to a certain time, place, and nature, anything that is produced could be produced from anything else. Therefore, it would be senseless to initiate any undertakings or make effort at anything.

Think about these reasons in relation to the things you do every day. It is no good just to think about them superficially, as if you had a blackboard in front of you. How would your life change if anything could be produced from anything else? If production were causeless and there were no certainty about anything, what would this mean for you?

[Chandrakīrti] says:[245]

> If it is viewed that [things] are only
>   produced causelessly,
> Then everything would always be produced
>   from even everything,
> And this world also would not gather in so
>   many ways
> Such things as seeds for the sake of their
>   effects.

We do many, many things in anticipation of their future effects. We make sure to buy toothpaste at the store so that it will be there when we want to brush our teeth that night at home.

> Through refuting production of the four extreme types in this way, production that is established by way of its own character is negated.

This reasoning is an analysis of causes. It investigates whether effects are produced from causes that are the same as the effect, other than the effect, both, or causelessly. Things, the subject, do not have inherently existent production because (1) they are not produced from themselves, (2) they are not produced from inherently existent others, (3) they are not produced from both, and (4) they are not produced causelessly. These four reasons are non-affirming negatives. Together they prove that there is no inherently existent production.

Once you have eliminated these four modes of production, then, since there are no more ways in which inherently existent production could take place, you come to the decision that there is no inherently existing production. Seeing that there is no inherently existing production, you can see that there is no inherent existence. For, if these things are going to inherently exist, then since they are products, they must be inherently produced. Once they are not inherently produced, they do not inherently exist. You have to make all these steps, follow out all these implications; they will not go into your mind by themselves, you have to make them. It is like a treasure hunt: you must have a map and follow that map, but when you get to the end, the treasure is there, not the map. At that point it has real force; you have reached a place where you are not trying to convince yourself of something. We are now, however, at the stage where we have to convince ourselves. This means that we have to sit down and actually do it; merely hearing about it is not enough.

The whole point of refuting other systems is to get at our own innate sense of the inherent existence of production and so forth. This is the hard point. For, Jang-gya has just said that although we have no innate sense of same, other, both, or neither about cause and effect, we should refute systems that propound these. Even though innately we do not analyze cause and effect to be inherently the same or different, this type of analysis covers all possibilities of inherently existent production; so, if these can be refuted, there is no place left for inherently existent production.

This analytical refutation of production will break down and destroy our sense of production that is established from its own side. Since, roughly speaking, inherently existing production is the only production that we now know, it may seem that once this has been destroyed there will be no production, resulting in nihilism. Thus, at this point when you are doing the analysis, you have to keep in mind that you are not denying all production but will, after understanding emptiness, gain a different sense of what a seed is, what a sprout is, and of what growing is.

However, the refutation of production of the four extreme types does not refute merely conventional production. For, merely conventional production does not have to be any of the four extreme types of production. Not only that, but also dependent production itself establishes that things are not produced from the four extremes. Dzong-ka-ba's *Great Commentary on (Nāgārjuna's) "Treatise on the Middle Way"* says:

> Therefore, that, by the very necessity of accepting that a sprout is produced in dependence on a seed, one is able to refute these four [extreme types of production] is a distinguishing feature of the reasoning of dependent-arising, the king of reasonings.

Earlier we talked about proving emptiness with non-affirming negatives. Here, something positive — that a sprout is produced in dependence on a seed — is used. Dependent production itself is able to refute production from self, other, both and neither. This suggests the way in which all the reasonings that prove emptiness meet back to the reasoning of dependent-arising.

Furthermore, the master Buddhapālita, who attained yogic feats, says:

> Here [an objector] says, "Show how this which is called production is only a convention."
>
> *Answer:* This is shown initially [in the first stanza of the first chapter of Nāgārjuna's *Treatise on the Middle Way*]:[246]
>
> > There is never production
> > Anywhere of any thing

From itself, from others,
From both, or causelessly.

According to Jam-yang-shay-ba,[247] this introduction by Buddhapālita to Nāgārjuna's first stanza is the source of a great deal of the debate between Bhāvaviveka (the founder of the Autonomy School) and Buddhapālita and Chandrakīrti (both Consequentialists). In the first chapter of the *Treatise on the Middle Way,* Nāgārjuna sets forth a non-affirming negative, the emptiness of phenomena in general. How is this proven? Through the emptiness of impermanent phenomena. How is that proven? Through a proof that things are not produced from self, from other, from both, or causelessly. Thus, there are four non-affirming negatives, realization of which leads to realizing one non-affirming negative. Four non-affirming negatives, that phenomena are not produced from themselves, from others, from both, or without cause, imply one non-affirming negative, that impermanent phenomena are not inherently produced. This non-affirming negative implies another non-affirming negative in its turn, that impermanent phenomena do not inherently exist. This implies still another non-affirming negative, that all phenomena do not inherently exist. Once impermanent phenomena do not inherently exist, permanent phenomena also do not inherently exist. For, permanent phenomena all have some relation to impermanent phenomena, such as the space of a pot and a pot.

Buddhapālita, however, seems to be saying that the first chapter of the *Treatise* was written in order to show how production is only a convention. Conventionally existent production is a positive phenomenon, not a non-affirming negative. Nāgārjuna would then be proving an affirming negative when he negated production from self, from other, from both, or without cause — that is, the four negations would negate inherently existent production but imply conventionally existent production. However, this was not Nāgārjuna's intention, for when you cognize emptiness you realize a mere elimination of all elaborations of inherent existence. If you come up with something in place of the object of negation, you would not be cognizing emptiness, but an affirming negative that implies a positive phenomenon. Thus, Bhāvaviveka very rightly rejected this. The question is whether Buddhapālita really meant what he seems to say.

Jam-yang-shay-ba defends Buddhapālita by pointing out that Buddhapālita's statement is not really a specific introduction to this reasoning, but a general statement that production does not exist ultimately but exists conventionally. However, Buddhapālita's statement does seem to have been given to clarify why this chapter was written. Chandrakīrti's defense of Buddhapālita is that even if Buddhapālita did seem to say that, he did not mean to say it. According to the conventions of discourse, one cannot be held to account for something one did not mean to say.

Also, the *Buddhapālita Commentary* says, "Hence, because there is no [inherently existent] production, this which is called production is only a convention."

This appears at the end of Buddhapālita's proof that things are not produced from themselves, from others, from both, or causelessly. Again, Buddhapālita speaks of this negation as if it were affirming conventionally existent production. He is drawing a positive conclusion from the fact that there is no inherently existent production.

The issue here is not just formal but has a great deal to do with how you meditate. Are you trying, through the reasoning, to come up with the conclusion that production is only conventionally existent? No, upon searching for production, you are not able to come up with anything that you can identify as production. What you are looking for in meditation is the vacuity that is the absence of analytically findable production. You are not at that time looking for a positive replacement. All that will be in your mind is that there is no such production, or that production as presently so boldly appears to your mind does not exist.

12 Inducing Realization

COMMENTS ON THE REFUTATION OF PRODUCTION

Though we live in the midst of these things appearing to exist inherently, somewhere deep in the mind, this solidity must bother us. Depending on our predispositions, the tension of questioning these concrete appearances is more or less near the surface, more or less affecting us. But in any case we have a feeling not to consider it, a feeling that it cannot be figured out. For, we are faced with the overwhelming appearance of things as inherently existent. Even when exposed to Buddha's teaching and to the reasonings that refute true existence, we still feel that these appearances are "there" and that these reasonings are incredible. What has appeared to us for countless lifetimes makes us resist coming to a conclusion, and eventually when we understand a little about emptiness, it seems even painful.

We have a network of anxiety and, based on it, a network of desires and hatreds. When we do not investigate objects and just take them at face value, it seems as if we are down to bare facts. We feel that here is something that matters, that, for example, our life, or future, or happiness is at stake.

In support of the inherently existent I and this network of desires and hatreds, we need inherently existent production of help and harm. However, emptiness means that there is no inherently existent production of harm when someone stops you on the street at midnight, beats you up, and takes your money. You would certainly feel that there was an inherently existent effect there — you were beaten up and you have no more money! However, if you understand it well, there is no way for any kind of production *as we understand it*, qualified by inherent existence, to occur.

We can destroy the exaggerations of harmer and the harmed that are created by the conception of true existence — these being almost all of what we experience. Still, we cannot deny conventionally existent harmer and harmed without deprecating what does indeed exist. Conventionally and validly, of course, there are help and harm. However, we have a strong sense that help and harm are analytically findable, existing from their own side, concretely, most palpably. Conventionally, within the context of cause and effect not being analytically findable, it is important to value cause and effect even though they are not analytically findable. For, though we exaggerate the status of cause and effect, the removal of that exaggeration does not mean that cause and effect are removed; rather, the removal of the exaggeration yields greater understanding and appreciation of cause and effect. This is difficult. How could you not concretely find that one person's arm was cut off and another's was not? But if you can probe these reasonings, it is said that you will be able to see your own arm being cut off, and there will be nothing to point to which is the cutting off of the arm, the person whose arm is being cut off, or the arm that is cut off, all within not denying that the arm is being cut off.

For instance, ultimately there is no production from other, but conventionally there is production of effects that are other than their causes. Still, this does not mean that there are two levels of reality, one that is the ultimate level of emptiness and one that is our normal world. It would be incorrect to say that when we rise from meditating on emptiness, forget the absence of inherent existence, and again fall into ignorance, we are then in the conventional level. For, our ordinary misperceptions of inherently existent objects do not constitute the conventional level. Inherent existence is an object of ignorance and does not exist, not even conventionally. Rather, we must see the compatibility of the ultimate and the conventional. We must *act within* the context of understanding the non-concreteness of phenomena, knowing that these things are unfindable.

Dzong-ka-ba and his followers say that the consciousness that certifies, or establishes, the existence of a conventional truth is a valid cognition. Others, however, say that conventionally existent phenomena are posited by ignorance. For the Ge-luk-ba system, ignorance falsely certifies the *portion* of perception that is the appearance of inherent existence, but there is also a portion of correct appearance that is certified by conventional valid cognition. The appearance of objects is partly right and partly wrong, but it is not that the underside is wrong and the topside is correct. Everything throughout the appearance is colored by falsity. In other interpretations of the Consequence School, it is felt that because every portion of the object is affected by the false appearance of inherent existence, the whole object is posited by ignorance.

From the way that many speak of conventional and ultimate truths, it might seem that they are two levels of operation on the same object. However, the aim is to practice a union of conventional truths and ultimate truths, realizing that conventional truths only nominally exist and that ultimate truths negate only inherent existence and not existence in general.

"Conventional truth" (*saṃvṛti-satya*) can also be translated as "concealer-truth" or "truth-for-a-concealing-consciousness". The "concealer" is ignorance because ignorance conceals, obscures, or obstructs perception of the actual nature of phenomena. These objects are truths for a concealing, ignorant consciousness; however, a "concealer-truth" is not an object that is posited by ignorance, but a phenomenon that is a *truth* for ignorance. A "truth" is what exists the way it appears, whereas conventional objects falsely appear — even in direct perception — to be inherently existent; hence, conventional objects are not truths in fact. Ignorance affirms this false appearance of inherent existence and, therefore, is the concealer of suchness. Everything that we see is a concealer-truth, taken by ignorance to exist the way it appears, but actually appearing one way and existing in another; these appearances are fraudulent. Meditative investigation is used to penetrate this falsity.

The Reasoning
Almost everything with which we come into contact is compounded, produced. We have a very firm sense that all these products are there in and of themselves. If we want to find out if these products are really there in the way that they appear, one technique is to examine how they are produced. For, if we can refute their substantially established production, we can negate this very solid, bold, and forthright appearance as if they are right there in their own right.

First, decide whether these appearances are permanent or not. This can be done easily. These are impermanent and hence must be products. Once they are products, we have only four choices. Production has to be either caused or causeless; if it is caused, then there are three choices — the effect has to be produced from a cause that is either the same as itself, different, or both same and different.

In order to succeed, you have to tie the reasoning to these very forceful appearances. What we usually do is to take the things appearing here as data, as facts, and then try to figure out an intellectual system that will accord with them. What is needed here is quite different. We have to figure out some way to extricate our minds from these wrong appearances so that we will quit assenting to them; then we have to destroy the wrong appearances themselves so that things will appear correctly. This Buddhist system is opposite to what we are accustomed to.

Many people talk about quieting the mind down, about ceasing the frozen overlay we put on things and experiencing them more the way they are. Perhaps this is a way of getting closer to the innate mind; artificial conceptions are being quieted, and the mind is being withdrawn from intellectually acquired ideas. There is no question that if we can do this, we will perceive the world differently. However, even if you could completely keep the mind away from even the innate conceptions, the appearance of phenomena would still be wrong. By sinking down into appearances, you are getting deeper into your problem and, in a sense, identifying it more, but your realization is getting no deeper. As mentioned before, it is insufficient merely to withdraw the mind from things. Although attempting to put people more into the present moment, these systems do not have any means of actually opposing our wrong conceptions and wrong appearances. Their method of opposing is merely to push them out of the way.

The system here, however, is to provide a weapon explicitly countering wrong conceptions. We have to get to the point where, when we look at our object of meditation, we will understand that one of its qualities is that it is not produced from self, other, both, or without causes. These four points have to move your mind deeply; they have to be able to show you that things do not exist in the way that they appear. The non-production of things in these four ways contradicts how things appear. Thus, with this, the very appearance of phenomena will begin to change. The refutation of production of the four extreme types is like a diamond weapon.

Whether this reasoning works for you or whether you will have to find some other reasoning is something to be discovered by playing with these reasonings and getting into them, learning how they work. The four positions of production from self, other, both, or causelessly are the only possibilities of inherently existent production. We get upset because it looks as if the Buddhists are forcing people like the Sāṃkhyas and Nihilists into positions they would not themselves accept. We may even feel to support the side being refuted. However, when you meditate, you have to throw yourself to the Buddhists' side; play the Buddhists' game for a while and get into it. This will work itself down into your mind and cause your natural resistance to come out. Then you really have to start looking at it, from inside.

Since these phenomena are not permanent, they must be products. If they are produced and this production is find-able — as being from self, other, both, or causelessly — then this appearance of things as findable is correct. If their production cannot be found, then what is appearing is not right. We have a very important matter to decide here; it will apply to all phenomena. Throw your mind completely into this, put all your energy behind it. There is a lot at stake: if there is no findable production, then we are wrong in our usual way of living. These meditations change the appearance of things. Normally, when things appear and we assent to the way they appear, the appearance becomes even more encrusted. Then, we make up systems and freeze this appearance of inherent existence all the more. Reasonings such as these that refute inherently existent production do just the opposite; they change the way things appear, making it easier not to assent to that appearance. Meditation on emptiness is a real antidote.

This reasoning in which the four extreme types of production are refuted is an analysis of causation. Jang-gya calls this both a "refutation of production from the four extremes"[248] and "diamond fragments".[249] The reasoning refuting production of an effect that is existent, non-existent, both existent and non-existent, or neither is also sometimes called a "refutation of production from the four extremes", though here Jang-gya calls it a "reasoning refuting production of the existent and the non-existent".[250] Such a reasoning is an investigation into effects. To investigate both causes and effects, one uses the reasoning Janggya calls a "refutation of production of the four alternatives"[251] — of one cause producing one effect, one cause producing many effects, many causes producing one effect, and many causes producing many effects. The reasoning of a lack of being one or many and the sevenfold reasoning are analyses of entities.

When analyzing causes, you are not taking what is in front of you and thinking of it as a cause but are thinking of the causes that produced it. Since its causes are not in front of you, in order to do this reasoning you must reflect on something you are not seeing. This, in my opinion, makes it difficult for the reasoning to appear to the mind. Although many treatises present this investigation of production by way of causation, Chandrakīrti advises yogis to start out using the sevenfold reasoning (which will be explained in chapters fourteen through nineteen). Perhaps it is easier to understand because it is an investigation into an entity, an investigation of the thing itself. As that entity presently appears to us, it is not necessary to think of something else.

Again, with the reasoning refuting production of the existent, the non-existent, both, and neither, you have to think of your object of meditation as an effect. You are not thinking just of the entity of the object itself but of the fact that it is an effect. You have to think about the object in terms of something else, not just the entity appearing to you. The same is true for the reasoning refuting production of the four alternative types — one cause producing one effect, one cause producing many effects, and many causes producing many effects. You have to think about something that is not appearing to you, and thus you may not have a sufficiently vivid sense of what is being refuted for the reasoning to affect it.

In the reasoning that refutes production from the four

extremes, or the reasoning that refutes the existent or non-existent, or the reasoning that refutes the four alternatives, you must think of something else in relation to the subject of the reasoning; they depend on your having understood that production is essential to that subject. In order for the diamond fragments, for instance, to work, your mind must be imbued with the fact that whatever you are taking as your object is indeed a product. Compared to the sevenfold reasoning, this can be almost abstract or imaginary for a beginner, even though it is not.

In the sevenfold reasoning, you are basically refuting two positions, sameness and difference of the basis of designation and the designated phenomenon, both of which are right there in your imagination. You can point to something right there, identifying the basis of designation — such as the collection of arms, legs, and a trunk, for example — and the designated phenomenon — the body. However, when you analyze causes, they are not quite in your field of vision. You have to put more thought into it. When you are analyzing effects, it is indeed true that your object is an effect, but this fact is not obvious just through its appearance. We are not always impressed by a thing's being an effect; however, we are impressed by the thing itself.

This is only to say that it can be difficult to apply the reasoning of the diamond fragments. Still, once you can use these reasonings, they will apply to what is right in front of you. If something exists in the way it appears, then it must be produced from itself, from some other, from both, or neither. If you can slowly go through these and eliminate them, you will see that the non-affirming negative that is the emptiness of truly existent production is a quality of this object itself. This will show you that its current solid appearance is incorrect and that you should not assent to this appearance. Although you have to approach this reasoning through a lot of thought, in the end you must bring it back to what you are seeing.

For instance, if you leave the analysis of production from

inherently existent others at mere words, it will not mean much. You have to develop the sense of other such that you can look at, for instance, your chair as being just other. Once you can see things as being, in their nature, other, then you can use these reasonings that get at inherently existent otherness.

We take things to be others from their own side and nevertheless designate a relationship between them despite their otherness. We need to investigate this feeling of otherness and see just how sensible it is. For example, if you write letters at random on a blackboard, it is easy to see that they are all other. But when you put them together in a word, you no longer perform the activity of making them so other. For instance, take the word "work". It is one word; the letters are related and are usually seen as one unit. However, if you put the same letters in the wrong order, they become very other. Put them back in the right order again, and you suddenly feel them coalesce. At some point when you are putting them together and they are very close, they come together and become locked into a unit. Something very powerful substantializes things over and beyond what is actually there.

If we did not substantialize things, if this coalescing were very light and were just considered a mental fabrication, we would be convinced of the error of such gross substantialization quite easily. However, this is not the case. This substantialization differentiates the external world from ourselves.

We might be willing to accept, at least philosophically, that the external world is not as grossly other as we see it, but when we are faced with an external existent that seems to have its own being, we definitely feel that it exists in its own right. At that time it impinges upon us with tremendous force, and we feel very strongly that we have to accept it as independent.

We go to sleep every night; appearances impinge on us, and we are totally convinced. The fact that dreams are wrong does not itself make waking life wrong, but the very same tendency towards substantialization that convinces us that dream objects are external real objects convinces us now that the external world exists from its own side.

Another way to look at this is to take all these things that appear and wipe out this sense of substantiality that convinces you they are there in and of themselves. Identify what it is in dreams that impinges on you; get at it, feel it, understand it, and then do away with it utterly in waking experience. When you have done that, try to come up with something that will prove to you that these waking appearances are substantially established external objects.

For instance, if a loud noise suddenly happens nearby, there is something very bold, forthright, and solid right there. If you are tuned into your experience, you will feel right then that the reasonings we are discussing here are wrong, that things do happen, that these happenings are findable. However, when you analyze and get into your investigation, intently attempting to find what is appearing to you, you will not be able to come up with such massive, solid, bold, seemingly findable and forthright happenings as are appearing to your mind. These forthright happenings are production — something that is appearing or happening in front of you. Moreover, production is not just production of an entity; the product's coming into your ken — your perception of it — is also produced.

These products cover a certain spot, but activities cover this spot also. When some bad event happens, that is production of trouble. It is produced, and then it ceases. It seems to be a findable thing, and then it is no longer there. Suppose, for instance, your house is destroyed. You have feelings of inherent existence about the house, about its destruction, about what it will cost to replace all your possessions, about what is there. This kind of harm, the harm induced by the conception of true existence, can be eliminated.

What if I were sitting next to you and someone came

along and cut off my ear? You would certainly feel that my ear was cut off, but even an experience of something as forceful as that, when you know how to analyze, becomes transformed. For, this analysis is not a vague process of turning your mind away from events. When you analyze, you are more engaged than you ever were before in your life. It is said, "One who knows emptiness is aware," more perceptive, more awake, more conscientious. It is not that when an event happens you superimpose emptiness on it or turn your head away from it in order to remember its emptiness. The only way that you can get into emptiness is to get more into objects. When you realize emptiness, you will become more familiar with objects; your mind will be more brilliant, more clear. By turning your mind away from experiences, you will never get to emptiness. You have to go right to the thing itself as it is happening and let it happen again and again mentally. Then, analyze. You can, without analyzing, turn the mind away to some sort of a vacuity, but in doing so you are just tricking yourself.

There is a different vacuity that is the absence of inherent existence in suffering. If suffering were not empty of true existence, if this vacuity were not there, suffering would be firm and massive. It would always be there, and you could never get over it; if it existed from its own side, it would be uncaused and, therefore, not caused by ignorance; it would not be a mistake of understanding. Once that were the case, then correct understanding could not get rid of suffering. However much we may now feel that pain is indeed massive and existing in and of itself, it is not that way at all. Suffering is empty of existing from its own side, it is caused by ignorance, and thoroughly understanding emptiness will get rid of it.

So much of our experience of pain is induced by our conception of inherent existence that if we were to get rid of some of this mistaken conception, we would say that there is no longer any pain, for whatever pain was left would be almost unrecognizable. Even beyond that, it is said that when you become fully accustomed to cognizing emptiness there is pleasure in everything. This is a special power of meditation; it is said that many who do not understand emptiness also have some of these powers.

When searching for an object with one of these reasonings, you are unable to find anything, and a vacuity appears to your mind. This vacuity is the absence of inherent existence, the analytical unfindability, of the object you are seeking. The appearance of such a vacuity is the mental image that is the "appearing object"[252] of the initial view of the middle way. As you become used to this vacuity, the image will disappear. Finally, only the vacuity will be left — the vacuity itself will be the appearing object. That is direct cognition. On the path of preparation (the second of the five paths of accumulation, preparation, seeing, meditation, and no more learning), the imagistic element as well as the sense of subject and object becomes less and less until it disappears completely at the path of seeing. Until that time, the vacuity that is a negation of inherent existence is realized through the medium of an image.

At the beginning of the path of preparation, yogis can ascertain a subject and an object — the wisdom consciousness and its object, emptiness. As they progress along the path of preparation, they can no longer ascertain the sense of an object, even if they were to reflect on it. By the time they have reached the end of the path of preparation, they can no longer ascertain the appearance of the subject either. Both subject and object are still appearing, but they can no longer ascertain either one. Finally, the sense of subject and object vanishes, and yogis have direct cognition of emptiness. At this point, they are on the path of seeing; their mental consciousness *is* a path of seeing.

All Buddhist schools of tenets speak of five paths: accumulation, preparation, seeing, meditation, and no more learning. These paths are developments of a consciousness over time. It helps to imagine them. Imagine finding the vacuity that is a negation of inherent existence — there still

being a sense of subject and object. Then imagine subject
and object disappearing in terms of ascertainment but still
subtly appearing to the mind. Then imagine there being
merely a vacuity fused with mind; this would be the path of
seeing, which is non-dual in the sense that there is no
appearance of subject and object, no appearance of conventional phenomena, no appearance of inherent existence, no
appearance of conceptual images, and no appearance of
difference. Then, imagine that the meaning of the vacuity is
so vivid that it eliminates a certain level of the conception of
inherent existence. The things that are overcome through
cognizing emptiness on the path of seeing are called objects
abandoned through seeing, and due to this one cognition,
you will no longer have that level of defilement for the rest
of infinite time. Among the four noble truths — true sufferings, true sources, true cessations, and true paths — these
abandonments are true cessations. True cessations last
forever.

When you take refuge in Buddha, his Doctrine, and the
Spiritual Community, your actual refuge is the Doctrine,
verbal and realizational — mainly the latter. Thus, when
you take refuge in the Doctrine, true cessations should
appear to your mind. These are not just something temporary, like having no desire for food at present. True cessations are absences of things that will never occur again.
There will be a time when, due to cognition of emptiness,
desire will never appear again. It will become utterly non-
existent through the power of its antidote, a consciousness
with an opposite mode of apprehension. True cessations are
not just absences of things due to the incompleteness of the
conditions for their production, such as the lack of desire
for food when intensely involved in some other activity;
they are absences of afflictive emotions brought about by
the realizations that act as their antidotes.

The main refuge is true cessations. How are they
achieved? Through true paths. Thus, true cessations and
paths are the actual objects of practice and hence the actual

refuge. The teacher of this refuge is Buddha, who laid out what should be practiced in order to attain exactly what he attained. The Spiritual Community are the indispensable friends who help us to understand and practice this refuge of true paths in order to attain true cessations.

The direct cognition of emptiness is such that it will bring about a true cessation of a certain level of the afflictions. Although meditative suppression can yield a sense of bliss, clarity, non-conceptuality, and even greater intellectual power, if you want utterly and forever to get rid of desire, hatred, and ignorance, merely suppressing them is not enough. You have to destroy them by means of their antidote, direct cognition of emptiness. How can you arrive at this direct cognition of emptiness? Through inference. The meaning of the vacuity that appears to an inferential cognition is that these concrete events and objects to which we are accustomed do not exist as they appear. This vacuity has to keep meaning this for you because otherwise, it will become a vacuity of nothingness.

At the level of direct cognition, you do not have to worry about sustaining the meaning of the cognition, you do not have to think about whether the force of the intent of your cognition is still there or not, you do not have to keep reminding yourself what you are looking for and not finding. Your mind is at a level where all these are there. However, with our kind of conceptual cognition or, even more so, with its precursor, correct assumption, we have to sustain the intention of our cognition.

A strong sense of being unable to find what you were formerly sure could be found must be maintained — once you are impressed, you have to sustain that impression. If, when meditating on emptiness, you merely race through the reasonings, get to the point of utter vacuity, and are no longer impressed with it, that vacuity has become mere nothingness. At that time you are cultivating a wrong view, an impediment to the path, because you have lost the sense of the object of negation, inherent existence, and are now becoming accustomed to a view that nothing exists.

When done properly, one is deeply impressed with not being able to find the object of negation. For instance, when I was studying at the Tibetan Buddhist Learning Center in New Jersey, a student came one day to see Geshe Wangyal, the founder and main teacher, at a time when Geshe-la was away. The student was very impressed by the fact that Geshe-la was not there. He went into the monastery and asked someone who would definitely have known of Geshe-la's presence if he was there. This person told him that he was not. The student probably even thought, "Geshe-la's car is not here," and he may have even wandered about the monastery and looked to see if he was there. The student was truly impressed by Geshe-la's absence — he was impressed by it for months. He did not forget that Geshe-la was not there because it meant something to him.

The absence of an object of negation is a negative. There is a negative right here with us which is our absence of inherent existence. This negative is not a negation performed by a person. "Negation" can be viewed in two ways, from the point of view of two types of agents: one type of negator — not the kind of negation we are speaking of here — is a person who is thinking about and meditating on the right view, thereby negating or ceasing the wrong view; the other type of negator is a negative that negates something in the sense of being the absence of it — here, an emptiness of inherent existence. This latter negative is not as if there is something there always punching away at inherent existence and destroying it. It is a mere absence of the object of negation.

This negative exists. It is not non-existent, as the word might seem to imply. Even non-affirming negatives are phenomena, but this does not mean that when emptiness is cognized, the meditator thinks that this negative *is* an emptiness. Realization of emptiness is merely the non-finding of the object of negation. You do not enter into any thought, "This is emptiness." A consciuusness that thinks such would be a valid cognition of conventional phenomena, for it is dealing with the *existence* of something, in this case emptiness.

Furthermore, even though a non-affirming negative exists, to cognize this non-affirming negative does not mean to cognize its existence. This is technical but very helpful to know. For example, when you cognize a book, you cognize the existence of that book. Your eye consciousness is both the certifier of the book and the certifier of the existence of that book. However, when you cognize emptiness, it is different, for you are not cognizing the existence of emptiness. Thus, the uncommon certifier of emptiness is a consciousness directly cognizing emptiness, and through its power — or also through the power of an inferential realization of emptiness — the existence of emptiness is later understood without any further cogitation.

When emptiness is directly cognized, the emptinesses of all phenomena including emptiness itself are directly cognized but without any sense of their difference. Because the cognition is direct, the cognition of the absence of inherent existence of all phenomena and the cognition of the absence of inherent existence of that absence of inherent existence do not have to be serial. With inferential cognition (which is necessarily a conceptual cognition) it is serial, but a direct cognition is a different type of mind. A direct cognition of emptiness is a wisdom consciousness of meditative equipoise that simultaneously realizes the emptiness of inherent existence of all phenomena.

The point of this discussion is to emphasize that we are searching to find the inherent existence of the object. This needs to be remembered; otherwise, when searching, you will think that you are seeking emptiness. In fact, you are searching to find the inherent existence of an object such as your body, but come up with an utter vacuity. This utter vacuity is called "emptiness", although you are not seeking to identify it as such. You are to remain with the feeling that concrete objects such as these now appearing to our minds do not exist. What the student saw and remembered was that Geshe-la was not at the monastery. He did not turn around and say, "This is the absence of Geshe-la at the monastery."

13 Other Reasonings

REFUTATION OF PRODUCTION OF THE FOUR ALTERNATIVES

This reasoning investigates both causes and effects. It is an analysis of whether or not ultimately one cause produces one effect, one cause produces many effects, many causes produce one effect, or many causes produce many effects. Jang-gya does not go into it here; so we will not go into it either.

[Some of] our own recent scholars apply the reasonings explained in the basic text and commentary of [the Middle Way Autonomist] Jñānagarbha's *Discrimination of the Two Truths* here [in the Middle Way Consequence School. However] most texts concerning the Consequence School describe just the reasons of the diamond fragments as a refutation of the four alternatives. Except for this, it does not appear that what Jñānagarbha explains in the *Discrimination of the Two Truths* is set forth with much emphasis in the Consequence School.

In the texts of the Consequence School, the diamond fragments (which Jang-gya also called a "refutation of production of the four extreme types") are also called a "refutation of production of the four alternatives". For, production from self, from other, from both, and without cause are, from the point of view of causes, four alternative types of production. Thus, when the four alternatives are discussed, they usually do not refer to Jñānagarbha's analysis of single or multiple effects from single or multiple causes.

All teachers have a reasoning that is their own diamond instrument for attacking the false appearance of objects, but it seems that none of the Indian masters of the Consequence School had particular interest in this reasoning explained by Jñānagarbha, an Autonomist. Ashvaghoṣha, in his *Cultivation of the Ultimate Mind of Enlightenment*, uses the diamond fragments. Chandrakīrti's favorites are the diamond fragments and the sevenfold reasoning. Āryadeva, in a work called *Length of a Forearm*, [253] teaches meditation on emptiness through an analysis of whole and parts, which is also said to be a favorite reasoning of the Autonomists, though Consequentialists also use it.

Still, it should not be felt that just because the analysis of whole and parts, for example, was a favorite of Shāntarakṣhita, it is unsuitable to use it in the context of the Consequence School. Āryadeva used it, and he is, in the end, a Consequentialist, at least according to the Consequentialists. Not only that, but also such a reasoning is very appropriate to the Consequentialist system, as is the reasoning that refutes production of single and multiple effects from single and multiple causes. Jam-yang-shay-ba's *Great Exposition of Tenets* explains this reasoning in the context of the Consequence School; he is among those whom Jang-gya implicitly criticizes for bringing it over to the Consequence School. [254]

REASONING REFUTING PRODUCTION OF THE EXISTENT AND NON-EXISTENT

As before, this reasoning could also be called a refutation of production of the four extreme types or of the four alternatives, since it is a refutation of inherently existent production through considering four alternative types.

This reasoning investigates an effect. What kind of effect is produced? Is it existent, non-existent, both existent and non-existent, or neither existent nor non-existent? The reasoning can be framed in two ways. In one way, you are considering an effect at the time of its causes. Is an effect produced that is existent at the time of its causes, non-existent at the time of the causes, both, or neither? Or, you can consider the effect at the time of the effect. Is an inherently existent effect produced, a non-existent effect, both, or neither?

In the first way, you consider a product at the time of its causes — whether that product was existent at that time, non-existent, both, or neither. Apart from these four, there are no other choices. A huge amount of production occurs — cars, buildings, buses, smells, sky, people; everything is a product. If these things exist, they must be products. We have already done away with uncaused products in the earlier reasoning; here we are considering caused products. How many choices do you have? The effect is either there at the time of its causes or it is not — that is about it. You can go on to consider that it is both there and not there, but that is silly. Or you can say that it is neither there nor not there, but that is also absurd. So it is either existent at the time of its causes or non-existent at the time of its causes. The only point in stretching the possibilities to four is that there are philosophical systems that assert such; still, the only sensible options to consider are existence and non-existence, because these are a dichotomy.

Do causes produce an existent effect? If the effect is existent at the time of its causes, there would be no point in its production, for production would be a senseless reproduction. On the other hand, if the effect is non-existent at the time of its causes, how could it be produced? How could causes produce that effect? We say "produce that effect", but there is no effect there to produce. In general, the

Ge-luk-ba Consequentialists say that conventionally a formerly non-existent effect is newly produced and that an existent effect is produced. Thus, a foot-high sprout which has a root system exists as the entity of the seed, but it is non-existent at the time of the seed. The seed exists, its effect does not; the sprout exists as the entity of the seed. This is how conventional production is asserted.

I am writing a book, *Emptiness Yoga*. If it were existent, it would be crazy for me to write it. If it were non-existent, how could I write it? It is as if there is a small child shouting in your ear, wanting to know how things are — it is almost unbearable. Yet this is the very perspective into which we are to sink our minds. We have to become convinced that despite the ever so solid appearance of production, there is no analytically findable production. This has to affect you, to impress you.

Causes do not produce inherently existent effects, for the inherently existent has no need for causes.[255]

Above, we investigated the possibility of an effect existing at the time of its causes. The analysis is also applicable at the time of the effect. If an effect were inherently existent, what would be the use of causes to produce it? We live in a world where things appear to be inherently existent; since if they did inherently exist, they would not be caused, we have to struggle to superimpose the idea that these inherently existing effects have causes. We have to keep learning and reminding ourselves about cause and effect. Why? Because cause and effect contradict the way in which things appear to us. Even if you can intellectually decide that an absence of cause and effect would be absurd, the fact still remains that the world appears to us to exist from its own side, and we assent to that appearance. Thus, if an effect inherently exists, what use are causes at any time? If this effect inherently exists at the time of the effect, it must exist at all times. If we are to accept the way things appear to us, we should give up cause and effect, but since cause and effect cannot be sensibly eliminated, we should give up believing in the concrete appearance of things as if they exist from their own side.

Non-existent effects also are not produced, because causes could not do anything for the non-existent.

Once you have exhausted those two options — inherently existent and non-existent effects — it can be decided that there is no production that exists in its own right, but the reasoning continues for the sake of generating a sense of thoroughness.

Effects that are both existent and non-existent also are not produced, because a composite of these two does not occur.

Nothing is both existent and non-existent from the same point of view.

Also, causes do not produce effects that are neither existent nor non-existent, for something that is neither of these two does not occur.

Something that is both existent and non-existent or is neither existent nor non-existent is impossible even conventionally.

This [reasoning] is explained in the basic text and commentary of Chandrakīrti's *Supplement*, in Shāntideva's *Engaging in the Bodhisattva Deeds*, and also in Atīsha's *Lamp for the Path to Enlightenment*.[256]

Now Jang-gya indicates that he will not give a separate explanation of the reasoning of the lack of being one or many — singular or plural — because an explanation of it is contained in the following, lengthy explanation of the sevenfold reasoning.

One can understand [the reasoning of] the lack of being one or many through the explanation of the sevenfold reasoning.

14 The Sevenfold Reasoning: Background

REASONING FOR ASCERTAINING THE SELFLESSNESS OF PERSONS

The explanation has three parts: (1) ascertaining the self as not inherently existent, (2) showing that this also establishes the mine as not inherently existent, (3) how this reasoning is applied to other [phenomena].

Wherever the term "self" occurs, it is necessary to determine which meaning of self is appropriate to the context. I, person, and self are, in general, synonyms. However, the self of "selflessness" is not synonymous with "person", but means inherent existence, the existence of something as covering its basis of designation. That type of "self" does not exist, whereas the self that is synonymous with "person" and "I" is the conventionally existent person. Thus, when Jang-gya speaks about reasonings for ascertaining the selflessness of persons, he is speaking of reasonings for ascertaining that persons are without inherent existence — "self" meaning inherent existence and "person" meaning conventionally existent beings. However, when he speaks

209

about ascertaining the absence of inherent existence of the self, "self" means conventionally existent persons.

Therefore, the object of observation of a consciousness[257] falsely conceiving oneself to be inherently existent is the mere I, the conventionally existent person; it is a phenomenon, it exists. The appearing object[258] — roughly speaking, the object that appears to such a misconceiving consciousness — is a mental image of an inherently existent I. The conceived object[259] of this wrong consciousness is an inherently existent I. The appearing object exists, as does the object of observation: the former is a mental image, and the latter is the conventionally existent I. However, the object to which this mental image seems to refer, the conceived object — an inherently existent I — does not exist.

In this way, selflessness is a predicate of something that exists. Persons exist, but the self that means inherent existence does not. Frank is a person, and there is a selflessness of an existent Frank. However, the Frank at whom you are pointing, this very thing at the end of your finger, is the appearance of Frank as if inherently existent. Thus, in order to discover the status of the conventionally existent person who is the basis of the predicate, selflessness, you have to realize selflessness, emptiness.

Not understanding this, when we hear Dzong-ka-ba's followers say that persons exist but self (inherent existence) does not, we will probably assume that persons exist the way they appear and that they have the predicate of selflessness. We thereby miss the boat entirely. Therefore, many teachers of other Tibetan orders have said that persons do not exist, since persons *as we know them* — within assenting to this appearance of objective existence — do not exist. However, if we can avoid this trap, Dzong-ka-ba can give us something to think about, for we then approach it from two sides. From the positive side, we are trying to figure out what this person is that does exist. Negatively, we are trying to get at the absence of inherent existence of that person. When you reflect on these two sides of selflessness, you become doubly uncomfortable with your ignorance. Even while working with the world, you try to figure out what would exist without any superimposition. Thus, you are always, directly or indirectly, working on emptiness.

In the Autonomy School, the conventionally existent person is a subtle form of the mental consciousness.[260] Autonomists also assert a temporary person that is the mere collection of the aggregates; this too exists conventionally. The conventional person that is a subtle mental consciousness is an impermanent phenomenon, but it is always there, making possible the continuity of karma. Consequentialists also accept this subtle mental consciousness, but for them it is not the person since it is a basis of designation of the person.

In the Consequentialist system, the conventionally existent person is the mere I that is imputed, or designated, in dependence on either four or five aggregates — actually, on however many aggregates you are dealing with at the time. "Four or five" is said because beings in the Desire Realm or the Form Realm have five aggregates — forms, feelings, discriminations, compositional factors, and consciousnesses — but beings in the Formless Realm have only the latter four, not having coarse form. However, it is not necessary for all four or five aggregates to appear to the mind in order to have a suitable basis of designation. The mind shifts around a great deal, and thus there are many different I's. Sometimes just feeling and sometimes just breath is the basis of designation. It could be form, the whole lump that another person identifies as you when he or she comes into the room and sees you. There are many, many others. For instance, when you bump into something in the dark, watch the sense of I there. You have to catch it in order to start reflecting on emptiness.

In the Consequentialists' system, these things that are the conventionally existent I for the Autonomists — the subtle mental consciousness and the mere collection of aggregates — are only bases of designation of I, not I itself. For the

Consequence School, the basis of designation and the phenomenon designated are different and mutually exclusive — the one is not the other. If you study this and seem to get an understanding of how it fits together — of what it means for the basis of designation and the phenomenon designated to be different — without its bothering you as if you had fallen on your head, it means that its import has not yet hit.

Ascertaining the Self as Not Inherently Existent
"Self" here is the conventional person, the conventionally existent I, your own or others'.

Nāgārjuna's *Treatise on the Middle Way* describes a fivefold reasoning:[261]

> The One Gone Thus is not the aggregates,
>   nor is he other than the aggregates.
> The aggregates are not in him, nor is he in
>   them.
> The One Gone Thus does not possess the
>   aggregates.
> What One Gone Thus is there?

This is from the twenty-second chapter of the *Treatise on the Middle Way*, the chapter on the One Gone Thus, "One who has, is, or will go thus," that is, a Buddha, since all proceed eventually on the same path to Buddhahood. A One Gone Thus is a person[262] just as you or I are persons.

The tantric abbot Kensur Lekden said that some people have objected saying you should not fool around with analyzing a Buddha, since a Buddha is a very special person. However, he said, that this objection is completely off the mark. The Dalai Lama said in a lecture that you should take someone such as your guru, someone who is highly respected and who means a great deal to you, and use him/her as an example. That is perhaps why Nāgārjuna used Buddha here. However, you may feel that such a highly realized person is not really there anyway, at least not as we are, and that this analysis thus could become an exercise in futility. Still, if Shākyamuni Buddha now walked into this room, you would have great feelings about *him.* Take someone you admire greatly. However deep you know his/her realization to be, or however great you feel he/she is, when he/she comes into the room, you would still have the feeling that he/she had come into the room.

If you search for the One Gone Thus in these five ways, you will realize that there is no One Gone Thus there to be found under such analysis. The most marvelous of all beings, the supreme person, is not findable either. One sure sign that Buddha was not a fake is that he did not claim himself to be truly existent. He said that he, too, is like a bubble.

> Three positions, the two of mutual dependence and the one of possession, are included in the two positions of sameness and difference.

Nāgārjuna said, "The One Gone Thus is not the aggregates, nor is he other than the aggregates." These are the first two positions — sameness and difference between the phenomenon designated and the basis of designation. Then he said, "The aggregates are not in him, nor is he in them." These are the two positions of mutual dependence: the One Gone Thus depends on the aggregates, the aggregates depend on the One Gone Thus. In one way, the aggregates are like a forest, and the person is like a lion in the forest — this is the person depending on the aggregates. The person and the aggregates are different just as the forest is a collection of trees and the lion is an animal somewhere among those trees, but not a part of them. In the other way, the person can be like snow that pervades the forest and extends beyond it. The forest is in the snow and, in a sense, depends on the snow. This is the aggregates depending on the self, the I.

This "depend" is like "is in" or "is on". For instance, you could imagine that your hand is an entity pervading its parts. Is it just a little bit bigger, enveloping all the fingers, and so on, which depend on it? Or is it just a little bit inside the parts that make up the hand and thus dependent on those parts?

A lion in a forest or a forest in snow are things that are radically different from each other. Reasonably, once there is dependence, there must be two things; that is, if the person depends on the aggregates, it has to be different from the aggregates. However, they may not appear to differ as much as a lion and a forest. It may be more that the person is the space pervading the whole of the forest and the aggregates are the forest — the aggregates in the person. Or, to reverse it and exemplify the person in the aggregates, it may be more like a person in a tent. These examples, even though they are exaggerated, are very helpful for catching the sense of self.

The two positions of dependence can be included in the position that the aggregates and the person are different. Indeed, if the person is inside the aggregates, you should be able to take it out and identify a person separate from aggregates. You can empty yogurt out of a bowl, a person can come out of a tent, a lion can come out of the forest, the forest can be chopped down and leave the snow.

We have five positions: same, different, two positions of dependence, and one of possession. The two positions of dependence are included in the position that the One Gone Thus and the aggregates that are bases of the designation "One Gone Thus" are different. That the One Gone Thus possesses the aggregates is included in both the positions of sameness and difference because there are two types of possession — either within sameness of entity or within difference of entity. A One Gone Thus could possess the aggregates in the way that Devadatta possesses a cow; this is a position of otherness — the person and the aggregates are different entities. Or, a One Gone Thus could possess the aggregates in the way that a tree possesses its core — a position that the person and the aggregates are one entity. This is a profound analysis of "have" — "I have a body,"

"I have a mind."

Thus the five positions can be reduced to two. So why bother with five?

However, in consideration of the modes of conception in which the [false] view of the transitory collection operates, five positions are set out in the tenth and twenty-second chapters [of Nāgārjuna's *Treatise on the Middle Way*].

The false view of a transitory collection is our conception of our own inherent existence. If we were merely doing a technical analysis for the sake of making a chart of the unfindable self that we could paste up on a wall, we could use just the positions of sameness and difference and dispense with the rest. However, there are many facets to the positions of sameness and difference in terms of the way in which the false view of the transitory collection works. Nāgārjuna teaches these reasonings not for the sake of debate or merely in order to set up a beautiful philosophical system, but for meditation. If this teaching were not for meditation, there would be no reason to give five positions.

Some of them will attract your mind more than others; the elaboration of five positions draws out the significance more than just the two positions of sameness and difference. For me, sameness and difference is usually too short, whereas the fivefold analysis opens it up and the sevenfold analysis does so even more. It tells more about what is involved in the two positions.

Remember that Dzong-ka-ba said that a consciousness innately misconceiving an inherently existent I does not conceive the I to be one with the mental and physical aggregates or different from them. Still, it sometimes *tends* towards one or the other.

> *Objection:* [Buddha] says in sūtra that (1) forms are not the self, (2) the self does not possess forms, (3) the self is not in forms, (4) nor are forms in the self, and he spoke similarly with respect to the remaining

four aggregates. In this way, he taught antidotes to the twenty parts of the [false] view of the transitory collection. Hence, would a fourfold analysis not be appropriate? Why is it explained as having five aspects?

Buddha spoke of twenty false views of the transitory collection, twenty ways in which the conception of the true existence of your own I operates. In consideration of these twenty mistaken consciousnesses, he taught twenty antidotes — the realizations that forms (or a form) are not the I, the I does not possess forms, the I is not in forms, forms are not in the I; feelings are not the I, the I does not possess feelings, the I is not in feelings, feelings are not in the I; discriminations are not the I, the I does not possess discriminations, the I is not in discriminations, discriminations are not in the I; compositional factors are not the I, the I does not possess compositional factors, the I is not in compositional factors,.compositional factors are not in the I; consciousnesses are not the I, the I does not possess consciousness, the I is not in the consciousnesses, consciousnesses are not in the I. The twenty false views of the transitory collection are like twenty mountain peaks. The twenty antidotes are like diamond instruments that crush and destroy these mountains. That the twenty wrong views are compared to mountains gives a sense of their solidity, how difficult it is to overcome them. Still, depending on your predispositions, you may be able to destroy them as soon as you get the antidote in your hand; more likely, you will have to hack away at them. Mostly, the process is very difficult due to thick, heavy predispositions and karmic obstructions.

Buddha taught twenty, not twenty-five; he spoke of four for each aggregate whereas Nāgārjuna gives five. In addition to the four in sūtra, Nāgārjuna teaches an antidote to the position that forms, and so forth, are *different* from the I. Jang-gya explains the discrepancy by pointing out that Buddha had already refuted that the mental and physical aggregates are a different entity from the I and thus did not mention this position when laying out the others.²⁶³

> *Answer:* [Buddha] spoke this way in sūtra because the [false] view of the transitory collection is unable to conceive of self without there being first an apprehension of the aggregates and, hence, within observing the aggregates in these four ways, it engages in [the conception of] self [inherent existence].

The aggregates have to be involved. Still, the object of observation of an innate conception of a truly existent I is not the aggregates but the conventionally existing I. Nevertheless, the I only comes into being in dependence on those aggregates, and, therefore, before we misconceive the nature of the I that is designated in dependence upon them, the aggregates that are the bases of designation of the I first have to be conceived to be inherently existent. A conception of a self of phenomena, taking the aggregates as its object of observation, comes first; then, within taking the I that is imputed in dependence on those aggregates as the object of observation, the I is conceived to exist inherently.

A difficult point here is that although the answer given to the objection raised is that Buddha did not refute the position that the I and the aggregates are different (as did Nāgārjuna) since he had already refuted this, Buddha, in fact, did set forth and refute several positions of difference — for instance, that the I is not in feelings, feelings are not in the I, and so forth. Perhaps we could say that none of these is an unrelated difference. You would have to say, then, that Buddha had earlier taught that there is no innate conception of an I as an unrelated other, even if the refutations of the positions of dependence and one type of possession revolve around and are reduced to refuting unrelated difference.

> Therefore, a fifth base of the apprehension of self as something other, beyond the aggregates, does not

occur except in [the philosophies of the non-Buddhist] Forders.[264] This is the reason why [Buddha] did not speak of a fifth position.

The Tibetan translation of the Sanskrit *tīrthika*, Forder, literally reads "one who has a ford (or platform or path for the sake of getting) to the end" (*mu stegs pa*). What is this end? Either liberation from cyclic existence or rebirth within cyclic existence in a high status as a human or god. Indian non-Buddhists called themselves Forders because they have a ford to the end, a path enabling them to get out of cyclic existence or at least to arrive at a higher state.

Only in non-Buddhist philosophies is there a conception of a person as a different entity from the aggregates that are its basis of designation, and it is said that when Buddha set forth the twenty views, he had already refuted the view that the self is a different entity from the mental and physical aggregates.

> Nāgārjuna spoke of a fifth position in the *Treatise on the Middle Way* because he wanted to refute the systems of the Forders as well.

Now the question comes, "Why bother to refute the non-Buddhist systems?"

> Furthermore, one should understand [the refutation of the Forders' systems] as a branch of the process of coming to a decisive conclusion when refuting the innate self within settling selflessness in one's own continuum.

Refutation of other systems is part of refuting our own conception of ourself as a truly existent person. For, if a person did truly exist, it must be either the same entity as or a different entity from the aggregates, and other systems take both those positions. Though a consciousness innately conceiving inherent existence does not itself specify its object as being a different entity from or the same entity as its basis of designation, still if that object did exist, it would have to be either the same as the aggregates or different from them. Thus, when you refute a system that holds the person to be other, you are refuting this possibility with respect to the inherently existent person who so vividly appears here and now. Indeed, you do not have to refute other systems; you can concentrate on just your own conception. Refuting other systems is a way of externalizing this negation and playing with it; however, we then have to turn it inside. This is very important because it is easy to get carried away with external refutation.

There is a difficult point here. The mind that conceives an inherently existent self does not itself enter into any kind of analysis. Therefore, it seems unnatural and unwarranted for us to analyze; it is as if we are opposing the very thread, the very warp and woof of the universe. Indeed, we are. Non-analysis is a great fault; thus, we are to analyze and oppose the usual way that we go about things.

Some urge us to become one with nature and open ourselves up, ceasing our analytical babbling and toying with the way things are. What they may be saying in fact is that we should flow with ignorance. A mind controlled by ignorance is like a ball on the surface of a swiftly running stream, going all over the place. Under those conditions it seems that it is the nature of the mind to get involved with everything that appears to it. However, this is really not its nature; rather, in order to get around this involvement to which we have become habituated, we have to oppose its "normal" course.

There are many techniques for opposing this wrong involvement. One is to try to hold that bobbing ball right in one place, as if you were trying to stop the stream. Another is to let the ball go wherever it wants but not become involved in anything, just watching the luminous and cognitive nature of the mind. This is very tricky, for you have to be careful not to enshrine the automatic ignorance that you already have. To get around this, it is helpful to analyze to try to find the person, developing a consciousness that does not find it and knows its unfindability very well. Then, let things appear without becoming involved with any of them but within understanding their unfindability. This seems to me to be the acme of the ways to oppose attached involvement with objects. By letting whatever wants to appear appear, you are letting the potencies of the mind develop without stifling them, letting the strength of the mind come to fruition. However, you are not being dragged down by this because, through first analyzing, you have understood the nature of things and then maintained that understanding. It is as if someone came into the room and was going through all sorts of antics, accusing you of different things and so on, and you just sat there, very attentive but not dragged into it. In the Nying-ma order of Tibetan Buddhism, this is said to be like a robber coming into an empty house; all of these manifold things appear to the mind, but the mind does not get caught in them, the mind does not become sunk in them.

We are not seeking to analyze forever. When you understand how to do this analysis, you do not sit talking to yourself all the time — you are understanding emptiness and applying this cognition to this and that phenomenon. You qualify everything you do with it; it is as if you are *feeling* emptiness. It is conceptual in the sense that you are not cognizing emptiness directly, but there is not a lot of verbalization. It seems to me that this also is a way to become one with or flow with nature.

> The honorable, glorious Chandrakīrti made a sevenfold reasoning, adding two more to those negations: that the mere collection [of the bases of designation] is the self and that the shape [of the body] is the self.

"Self" here means "person". Both of these positions are variations on the first position that the person and the mental and physical aggregates are the same. The position that a person is the mere collection of his/her bases of designation is that of lower Buddhist schools. The position that the shape of the body is the person is perhaps that of one of the Great Exposition Schools which asserts that the five aggregates *individually* are the person. When we see certain shapes, we say, "That is Bob, and the other one is Bill." Kensur Lekden's favorite example was a cow (cows are sentient beings and persons): we see something with four legs and a thing jutting out on its neck, teats hanging down, and so forth, and we say, "That is a cow." How can you not say that the shape is the cow, the person?

> [Chandrakīrti] added [these two refutations] in order to refute the Buddhist schools of tenets that propound true existence and certain Autonomists who posit the mind as the self or who posit some attribute of a person such as the collection of the aggregates or their shape [to be the self].

Jang-gya literally says "the Buddhist schools of tenets propounding *bhāva*". *Bhāva* (*dngos po*) is usually translated as "thing", meaning that which is able to perform a function, an impermanent phenomenon; here, however, it is taken to mean "true existence". The word *bhāva* has three meanings: (1) an existent phenomenon that may be either permanent or impermanent, as when in the Perfection of Wisdom Sūtras it is said that all "things" (*dngos po, bhāva*) are empty, (2) an impermanent phenomenon, or (3) true existence. Here, it is the third; thus *bhāvavādins* are Proponents of True Existence. The Buddhist *bhāvavādins* are the Proponents of the Great Exposition, Proponents of Sūtra, and Proponents of Mind Only; sometimes the term also includes the Autonomists.[265]

> Furthermore, sūtra teaches that the conventionalities of self and chariot are posited similarly:
>
> "Self" is a devilish mind.
> You are under the control of a [bad] view.
> These conditioned aggregates are empty.
> There is no sentient being here.

Just as a chariot is designated
In dependence upon collections of parts,
So, conventionally, a sentient being
[Is designated] in dependence upon the
    aggregates.

Moreover, Chandrakīrti sets forth the sevenfold
reasoning to clarify that [the Consequence School]
has a special mode of positing the similarity [be-
tween a chariot and a person] that is not shared with
the Autonomists or the other lower [systems of
tenets]. This can be understood in detail from one
who has become skilled in the word of the Foremost
[Dzong-ka-ba].

Consequentialists say that a person conventionally exists
but is not any of the things that are its bases of designation
even conventionally. A person is only imputed in dependence upon the mental and physical aggregates; it is not any
of them. This is so for both persons and other phenomena.

Thus, the sevenfold reasoning is neither too extensive nor too brief and has many features. Dzong-ka-
ba's *Great Exposition of the Stages of the Path to
Enlightenment* says:

This presentation, as explained earlier,
starting from [examining] a chariot, has, in
brief, three features: (1) the feature of easily
refuting the view of permanence which is
the superimposition of inherent existence
on phenomena, (2) the feature of easily refuting the view of annihilation which is to
think that dependent-arisings are not feasible in the context of no inherent existence,
and (3) the stages of a yogi's analysis,
through the practice of which the first two
features are achieved.

The third is explained to be the feature of easily

gaining conviction about illusory-like dependent-arisings when one analyzes with this mode of analysis.

Even though non-affirming negatives prove nothing positive, this does not mean that nothing positive is going to come out of *meditating* on these reasonings. Through this reasoning process, it is understood that dependent-arisings are like illusions in that they appear one way but exist another way — they appear to exist inherently but do not.

The sevenfold reasoning has nine essentials. The first essential is to ascertain the object of negation. The second is to ascertain the entailment, the pervasion. The third through ninth essentials are to ascertain the seven reasons each in its turn.

We have already discussed the ascertainment of the object of negation, the essence of which is that the image of the inherently existent I that we believe in so strongly must appear clearly to the mind. The essential of ascertaining the entailment, or pervasion, is to develop reasoned conviction that whatever does not exist in any of these seven ways is necessarily not inherently existent. If the I and the aggregates inherently exist, they must exist in one or more of these seven ways.

Every type of reasoning — the diamond fragments, the lack of being one or many, the sevenfold reasoning, etc. — involves the first two essentials. The remaining essentials vary in number according to the number of the reasons to be ascertained. The first essential is to get in focus whatever is being negated. The second is to ascertain that if it did exist, it would have to be this, that, the other, etc. and if it is none of those, it does not exist. The remaining essentials are the refutations that it is this, that, the other, etc. After the first two essentials, or key points, there are as many steps as there are possible positions. Sometimes there are four, as in the diamond fragments, sometimes there are two, as in the lack of being one or many; here, there are seven.

15 The Example: A Chariot

Now I will explain the sevenfold reasoning itself. The explanation is in two parts: stating the example and applying it to the meaning.

STATING THE EXAMPLE

Chandrakīrti's *Supplement* says that although upon analyzing a chariot in the seven ways — whether it is one with its own parts, different from them, and so forth — it is not found, it is permissible for valid cognition to posit, without invalidation, a chariot designated in dependence upon the parts of the chariot, and that likewise the self, the aggregates, and so forth are posited in a similar manner. The *Supplement* says:[265a]

> A chariot is not asserted to be other than its
>   parts,
> Nor non-other. It also does not possess
>   them.
> It is not in the parts, nor are the parts in it.
> It is not the mere collection [of its parts],
>   nor is it [their] shape.
> [The self and the aggregates are] similar.

"Similar" at the end indicates that the chariot and its parts are an example. Just as a chariot is not accepted as being other than its parts or non-other and so forth, so the self and the aggregates that are its bases of designation cannot be accepted as being the same, different, and so forth.

A chariot that cannot be found but is designated in dependence upon its parts is nevertheless validly established. The view of the Middle Way is a composite of analytical unfindability and valid nominal establishment of an object. These two are not at all contradictory. The valid establishment of an object does not mean that it can be found under analysis.

Jang-gya now goes through each of the reasons in the sevenfold reasoning and, through showing the faults and fallacies that would arise if each were the case, proves that a chariot and its parts could not exist in any of these seven ways.

> Concerning this, the subject, a chariot, is not inherently the same as its parts — axles, wheels, nails, and so forth — because, if it were, there would be the fallacies that (1) just as there are many parts, so there also would be many chariots, (2) or in another way, just as the chariot is one, so the parts also would be one, and (3) agent and object would be one, etc.

This is the first of the seven reasons. The basic syllogism is: The subject, a chariot, is not established by way of its own character, because of these seven reasons. The reasons themselves are not obvious, so they have to be proved individually, beginning with the first, sameness. The proof will not be endless because all reasoning must eventually come down to something that is obvious. As the Dalai Lama says in his *Key to the Middle Way:*[266]

With respect to a non-conceptual wisdom that apprehends a profound emptiness, one first cultivates a conceptual consciousness that apprehends an emptiness, and when a clear perception of the object of meditation arises, this becomes a non-conceptual wisdom. Moreover, the initial generation of that conceptual consciousness must depend solely on a correct reasoning. Fundamentally, therefore, this process traces back solely to a reasoning, which itself must fundamentally trace back to valid experiences common to ourselves and others. Thus, it is the thought of Dignāga and Dharmakīrti, the kings of reasoning, that fundamentally a reasoning derives from an obvious experience.

If every reason had to be proven with another reason *ad infinitum,* one could never get back to realizing the original thesis; one would always have to be proving the reasons. Thus, at some point in the process you have to arrive at something that is obvious. Reasoning has to have a floor. We start with the end point, "Such and such is not inherently existent because ..." We then add a few "because"s, but eventually it gets down to something that is obvious. It is like someone showing you a place you had never been to before, taking you some place that is deeper by building on what is already known.

If, for you, the reasoning does not come down to something obvious, then this is not the proper time for cognizing this thesis. Thus, even though the process finally depends on basic shared experience, some persons cannot draw on such experience, in which case further reasoning is not appropriate; for them, a teacher will have to approach the topic in a roundabout way, do some activity with them, lead them some other way, and then bring them back to the realization another time. The correctness of a reasoning depends upon the suitability of the person who is hearing it; reasoning is not abstractly coercive.

Jang-gya has given the reasoning showing why a chariot is not the same as its parts. Let us go over it, step by step.

The subject, a chariot, is not inherently the same as
its parts — axles, wheels, nails, and so forth.

Let a car appear to your mind; run your finger over it. Is

the car one with the many parts that are appearing to you? The way I feel right now, it is. The important thing is to have something to point to. You have to be able to say, "These are the parts: the wheels, axles, doors, floor, sides, engine," and "This is the car." You cannot pass to something abstract, not if you are to come up with a concrete car.

Why is this car not the same as its parts?

> Because, if it were, there would be the fallacies that
> (1) just as there are many parts, so there also would
> be many chariots.

For example, is the left door of your car your car? I sometimes feel yes and sometimes no. Right now I feel yes, it is. Is the other door your car? If you feel that it is, then looking at it, sink "car" into the door. Take the name or maybe even take a little picture of an entire car and sink it right into the door. There are many things you could do here to stimulate the mind.

Thus, you have sunk the whole name, "car", in one part. This is not bad; many people would say that any part of a whole thing is the thing. If you were to stick a pin in my finger, I would say that you stuck a pin in me. Someone playing with this sort of analysis might reply, "That's not you, that's your finger." And I might respond, "Of course that's me; it's certainly not you." Though I am conceiving me, I do not think, "The finger is me," unless pressed. It seems that the later response is an artificial feeling whereas the first is innate. We have both.

When the object of analysis is a chariot or a car, it is fairly clear. If, on the other hand, you are considering something like a banana, you have to be sure to identify what you are dealing with. You may be considering either a banana that is six inches long and has a peel and can be cut into ten pieces of about the same size *or* a certain substance called banana. When searching to find whether or not a banana inherently exists, it is first necessary to identify which banana you are taking as your object. Otherwise, you may rightly feel that when you slice the banana, each slice is definitely banana. Indeed, it is the substance, banana. You have switched from an analysis of one thing to that of another.

The same holds with tea. What you are considering has to be clear. Are you thinking of a cup of tea, or are you thinking of the substance, tea? In general, it seems easier to work with something like a banana by identifying it as a single whole banana that can be cut up into however many pieces, or, if you are dealing with tea, it is easier to work with a cup of tea. Still, even if you decide to search for the inherent existence of the substance banana, you have a certain amount in mind. Likewise, if you have trouble thinking about what a car is, you can specify attributes as in "my car that has four wheels, an engine and is capable of carrying six people". Once "car" is not just a vague idea, you can decide with certainty that the left door is not this car. The door is not a car that has four wheels, an engine, and can carry six people.

Go over the object of meditation piece by piece, carefully. We deal with our cars often, and we have to determine whether or not the thing that we are dealing with exists as concretely as it appears. If my car and its parts are exactly the same, then, since my car has all these many parts, there must be just that many cars. Since my friend needs a car and I have ten cars — for there are at least ten parts to my car — I can give him a car and still have nine! But that is foolish.

Go over the whole thing with your mind's eye and see whether or not each of these individual parts is your car. We will not, at this point, consider the collection of those parts; right now, consider each one of them individually, until generating the idea of non-car with respect to each — each is non-car, it is not car. You are not determining that these parts are anything else, just that they are not car. "Non-car" and "not car" here are the same; whether or not something positive is implied depends on context. All of the parts must appear to you as non-car. This is a very important stage of the reasoning. The door must be non-car, the engine non-car, the windshield non-car, the back doors non-car, the frame non-car, the top non-car, the trunk non-car, the wheels non-car, all the bolts non-car, and so forth. Every single part of it should be clear as non-car.

At this point, you are not considering whether or not the bases of designation of the bolts and so forth are bolts or anything else. You are merely considering whether or not they are car. If you let your mind immediately go on to something else, you will miss the point. Here you should try to stay with non-car.

Take this analysis to the point where you can see everything appearing there as non-car, from its very innards. Non-car is obvious from every part. If you do this well, it will also take care of the refutation that the composite of the parts is the car. For, once everything appearing to you is non-car, you will feel uncomfortable saying that the whole is the car. You would have to deny this non-car-ness. You understand that this butter or mayonnaise that you spread over all the parts and call the whole does not exist; it is just a mental fabrication. If you see each part and then speak of "all" or "whole", moving your hand over them as if to bring them together in one mass, this is a substantialization beyond what is actually there, an exaggeration of consciousness.

During a lecture in Dharmsala, the Dalai Lama said that if this person sitting and talking in a certain way were the Dalai Lama in and of himself, then he would be unable to make any change such as in lifting his hand. If you do not already see such inconsistencies in your usual perception, this analysis should help. You will come to feel that if things existed the way they appear, it would be impossible for any change to happen, or that because change has occurred you must have been deceived earlier. Then, you will wonder how you could have been tricked, since the appearance of the car or of the banana was one of the givens. Either a change in appearances is impossible or the original appearance was a deception. In one way you feel that the cut up banana is a deception because a banana encased in a skin was vividly appearing to you previously. Or, emphasizing the cut up banana, you will feel that you were deceived previously when the whole banana appeared to you. But, since they are both equally givens, how could you be deceived? This is where the intellect becomes weak. It cannot figure these things out and so withdraws from thinking about them.

When we look at ourselves in a full length mirror, we are telling ourselves all the time, "It is a mirror image; it is a mirror image. ..." However, when we quiet down and stare in the mirror for awhile, there is a person there. From every quarter there is a person in front of us, vividly appearing. Cultivate a sense of that person and then reassert your realization that although it is appearing to be a person from its every part, it is not — "This mirror image is not a person." Or, when you wake up from a dream, let the person who appeared in the dream still appear to you; then, deliberately reflect on the fact that every part of that person whom, when you were dreaming, you felt to be a person, is qualified by not being a person. In just the same way, phenomena appear to be findable, they appear concretely, but from every quarter, from every part, they are qualified by not being so.

Jang-gya continues:

> (2) Or in another way, just as the chariot is one, so the parts also would be one.

Sometimes these things seem to be many; sometimes they seem to be one. Sometimes, for instance, when it needs a lot of repair, you feel that your car is many things; at other times you look upon it as one thing. People do this with countries. For example, we sometimes see all the parts as just one nation. Listening to some politicians, you can tell that although they are not consciously ignoring the other things, the states, the towns, the streets, the families, the individual people, and so on, they stress the single nation to the exclusion of these other things. Everything between the Atlantic and the Pacific generates the thought of America; there is an unconscious absence of distinctions. If you reflect on this single America, you will find yourself in trouble almost immediately. Perhaps one state will appear to you. What then? "Is this America, or is it Wisconsin?" Some say that it is essentially Wisconsin, and others say that it is essentially America. America covers the whole expanse; Wisconsin, however, does not cover the whole, only a part. Try keeping these two at the same time. When you have one part that is generating the thought, "Wisconsin," can the whole, including that part, generate the thought, "America"? Which is it? You cannot have both at the same time in such a substantial way; you seem to have to disregard one in order to do the other.

If you identify that this area *itself* generates the sense "America" and that this area *itself* generates the sense "Wisconsin", you will find that in itself it cannot be both at the same time, that there is something wrong. America and Wisconsin are in fact just nominalities, things designated in dependence on their parts, capable of performing functions but not existing in their own right.

Jang-gya continues:

(3) Agent and object would be one.

The agent is the chariot; it may seem a bit silly, but it does convey its parts. The activity of the chariot is the conveying, and the object of that activity is the conveyed parts of the chariot. A chariot, or a car, can convey many things, but, in any case, its parts are conveyed. Similarly, when you yourself move, the conveyer is you, the person, and what is conveyed is your body.

Conveyer and conveyed, when they are taken in this sense, cannot be completely separate. You cannot have a car over here conveying its parts over there as if it were hauling them in a trailer. For example, it is undeniable that when your hand moves, your index finger is carried along with it. This division into conveyer and conveyed is provocative because it shows the absurdity of this hand that appears to us to cover a certain area. If that hand is one with its parts, then all of that area is hand, which is absurd, but it is also undeniable that when you move this hand from one place to another, the fingers are conveyed along with the hand.

If you pour your mind into this reasoning, you will get a funny sense that you cannot point to anything that could be called the "conveyer". Just so, with anything that performs a function, it is hard to point to the thing that performs that function. Functionality, however, is not what is being refuted; rather, it is the object's seeming to exist in its own right.

The second of the seven reasonings is that a chariot is not inherently different from its parts. As before, this assertion is stated, in order to prove it, as the thesis of a syllogism.

> The subject, a chariot, is not inherently different from its parts because otherwise they would be different entities and whatever are different entities and simultaneous must be unrelated other factualities; hence, like a horse and an ox, a chariot would have to be observed separately from its parts but it is not.

When we think that a chariot is different from its parts, we imagine a chariot and parts at which we can point. Thus we have already wrongly concretized the chariot into a findable chariot different from its findable parts. We have imagined an analytically findable or inherently existent difference.

The syllogism speaks of these being *inherently* different in order to avoid refuting all difference between the phenomenon designated and its basis of designation. For, the chariot and its parts are indeed not the same; they are not different entities, but they are conventionally different. *Inherently established* difference entails that a chariot would be a different entity from its parts.

Ge-luk-ba Consequentialists speak a great deal about nominal difference and conventional difference, but negatively speaking, what these terms mean in the end is that there is no analytically findable difference. This is why so many non-Ge-luk-ba teachers do not bother to qualify the term "difference" with "inherently existent", instead just saying that a chariot is not different from its parts. They feel that we are investigating the ultimate nature of things and, thus, there is no need to affix the qualification "inherently" because if we did, we would, in our minds, not deal with our sense of difference — which we already misconceive as findable — but consider it to be something beyond that, feeling that we need only negate some inherent existence that is in addition to what is appearing. Once the refutation is viewed that way, nothing significant is negated. Therefore, it should be understood that when the qualification "inherently existent" is tacked onto the refutation, it is not done in order to exclude our ordinary sense of difference, which is imbued with a sense of objects existing in their own right.

"Ordinary" does not mean conventional, and vice versa. In the end, when you understand conventional difference, merely seeing that the hand and its parts — fingers and palm — are conventionally different is sufficient to generate continual cognition that neither the hand nor its parts can be found.

A prevalent misconception about emptiness is to think that, when we meditate using these reasonings, we have decided something intellectually in an abstract realm and that, once we understand unfindability, we must return to our ignorant presuppositions to work with phenomena. We must work with phenomena, but with a mind that is conjoined with an understanding of unfindability. Thus, realization of emptiness can be a continuous, meaningful, eventful cognition that eventually can last forever. We have to figure out how to blend realization of unfindability with every aspect of our life. It is not easy.

Let us go over the refutation of inherently established difference point by point:

> The subject, a chariot, is not inherently different from its parts because otherwise they would be different entities.

Inherently established difference results in difference of entity. Many times it seems that these rules which have been made for inherent existence are so absurd that they do not relate to the way in which we usually conceive things. However, difference of entity just means that it is possible to point out, "This is the chariot, and these are the parts of the chariot," with a sense of concrete findability of each. Difference of entity means that you can point to two separate things.

In visualization, turn the chariot blue and then the basis of designation of the chariot, its parts, red. You first have chariot there, a blue one, and now you make all the parts red. What have you got left over that you can say is the chariot? There is no chariot separate from its parts.

Jang-gya continues:

> And whatever are different entities and simultaneous must be unrelated other factualities; ...

This is so even conventionally.

If the chariot and its parts were different entities, it would mean that the chariot could be here and its parts over there in another place. That may seem a little crazy since you would never feel that the parts of your car — the bumper, the body, the seats, the engine, and all its other parts — are over there and that your car is over here. However, we do sometimes have feelings that although somehow the car and its parts are in the same spot, the car is a pervasive entity tying everything together. This cohesive entity is the car.

Such can certainly be imagined, but if it were the case

that the car and its basis of designation were like that, we should be able to take all the parts and throw them away and still have the car.

> ... hence, like a horse and an ox, a chariot would have to be observed separately from its parts but it is not.

For instance, in the conception of an I that is a self-sufficient or substantially existent entity, there is a strong sense of an I with a definite location. Sometimes it even feels as if you could get rid of mind and body, and this person would still be there, just in space. We should consider whether this feeling is sensible.

If you end up with a persistent vivid thing left over after having gotten rid of mind and body, you can use another analysis: Is this self-sufficient person the right half of its vivid appearance or the left half? It is forthright and forceful, but since it is something spread out, a line can be drawn down the middle. Is the right half me? Yes. Then what about the left half? If they are both self-sufficient persons, there must be two me's. In another way, if the whole thing just generates the thought "me", how could I possibly have even the idea that there are sides to it? "Me", then, is just designated in dependence upon its basis of designation and does not exist from its own side, in its own right.

That was the second of the seven reasonings, that a chariot and its parts are not inherently different. Now Jang-gya quickly presents the third and fourth reasonings — that a chariot does not inherently depend on its parts and that the parts of the chariot do not inherently depend on it.

> With regard to a chariot, the subject, the two positions of dependence — that a chariot inherently depends on its parts or that its parts inherently depend on it — also are not feasible. For, if [either of] these two [positions] were the case, [the chariot and its parts] would have to be inherently different,

whereas this has already been explained as not feasible.

We have just decided that the chariot and its parts cannot be established by way of their own character as different because, if they were, we would have to be able to apprehend the chariot aside from its parts. That reasoning is sufficient to refute these two positions, but it has to be repeated here in detail. When the reasoning of the lack of inherently established difference works well, its application to these positions of dependence is startling.

That the parts of the chariot depend on the chariot is like a forest in snow. The snow stretches throughout and beyond the forest. The chariot or car is the place where all these parts are as if hung; it is the cohesive entity.

A chariot depending on its parts is similar to yogurt in a bowl. The chariot or car depends on them from within. They hold this whole thing together.

Both of these require that the chariot and its parts be different. Hence, the above refutation of difference is to be applied here, step by step.

The fifth reasoning refutes the possession of the parts by the chariot. Again, there are two modes, one in which the possessor and the possessed are the same entity and one in which they are different entities.

> With regard to a chariot, the subject, either way in which the chariot could inherently possess its parts — in the sense that, for instance, Devadatta possesses an ox or in the sense that Devadatta possesses ears — also is not feasible. For, according to the former mode of possession, they would be inherently established as different entities, and, according to the latter, they would be inherently established as one entity, and both of these have already been refuted.

In the case of Devadatta possessing his ox, Devadatta and

the ox are different entities. Devadatta possessing his ears is an instance of possession of something that is the same entity. Still, where is the Devadatta who has ears? You almost have to withdraw your sense of Devadatta from his ears so that he can possess them.

Both of these positions have been refuted by the first two reasonings. However, we have to apply those refutations slowly and carefully in this context and come gradually to feel that it is impossible for a chariot to possess its parts within the context of findable establishment. We have to *feel* that a car could not possess its parts in the way that a person possesses an ox because, if it did, we would have to be able to apprehend the two separately but we cannot. On the other hand, if the car inherently possessed its parts as a human possesses ears, then there is the problem of the car and its parts being one. We would not be able to point to the individual parts and say, "This is the trunk," "This is the door," and so forth. Or, from another point of view, we would have as many cars as there are parts.

It is necessary to go through the same refutations that we discussed with the first and second reasonings, taking as the thing to be eradicated the feeling of a car inherently established as possessing its parts. It cannot just be decided that this refutation has already been covered at the time of refuting the sameness and difference of the car and its parts. Rather, it has to be done again with intense involvement. We have two possibilities, and if neither of them works out, the car does not possess its parts in the way we thought it did; we have been deceived. You have to do this as if you were putting your life as stake; you are making a momentous decision.

We have felt all along that people possess parts, cars possess parts, books possess parts. We have felt that this was part of the stuff of reality. As a child, I based my life a good deal on the fact that my family's home had ten rooms. I have certainly based much on my feeling that I have a leg. It is almost unthinkable that this might not be something in the very fabric of reality. "What do you mean? I'm supposed not to care if I lose a leg?" We immediately draw absurd conclusions which fortify the sense that I must inherently possess my leg.

This room has four walls, but where is the room that has four walls? If a crane comes and knocks down one of your walls, you would think, "Consequentialists say that the 'have' relationship cannot bear analysis. Let *them* come over and freeze." Consequentialists are not denying functionality; in fact, they are providing for functionality.

For me, analysis of possession is one of the most moving and helpful parts of the sevenfold reasoning. Within possession are the positions of sameness and difference. Thus, you can do the whole reasoning within the reasoning on possession. The meaning of the sevenfold reasoning is right within "have". This is particularly helpful for developing altruism because upon seeing how much suffering is induced by believing in these so solid appearances, we can have a stronger, more realistic wish that others could be free from the suffering induced by such misperception.

We have now reached the sixth of the seven reasonings.

> With regard to a chariot, the subject, it is not feasible to posit the mere collection of its parts as it, because in that case it would [absurdly] follow that once all the parts of the chariot — wheels, axles, etc. — without anything missing were piled unassembled, in one place, there would be a chariot even in that mere collection.

The position being refuted here is just what in the end you would think was the fact — that things are the collections of their parts. There may be no prominent collection of parts sticking out separately, but there is a collection of parts that is right there and that *is* the chariot. This is what we commonly think.

However, if a chariot were the collection, the composite,

or the whole of its parts, then if you dumped all the parts into a pile, you should have a chariot. It is fairly easy to take a wooden chair apart. When you put it back together, there is a point at which you feel that the chair comes together — something compelling and convincing right there in the basis of designation.

> Our own [Buddhist] Proponents of True Existence [that is, Great Exposition School, Sūtra School, and Mind Only School] maintain that although there is no whole,[267] there is a mere composite[268] of the parts. However, even this [composite] is not feasible [as a chariot] because [according to them] the whole does not exist and, therefore, the parts also would not exist.

The non-Middle Way schools say that there is no separate whole — there is merely a composite of parts. Refutation of their position depends on the fact that parts themselves only exist in relation to a whole. We have different words evoking a feeling of wholeness; it may be "whole" or "collection" or "all". In the latter case, make "all" the subject of the reasoning and see if you can find the relationship between all and the parts. Is this one part all? Is that one all? Having dispensed with these, you may then feel that the mere collection is all. At that point, turn around and look for the collection.

In kindergarten, I used to ask the teacher about the word "dozen" as in a dozen eggs. It seemed to me that she felt there was some sort of dozen right there. I remember looking at home at a basket of eggs in the refrigerator to see if I could find the dozen, taking the eggs out and seeing at what point the dozen disappeared.

Since the dozen is just designated in dependence upon a collection of twelve eggs, egg also is just designated in dependence upon a collection made up of shell and so forth. Following the reasoning, you finally get down to the little particles, and at some point it seems that you can go no further. A wrenching occurs inside, a feeling that there has to be something there, existing from its own side.

The last of the seven reasonings is to refute that the shape of the parts is a chariot.

> With regard to the subject, a chariot, it is also not admissable to posit the special shape of its parts to be it. For, it is not feasible for the shapes of the individual parts to be the chariot, nor is it feasible for the shape of the collection of the parts to be the chariot.

You may feel that the chariot is its own particular shape. When you are going down the street wanting to find someone's house, you know that the house has a certain shape that identifies it. Are you going to say that this shape is not the house? Then what is the house?

There are several possibilities in this reasoning about shape. Some seem silly, but it is necessary to go through them all. A house is in front of you; are the individual shapes of the parts, etc., the house? Or perhaps the shape of all the parts together? Having indicated these two ways in which a chariot might be considered to be shape, Jang-gya now shows individually that each is impossible.

> The first [reasoning, that it is not feasible for the shapes of the individual parts to be the chariot] is established because it is not feasible for shapes that are not different from the shapes of the parts before they were assembled to be a chariot, nor is it feasible for some other shapes that are unlike the shapes previous [to their being assembled] to be a chariot.

The shapes of the individual parts before they were assembled and made into a chariot cannot be a chariot. Also, after assembly, there are no new shapes of the parts, different from the shapes of the parts before they were assembled, that could now be the chariot. You have wheels, an axle, doors, and so forth, all lying on the ground in front of you. Do they individually have different shapes when you put them together? We certainly feel that the shape of the parts assembled is the chariot. However, do they individually get new shapes when they are assembled? It is an incontrovertible fact that the individual parts do not get a different shape when you put them together.

Jang-gya just gave two reasons showing why it is not possible for the shapes of the individual parts to be a chariot; he will now prove each of these.

> The first [reason, that it is not feasible for shapes that are not different from the shapes of the parts before they were assembled to be a chariot] is established because, otherwise, since there is no difference in the shapes of the wheels and so forth before being assembled and afterwards, just as there was no chariot before [the parts] were assembled, so there would be no chariot even after [the parts] are assembled.

All these parts have their individual shapes, and the shapes after arrangement are the same as before they were arranged. Thus, just as there is no chariot before the parts of the chariot are assembled, so there would be no chariot after the parts are assembled.

> The second [reason, that it is not feasible for some other shapes that are unlike the shapes previous to their being assembled to be a chariot] is established because if the wheels, axles, and so forth have some other, different shapes after they have been assembled that they did not have before they were assembled, this would have to be observed, but it is not.

Remember that this is part of the reasoning refuting the position that the shapes of the individual parts of the chariot are the chariot. If the chariot were the shapes of its parts, then, since the chariot is obviously there after its parts are assembled and not before, the parts would have to have a new shape after they were put together. If the parts indeed do have new shapes, these must be observable. However, when you look at each part, you can see that no part has changed shape.

> The second part of the earlier reason — that the shape of the collection of its parts cannot be posited as the chariot — is so because in the systems of the Proponents of True Existence the collection is not substantially established, and, therefore, it is not feasible for the shape of that [collection] to be substantially established, whereas they assert that a chariot is substantially established.

Once you cannot find a substantially existent collection, there is no way to find a substantially existent shape of that collection.

Another way to get at this is to consider, as before with the first of the seven reasonings, whether the shape of the whole chariot is the shapes of the individual parts. A chariot has many shapes; is the general shape inherently the same as or different from them?

We have to keep hacking away at this. If appearances were not like magnets attracting our minds and making us believe in them, we would never have become involved in the mess we are in. We would have learned a long time ago that this is wrong; even if we had started out ignorant of this, we could have figured it out much earlier. However, there is a basic attraction, like a need to eat or drink, a magnet that makes us conceive these things to exist as they appear.

For us, this overpowering sense of findable things is incontrovertible evidence. How could we live if these things were not true as they appear? What would we do? What would we be? We would have to change so radically that it is almost as if the ground itself were being cut out from underneath us. What we take as home, where we are in time, space, and so on, would all come into question. Thus, the Great Vehicle is said to be baseless, allowing no base for a sense of inherent existence. The Consequentialists are saying that the mind is competent to figure out that the status of objects that appears to us is false.

Jang-gya has mentioned the systems that assert true existence. If we can refute them, it will help in refuting our own innate sense of true existence.

> Moreover, it is the case [that they assert a substantially existent chariot] because those systems maintain that the bases of designation of all imputed existents are substantially existent. Furthermore, in our own system, in which the basis of designation of an imputed existent is not asserted to be substantially existent, the shape of the collection of parts is the basis of designation of a chariot, not a chariot.

Many different things can be identified as the basis of designation of a chariot, among which are the collection of the parts and the shape of the collection of the parts. Again, the basis of designation varies according to the observer and that to which he or she is directing attention at a specific time. For example, you do not ever see the shape of a car in its entirety. You see only a portion, an angle on it; this is what the basis of the designation "car" is for you at that time.

A collection of parts that is non-car is correctly designated "car". This means that within acting in the world we can make an understanding of the actual conventional nature of objects and activities the very means of furthering the understanding of emptiness. It is not that we have to act in ignorance when we act in the world.

> *Objection:* When sought thus in these seven ways, a chariot is not found, and, therefore, a chariot does not exist. However, this is not feasible, for such [expressions as] "Bring the chariot!" "Buy a chariot!" and "Prepare the chariot!" are renowned in

the conventions of the world.

Can you think of persons who would agree that a chariot exists despite there not being anything at all at which to point and say, "This is a chariot"? This is the main qualm that anyone has to work through in order to become a Proponent of the Middle Way. As long as we have the feeling that because of analytical unfindability there can be no chariot, we are not Proponents of the Middle Way.

> *Answer:* There is no such fallacy. In our system, when a chariot is analyzed in these seven ways, it is not found, and it is not found either as an ultimate truth or as a conventional truth, but this does not make a chariot non-existent. For, (1) the assertion of a chariot is not made due to [the chariot's] being established by reasoning analyzing whether it inherently exists or not, but is established by only a non-defective, ordinary, worldly — that is, conventional — consciousness without any analysis that searches for the object designated, and (2) moreover, the way in which [a chariot] *is* posited is that it is established as only existing imputedly in the sense of being designated in dependence upon its parts, wheels and so forth.

A chariot is not asserted from the viewpoint of its being established by that consciousness qualified to determine whether it is analytically findable or not; rather, it is asserted as existing from the viewpoint of an ordinary, non-defective consciousness. There are conventional consciousnesses that apprehend unusual objects such as the existence of emptiness or that Jang-gya's book on tenets exists merely designatedly; these are conventional consciousnesses, but not *ordinary* ones. An *ordinary* conventional consciousness is a conventional consciousness of a person who has not turned his or her mind toward emptiness; it does not search for its objects in any of the ways that we have just discussed. Since it is what establishes a chariot as existing, not finding a phenomenon when you search for it in the seven ways does not make that phenomenon non-existent.

Sometimes it seems that in the Middle Way School a chariot is accepted when there is no analysis and not when there is. This is partially so, for, when there is analysis, it is not possible to come up with anything that is even a conventionally existent chariot. Under ultimate analysis, you cannot come up with the designator, you cannot come up with the designation, and you cannot come up with the act of designating. The conventionally existent chariot is something perceived by a valid consciousness that does not perform such analysis. Nevertheless, this does not mean that the chariot which is asserted when there is no analysis exists in the way that it *appears* to our minds, for it appears to exist from its own side even when we are not actively assenting to that appearance. What would it mean always to know that chariots and all other phenomena are analytically unfindable and always to be able to act within such understanding? This is what we have to work for: to know conventional existents as only conventional existents, as fraudulent.

Chandrakīrti's *Supplement* says:[269]

> That [chariot] is not established in these
>   seven ways
> Either as [its own] suchness or in the world,
> But without analysis it is designated here
> From [the viewpoint of] the world in
>   dependence upon its parts.

Chandrakīrti's *Autocommentary on the "Supplement to (Nāgārjuna's) 'Treatise on the Middle Way'"* clearly speaks of how [phenomena] are established in a nominal way:

> Not only does this position just very clearly establish the designation of the convention,

chariot, from the viewpoint of what is renowned in the world, but also these nominalities should be asserted from the viewpoint of worldly renown without analysis.

Chandrakīrti's speaking of the necessity to assert these
nominalities refutes those who say that Consequentialists
have no positive assertions. It is clear that in Chandrakīrti's
own system he accepts interdependent, analytically unfindable, conventionally existent things.

The Autonomists and the other lower tenet systems — having seen that if the collection of parts,
etc., were not posited as an illustration of a whole,
etc., [no phenomenon could be posited at all since]
there is no whole, etc., which is a separate entity
from those — assert that [something] from within[270]
the bases of designation is posited as this and that
phenomenon.

The lower tenet systems feel that if you cannot posit something — the collection of the parts or one of those parts —
as the phenomenon itself, then that phenomenon does not
exist. However, they do refute non-Buddhists such as the
Vaisheṣhikas who say that there is a whole that is a separate
entity from the parts. We tend to feel that the whole is
indeed something separate from its parts because when you
put something together, you are able to do something new;
for such reasons, these systems conclude that the whole has
a separate substantial entity. But, where is this new substantial entity? The Buddhists have seen that you can find
no whole as a separate entity from the parts, a separate
entity from the basis of the designation, but the non-
Consequentialist Buddhist schools then assert that a chariot
is some phenomenon from among the bases of designation
— in this case, the collection itself.

They do not know how to posit a phenomenon if an
object that is designated as that phenomenon is not

found when sought.

They feel that a phenomenon cannot be said to exist at all if you cannot point to something that is the thing designated. This is the crux of it all; we do not know how to live with such non-objectively established phenomena. Our test for something being inherently existent has been whether it can perform its function or not. If it performs its function, then it covers that place. If it cannot perform its function, then it does not. This is our extreme way of identifying an existent; we do not know how things could perform functions and yet be without inherent existence.

> Therefore, because they do not accept that chariots and so forth are mere nominal designations, they assert that chariots and so forth conventionally are established by way of their own character.

The Autonomists and below feel that no phenomenon would have any more standing than a snake mistakenly imputed to a rope if phenomena were all merely designatedly existent. We feel this too. Verbally, the Autonomists might accept that things exist merely as designations, but for them this means only that they are not separate from their bases of designation, for they assert that a phenomenon can be found from among its bases of designation; Bhāvaviveka, for instance, says that the mental consciousness *is* the person,[271] whereas Chandrakīrti does not allow that any of the bases of designation of a phenomenon is that phenomenon. This is the core difference between the Autonomy and the Consequence Schools.

> Although this supreme system does not hold that anything such as the collection of parts or something within it is an illustration of the whole and so forth, it is able to present well all actions and agents within the context of mere nominal designation of whole, etc. The Foremost Omniscient [Dzong-ka-ba] advised that since this mode of commenting on

> the meaning of the scriptures is the Subduer [Buddha's] own uncommon thought, those who are discriminating should train in this system of interpreting Buddha's thought. It appears that this way [of positing phenomena within the context of mere nominal designation] is a supremely difficult point that was not in the province of mind of many who were famed as great paṇḍits in the land of the Superiors [India], and except for the Omniscient Father [Dzong-ka-ba] and his spiritual sons [Gyel-tsap and Kay-drup] most of the scholars and adepts in snowy Tibet also were unable to see even a part of this.

This is an advertisement for the particular way in which Dzong-ka-ba presents emptiness and conventional phenomena. I try to bear in mind the present Dalai Lama's statement that all the different orders in Tibet have weapons for destroying the conception of inherent existence and that such a weapon is all that is needed. Some of these weapons might be described better than others; some might be more appropriate for certain people than for others. However, all have weapons that get at inherent existence. How this could be so despite the history of controversy needs to be investigated.

> This mode of analysis is a profound means of quickly finding the view of emptiness. Chandrakīrti's *Autocommentary on the "Supplement to (Nāgārjuna's) 'Treatise on the Middle Way' "* says:[272]

>> Because these worldly conventionalities do not exist when investigated in this way but do exist by way of non-analytical renown, yogis, when they analyze these in these stages, will penetrate very quickly to the depths of suchness.

The sevenfold reasoning is used first because it bestows understanding quickly.

16 Bringing the Reasoning to Life

COMMENTS

An example is easier to understand than the thing itself. Taken at face value, this should mean that it is easier to understand the absence of inherent existence of a chariot than it is to understand the absence of inherent existence of a person. However, it is traditionally said that the selflessness of persons is easier to understand than the selflessness of phenomena and that this is the reason why one meditates on the selflessness of persons first. As Dzong-ka-ba says in his *Middling Exposition of Special Insight:*[273]

Chandrakīrti's *Clear Words* and Buddhapālita's *Commentary on (Nāgārjuna's) "Treatise on the Middle Way"* explain that when entering into suchness, one initially enters by way of the selflessness of persons. Shāntideva also says the same. The reason why it must be done this way is that, although there is no difference in subtlety with regard to the selflessness to be ascertained in terms of the persons or the phenomena that are its base, selflessness is easier to ascertain in terms of a person, due to essentials of the substratum, whereas it is more difficult to ascertain in terms of [other] phenomena. For example, since it is more difficult to ascertain the selflessness of phenomena in terms of an eye, ear, and so forth and easier to ascertain it it terms of a reflection and so forth, the latter are posited as examples for settling selflessness in terms of the former.

Dzong-ka-ba clearly says that selflessness is to be ascertained first with respect to persons and then with respect to other phenomena; he says that this is due to "essentials of the substratum" but does not say what these essentials are. Lati Rinbochay, recently abbot of the Shar-dzay College of Gan-den Monastic University in Mundgod, Karnataka State, in South India, explained that the person is always present and thus it is easier to realize its emptiness than that of other phenomena. However, our minds are also always present, and they are phenomena other than persons.

The Dalai Lama explained that we already have some suspicions about the status of the person, since the lower Buddhist schools hold that only persons are empty of self-sufficient, substantial existence. Because we already have suspicions that persons do not exist in accordance with their appearance, it is easier to realize emptiness in terms of a person than in terms of other phenomena.

Still, Chandrakīrti seems to use a selflessness of a phenomenon other than a person (a chariot) as the example for the selflessness of persons in the sevenfold reasoning. Putting this together with what Dzong-ka-ba and the Dalai Lama have said, perhaps it is that although, in the strict usage of examples in Buddhist reasoning, the predicate of a thesis (such as the absence of inherent existence) is realized first in terms of the example and then in terms of the subject, here that is not case; rather, you are not fully cognizing the emptiness of a chariot but are merely gaining some familiarity with the procedure of the reasoning. Perhaps the tradition first examines a chariot because it is an external object, such that when we analyze it and take it apart, it does not affect us quite as much as would taking apart our own sense of self and thus is easier for getting a sense of how the reasoning works.

In any case, we have to throw ourselves into the analysis of a chariot, after which that understanding is to be applied to the person, oneself. Since it is the person who travels in cyclic existence and who is the focus, or the knot, of all the trouble, emphasis has to be put on it. It may be the case that until we work on breaking through the heavy encrustations of inherent existence that are superimposed on this I which is most important in terms of being caught in cyclic existence, it is impossible to *realize* the selflessness of another phenomenon no matter how facilely the format of the reasoning may appear to our minds.

It is a basic tenet of the Consequence School that when the emptiness of inherent existence of one subject is realized, all superimpositions of inherent existence have been removed with respect to all other phenomena, due to which you need only turn your mind to other phenomena in order to realize their emptiness. Thus, overcoming the superimpositions of inherent existence and realizing emptiness is an horrendous task, and without explicitly taking the person, I, which is the center of all the troubles of cyclic existence as the basis of your meditation, it is impossible to penetrate the webs, veils, and encrustations of the superimpositions of inherent existence with respect to another phenomenon to the point of *realizing* emptiness. Although it is the case that when you apply the sevenfold reasoning to a chariot, or a car, you can be shocked to the very depth of your being that it is not an analytically findable entity as you previously thought, still actual *realization* of emptiness is even more profound. The Dalai Lama described developing a correct assumption of emptiness as like being hit by lightning, and thus the development of inferential realization must be a thousand times more shocking. Therefore, the reason why the emptiness of a chariot is given as an example of the emptiness of a person may be that it is easier to learn the *format* of the reasoning with this less touchy subject even though it is not easier to realize the *emptiness* of this less touchy subject.[274]

Being Unfindable and Yet Being Validly Established

A chariot is analytically unfindable but is nevertheless validly established. We usually think that if something is valid, it must be findable. For instance, a valid car must be usable, able to perform its functions. Suppose I told you that I had bought a great new car and would take you for a ride. If we went outside, and there was only a bumper and a part of an engine, you would say, "That is not a car, it cannot perform the functions of a car." This is not the unfindability the Proponents of the Middle Way are talking about. A car that has valid nominal establishment can perform the functions of a car, even though it cannot be found under the sevenfold analysis.

If you went to a movie and the film was ripped so badly that you could see only the left half of the picture, there is no question that the film would not be performing its proper function. You would get fed up with it and leave the theatre, maybe go to another movie. You would have become discouraged about that movie. Or, suppose you go to a store and buy a lot of heavy things, canned goods, milk, and so on, and the clerk gives you a wet paper bag to put them in. You would say, "This is not a paper bag," and would start thinking about how you could get a paper bag to put your groceries in. Your mind would race to something else. Just so, because we are not accustomed to the Middle Way view, when we search to find things and do not find them, we become discouraged and depressed. Our minds want to race on to something else and are not impressed by this unfindability since we take it to be a type of non-finding that we are already used to.

We have little choice but to work within the context of our own mind, and indeed this is the way in which our minds have been conditioned to operate. However, discouragement at the lack of analytical findability is mistaken; it comes from our foolish habituation to the sense of inherent existence. In this vein, the Fifth Dalai Lama says that for a beginner the experience of emptiness carries with it a sense of loss:[275]

If you have no predispositions for emptiness from a former life, it seems that a thing which was in the hand has suddenly been lost. If you have predispositions, it seems that a lost jewel which had been in the hand has suddenly been found.

Emptiness is the key to mental and physical transformation; thus, for someone who is used to it, it is not at all like losing something. Rank beginners, however, would have a hard time staying with the process of realization due to their sense of loss; we have ingrained tendencies to leave such a state.

We have to be able to search for objects, not find them, and then remain in the vivid realization that they cannot be found. We have to realize, for instance, that there is a book here, Jang-gya's *Presentation of Tenets*, which he wrote and yet we cannot analytically find any writer who wrote it, subject written about, or readers for whom it was written. We have to understand, moreover, that this unfindable writing nominally performs a function and realize that unfindability is not a reason for giving something up.

Thus, it is within the context of their being unfindable that things are validly established. It is not that unfindability contradicts the valid establishment of the object; it contradicts the object's inherent existence. Also, it is not that you first develop a wisdom consciousness that does not find inherent existence and then, when you cease meditating, ignorance comes back, within the context of which things are validly established and exist.

We can also say that a conventionally existent table is refuted as ultimately existing, but this only means that an *inherently existent* table is refuted as being conventionally existent. Ultimate analysis cannot negate a conventionally existent table. It can only negate a findable, ultimately existing table. We also need to counteract the tendency to consider even nominal existence as if it were findable, as if it could bear ultimate analysis.

The cognition of emptiness has great meaning; in time, it will get us out of cyclic existence. If we immediately cognized it *directly*, we would naturally appreciate its significance, but when we set out on a path to this direct realization and get to a point where we tend toward depression or want to turn away to something new, we have to be careful not to veer off this path. Thus, you need firm motivation for meditation, as well as perseverance. If you have tremendously good predispositions, you will appreciate the significance of this unfindability right away. If you do not, you just have to keep reminding yourself that this is the real nature of objects, or, if you have the wish to help others, that this is a supreme way to bring that about. In cultivating altruism you are developing love and compassion for all sentient beings and the determination to attain enlightenment in order to help them. Necessary for attaining this position through which you can help sentient beings on a vast scale is direct cognition of emptiness. If you cannot make effort at realizing emptiness, then your desire to help all beings is merely words. So, here is something you can do: you can stay with this realization that will help clear up your mind so that eventually you can liberate all other beings. If you do not do this, what are you going to do?

In his *Precious Garland*,[276] Nāgārjuna says that if you saw a mirage in the distance and, after going over to see if water was there and finding none, thought, "That water no longer exists," you would be very stupid, for that water never existed. You were living with a mistake, a dream; now you have awakened, and you mourn the loss of the dream-objects. Similarly, although since beginningless time we have been convinced that the object of negation, inherent existence, has existed, we have to realize that it is just made up, that it was not there at all, and that now we are seeing the reality that was there all the time. Proud people do not have the slightest hope of realizing this. People who insist on being right have no hope at all. It must be that when you realize emptiness, you understand that you were mistaken in every perception you have ever had. We are wrong from beginning to end, completely foolish in terms of the status of objects. Ignorance may actually be a small thing when you see the truth — wisdom and ignorance being as if you could have gone this way or that way; still, it produces a huge error. Those who are proud and want to be right all the time just cannot face how wrong they have been. It is no one's fault but our own.

At the beginning of 1965 at the Tibetan Buddhist Learning Center in New Jersey, I spent a lot of time just meditating on the fact that I was wrong, given that in all my perceptions everything appeared to exist from its own side. I kept repeating to myself, "I am wrong, I am wrong, I am wrong," imagining people pointing their fingers at me and saying that I was wrong. In time, I was able to think, "There is just no question about it. I accept it completely, I am wrong." We are afraid to be wrong; it takes courage to be wrong, to be able to take being wrong. If you are willing to accept your error, you develop greater strength of character just from the fact that you are wrong. You can even carry it further and let yourself be wrong in every instance where someone thought it was a question of right or wrong, for no matter what the situation was, you really were wrong — about the mode of existence of the object. Which is more important, the way in which the whole world exists or whether so-and-so said this or said that? Even if you win the argument, you are still wrong; you should face the fact that you are wrong.

You might become proud that you are facing the fact that you are wrong, but this means that you are looking at it incorrectly. You have to take this vastly, as when you do everything for the sake of all beings. You can take the very pride that swells up and meditate from within that, thinking that this pride itself is for the sake of all sentient beings. Inside, where you want it for yourself, it is all knotted up; if you take this pride outside for the sake of all sentient beings, the knot will loosen. It is no longer the same kind of pride that it used to be.

The main point is to realize how wrong one is. We have to get rid of the pride that always wants to be right and accept being wrong about the most important thing. Suppose that when you were a child you learned that all people of a certain country were bad. This was reinforced over and over again in newspapers and so on. If you later studied and found out that all people of that country are not bad, you would go back in your memory through your whole lifetime to undo this conditioning, seeing yourself as wrong in every single one of these instances where the opinion that all those people are bad was reinforced. The meditation on wrongness is similar.

Determining the Entailment
Once you understand something about how these seven reasons work, it can be determined whether or not it follows from them that a chariot is not inherently existent: if something does not exist in any of these seven ways, does it then follow that it is not inherently existent? First, you have to be able to decide that if a chariot exists in accordance with its concrete appearance to you — like your car or your house — you ought to be able to find it. Once you have determined this, the question becomes, "What kind of a mind is qualified to find such concrete existence?" If you thought, for example, that you had termites in your house, you would put a lot of energy into trying to find out whether or not you actually did have termites. You would try to find someone who knew where the termites would likely be found. Just so, you have to give inherent existence every possible chance there is. Go out to your car and try to find it, really.

If you determine that the object must not inherently exist if, after looking in all seven of these places, you still do not find it, then you have established the entailment, the second of the nine essentials. For me, these seven ways cover all possibilities. Take a car, for example. You have some parts: metal, paint, seat, an engine and so forth, and you have a car. This car, if it is really there, must either be, in brief, the same as these parts or different from them. This is so; there is nothing unfair in saying that. Still, as soon as you realize that if something inherently exists, it must exist in one of these seven ways, you already have some doubt about its inherent existence. When you realize the entailment, the pervasion, you have already changed a bit. You have not yet found that the car does not exist in any of these seven ways, but your usual mind that is overwhelmed by the appearance of a car is interrupted.

There is no question that we are now overwhelmed by what appears to us. Why else would we be so deceived by dreams unless we were overwhelmed by appearances? We feel that the basic stuff of the universe is impinging on us and that we are correct in responding to these appearances. I have had many dreams about getting on and off buses searching for a place; all of a sudden there I am, there is a bus, and I am getting on it. The wish to get on it and the wish to find a certain place are already there. I do not even consider whether I want to find the place or not; the mind to do so already exists right there. I am already completely inside this unfolding scene, and yet it is merely beginning. I accept it as if it were all logical and sensible, as if there were a whole sequence of events that led up to it. But, actually, all I have done is to lay my head on a pillow. For us to agree with it, the appearance must be very powerful; we must be addicted to accepting appearances. We have acquired a need and have to fulfill it. In meditation on emptiness, reason is being used to counteract this.

If something were inherently existent, it would have to exist in one of these seven ways. If it does not exist in one of these seven, it is not inherently existent and, therefore, does not exist the way it appears. What seems so bothersome about the reasoning is its decisiveness. We could decide that although it is possible to consider these things from many points of view, there is nothing that one can really do about the basic appearance, and thus we should just put up with it. Or, we could decide that the reasoning simply is incapable of indicating anything about the basic appearance. However, what we are doing here is the opposite; we are getting down to the raw stuff of existence itself, challenging through reasoning the very way that things appear to us, not just abstractly dealing in theories. Many people nowadays think that reasoning is useless with respect to direct experience; however, here reasoning is used to refute direct experience by telling us something earth-shattering about it: that is, that objects falsely appear to have a far more substantial status than they actually do.

Presently, we are part of the end result of a process of over-concretization. Object and subject are already there, appearing to us. Thus, to make any kind of decision about the way in which things appear seems to contradict our own status. Nevermind searching, in seven ways, for the phenomenon designated, even to ascertain the entailment is for us like challenging the process of appearance. Who are we to make such a judgment? It seems tantamount to creating our own data. We feel as if this is not our place at all, that our place is to be someone who is just a responder.

Our usual sense is of a reality that is there like Mother Nature herself; we feel that there is nothing we can do about it, it is just there. The sevenfold analysis interferes with all this. It changes our position in the carnival of appearance — instead of being the end result of appearance, we are going back down inside it. We are taking this end-result, the responder-mind that agrees with things as they appear, and analyzing, "Do these things exist the way that they appear?"

Upon initially analyzing in this manner, it is not as if we

suddenly have a new kind of mind. We are consuming the fuel of wrong conception with the fire of conception itself. We are lighting the fire of right thought which will burn away wrong thought so that in the end there will be no conceptual thought left at all. The "Kāshyapa Chapter" of the *Pile of Jewels Sūtra* says:[277]

Kāshyapa, it is thus: For example, fire arises when the wind rubs two branches together. Once the fire has arisen, the two branches are burned. Just so Kāshyapa, if you have the correct analytical intellect, a Superior's faculty of wisdom is generated. Through its generation, the correct analytical intellect is consumed.

By using conceptuality to burn conceptuality away, only direct perception is left at Buddhahood.

This kind of practice is emotionally harrowing, for our mind has been convinced to remain in its place for eons and eons. Over and over and over again everything has convinced us that it would be better to stay as we are and leave things be. The inertia to stay with the status quo is great. We feel that otherwise there would be no way at all for us to get along, whereas in fact we would get along much better if we could figure out the actual status of objects.

This conceptual mind, the mental consciousness, has to make a decision, has to do some unusual thinking. Instead of taking everything as given, it must challenge appearances. Children often enter into these kinds of probing thoughts; eventually, however, they are conditioned such that they no longer ask these questions. At a certain point, we accept things as reality, no longer feeling to question. For, "reality" will not bear these questions. If this is going to be reality, its very precondition is that you will not ask such questions of it. Thus, when you do ask them, it is upsetting. We have become used to it this way. We need a willingness for new experience even if it entails the reopening of wounds of emotions built on views of reality. This analysis involves anxiety, fear. It is necessary to build the kind of mind that will not want to sink back and be overcome by inertia, a mind willing to change, willing to see everything change.

Practices that are a great help in the midst of these changes are love, compassion, and the altruistic intention to become enlightened. Realizing emptiness helps to develop such altruism, but altruism also helps in understanding emptiness. No matter what type of practice you are doing, meritorious power helps, and altruism is the best kind of merit. It loosens up the mind and relaxes it so that, when these changes in state occur, bad events do not have the chance to take over.

If you can challenge appearances, you can ask whether these seven questions are sufficient. We have to determine whether, through employing these seven reasonings, we can create a consciousness that is like a pest control person who knows how to find cockroaches. Is this consciousness that applies these seven criteria sufficient to find inherent existence? A policeman, for example, applies criteria in order to find out if someone is the killer or not. Are these seven criteria sufficient to investigate inherent existence?

If you leave it for the rest of the world to decide, people will say that you should not ask these questions. They will say that you are being too literal, that since everything is related and mutually dependent, it is not necessary to be so literal. Dependence for them means inherent existence. They feel that the way things appear is correct. Furthermore, if you were to ask philosophy experts how many agree that these seven criteria are sufficient to establish or reject, once and for all, the existence of things as we conceive of them, I think that not many would feel they are; it is too conclusive.

We need a competent mind, one that could find inherent existence if it were there. You will perhaps feel that you already have a mind that is finding inherent existence. For when you think about your car, there it is. You already have a mind capable of finding it, why look for another one? Why structure one, why use a whole lot of words? This car is a valid appearance, isn't it? This, however, is to accept the given, living in the end result of appearance. Is such a mind actually competent? Just because when you go out, the car appears to you to exist from its own side and you think about it that way, is such a thing valid?

The Nying-ma lama Khetsun Sangpo tells a story about someone who finds a scorpion and, not knowing that it is a scorpion, puts it in his hand. Looking at it, he says, "How fantastic! How beautiful, how black!" Then someone says, "That's a scorpion," and he goes, "Eek!" Now what was that lovely thing he saw? Was such a mind competent? Suppose you think that you have termites in your house and want to find out where they are. Some person comes up to your door, a real bum, who comes into your house and says, "Man, that's a termite trail; you give me five hundred dollars, and I'll get rid of your termites for you." You will wonder if he is competent. He has come in, and he is definitely there; he is very vividly appearing to you. However, is he competent? Does he have the materials? Does he have the training, and could he get rid of the termites? Is five hundred dollars a fair price?

Is the dream-mind that accepts the so vivid appearances of dreams competent? Usually we do not stop in dreams and think about them; it is rare to have a mind that can relate to dreams in this fashion. However, is our dream-mind a competent mind? When, in a dream, I try to find out if I am dreaming or not, whether these things are false appearances or not, I find that at times I am just overwhelmed by appearances. Though I start out realizing that I am dreaming, having the very strong thought, "Dream, dream, dream ...", after a while it is as if I am being pressured out of retaining the thought that I am in a dream, and I capitulate. Eventually, I wake up, see that it was a dream, and feel like a fool. This experience makes me question whether these non-dream minds are competent or not in that they accept how things appear just because they appear vividly.

Here you might think, "Since our minds have been conditioned from time without beginning to assent to this appearance of objects as if they are established by way of their own character, how can we possibly have a mind competent to determine the truth or falsity of this appearance?" If it were possible to develop ignorance limitlessly, which it is not, we would indeed be without any hope. If you could bring ignorance to full, utter completion, there would be no point in trying to overcome it. But ignorance does not accord with the fact, whereas what does accord with the fact can, over time, develop force. Emptiness has valid backing. Therefore, the wisdom that cognizes emptiness also has valid backing and can be developed limitlessly and brought to full fruition.

The beginning of a wisdom consciousness cognizing emptiness is developed by reflecting on the reasons proving an emptiness. The reasoning process is a chain leading from what is in experience to something that is not obvious. Still, you do not take two obvious things and put them together and have another obvious thing. You have to go through what may seem like a dark passage where you start with a few obvious things and then progress to the unknown. It is not like passing from one room to another, but is more like finding out that there is a palace of jewels right here under your basement. The reasoning is not like reading a map in order to learn the route to go to some *other* city. It seems that when emptiness is realized, you are doing something the very type of which you have not done before.

17 I As a Basis of Emptiness

We have studied the example, a chariot; now, let us consider the meaning exemplified, the person.

APPLYING THE EXAMPLE TO THE MEANING

One should consider whether this so-called person or self which is the basis of the conception thinking "I" is the same as one's own [mental and physical] aggregates or different from them.

The person or self is the basis of a consciousness conceiving "I" and is the object that generates the thought "I". It is the conventionally existent I. A consciousness that apprehends or conceives it is correct, valid, because a conventionally existent I does indeed exist. This explanation, despite the fact that it is technically correct, is, at this point, only theoretical since, prior to realizing emptiness, it is impossible to realize that a person or any other phenomenon only conventionally exists.

As with the chariot, what we are considering is the relationship between the phenomenon designated and its basis of designation. A person in our realm, the Desire Realm, is inextricably involved with mental and physical aggregates that are his or her basis of designation. Any intelligent estimation of what a person is has to come to terms with mind and/or body.

> [One should consider whether the person is the same as or different from the mental and physical aggregates] because, if it exists, it must be one of those two. For, in general, it is seen in the world that if something is affirmed by the mind to have a counterpart, it is excluded from being without a counterpart; and, if something is affirmed as not having a counterpart, it is excluded from having a counterpart. Therefore, oneness and otherness are a mutually exclusive dichotomy.

If the self solidly exists, it is either one with its basis of designation — mind and body — or different. These are the only possibilities.

[Refutation of Oneness]
> If the self and the aggregates were one, there would be three fallacies:

> (1) asserting a self would be senseless;

If the self is the aggregates, then why make such a big deal about the self? It would then be just a synonym for mind and body or for some part of mind and body.

> (2) there would be many selves;

Even if we say that the I is just the mental consciousness, we have to take into account the individual moments of the mental consciousness. Even then, if we take it down to what we consider the smallest moment of consciousness and say that this is what the self is, that moment also has parts — a beginning, a middle, and an end.

> and (3) the self would have production and disintegration.

If this production and disintegration were inherently existent, then, when the self disintegrates or ceases, it would utterly cease, never to appear again.

Jang-gya now elaborates on these three reasonings.

(1) If the self and the aggregates were inherently one, asserting a self would be senseless because "self" would merely be a synonym of "aggregates", like "moon" and "rabbit-bearer".

Take whatever you consider to be the basis of designation of this I. If the I is the same as its basis of designation, then it is senseless to posit it. Jang-gya's example is that it would be like "moon" and "rabbit-bearer". "Rabbit-bearer" is a Tibetan and Sanskrit name for the moon. We say there is a man in the moon; they say there is a rabbit. So it would be silly to make a big deal about both the moon and the "rabbit-bearer" since they are the same thing. Such is also the case when we place a great deal of importance on mind and body and also on I. If the I is mind and body, then of what use is I?

Nāgārjuna's *Treatise on the Middle Way, Called "Wisdom"* says:[278]

When it is taken that there is no self
Except for the appropriated [aggregates],
Then just the appropriated [aggregates] are
  the self,
In which case your self is non-existent.

The appropriated are the mental and physical aggregates; they are what we appropriate in rebirth.

Is there something at which you can point that is rabbit-bearer but not moon? Further, if you have nothing at which to point, will you be satisfied? Will this mind thinking that there is something findable there be satisfied with something not findable?

(2) If the self and the aggregates were inherently

one, then just as there are many aggregates, so there would be many selves.

Milk this for all the experience you can get. For example, if Frank were the same as his aggregates, then there would be many Franks. Then, if someone came to the door and asked, "Is Frank here?" he would have to decide which Frank should answer. It is important to be playful, because you can put I here and I there and be quite satisfied despite the fact that it is not consistent. It is easy to feel that you pervade your entire body if you do not think about it.

When you get down to the subtle object of negation where the self and the mental and physical aggregates seem fused and undifferentiable, the sense of self seems so right and natural that effort must be made in order to decide which one of these many you's should answer the door.

> Chandrakīrti's *Supplement to (Nāgārjuna's) "Treatise on the Middle Way"* says:[279]

> > If the self were the aggregates, then,
> > Since they are many, those selves would also
> > be many.

(3) If the self and the aggregates were one, it would [absurdly] follow that the self would be subject to production and disintegration. For, the aggregates are subject to production and disintegration. Nāgārjuna's *Treatise on the Middle Way* says:[280]

> > If the self were the aggregates,
> > It would have production and
> > disintegration.

What's wrong with that? What should the self be, permanent?

> *Objection:* What fallacy is there in the self's having production and disintegration?

> > *Answer:* If production and disintegration are only conventions, there is no fallacy.

There is indeed no fallacy for the self to be produced and to disintegrate if production and disintegration are only analytically unfindable nominalities. For, conventionally it is indeed asserted that the self has nominally existent production and disintegration.

> However, if the self has production and disintegration that are established by way of their own character, there would be three fallacies: (a) remembering [former] births would be impossible;

How could we ever remember another life once we conceive of our present life to be so concrete? However, if we understood that this I is a mere nominality, without inherent existence, it would probably be easy to remember past lives since the I would not be fused with a particular form.

> (b) actions done would be wasted;

Karma would be lost; it would be pointless to do virtuous actions and avoid non-virtues.

> (c) one would meet with [the effects of] actions not performed [by oneself].

We would experience the effects of actions that we ourselves had not done.

> Moreover, those three fallacies arise due to [the consequence that] if the selves of former and later births were individuals that are established by way of their own character, they would be unrelated other factualities.

Once the selves of different lives are, in and of themselves, individual, then they are completely unrelated. You can feel it — there is this life here and that life there, and they are separate in and of themselves. Because they would be so isolatedly separate, we would not be able to remember another life. Also, what we did in a former life would be wasted in that it would not come over into this life — there would be no connection. Because lives would be unrelated, effects of actions in a former life would not emerge in this life. Moreover, the good and bad features of body and mind that we now have and that must have arisen from causes, would absurdly arise from karma that we did not do. It would come from a past life that is not in a continuum with this life — "Look at all that I have to put up with now because that guy was a murderer!" That is to see "me" as covering this spot here (this life) and the previous "guy" as covering that spot there (the former life). How could they possibly be related?

> *Objection:* There is no fallacy. For, although [former and later births] are individuals that are established by way of their own character, they are of one continuum.
>
> *Answer:* That also is not feasible because if [former and later lives] were different by way of their own entities, they could not be one continuum just as, for example, with Maitreya and Upagupta are not. Chandrakīrti's *Supplement* says:[281]
>
>> The phenomena dependent on Maitreya
>>   and Upagupta
>> Are just other and thus do not belong to one
>>   continuum.
>> It is inadmissible for things that are
>>   individual
>> By way of their own character to belong to
>>   one continuum.

Maitreya and Upagupta are two contemporaries, like Dick and Jane; thus they cannot be one continuum. How can one continuum be superimposed over such inherently separate lives? Otherness is their nature; how can continuity occur in them?

Refutation of the Position That the Self and the Aggregates Are Different

If the self were established by way of its own character as different from the [mental and physical] aggregates, it would not have the character of the aggregates: production, abiding, and disintegration. For, [the self] would be an other factuality unrelated to the aggregates. It is like, for example, a horse, which, since it is different from an ox, does not have [the specific characteristics of an ox, which are] a hump [on the shoulders] and so forth.

If the [mental and physical] aggregates, which are the basis of designation of the self, and the self are two different things, then the self cannot have the character of the aggregates. "Aggregates" here mean the aggregates that are the specific bases of designation of the person; if the person is other than them, it cannot partake of their character. Also, if the self or person is not an aggregate itself, it cannot have the production, disintegration, impermanence, and so forth that are characteristics specifically of aggregates, which include all produced phenomena.

If this is interpreted in the latter sense as refuting that the person is other than the aggregates in general rather than the specific aggregates that are its basis of designation, then it is clear that the person could not at all have the character of being born, living, and dying, since it could not be impermanent. For, it would be totally other than the aggregates, which include all impermanent things. However, if this is interpreted in the first sense as a consideration of whether the person is other than the aggregates that are its own basis of designation, then it does not follow that it could not have birth, dying, and so forth because things other than these specific aggregates which are my basis of designation — such as a tree — have production and cessation. Still, I would not have the characteristics of production and disintegration of those aggregates that are my own basis of designation. I would not have the same dying that the body does, but would absurdly have some other dying.

> If this were the case, [the mental and physical aggregates] would not exist as the basis for the designation of the convention of a self, nor would they exist as an object of a [consciousness] conceiving self. For, the self would be uncompounded, like a sky-flower.

Who would ever call something that is uncompounded and a non-product a self? A non-product has neither causes nor effects, whereas the self has to go here and there, know this and know that, be born and die, etc.

A sky-flower is like a pie in the sky, a non-existent; if the self were different from the mental and physical aggregates, it would be like a pie in the sky, or like nirvana which, despite being existent, is uncompounded and such that no one would ever call it "I" or "self".

> Chandrakīrti sets this forth in his *Clear Words* in the form of an other-renowned syllogism.

Chandrakīrti taught this in syllogistic form; he did not make it into a consequence. This kind of syllogism is called "other-renowned" because in a debate the other, the opponent, agrees with the reason and agrees that the predicate of the thesis follows from the reason — or at least he or she should, based on previous assertions.

> Moreover, if the self and the aggregates were inherently different, [the self] would have to be observed as a different factuality from the characteristics of the aggregates, such as being suitable [to be called] form, just as form and consciousness, for example, are observed as different.

This is basically the same argument as before. If the self is inherently different from the mental and physical aggregates, it cannot have their characteristics. Before, the general characteristics of all the aggregates — production, abiding, and disintegration — were considered. Here, the reference is to the characteristics of the individual aggregates.

The standard definition of form as found in the elementary texts called the *Collected Topics of Valid Cognition* is "that which is suitable as form."[282] Some Tibetan scholars say that this means "that which is suitable to be called 'form' ". Thus the definition says little. You could then say that the definition of a dress is what is suitable to be called "dress". The Sanskrit for "being suitable as form" is *rupaṇā*, and some scholars, such as Ajitamitra, the sole Indian commentator on Nāgārjuna's *Precious Garland*, took it as meaning "what is breakable" since the verbal root *rup* means "break". However, that perhaps incurs a technical problem, in that, according to Geshe Gedun Lodrö, a single particle cannot be physically broken and still have form. Perhaps this is why, eventually, *rupaṇā* was taken merely to mean "that which is suitable to be called form" instead of "that which is breakable".

In Chandrakīrti's presentation of the defining characteristics of the remaining aggregates in his *Clear Words*, the characteristic of feeling is that it experiences; the characteristic of discrimination is that it apprehends signs or differences. The characteristic of compositional factors is that they compose, or compound, things. The characteristic of consciousness is that it knows its object.

If the self and the mental and physical aggregates were different entities, they would be like form and consciousness. For, since form has certain characteristics and mind has certain other characteristics, they can be apprehended separately. Similarly, if the self were a different entity from its basis of designation, it would have to be observable separate from them. Is there any self that can be perceived separate from knower, thinker, doer, feeler, having body, and so forth? Certainly not the self that we take to be the person who came into the room.

This reasoning proves that there is no I that is inherently

established as separate from mind and body, but it does not prove that there are no states in which we do not perceive our body. For, there are many times when we pay attention just to mind, and not body. Also, when emptiness is directly cognized, just emptiness is perceived; at that time the meditator does not cognize the body, mind, or anything else, just emptiness. Similarly, when one meditates on infinite space, the first of the formless meditative absorptions, one intentionally does not pay attention to body or mind; there is just space.

The former reasoning is taught in the eighteenth chapter [of Nāgārjuna's *Treatise on the Middle Way*] with:[283]

If [the self] were other than the aggregates,
It would not have the character of the
  aggregates.

Sometimes it seems as if we can put everything aside and still be left with a distinct feeling of self. But we would have to say that this distinct self is not a knower because the mind has been set aside. We would have to say that this distinct self is without a body since the body has already been set aside, and so on. Would anyone ever call this a self? Is this reasonable?

The latter reasoning is taught in the twenty-seventh chapter [of Nāgārjuna's *Treatise on the Middle Way*] with:[284]

If [the self] is other, then it should be
  apprehended
Without the appropriation; but it is not [so]
  apprehended.

"Appropriation" means the mental and physical aggregates. If the self were a different entity from the aggregates, we should be able to apprehend it separately whereas we cannot.

There are a great many difficult points to be explained with regard to these reasonings refuting oneness and difference, but I will not elaborate on them here.

How the Remaining Positions Are Refuted By These Reasonings

Through having refuted those two [positions of] oneness and difference of entity, the two positions of dependence — that the self exists in dependence on the aggregates and that the aggregates exist in dependence on the self — also are refuted.

Through negating inherently established oneness and difference, all the remaining five reasonings are established, since they are permutations of those two positions. The two positions of dependence are variations only of the position that the self and the aggregates are inherently established as different and are, therefore, completely negated by the reasoning that refutes inherently established difference.

For, although these two [positions of dependence] would be feasible if [the self and the aggregates] were different entities, the position that they are different entities has already been refuted.

If we refute that the self and the aggregates are inherently existent others, we have also refuted these two possibilities, but it is necessary to go through the refutation of otherness again so that its import is felt.

The position that the self possesses the aggregates is also not feasible. For, as was explained at the time of the chariot, the two modes of possession do not pass beyond the positions of oneness and difference.

When my head aches, I am sure that I possess a head. Do I possess this head as if I were something separate from it, as a man possesses a table, a cow, or a house? Or do I possess it in the sense of sameness of entity, in the way that I possess an ear or a body, or the way that a table possesses a leg?

I have a head. Have. *I* have a head. I have a head. I have a *head*. Where is this I who has the head? Is it the head? Is the head part of me? I have one head that is the head as well as one head that is at least part of the I possessing the head. So then I have two heads.

This analysis challenges the meaning of possession; possession turns into being. This can be seen clearly by considering a house having ten rooms. There is nothing else but the ten rooms. What *house* is there that could possess the ten rooms? When I say that I possess my head, there is enough body below it so that I can identify with that and from that perspective possess my head. But when I consider possession of the trunk, the two arms, the head, and the two legs, where is the I that possesses all of these?

I am then pushed into taking the position that I am like a marble that has been dropped down inside this mind and body. This is just a fabricated, and not innate, way of viewing the self, but I often come close to conceiving this. Indeed, even if a marble came rolling into the room, no one would say that this is Jeffrey. It is as if you dropped a marble down inside a mass of meat and somehow came up with the foolish idea that the marble owned the meat. Take away all the meat of the body; this marble is left. Then take this round thing: you have a sense of something that makes the whole thing cohere, but it has a top half and a bottom half. Is this cohering thing the same at the top as it is on the bottom?

Stop at whatever point the message gets through; the other reasonings are not necessary, though later on they can enhance understanding. Once it is known that the self is not findable, it is not necessary to keep applying different reasonings. Stay with that realization; then, when that knowledge diminishes in feeling, refurbish it with more reasoning.

> Moreover, it is also not feasible that the mere collection of the aggregates is the self. For since it is said

that the self is designated in dependence upon the five aggregates, the five aggregates are the basis of designation and the person is the phenomenon designated, and it is not feasible that the basis of designation be the phenomenon designated.

This is the reason why the mere collection cannot be the self. The collection of the mental and physical aggregates is the basis of designation, and the person is the phenomenon designated; therefore, the former cannot be the latter.

The thrust of this reasoning [that the basis of designation cannot be the phenomenon designated] is slightly difficult to realize. Moreover, this should be understood from (1) the [Consequence School's] uncommon way of interpreting the force of the words in the previously quoted sūtra:

> Just as a chariot is designated
> In dependence upon collections of parts,
> So conventionally a sentient being
> [Is designated] in dependence upon the
>   aggregates.

The lower schools take this passage to mean that just as a chariot is merely the collection of its parts and is not anything separate from them, so a person is to be found from among its bases of designation, either all five mental and physical aggregates, or a consciousness, or a continuum of consciousness, etc. The Consequence School, however, sees this passage as indicating that just as a chariot is designated in dependence upon bases of designation and cannot be posited as anything separate from or among those bases of designation, so a person is designated in dependence upon the mental and physical aggregates but cannot be posited as something other than or something among those aggregates.

And (2) from detailed[285] realization of the essentials of reasoning in Chandrakīrti's *Autocommentary on* the *"Supplement to (Nāgārjuna's) 'Treatise on the Middle Way' "* that illuminate this reasoning through proof statements.

Moreover, if the collection [of the aggregates] is the self, there is also the fallacy that agent and object would be one.

The appropriated and the appropriator would be one. "He/she took a new life," means that the person took a new mind and body. The mental and physical aggregates are the appropriated, and he or she is the appropriator. If the collection of mind and body were the self, appropriated and appropriator would absurdly be one.

This also refutes the assertion made by some of our own [Buddhist] schools of tenets that the self is the continuum of the aggregates.

It is also not feasible to assert that the shape of the aggregates is the self. For, shape exists only in physical things, and, therefore, [if the self were shape] the self could not be posited [in dependence] upon mind and so forth.

We often associate persons with shape — especially other people and sometimes ourselves. However, a person is not just physical.

COMMENTS

On this one spot are mind, body, and person. We have, therefore, to take account of their relationship. To talk about a table, it is not necessary to consider an elephant, but it is necessary to consider the table's parts. Similarly, to posit a person, mind and body must be taken into account.

A mind that conceives a person to be truly existent merely conceives the person to be there in its own right; hence, to start thinking about mind and body interferes with this conception of true existence. The problem is: given that mind and body are here, as well as the person, what is their relationship? Usually, we merely accept whatever appears, constantly switching from one conception to another, at one time paying attention to the body, at another time paying attention to the mind, at yet another paying attention to the I — never questioning whether these are coherent.

Jang-gya says that we should consider whether the person is the same as the mental and physical aggregates or different from them. If you were to ask, "Is the conventionally existent person different from or the same as the aggregates?" the question would be framed as if you knew what a conventionally existent person is. However, when this analysis is done, it is necessary to start with the person that is appearing to our minds, and according to this system, this person whom we are considering is *appearing* incorrectly — in that it seems to exist inherently — and is *misconceived* to be inherently existent by assenting to that appearance. Thus the very base, our subject, is already wrong in the sense that it appears to be inherently existent. Although it is said that sometimes we do not specifically qualify it as inherently existent, it always appears as if it were.

This seemingly solidly existent I is the object to be negated; once you get it in sight, you can almost put your hand on it. Its basis of designation is right here — the body, mind, or whatever the basis of designation is at the moment. Is this person the same as its basis of designation or not? If we are to be able to point and say, "This is the I, and that is its basis of designation," we must point to the same thing or to two things.

To decide whether the person and the aggregates are the same or different is to commit yourself to think the unthinkable. People draw back from this — feeling that they cannot come to a conclusion, that neither of these options is right. There is this overwhelming experience of concretely existent objects, and since neither of these two is correct, what is the point of thinking about it anyway!

However, if we exist the way we appear, we must be findably either the same as mind and body or different. If we are neither, then we do not exist the way we seem to. To make such a decision is to cut into the very fabric of the world.

If we are to oppose the whole weight of cyclic existence, we have to become convinced that coming to a decision about inherently existent oneness and difference, for instance, is sufficient for making a decision as to the truth or falsity of the appearance of concrete existence. We have to become certain that a mind searching for inherently existent oneness and difference is qualified to come to a conclusion about the things that are appearing. It is as if we have become superliteral and are no longer moving with the punch, not accepting things as they come. (Eventually, however, when we stop superimposing concrete existence on things, we can then move with the punch; anything can appear without our being overpowered by it.)

Therefore, the first step is to make this decision: "There is no choice but that I am one with this mind and body, which are definitely there, or different from them." Moreover, the I does not have to be one with or different from the whole complex of mind and body aggregates; it could be one with a part of the complex, or it could be one part now and another part later.

This method puts a tremendous amount of faith in the mind. Here we are, tiny little persons, establishing criteria for the other four billion humans in this world, saying that if they exist the way they appear, then they must satisfy certain qualifications. It is as if we were taking job applications from the rest of the world.

It is helpful to decide in the beginning that something is wrong. Why is it that people write so much poetry about impermanence? Why do all religions keep drumming transitoriness home? Is it perhaps because we are tricked by experiencing things in a way other than their actual condition? If we can decide that there must be something wrong with our usual perceptions, then limiting everything to these two possibilities and analyzing whether the world lives up to them promote a courageous attitude. Then, we can see that the problem is not external, but internal because it is our own mistake. It is said that if we clean our own error, the whole process will appear differently. It takes courage; there is a lot of inertia. It often seems that I am such a tiny thing, maybe I should let the solid appearance of the world win. It becomes a question of who is to prevail.

This is a reason why meditators make their lives more simple, why they go off to the mountains or another quiet place to meditate. They do not want to have so many different objects appearing to them; they want a place where running through everything that appears will not involve an excessive amount of variation. Also, in quiet places things are not so pressing, there is no one coming in to visit you, rob you, and so forth, as in the city. You can stay out of the marketplace.

This does not mean that emptiness is not true everywhere. It is just that usually, unless well trained in prior lives, we do not find the truth to be that powerful. We have to get used to the truth and build it up, strengthen it. When we understand emptiness and gain some experience with a limited number of objects in a quiet situation, then we can go back into the marketplace for a little while and, eventually, will even be able to stay in the marketplace.

It is good to have a place for retreat and also to keep coming back to the marketplace to test your realization. Further, it is good not to be too surprised if, when you come back, you are overwhelmed by the opposite of what you thought you had understood. Also, it is said that as we penetrate more deeply into the nature of things, strong resistance and strong problems arise. For instance, hatred may manifest so strongly that you will feel you could never overcome it, hatred so strong that you may wonder how you could ever think about its not existing from its own side. Training is required to know that such experience does not mean that it is existent in its own right.

For instance, the mind must become involved in this reasoning dealing with oneness and especially in the part showing the fallacy of many selves. Go ahead and think, "Okay, there are as many I's as there are aggregates," and live with this for awhile. Eventually you want to find out whether or not it is sensible, but first live with it for a while in order to explore the possibility.

Be like a man in the desert who sees mirages in all four directions. He sees four beautiful lakes and goes to each, desperate to find water. In the end, though he wants water, he knows for sure it is not there. We have to get down to just such an inner mind that wants the inherently existing self to be there and then, with that mind, go search for it. Each time you lose a possibility, you get more desperate. We have to become desperately, deeply convinced. To be desperate means to have no other hope.

Den-dar-hla-ram-ba, a great Mongolian scholar and adept (who is said to have hung his pipe on a shaft of light in his tent when someone came to discipline him, a monk, for smoking), said that when searching to find inherent existence, you have to bring it to the point where you actually generate fear at finding nothing.[286] If you cannot bring it to the point of desperation but, instead, are satisfied not to come up with anything, then you are just daydreaming, oblivious to all the emotions and all the activities that are built on being utterly convinced of inherent existence. The analysis ought to move us deeply.

Indeed, sometimes this kind of analysis can be just fantastic; however, at other times it seems as if you are carving out your own heart. You are rending the fabric of cyclic existence, and since this fabric is your own, it is difficult to bear. All experience of emptiness is not like this, but great scholar-yogis such as the Fifth Dalai Lama and Den-dar-hla-ram-ba have spoken of initial understanding this way. On the other hand, it is also said that there are people who can easily put it together; the rich revelatory nature of emptiness as the key to transformation confirms itself in vivid experience. In an evening, such people can make sense out of it. These are unusual people, who know how to apply what they learn, who can take it and reach back through their whole lives and apply the significance everywhere. This is said to take a person of great awareness, great consciousness.

However, most people are not such. Most of us have to keep going through experiences where we want something but find that it does not exist that way — we need repeatedly to find out how wrong we were, to be destroyed again and again. Still, at other times it can be just plain thrilling to find that you do not have to cover this area, that you do not have to exist so concretely. Meditation on emptiness can reveal the subtle elements that are in the mind-body complex, making it possible to be useful to other people, getting a sense of how activities could be spontaneous. There is certainly little spontaneous in the lives that we now live, except for spontaneous expression of afflictive emotions that masquerade as being natural to our minds.

18 Compatibility of Emptiness and Nominal Existence

The non-finding of a self anywhere, when analyzed thus with reasoning in these seven ways, is the meaning of the absence of inherent existence of the self.

Here "self" means "person". We have talked a lot about selflessness, emptiness, absence of inherent existence, and so on; this is it — the non-finding of the person or any other phenomenon when analyzed in this way.

Since this fact is similar in terms of both of the two truths, there is no self established by way of its own character even conventionally. Nevertheless, when there is no analysis seeking the object designated, the self or person is established by valid cognition, with no possibility of denial, as being able to perform activities.

Here, "self" and "person" refer to the same thing, the conventionally existent I.

Therefore, persons exist conventionally. Moreover, when an awareness thinking, "I," is produced, it is produced in dependence on having taken the five aggregates in one's own continuum as a basis. Therefore, [the I] exists as a mere designation in dependence upon the five aggregates. Moreover, these [points] are the thought of the root text and autocommentary of Chandrakīrti's *Supplement* quoted earlier:[287]

> That [chariot] is not established in these
>   seven ways
> Either as [its own] suchness or in the world,
> But without analysis it is designated here
> From [the viewpoint of] the world in
>   dependence upon its parts.

Chandrakīrti's *Commentary on (Āryadeva's) "Four Hundred"* says that something illusory must be left over as a remainder:

> For that reason, when analyzed thus, the inherent existence of things is not established. Hence, just an illusory-like nature is left over as a remainder with respect to things individually.

The Foremost Omniscient [Dzong-ka-ba] says:

> This combination of the following two [factors] barely occurs — (1) refuting, without residue, the object of negation [inherent existence] through reasoned analysis and (2) the feasibility of positing, as left after the negation, without losing anything, all the functionalities of dependently arisen causes and effects as like illusions. Therefore, it is very difficult to gain the view of the Middle Way.

An understanding of this combination is almost nonexistent because we tend to fall to one extreme or the other, either refuting objects along with their inherent existence or not refuting enough.

An illusory-like object is left over when inherent existence is negated, but no inherent existence is left over. Inherent existence must be totally refuted; its complete negation must be realized. Subsequently, an illusory-like object is realized. It is called illusory-like because it appears to be inherently existent but is not. When yogis have this realization of illusory-like objects, they are like magicians who have put salve on a stone and a spell on everyone's eye consciousness, including their own, so that the stone appears to be an elephant. Even though it vividly appears to be an elephant, they know that it is not, that it is only a stone.

The understanding of phenomena as like illusions is called illusory-like subsequent attainment. When yogis rise from cognition of emptiness, things again vividly appear, but they do not believe in their seeming inherent existence. There are, nevertheless, many differences between the non-existence of an illusory elephant, man, or woman and the absence of inherent existence of a person, or any other phenomenon. The illusory elephant created by the magician cannot perform the functions of an elephant even conventionally, whereas a person can perform the functions of a person. Still, they are both the same in that neither the illusory elephant nor the non-inherently existent person can cover the spot that they seem to cover. In this way, understanding gained from looking at dream-objects and deciding that they do not exist the way they vividly appear to exist can be applied to the phenomena of the world.

The sense of inherent existence acts like a magnet towards the mind, and we are also as if magnetized by our previous actions. Thus, to realize that something does not inherently exist, it is, so to speak, necessary to demagnetize. Nevertheless, making progress toward understanding the absence of inherent existence makes one more engaged. In ordinary, mistaken perception we are both being pushed away and at the same time pulled into something. We are being attracted, but there is a great distance between us and the magnetic object. It is as if two very different things are strongly magnetized to each other. However, when it is understood that oneself and the object are unfindable, it is much more direct, like intimately looking someone in the eye. It is as if you had two magnets but one of them has disappeared into the other. Objects can be seen as never before. In our usual perceptions, the object is as if covered or protected; it stops you before you can get to it. It is as if you had put on sunglasses; something has been put in the way, covering it up. Here, after understanding that an object is unfindable and empty of inherent existence, you can be thoroughly engaged in the object with nothing in the way.

Thus, when we meditate on emptiness, searching, for example, to find this book, we carefully go over the basis of designation of the book, doing the sevenfold analysis, deeply involved in searching to find the book. Finally, when we are impressed with not finding the book, it even becomes such that when the book later reappears, its very appearance means for you that it cannot be found. If, prior to such analysis, we thought a lot about the unfindability of this book, we would have to disengage ourselves from it, because right now we are utterly convinced that this book is here, covering its spot. However, when the sevenfold analysis is done correctly, we become even more engaged. At that point, the mind does not have to be withdrawn in order to reflect on reality. The very appearance of the book itself fortifies our sense of the absence of inherent existence; it can then be understood that a book is only imputed and is utterly unfindable under such analysis. These conventional phenomena are understood as mere conventionalities, as falsities, as fraudulent, appearing one way and existing another.

At present, we lock a general assent onto our everyday perceptions. For example, we lock in the feeling, "I am awake." When we go to sleep, even in our dreams we still have this sense of being awake; otherwise, why would we enter into dream activities, believing them to be real? Similarly, we constantly lock into the present scene an acceptance that it exists the way it appears. We usually even *practice* sinking ourselves into objects, even into what is known in the world to be false. We buy mirrors and put them up in front of ourselves, developing a relationship with the person in the mirror. We go to the movies and get deeply involved with the characters; we want movies in which we can get to the point where we feel that the figures on the screen are real people. We cultivate this.

However, with an understanding of things as like illusions, we can infuse all appearances and events with an appreciation of them as being illusory-like. In the same way that we experience someone or something that appears in a dream when we know we are dreaming, so we can experience everything when awake as appearing one way and existing another way. Whereas presently the mind is sunk into the objects that we believe to exist in their own right, when we no longer believe in such concrete, solid objects, they will appear to our mind, but it will not sink into them. The mind is then in a state that is more vast. There is a feeling of being everywhere and of not being so different from things — and this heavy sunk-in feeling is not there. Though objects have not disappeared, attraction to them is removed.

If, after searching for and not being able to find an object, this presentation of effective, validly existent nominalities is remembered, we can *feel* that the book is merely designated in dependence upon the collection of its parts. Having meditated with full concentration on the unfindability of the object, when we relax the meditation and consideration of things comes back, we will not experience them in the way that we did before. Our understanding of emptiness will affect the way appearances are perceived. This cognition when we rise from meditation, that is, when we end single-pointed concentration on emptiness, is a valid cognition of conventional phenomena as conventional phenomena, as falsities, appearing one way and existing another way.

Yogis who have been meditating on emptiness rise from meditation and see everything to be like objects in a dream. They take these appearances that suck us into them in a different way than we do, without this hardening of appearance. We can illustrate this by sustaining visualization of dream-objects after awakening; they appear but are empty.

It is important to remember, when studying nominal existence, that nominally existent objects are not findable under ultimate analysis either. Nominal existence is itself nominally existent. Thus, it should not be felt that nominal existence, conventional existence, somehow preserves our old way of seeing things.

Such a combination of an utter negation of the object of negation with a presentation of the illusory-like objects of dependent-arising, as described in the Consequence School, is very rare.

> Regarding that, all proponents of tenets among our own schools of the high and low vehicles, present their own systems as systems that are free from the extremes.

Even non-Buddhist schools of tenets, such as the Indian Nihilists, present their system as being free from the extremes, for they say that they avoid the extreme of permanence — reification of what does not exist as existent — through rejecting inference and avoid the extreme of non-existence — denial of what does exist — through accepting direct perception. They say that what you can see exists. You can see that a pot is made; therefore, the maker of the pot and the making of the pot exist. You cannot see anyone putting color on flowers; therefore, a flower's color arises merely by way of its own nature. Each system has its own way of avoiding the two extremes.

And, in particular, the other [i.e., non-Consequentialist] great chariots of the Mind Only and Middle Way Schools have ways of presenting the meaning of the middle free from extremes and of presenting illusory-like [appearances]. If you understand well how assertions on these by the higher schools of tenets are more to the point[288] and more difficult to realize than those of the lower systems of tenets and that nevertheless all of those [non-Consequentialist schools] do not contain the essentials of being free from all extremes as in the presentation of the two truths in this supreme system and if you understand well how only this system avoids all the very subtle extremes and how it also has profound features totally unlike the other systems in its positing illusory-like [appearances], you will develop firm and genuine faith, induced through the path of reasoning, in general in the texts of the father [Nāgārjuna] and his spiritual sons and in particular in the texts of the great lords of adepts who properly expounded the Consequentialist system as well as in the high sayings of the father, the Foremost Great Being [Dzong-ka-ba] and his spiritual sons [Gyel-tsap and Kay-drup].

Jang-gya is emphasizing that the presentations of the Mind Only and Autonomy Schools come much closer to hitting the mark than do those of the Low Vehicle philosophers; nevertheless, they do not penetrate directly to the essence and present emptiness and illusory-like appearances such that all extremes are destroyed. Jang-gya is saying that when someone knows well the differences between the Middle Way School as Nāgārjuna explained it and what the other schools say, and also knows the differences between the Consequentialist system and the other systems, as well as knowing how well Chandrakīrti, Buddhapālita, Shāntideva, and so forth elaborated on the Consequence School and how well Dzong-ka-ba and his two chief disciples explained this system, firm faith comes naturally. Jang-gya must be speaking from experience.

You must understand, just as they are, the essentials of the reasonings explained previously and the essentials of the presentation [of appearances] as like illusions, and you must also understand the stages in which these are properly taken to mind as well as the subtle distinctions in generating experience of them. These understandings come (1) through penetrating well in depth, not just superficially, the scriptures of the Foremost [Dzong-ka-ba] in general and his great and small *Expositions of the Stages of the Path to Enlightenment* in particular; (2) through properly relying on excellent spiritual friends who, along with meeting [exalted beings in meditative vision], have obtained certain subtle and secret essentials of the speech of the Foremost Great Being [Dzong-ka-ba] which were given orally to the excellent among his spiritual children, great Bodhisattvas abiding on the grounds, transmitted in stages and put down in writing by the scholars and adepts of this system; (3) through taking to mind the meaning of these texts again and again by means of properly thought out reasoning; and moreover (4) through engendering unusually great effort in the many external and internal causal collections. Moreover, it is very right to strive in this way.

Jang-gya is recommending that the fundamental works of the system be understood by meeting with scholars and adepts who are in the lineage and then by putting in mind the meaning of these books again and again with reasoning. Also, great effort at accumulating merit is important, for to meditate on emptiness, much positive power is needed. Such practices would include the seven-limbed service (prostration, offering, disclosure of ill-deeds, admiring one's own and others' virtue, entreating, supplication, and dedication). Emptiness is very difficult to understand, and the practices in the seven-limbed service create positive feelings and altruistically based relationships with other people and with teachers. Through these, a firm basis develops for meditation on emptiness.

Jang-gya emphasizes the greatness of Dzong-ka-ba's presentation of the compatibility of dependent-arising and emptiness.

For the omniscient Gyel-tsap says:[289]

> Until I found the Foremost Holy
> [Dzong-ka-ba],
> I had not even partially realized
> Dependent-arising, the middle free from
> extremes
> The path severing the root of cyclic
> existence.

Even [Gyel-tsap] the Great Lord of Reasoning who rivals the likes of the six ornaments[290] of Jambudvīpa, the land of Superiors [India], did not realize even a portion of this view of the Middle Way free from extremes, prior to meeting the Foremost Great Being [Dzong-ka-ba]. Also, [Gyel-tsap] says that he realized the meaning of the middle free from extremes through the kindness of the Foremost Omniscient [Dzong-ka-ba]:[291]

> In the good explanations of the excellent
> spiritual friend
> Is explained, just as it is, the meaning of
> dependent-arising, the middle free from
> extremes
> Which is just as asserted by the protector
> Nāgārjuna,
> And is the single thought of Buddhapālita,
> Chandrakīrti, and Shāntideva.

[Gyel-tsap] also says that it is necessary to work hard at this[292] way because it is the excellent life of the path of liberation and omniscience:[293]

Without realizing the principle of the
middle free from the extremes,
One cannot reach the levels[294] of the
supreme Superiors.
Therefore, having concluded that emptiness
means dependent-arising,
Make effort at practice, striving in the
proper way.

[Gyel-tsap] also says that upon understanding that
this supreme system is difficult to find and that in
not very long it will disappear, discriminating people should generate effort quickly, quickly:[295]

Since proponents of the two truths of
Nāgārjuna's good system,
Difficult to find in even a billion eons,
In not long will disappear from this world,
The discriminating should quickly generate
effort.

These points are very important, appearing to be
advice of the utmost profundity.

When we notice how Buddhism has diminished in Tibet
and China and how it is disappearing in other places due to
materialistic pursuits, we see how difficult it is to find this
teaching.

Suppose that you make great effort in meditating on
emptiness and then die, taking rebirth somewhere and remembering, "I was studying Nāgārjuna's system; it was
directing me toward reality. Now I have to find someone
who can teach me this." You would then go about trying to
find someone who could teach you. You might think that
your parents could teach you; you would ask them questions to see if they knew about emptiness, but they would
only think that the questions were strange. You might ask
people at school or church. Whom could you find? No

matter where you were born, it would be very hard to find such a teacher. If you were born in America thirty or forty years ago, impossible. Today, next to impossible.

Although we might read several books of the Middle Way School and give them a great deal of thought, the most important teaching we can get on the Middle Way School is from someone who shows it in such a way that we actually meditate on it and realize it.

Since I wish to explain about the Consequence School[296] only briefly here, you should understand the essentials of the tenets of this system at length from other [texts].

19 Extending the Realization

Showing That This [Ascertainment of Persons as Not Inherently Existent] Also Establishes the Mine as Not Inherently Existent
When the self is sought in this way by means of reasoning that examines whether or not it is inherently existent, it is not found to be any of these seven, whereby inherent existence is negated with respect to the self. At this point, that the mine is established by way of its own character is also easily negated.

Once there is no I, there can no longer be any inherently existent mine. However, at our stage, when we understand a little about the absence of an inherently existent I, we usually have to extend this realization deliberately to other phenomena; for, if it were not forcibly extended, it would not be extended at all.

Sometimes, however, it is automatically extended due to the importance of a particular instance of mine right at that time. If we are getting into a lot of trouble over a certain phenomenon which is ours, then, when we search to find the I and do not find it, it is as though right away there can be no such inherently established mine. Still, the under-

293

standing, being weak, will probably not be extended to neutral things or things that are not causing much trouble. At that time, deliberately extend this preliminary "realization" to other phenomena. Ask, "Who owns this?" In the midst of realizing that the I cannot be found, ask yourself, "Who owns these pants?", "Who owns this shirt?", "Who owns this skin?", "Who owns these fingernails?", "Who owns this hair?", "Who owns these glasses?"

Nāgārjuna's *Fundamental Text Called "Wisdom"* says:[297]

> If [an inherently existent] self does not
>   exist,
> How could [inherently existent] mine exist?

As mentioned earlier, it may help, in English, to consider "mine" two ways, as "my" and as "mine". "My" differs from "mine" in that "my" is the owning person whereas "mine" is a phenomenon owned. In one interpretation, "mine" refers to those things within the continuum that are qualified by being your possessions. Thus, your own mind and body are "mine". Still, a conception of inherently existent mine is a conception of a self of persons because it refers to the conception of the inherently existent I that is necessarily involved in understanding, or qualifying, this hand, for instance, as mine.

We can consider "my" to be another name for "I", the person who makes things into mine. "My" is a more active and extensive version of I.[298]

> Moreover, although just an awareness that realizes the I to be without inherent existence does not explicitly apprehend the mine to be without inherent existence, when the mind turns to the mine in a manner of analyzing whether inherent existence exists or not, based on the functioning of the former awareness, [the mine] is easily established as without inherent existence. Because [this mind] does not

consider another proof, no separate reasoning [for refuting the inherent existence of the mine] is set forth in the great texts.

Another reasoning is not needed. The functioning of the awareness that, through the sevenfold reasoning, understood the absence of inherent existence of the I is such that by merely moving to a new object, it understands that object's absence of inherent existence.

Two different ways of asserting [mine] appear. [One system explains that] the eyes, ears, and so forth included in one's own continuum are illustrations of mine but are not objects of observation of an innate [false] view of the transitory collection that conceives [inherently existent] mine. They explain that this is the thought of the Foremost Father [Dzong-ka-ba] and his spiritual sons [Gyel-tsap and Kay-drup].

Jang-gya then refers to Jam-yang-shay-ba's *Great Exposition of Tenets*:[299]

[Another system explains that] the eyes, ears, and so forth are the bases of designation[300] of the mine but are not illustrations[301] of mine because it is not feasible for a basis of designation to be the phenomenon designated. [Jam-yang-shay-ba says that] the explanation in Kay-drup's *Opening the Eyes of the Fortunate* that eyes, ears, and so forth are illustrations of mine merely indicates that these are illustrations of things taken as mine; it does not indicate they are mine itself.[302] [Jam-yang-shay-ba says that] this way of explaining [mine] is the thought of Dzong-ka-ba's *Great Commentary on (Nāgārjuna's) "Fundamental Text Called 'Wisdom' "*.[303] Although there appears to be much to be investigated in both these assertions, I wish to elaborate on them elsewhere.

In the first explanation, the objects themselves are mine. In the second explanation, eyes, ears, and so forth are just things that are made into mine and not mine; in the latter system "mine" is more like "my", a person.

Phenomena are divided into persons and other phenomena because persons are the users, the enjoyers, and other phenomena are what they use or enjoy. From the viewpoint of the conception of true existence and of meditation on emptiness, the mine (when not considered to be a person) are the most important phenomena other than the person. Within the mine, that is, from between the external and internal mine, those which are internal, included within our own continuum, are the most important — our body, mind, teeth, and so forth.

Jang-gya has described two ways of thinking about mine. In the first interpretation, the object of observation of an innate false view of the transitory collection that conceives inherently existent mine is the mineness of eyes, ears and so forth *which are qualified by being mine*. Our own eyes and ears *per se* are, therefore, not the objects of observation of an innate conception of the inherent existence of mine. They must first be seen as mine, and then that mineness is apprehended to be inherently existent. Eyes and ears qualified as being mine are illustrations of mine, that is, they are mine. Mine is not another name for "person" in this interpretation.

The second way of explaining mine is Jam-yang-shay-ba's. Despite Kay-drup's saying in his *Opening the Eyes of the Fortunate* that eyes, ears and so forth *are* illustrations of mine which means that they must be mine, Jam-yang-shay-ba holds that Kay-drup's meaning is that these things are illustrations of that which is taken as or made into mine rather than illustrations of mine itself. The mine (or, more properly, my) is the person who takes these things to be mine. The controversy over what "mine" is draws us into noticing that we qualify our own eyes and ears as being mine, that an inherently existent I is the owner of things that are considered mine, that "my" is a person actively owning things, and that, conversely, "I" is not as active. In this way, both sides of the controversy are useful in identifying common workings of the mind.

How This Reasoning Is Applied to Other Phenomena
We have been talking about a sevenfold analysis that has nine essentials, the first two being the identification of the object of negation (inherent existence) and the ascertainment of entailment (that if something is not findable in these seven ways, it does not inherently exist) and the last seven being the establishment of the seven reasons. These nine keys open the door, as it were, to realization of the thesis that the I does not inherently exist.

This reasoning is mainly applied to persons, but it can also be applied to other phenomena; for, every phenomenon can be seen from the viewpoint of basis of designation and phenomenon designated, and this reasoning is an analysis of those two. With the mental and physical aggregates and the person, the aggregates are the basis of designation, and the person is the phenomenon designated. With a house, its many rooms are its basis of designation, and the house is imputed in dependence upon those rooms. If the house and the rooms inherently exist, there are seven possible ways in which they could exist. If they do not exist in one of those seven ways, then the house does not inherently exist.

There is nothing to which this sevenfold analysis cannot be applied. When we sit down to try to meditate, our minds take off on a circle through a certain number of things. Whatever the number of things in that circle is, eventually we get back to the first one again and think about it. This sevenfold analysis can be applied to everything in that circle, everything upon which the mind alights.

Thus, after going through the sevenfold analysis with regard to the person, let the mind wander wherever it wants, but, within that, apply this analysis to everything.

This establishes a center in the mind. What normally happens is that our minds wander and the center goes right along with it. Here we are retaining the center, applying this ultimate analysis to whatever appears.

Shibayama Roshi in a lecture at Haverford College in 1968 said that ordinary thinking is like grinding the grinding wheel rather than grinding the corn or the wheat. We are unable to leave our minds set on memory of reality. Never mind when we are working hard on something, even when we are meditating, the mind goes off here and there. Keep in memory the sevenfold analysis, its conclusion, or even just a part of it — just that there is a basis of designation and a phenomenon designated. For a few hours let things appear to your mind. It is good to do this even verbally, not just when you have more profound understanding that you can apply to everything that appears. Just let things appear to your mind, identifying the basis of designation and the phenomenon designated.

When Jang-gya says that this reasoning applies to other phenomena, he means that we should apply it to all phenomena. Once the sevenfold reasoning has been internalized, we need no other reasoning to get at the selflessness of other phenomena.

Still, some people think that there is a conventional level and an absolute level and that you cannot live on the absolute level all the time, that it would expend too much energy. By elevating the ultimate to the level of an independent absolute, they make such extension of ultimate reasoning an impossibility. In this system, however, the ultimate is the nature of the conventional; thus, it should be possible to work with both levels together, since the effect in any situation is to cancel a wrong way of perceiving things.

Chandrakīti's *Supplement to (Nāgārjuna's) "Treatise on the Middle Way"* says that all these phenomena, renowned in the world, do not exist when sought in the seven ways and that they are posited as existent for a non-analytical, conventional consciousness:[304]

> Parts, qualities, passion, definition, fuel,
> and so forth
> As well as whole, qualificand, the
> impassioned,[305] illustration,[306] fire, and
> so forth —
> These do not exist in the seven ways when
> subjected to the analysis of the chariot;
> They exist through worldly renown which is
> other than that.

The first line is a list of bases of designation; the second is a list of the phenomena designated in dependence upon them. Whole is designated in dependence upon parts; qualificand is designated in dependence upon qualities. An impassioned person is designated in dependence upon passion, and so forth.

Take a table, for instance. We feel that a table is a qualificand or substance, a base of many qualities. Green, gold, flat, wide, long, high, being capable of doing this and that, and so on are qualities of the table. If we enumerate the qualities long enough, it will be hard to come up with something that is the table apart from those qualities; we will eventually become perplexed over what the table that is the basis of those qualities is. Once color and shape are qualities, where is the table that possesses these qualities? Upon listing off several qualities, any sense of the substance is crowded out.

Take definition, i.e., a defining characteristic, and illustration of what is defined. Is the definition inherently established as the same as what it defines or is it different?

Is fire the same as fuel? Is fire different from fuel? Is fire based on fuel? Is fuel based on fire? Does fire possess fuel? Does fuel possess fire? Is fire the shape of fuel? Is fire the collection of fuel?

People often say that it is impossible to figure out the

relationship between things — that reason is inadequate to the task. Yet they still believe in solidly existent things. They search for them in seven ways but still leave fire and fuel, or self and aggregates. Analysis does not disturb their basic notions. They do not see that it is their notion that constructs their very experience of these objects.

It seems to me that it was to counteract this that Nāgārjuna presented many reasonings proving emptiness with many examples in his *Treatise on the Middle Way*. The many formats provide different avenues of analysis so that the message can get through.

In the last line of Jang-gya's citation, Chandrakīrti says that although phenomena cannot be found under such analysis, they are posited as existing for worldly renown, this being interpreted as a non-analytical, conventional consciousness. This statement sometimes leads people to believe that we are supposed to cultivate a consciousness that does not analyze, and in a sense we *are* to cultivate a consciousness that is satisfied with things as mere nominalities. However, this is fraught with problems, for awareness of objects can lead quickly to a conception of inherent existence because objects appear to be inherently existent even in raw sensation.

Still, if we analyze everything, we will not find anything, and thus if we always performed ultimate reasoning, not taking it around to the positive side, which is the valid cognition of conventional phenomena that sees that objects exist but are not their bases of designation, we would never have a chance to act. Moreover, it is said that we are to see everything as like a magician's illusions, as illusory-like; we are to generate a conventional type of mind that sees objects as like illusions. That understanding is highly influenced by understanding emptiness; otherwise, we would not see objects as like illusions. Such penetrative understanding must be kept alive whenever we act in the world.

Therefore, although the statement that the objects are posited in the face of non-analysis would seem to encourage non-analysis, it cannot be realized that these things are like illusions — that although they appear to inherently exist they do not — without having done analysis first. Hence, rather than non-analysis, intense analysis is needed for proper understanding of conventional objects; ultimate analysis must first be done before you can understand that these things, though existent, are falsities — before you can understand that these things are truths, things that exist the way they appear, only for an ignorant consciousness. Therefore, the statement that these things are posited only for non-analytical worldly renown is not a call for non-analysis but rather a call for analysis, because the only way we can understand this fact is to analyze. Having analyzed, we find emptiness, after which, conjoined with the force of realizing emptiness but no longer engaging in ultimate analysis, we allow the bases of designation of these objects to reappear, at which point we realize their nominal existence.

Thus, it is possible to have the effect of analysis and still act in the world. For, what is refuted ultimately is refuted conventionally as well. Instead of paying attention solely to the emptiness of an object, we are now acting and paying attention to the object's being nominally existent. If this were not how to act with objects, we would have the feeling that things only exist for ignorance. If that were the case, how could analysis have even the slightest effect when you are dealing with objects? And in that case, meditation on emptiness would be useless with regard to stilling afflictive emotions. Analysis is the core of both meditative and post-meditative experience.

In the *Chapter Showing the Three Vows Sūtra* [Buddha] says that what is renowned in the world is not refuted by reasoning:

The world argues with me, I do not argue with the world. Whatever is accepted in the world as existent and non-existent, that I also accept in that way.

The world says, "This exists, that exists; this does not exist, that does not exist," — that is the extent to which Buddha accepts what the world accepts. Buddha does not at all accept the way in which the world feels or conceives these things to exist. Furthermore, the world thinks that if you take a shower, your body is clean; it is generally accepted that the washed body of a young and beautiful man or woman is clean. A yogi, however, holds that it is filthy, no matter how much it has been washed. Nāgārjuna himself makes the point in his *Precious Garland* that you are to see the body as dirty, asking whether we would consider a beautiful pot filled with excrement to be clean.[307] Thus, Buddha does not accept everything that the world says is so.

The world might argue with Buddha because he taught many special things beyond what the world says about the mode of existence of things. Nonetheless, he does not debate with what is certified by worldly, conventional valid cognition. A Buddha accepts that this grows from that, but has a radically different perspective on the mode of being of these things. Buddhas do not hold that objects are their own mode of being. The mode of subsistence of objects is an emptiness of inherent existence, the foundation of phenomena, totally at odds with ordinary assent to these seemingly concrete objects. Within realization of this, change can be known and the Buddha nature allowing transformation into compassionate appearance can be fulfilled.

20 Dependent-Arising

THE KING OF REASONINGS, THE REASON OF DEPENDENT-ARISING

This section has two parts: the actual explanation and how the other reasonings derive from this.

Actual Explanation of Dependent-Arising
The *Questions of Sāgaramati Sūtra*[308] says that inherent establishment is refuted through the reasoning of dependent-arising:

> Those which arise dependently
> Are free of inherent existence.

And the *Questions of Anavatapta, the King of Nāgas, Sūtra* says:

> Those which are produced from conditions
>   are not produced.
> They do not have an inherent nature of
>   production.
> Those which depend on conditions are said
>   to be empty.
> One who knows emptiness is aware.

The second line explains the meaning of the first line; no production means not having an inherent nature of production.

> In that, production from conditions is the reason. No production is the probandum. The meaning of not being produced is indicated by the second line. It is not that mere production is being eliminated; inherently established production is being eliminated.

The syllogism is, "Things are not inherently produced because of being produced from conditions."

We feel the opposite — that a thing's being produced is a sign of its inherent existence. Somebody painted this. The seed produced it. Production is right there — that is, production seems to be right there, findable from its own side. We feel that a house is being built right there, and we can point to its production. If, during a lull in building, someone says, "They are not working on the house today," we say, "You'd better believe they are working today. They are making so much noise I can hardly stand it."

> Moreoever, in the *Descent into Laṅkā Sūtra*, the Teacher [Buddha] himself clarifies his thought:
>
> > O Mahāmati, thinking of no *inherently existent* production, I said that all phenomena are not produced.
>
> [In the passage from the *Questions of Anavatapta Sūtra*,] through the relating of [the relative] "which" and [the correlative] "those", the subjects that are the substrata [of an absence of inherently existent production] are indicated. They are external things such as sprouts and internal things such as compositional activity.

Dependent upon a seed, a sprout is produced, and dependent upon ignorance of the nature of things, we initiate activities. The subjects being indicated to lack inherent existence here are such external and internal phenomena.

The third line means that just dependence and reliance on conditions is the meaning of [being] empty of inherent existence. This statement indicates that an emptiness of inherent existence is the meaning of dependent-arising. It does not indicate an emptiness that is the absence of the capacity to perform functions — that is, a negative of mere production.

How could emptiness and dependent-arising ever be considered to have the same import if emptiness were an absence of mere production! Mere production is analytically unfindable production, conventionally existent production. If emptiness were a refutation of that, then dependent-arising would have no meaning at all. How, then, could emptiness have the same import? Some who present the Middle Way School say that since there are not any dependent-arisings anyway, emptiness can have the same meaning as dependent-arising, but that is absurd.

Still, *how* can emptiness have the same import as dependent-arising? How could the emptiness of this table, which is permanent in the sense of not disintegrating moment by moment, be synonymous with a table, which is a dependently arisen impermanent phenomenon? Emptiness itself is a dependent-arising, but it is a permanent one. The table is an impermanent one. How could a permanent thing and an impermanent thing be synonymous? In brief, the answer is that for Proponents of the Middle Way School — that is, for those who have understood the view of the middle way — cognizing something's dependence on causes furthers their cognition that the thing is not inherently existent, and not only that, what is more difficult: cognizing that a thing is not inherently existent furthers their cognition of it as a dependent-arising.

Dependent-arising is the king of reasonings because it refutes both extremes — inherent existence and utter non-existence — simultaneously and explicitly. Take, for instance, the syllogism, "This tea is not inherently existent because of being a dependent-arising." When the thesis is understood, the extreme of inherent existence is eliminated; when you understand that it is a dependent-arising, the extreme of non-existence is avoided. Also, if you take dependent-arising itself, "dependent" eliminates the extreme of existence because it shows that the tea is not inherently existent. "Arising" eliminates the extreme of non-existence because it shows that the tea does exist.

> Seeing that just this teaching of this reasoning as refuting all extremes is an unsurpassed distinctive feature elevating his teacher, the Supramundane Victor, above all other teachers, Nāgārjuna's mind was captivated by this mode [of dependent-arising], whereupon the glorious protector, the Superior Nāgārjuna — in his *Fundamental Text Called "Wisdom"*, *Sixty Stanzas of Reasoning*, his Collection of Praises, and so forth — praised the Supramundane Victor from the viewpoint of just his speaking of dependent-arising.

For instance, at the beginning of his *Fundamental Text Called "Wisdom"*, also called the *Treatise on the Middle Way*, Nāgārjuna says:

I bow down to the perfect Buddha,
The best of propounders, who taught
That what dependently arises
Has no cessation, no production,
No annihilation, no permanence, no coming,
No going, no difference, no sameness,
Is free of the elaborations [of inherent
Existence and of duality] and is at peace.

> Also, our own excellent leader, the Foremost Great Being [Dzong-ka-ba] says:[309]

> Homage to the Conqueror who perceived

And gave instruction on dependent-arising.
Through perceiving and setting forth such
He has unsurpassed wisdom and is the
    unsurpassed teacher.

And so on. Praising Buddha in this way is pure
speech of praise induced by genuine faith induced
by the path of reasoning; therefore, these are not
artificial words or words of flattery.

As the Dalai Lama says in his *Key to the Middle Way*,[310]
dependent-arising is the slogan of the Buddha; "slogan"
was his own translation choice for *gtam* which usually is
translated as "discourse" or "talk". Without it, there is no
Buddha and no teaching of the Buddha. It is the heart,
core, stuff, motto, and cornerstone of the Buddha's
teaching.

The Sanskrit original of dependent-arising is *pra-
tītyasamutpādaḥ*.[311] Most earlier masters said that
prati is a distributive, [meaning] diversely, and that
i, [the verbal root meaning] going, is used [to mean]
departing and disintegrating.

Chandrakīrti takes *pratītya* to mean "having depended" by
identifying *ya* as indicating a continuative. Earlier scholars,
however, took *pratītya* to be a noun in a compound and said
that, when taken out of the compound, it is a genitive
plural, *pratītyānām*, "of these things which go and depart
diversely". They identified *ya* as forming a secondary derivative noun, not a continuative.

Through adding the affix *ya* to that [verbal root *i*],
itya is taken as a secondary derivative noun, which
comes to mean "that which goes". Hence, they say
that [*pratītyasamutpāda* means] the arising of what
possess going and disintegration diversely.

The term thereby refers to the composition and arising of
effects that disintegrate in each diverse moment and have

definite, diverse causes and conditions.

The "other masters" who interpret *pratītyasamutpāda* this way are identified by Bhāvaviveka's commentator, Avalokitavrata,[312] as other Proponents of the Middle Way School, which means persons other than Buddhapālita and Bhāvaviveka (and, by extension, Chandrakīrti). As Janggya will explain, Bhāvaviveka implies that the term *pratītyasamutpāda* should not be etymologized by breaking it down into its parts because, for him, it does not make sense that way. Chandrakīrti speculates that for Bhāvaviveka, it is like the term "wild sesame" (*dgon pa'i thig le, araṇ-yetilaka*)[313] which would be etymologized as "sesame found in the forest" but means anything that does not answer to expectations (just as wild sesame yields no oil). For example, if a meal is unsuitable, I could call it "wild sesame" without meaning that there is any sesame, wild or otherwise, on the plate. The meaning comes from conventional usage and does not accord with a literal rendering of the words. Similarly, according to Bhāvaviveka, *pratītyasamutpāda* gains its meaning through conventional usage. For Chandrakīrti, however, the etymology of *pratītyasamutpāda* "having depended, arising" accords with its meaning.

The other commentators interpret *prati* as a distributive, meaning "diversely", rather than as part of a continuative *pratītya* meaning "having depended" as Chandrakīrti takes it. "Diversely", in turn, refers to a multiplicity of effects relying on causes and conditions. Chandrakīrti objects to this interpretation of *prati* (1) because then *pratītyasamutpāda* could not refer to a specific instance of the arising of a single object since a specific one would not have the sense of multiple objects arising in dependence upon causes and conditions and (2) because *pratītya* is often used outside of a compound as a continuative, without any case ending at all, whereas a case ending would be required if it were a noun. As an example of such usage outside of a compound and without a case ending, Chandrakīrti gives "Having depended on an eye sense power and forms, an eye consciousness is produced" (*cakṣuḥ pratītya rūpāṇi ca utpadyate cak-ṣurvijñānaṃ*). That *pratītya* is used in this way outside of a compound as a continuative strongly suggests that it should be treated the same way in a compound and not be interpreted as a noun having an implicit case ending; Chandrakīrti's evidence is very good.

In that case, except for the general dependent-arising, which is the arising of effects from causes, when each particular case is specified such as in "A consciousness arises in dependence upon an eye [sense power]," [the etymology] is not suitable because within one thing there is no way to explain the term "diversely". Taking it as a secondary derivative noun is not feasible also because, in that case, it would be wrong [for the text] to read, "Having depended on an eye sense power and forms" (*cakṣuḥ pratītya rūpāṇi ca*) and would instead have to read on all occasions, "A consciousness which departs to an eye [sense power] and forms" (*cakṣuḥ pratītyaṃ vijñānaṃ rūpāṇi ca*) [and it is obvious to anyone who has seen the text that it is not written that way]. Since no case ending is to be seen [with *pratītya*],[314] it is suitable only to be a continuative with an indeclinable ending.

Because *pratītya* in *cakṣuḥ pratītya rūpāṇi ca utpadyate cakṣurvijñānaṃ* is obviously not in a compound and has no case ending, it has to be an indeclinable, a continuative.[315]

Also, the master Bhāvaviveka does not make individual explanations of the meanings of *prati*, and so forth. He explains it only as a term used to mean that "When this is, that arises," or "Due to having this condition, that arises," like [the term] wild sesame. For Chandrakīrti's *Clear Words* says:

Such is said [by Bhāvaviveka] having asserted *pratītyasamutpāda* to be a conventional term [not necessarily following its etymological meaning] like *araṇyetilaka*, etc.

Chandrakīrti *speculates*, based on Bhāvaviveka's lack of an explicit etymology, that for Bhāvaviveka *pratītyasamutpāda* is a term that gets its meaning through conventional usage. That also is not feasible because the master, the Superior Nāgārjuna spoke within dividing [the term] into its individual components, *pratītya (brten pa)* and *samutpāda ('byung ba)* [in his *Sixty Stanzas of Reasoning*]:[316]

That which is produced having met this and
that [collection of causes and conditions]
Is not inherently produced.
(*Tat tat prāpya yad utpannaṃ notpannaṃ tat svabhāvataḥ.*)[317]

Nāgārjuna is clearly using *prāpya*, a continuative meaning "having met" or "having relied", for *pratītya* and is clearly using *utpannaṃ* for *samutpāda*, *utpannaṃ* being the past participle without *sam*. It is obvious that Nāgārjuna is etymologizing *pratītyasamutpāda* by glossing its two parts, and thus Bhāvaviveka, his follower, would be wrong to avoid etymologizing the term by claiming that it gains its meaning only through conventional usage. Since *prāpya* is used as an alternative for *pratītya* and it is an indeclinable continuative, Nāgārjuna also gives clear evidence that he does not take *pratītya* to be a noun with a non-manifest case ending due to being in a compound. Since Bhāvaviveka is a follower of Nāgārjuna and Nāgārjuna is obviously etymologizing *pratītyasamutpāda*, Chandrakīrti's evidence for the unsuitability of Bhāvaviveka's not etymologizing *pratītyasamutpāda* is sound.

Chandrakīrti, thereby, has excellent backing for his argument. However, Nāgārjuna's etymology does not seem to support another part of Chandrakīrti's argument, namely, that the term *prati* of *pratītya* does not have a distributive meaning, in which case it would refer to this and that collection of causes and conditions. Chandrakīrti holds that in combination with *itya*, *pratītya* comes to mean only "having depended", but this seems to be contradicted by Nāgārjuna's using *tat tat* "this and that" as a seeming substitute for *prati*. Nāgārjuna seems to be glossing *prati* with *tat tat* and *itya* with *prāpya*, whereas Chandrakīrti's position is that Nāgārjuna is glossing *pratītya* with *prāpya*. As has already been explained, Chandrakīrti does not accept that *prati* has a distributive meaning because then it would apply only in general references since one effect has just one collection of causes and conditions. Perhaps, Chandrakīrti could say that with *tat tat* Nāgārjuna is giving an example, not part of the etymology.

Note that in "That which is produced having met this and that [collection of causes and conditions] is not inherently produced" (*tat tat prāpya yad utpannaṃ notpannaṃ tat svabhāvataḥ*), Nāgārjuna himself, by using the qualification *inherently* (*svabhāvataḥ*), specifies the production that dependent phenomena do not have as inherently existent production.

> Even if [Bhāvaviveka] wants to set forth [this position] as the meaning of the passage in Nāgārjuna's *Precious Garland*,[318] "When this[319] is, that arises, like long when there is short," he has to explain [*pratītya*] as having the meaning of "meeting" (*'phrad pa*, *prāpya/prāpti*). This is because[320] he has to assert just that long comes to be having met short and having depended on short, or in reliance upon short.

Jam-yang-shay-ba makes the point that the three phrasings "in dependence upon this, that arises," "meeting with this, that arises," and "in reliance upon this, that arises," are synonymous.[321] Chandrakīrti, based on Nāgārjuna's using "having met" (*prāpya*) in the passage cited above from his

Sixty Stanzas of Reasoning, emphasizes that "having met" is a suitable synonym for "having depended". Chandrakīrti does this because Bhāvaviveka criticized Buddhapālita for using the term. Although Bhāvaviveka does not explain the reasons behind his criticism, his commentator, Avalokitavrata, says that it is because only the simultaneous can meet and thus cause and effect cannot meet.[322] Because of Bhāvaviveka's criticism, Chandrakīrti repeatedly emphasizes the suitability of "having met" *(prāpya)* as a synonym for "having depended" *(pratītya).*

> Therefore, the honorable master Chandrakīrti's own system is: Because *prati* is used for "meeting" and *i* is used for "going", *pratītya* — which has the continuative affix *ya*[323] on that [*i* base] — through being modified by the modifier [*prati*], is used for "meeting", that is to say, "depending" or "relying". [The verbal root] *i* alone is generally used for "going", but when it is combined with *prati,*[324] it comes to mean "meeting" and so forth. That this is so is like, for example, the fact that the water of the Ganges is extremely sweet, but when it mixes with the ocean, it comes to have a salty taste. Moreover, in that way, Chandrakīrti's *Clear Words* says:

>> In that, *prati* has the meaning of meeting *('phrad pa, prāpti).* [The verbal root] *i* has the meaning of going. The term *pratītya,* a continuative, is used for "meeting" — that is, "relying" — because the root is completely modified by a modifier [i.e., the prefix *prati*]. It is explained:

>>> Through the force of a modifier
>>> The meaning of the verbal root is
>>>   completely changed.
>>> Just as, though the water of the
>>>   Ganges is sweet,

[It is completely changed] by the
water of the ocean.

In brief, *pratītyasamutpāda* means dependent-arising. If *pratītya* were not a continuative but a derivative noun, it would not mean dependent-arising but the arising of that which disintegrates. When you know that *pratītya* is a continuative, and not a derivative noun, you can understand the meaning of depending on causes, parts, and an imputing consciousness. Otherwise, you could not get that meaning; thus, it is important to understand how the term is formed.

The term *pāda*, which has *samut* preceding it, is used for "arising". It is also suitable to be explained as "existing" (*yod pa, sat*) and "established" (*grub pa, siddha*).

If the term "arising" in "dependent-arising" always had to mean arising or being produced from causes and conditions, then permanent things could not be dependent-arisings. However, by taking *samutpāda* as meaning "existing" or "established", *pratītyasamutpāda* comes to mean "existing in dependence" or "established in dependence" and thereby also includes permanent phenomena. In the Middle Way School, all phenomena — permanent and impermanent — are dependent-arisings. Even among impermanent phenomena, that an agent arises in dependence upon an action does not mean that an action produces an agent, with the action first and then the agent second as would be the case in actual production. Rather, an agent is established in dependence upon an action, is designated in dependence upon an action. An action also is designated in dependence upon an agent; the two are interdependent in a way such that one cannot arise before the other.

In this sense, going is a "cause" of a goer, not as a cause producing a goer, but as a necessary condition for designation of a goer. This broader type of "causation" is that which pertains to designation. We could not call this a table unless somebody made it; that is causation that precedes.

There is also "causation" at the same time, as in the conditions necessary for designation, but since Buddhists do not accept simultaneous causation, it is not actual causation.

Since the production of an effect depends upon causes, the effect is dependent on those causes. Causes do not depend on their effects for their production but are nevertheless dependent upon them in the sense that, for example, a cause of an apple, an apple seed, is designated relative to its effect, an apple. A cause of the designation of "apple seed" is an apple. Hence, an apple seed arises in dependence upon the apple that it will produce (or has the capacity to produce), but it is not produced by that apple. This makes causation and dependent-arising far more internal, related to thought.

> Therefore, in brief, our own system is this: The meaning of *pratītyasamutpāda* is the existence, establishment, or arising of things in dependence upon causes and conditions. Chandrakīrti's *Clear Words* says, "Hence, the meaning of *pratītyasamutpāda*[325] is the arising of things in reliance upon causes and conditions."

Notice the use of the word "things",[326] which usually means impermanent things. It is as if, in Chandrakīrti's system, there were no permanent phenomena at all because everything arises in designation. *In this sense,* everything is compounded, a product. However, there still are uncompounded phenomena, non-products, in the sense that there are phenomena that are not produced by causes and conditions in the usual sense.

> In that way, it is very important to know well the many different ways that [those great scholars, called] great chariots, etymologized *pratītyasamutpāda* because, in dependence upon their etymologies, there are many essential points of the different ways of generating ascertainment about the extent of the meaning of dependent-arising and

about the depth of penetration of suchness.

Dependence upon causes and conditions is narrower; dependence upon parts is as wide as everything in all universes; dependence upon an imputing consciousness, though just as wide in its scope of application, is more difficult to realize.

> Furthermore, since I wish to explain this extensively elsewhere, I will express [here] just a little about the assertions of the glorious Chandrakīrti. The meaning of dependent-arising is explained in that way as meeting, relying, and depending. The reason for this is as follows. In general, meet, rely, and depend are said even to be synonymous. However, if we separate them in order to facilitate understanding, "meeting" as a reason [for the absence of inherent existence of things] bears within it the sense of dependent-arising as the production of things from their own causes. This is [an assertion held in] common also with lower tenet systems. Moreover, since [the Middle Way School and the lower tenet systems] are similar in their assertions of the meaning of dependent-arising just to that point, this is said to be "common". However, [Proponents of the Middle Way School] do not [assert] the truly existent dependent-arising that those [of the lower systems] assert; also, [in lower tenet systems] they do not assert that the absence of true existence is what is proved [by dependent-arising].

The lower systems say that, to the contrary, dependent-arising is a reason proving true existence. When a Proponent of the Middle Way School says, "The subject, I, is not truly existent because of being a dependent-arising," the lower systems answer that there is contradictory entailment. For them, whatever is a dependent-arising must be truly existent.

What meet? The effect and the cause do not meet because

they do not exist simultaneously. However, the cause's approaching cessation and the effect's approaching production exist at the same time and, therefore, can meet. When the cause is about to cease, the cause exists, but when the effect is about to be produced, the effect does not exist; still, the two actions of approaching cessation and approaching production exist at the same time. Conventionally, such is possible, but when you apply ultimate analysis, if something is approaching production it must be there; otherwise, what is approaching? Anne showed me a seed this morning and said, "I'm growing a magnolia tree to take down to Virginia," and she held it out in her hands. Now what is growing there? If there is an action of growing there, and a magnolia tree is doing it, a magnolia tree must be present.

> "Meeting" refers to the meeting of the actions of production of the effect and cessation of the cause; it is not that cause and effect meet.
> "Relying" indicates a reason [for the absence of inherent existence of phenomena] that is the attainment by compounded and uncompounded phenomena of their own entities in reliance upon their own parts.

I find this reasoning astounding. Certainly, things appear as if they have their own entity; they do not appear to me as if they are dependent on their parts. Now if you think about it, things, of course, have to depend on their parts, but we are presented with a picture that we then freeze as the whole reality. It is as if there is a curtain. Why would seeing the outside of the body almost convince us that there are no insides to the body? Then, when a surgeon drills a hole in someone's skull and we look inside, we are flabbergasted. We might vomit. We might start shaking. Our perception is not only a non-seeing of the inside, but also it prevents any thinking that there *is* an inside. It is incredible. Although the appearance of inherent existence entails this, there is nothing about appearance in itself that requires it to be this way. This is why it can be cleansed. I used to think that this is all that we could see and that therefore we are stuck with such perceptions, but the Consequentialist claim is that *we* are somehow making up this mistake.

Kensur Lekden, the late abbot of the Tantric College of Lower Hla-sa, used to say that the obstructions to omniscience are like the mind's hitting a barrier due to seeing one thing; the perception of this wall blocks seeing what is beyond it. Our perceptions, therefore, are such that we are continually locked into something that is superficial. We are forced into this by how things appear to us and are practically prevented from even surmising that there is anything beyond what we are perceiving. We have to reflect intentionally on even the fact that we have guts inside our skin. We have to remind ourselves constantly, as if we were under a strong spell.

When dependent-arising is taken as an object's being established or existent in reliance upon its parts, it dramatically shows the absence of inherent existence — that objects do not exist in the concrete, solid manner that they seem to possess. In order to include all phenomena, and not just the impermanent, *samutpāda* here is said to mean not just "arising" but "establishment".

> This is in terms of explaining *samutpāda* as [meaning] "established".[327] [Here, the meaning of dependent-arising] has a wider application than the former [because it applies to all phenomena, both the permanent and impermanent]. The mere meaning that is explicitly indicated [in "establishment-in-reliance"] is in common with other Proponents of the Middle Way School.

Why is only the *explicit* meaning shared between the Autonomists and the Consequentialists? The Autonomists do not hold that establishment-in-reliance, by extension, means that things are not the mere collection of their parts.

"Dependence" indicates a reason [for the absence
of inherent existence of things] that is the dependent designation of all phenomena — their being
established as mere designations in dependence
upon their own bases of designation.

Usually, this third one is explained as establishment as mere
designations (or imputations) in dependence upon the *conceptual consciousnesses that designate them* rather than "in
dependence upon their own bases of designation". The
second one, then, is described as dependence, reliance, on
parts *or* bases of designation. The parts are the basis of
imputation, but you can pay attention to the parts merely as
parts or as the basis of imputation. "Basis of imputation"
(or "basis of designation") brings to mind the process of the
imputation of names, whereas just talking about the parts as
parts does not necessarily do that. Still, for a Consequentialist, dependence on causes, dependence on parts, dependence on basis of imputation, and dependence on imputing
consciousness all draw in the topic of the process of designation. This third interpretation of dependent-arising as "the
dependent designation of all phenomena" is unique to the
Consequence School.

This is a feature of only this supreme system; it is
not common to Autonomists and below.

Although the third interpretation of dependent-arising is
distinctive to the Consequentialists, this does not mean that
you cannot take the second, for example, and find in it the
Consequentialists' distinctive meaning, the third interpretation. Although the Consequentialists use all three and see
all three as deep, Jang-gya is speaking within the context of
differentiating three levels of meaning of increasing profundity.

Accordingly, if you take the meaning of arising in
the phrase "arising of things" from that passage in
Chandrakīrti's *Clear Words* to be mere production,

it then indicates the first reason, and if you take it as establishment or existence, then it also indicates the two latter reasons. If you take "causes and conditions" as merely the seed that is the substantial cause of a sprout and the water, manure, and so forth that are its contributing conditions, then it indicates the former reason. If you take "causes and conditions" to mean the cause for something's achieving its own entity — its basis of imputation or parts — then it indicates the middle reason.

Notice that here he includes basis of imputation in the second reason instead of the third.

If you take "causes and conditions" to be the respective conceptual consciousnesses that impute phenomena, then it indicates the last reason.

Thus, "causes and conditions" has a threefold meaning — first, as the producers of an object, then as the parts that are the bases of designation of an object, and then as the conceptual consciousness that designates an object. If you understand the arising of an object in dependence upon its parts, try viewing those parts as the basis of imputation of the object, and then shift your attention to the imputing awareness. Through this route, the full force of things' dependence on the mind will come home. The basis of imputation is not the phenomenon imputed; thus, a conceptual consciousness is needed to impute the imputed phenomenon in dependence upon that basis of imputation. If such were not needed, it could exist independently.

Therefore, the "causes and conditions" in Chandrakīrti's phrase "in reliance upon causes and conditions" should not be taken as only the causes and conditions of compounded phenomena such as seeds, water, manure, and so forth. That it must also refer to the imputing conceptual consciousness is the special thought of the glorious Chandrakīrti

and the Foremost Great Being [Dzong-ka-ba].
Nevertheless, most of those discriminating persons
whose heads are adorned with paṇḍita hats with
very sharp points have still not drawn out[328] [this
topic]. There also is a mode of explanation — that
others have not drawn out[329] — in which meeting,
relying, and depending [are taken as indicating]
only the third reason from the viewpoint of treating
them as synonyms. I will not elaborate on this here.

Also, regarding those, the Foremost Great Being
[Dzong-ka-ba] says in his *Small Exposition of the
Stages of the Path To Enlightenment:*

> Therefore, external things, such as sprouts,
> and internal things, such as compositional
> activity, arise in dependence upon, respec-
> tively, seeds, etc., and ignorance, etc.

This indicates the first reason. Also, that same work
says:

> [Whatever is established by way of its own
> entityness] must be inherently established,
> that is, be able to set itself up under its own
> power, whereby it is contradictory for it to
> rely on causes and conditions.

This indicates the middle reason.

As Jam-yang-shay-ba's annotator, the Mongolian scholar
Nga-wang-bel-den, says,[330] Jang-gya's citation here is a bit
of a mystery. For, the middle reason is dependence on parts
and basis of imputation, and the only way that this particular citation could indicate the second reason would be if
"causes and conditions" could mean parts and basis of
imputation, but since it follows the previous quote, where
the meaning is restricted to usual causation in which one
thing produces another, this seems unlikely. Perhaps, Jang-
gya is taking "be able to set itself up under its own power"

as the opposite of having a basis of imputation, which he, just above, described as "the cause for something's achieving its own entity". Still, it is hard to bend Dzong-ka-ba's words to mean this.

Also, that work says:

> Through this, you should understand that persons, pots, and so forth are without inhe-rent establishment because of being im-puted in dependence on their own collec-tions [of parts].

This indicates the third reason.

Because this statement is concerned with designation in dependence upon a basis of imputation, it indicates the third reason according to Jang-gya's first explanation but the middle reason according to his second explanation.

> However, [Dzong-ka-ba,] collecting them all into the common and the uncommon, says in that same work, "Those are the *two* presentations of the reasoning of dependent-arising."

From among the three reasons, the first is in common with the Autonomy School and below, and the second is in common with only the Autonomy School; thus, the first two can be considered reasons used in common with the lower schools, whereas the third is uncommon to the Con-sequence School. In this sense, the three interpretations are included in two groups.

Still, the passages, when put together, do not seem to indicate clearly all three reasons. Let us cite the entire quotation from Dzong-ka-ba in one unit:[331]

Therefore, external things, such as sprouts, and internal things, such as compositional activity, arise in dependence respectively on seeds, etc., and ignorance, etc. If that is so, that those [sprouts, compositional activity, and so forth] are established by way of their own nature is not feasible because whatever is established by way of its own entityness must be inherently established, that is, be able to set itself up under its own power, whereby it is contradictory for it to rely on causes and conditions. Āryadeva's *Four Hundred* says:

> That which has a dependent arising
> Is not under its own power.
> All these are not under their own power;
> Therefore, self [inherent existence] does not exist.

Through this you should understand that persons, pots, and so forth are without inherent establishment because of being imputed in dependence on their own collections [of parts]. Those are the two presentations of the reasoning of dependent-arising.

Perhaps we could say that once something has a self-established entity, it will not depend on its parts. In this case, "causes and conditions" will mean "parts". And for the third one, once it is imputed in dependence on its parts, there will have to be an imputing consciousness. It seems to me that only with such creative, but probably unwarranted, maneuvering can the passage yield the three reasons. As Nga-wang-bel-den says:[332]

That the earlier two sets of three scriptural passages [i.e., the three just given and three that Jang-gya is about to cite] respectively indicate those three [interpretations of dependent-arising] and, in particular, that the middle passage from the *Small Exposition of the Stages of the Path* indicates the middle reasoning does not appear to my obscured, dull mind; hence, it would be good if unbiased [scholars] analyzed these further.

Jang-gya proceeds to cite three more problematic passages, these being the other set to which Nga-wang-bel-den refers.

Not only that, but also Dzong-ka-ba's *Great Explanation of (Chandrakīrti's) "Supplement to (Nāgārjuna's) 'Treatise on the Middle Way'* " says:

> The Supramundane Victor said, "The essence of phenomena is this: When this is, that arises; because this is produced, that is produced. Through the condition of ignorance, there are compositional activities," and so forth. And Nāgārjuna's *Precious Garland* says:[333]

> > When this is, that arises,
> > Like short when there is long.
> > When this is produced, that is
> > produced,
> > Like light from the arising of a
> > flame.

And Nāgārjuna's *Fundamental Text Called "Wisdom"* also says:[334]

> A doer arises in dependence on a
> doing
> And a doing arises in dependence
> upon just that doer.
> Except for that, we do not see
> Another cause for their
> establishment.

Even each of these three passages which [Dzong-ka-ba] cites in series are suitable to indicate all three presentations [of the meaning of dependent-arising], but in terms of what they mainly indicate and in terms of sequence, they set forth the three different presentations of the reasoning [of dependent-arising].

The first citation indicates the first reason, the production of things from their own causes. The second is supposed to indicate the second reason, designation in dependence upon parts or basis of designation: although long and short are not each other's basis of designation in the sense of being the collection of parts in dependence upon which the other is designated, each is that in relation to which the other is designated. The third citation indicates the establishment of phenomena in dependence upon designation.

If a doer is to do something, it means that he or she already has an action of doing by which the person is a doer. A typist is called a typist because of typing. Does a typist have two typings — the typing by which he or she is a typist as well as the activity of typing to be performed? Today the typist of *Meditation on Emptiness* told me that she wants double pay because she is a typist and she also types. I had to agree, provided she was an inherently existent typist.

Who begins to read? Who begins to talk? Does a talker begin to talk? It is easy to see that the world can be divided into talkers and non-talkers. A listener is a non-talker. Who begins to talk? If a talker is already talking, how can he or she begin to talk? But a non-talker, by definition, does not talk.

You may feel, "Well, that is all right, but there is something said; therefore, there must be a talker." Do you begin to talk that which you have already talked? Or do you talk the yet-to-be-talked? Or do you talk the being-talked? If you talk the already talked, that is foolish. I do not mean that saying something again is foolish. The talked is something whose action has ceased; it hardly makes sense to begin it. Also, it could not be that the being-talked is begun to be talked, because if it is being talked, what is the point of beginning to talk it? And how could you begin to talk the yet-to-be-talked?

Still, you feel that talk must concretely exist because you hear something. But what do you hear presently? That which is being heard? You are the hearer of this. The guy in the next room does not hear it. And what you hear is not what is being said downstairs. There has to be one action of hearing to make this the being-heard and one to make you the hearer. Thus, there are two hearings. But where are the two hearers for these two hearings? Maybe one ear goes with the action of the being-heard and one ear goes with the agent! These are all intertwined.

Again, when we look at something, it is almost as if there is a spread out looking that extends from our eyes to the object seen. The part that you possess to make you the seer is not the part that the wall possesses to make it the seen. Then, is the seeing that makes the wall the seen performed by you? If you do not possess the part of the seeing that is over there, can you say that you are performing it? It should be *your* seeing.

The part of the entity that makes the seen is not the part that makes the seer. The seeing that makes that area the seen is not performed by that seer. There is a seeing that makes that the seen. When you get right down to it, in your own mind, there is such a seeing. That part of the big seeing that makes that area over there the seen is not the part that makes me the seer. You get half an egg. Each guy eats half and cannot eat the half that the other guy eats. Whatever you do, it comes down to two. You cannot avoid it.

You might feel that first the seeing is here with you, and then it goes over there to the object. Whoosh, like waves. But, if at the first moment, when you are the seer of that object, the seeing is here with you and not with the object, then at the first moment the object does not have the seeing. So you have a seer without a seen. You would be seeing what is yet to be seen because it has not received the seeing yet. And then again, if at the same instant when the stream of seeing starts from here, the stream of being seen starts from there, seer and seen would be independent, and the seeing by which the object is said to be seen would not be performed by the seer.

To return to hearing, if there is hearing, there has to be a beginning of hearing. If you can eliminate a beginning of hearing, you can eliminate hearing. You might think that it would then follow that there is no hearing of the doctrine Buddha taught, and, indeed, if inherently existent hearing were required, *then* there cannot be any doctrine to be heard. This consequence is flung back at the lower systems. Something that inherently exists could not affect you because of existing in and of itself. Thus, although there is no inherently existent hearing, nominally existent hearing unfindable by such analysis exists.

My typist said to me, "You didn't tell me to do those corrections," and I said, "I told you!" I possess that past talking. I talked it. I definitely feel that there is a certain talking that I have. And what did I say? "If you run out of things to do, do the material on the shelf." That is what I said. But my typist feels that there is definitely a Jeffrey who does not possess that talking. From one tiny action the whole rotten flower of cyclic existence appears.

This type of analysis has to be done frequently because it is the one thing to get us out of manifold problems. Otherwise, we will be convinced that things exist as they appear. Unless this becomes an instrument that pierces down inside our mind, we will never really believe it. As soon as there is one thing we feel is findable, we will revert to confirming that everything is inherently existent. If, on the other hand, the absence of inherent existence seems immediately obvious to you, I doubt that you have understood it. If it were so obvious, we would have given up these ideas and cyclic existence a long time ago.

When, in the passage Jang-gya cited, Nāgārjuna says, "We do not see another cause for their establishment," this means any cause for their designation. We do not see any cause for their existence "except for the arising of action in dependence on an agent". This means that when you have analyzed and cannot find anything, then, afterwards, you understand what nominal existence is. This shows that Nāgārjuna accepts what the world accepts. The world says that there are agents and actions. That he says *"Except for that,* we do not see another cause for their establishment," means there is a cause for their establishment. It is that action depends on agent and agent depends on action. This shows that Nāgārjuna accepted nominally existent, interdependent, non-concrete agent and action.

This [threefold interpretation of dependent-arising] is also the assertion of the glorious Chandrakīrti. Chandrakīrti's *Commentary on (Āryadeva's) "Four Hundred"* says:[335]

> Here, that which has its own intrinsic existence, has inherent existence, has its own power, or has no dependence on others would be self-established; therefore, it would not have a dependent arising. However, all compounded things are dependent-arisings. In that way, things that have dependent arising are not self-powered because they are produced in dependence upon causes and conditions. All these [phenomena] are not self-powered; therefore, no things have self, inherent existence.

In the phrase "dependence on others", the "others" are causes, parts, bases of imputation, and imputing consciousnesses. We do not see things within a full understanding of dependent-arising. This is why we react the way we do; this is why we have desire and hatred. There would be no afflictive desire and no hatred if we saw dependent-arising and all of its implications. It is not just that the conception of inherent existence makes desire and hatred stronger; rather, it is their whole foundation.

All things, even permanent phenomena, are compounded phenomena in this special sense because everything has a basis of designation and a designating consciousness that are considered to be its "causes and conditions".

If you know in detail [Dzong-ka-ba's] mode of interpretation of the meaning of this citation [as set

forth] in his *Great Exposition of Special Insight,* you
will understand [how the passage indicates the
threefold interpretation of dependent-arising].

In dependence on certain such special points, the
definitive great scholar Nor-sang-gya-tso[336] is renowned to have said, "Whatever is an established
base [i.e., whatever exists] is a compounded phenomenon." About this, many skilled and unskilled
people have said, "It [absurdly] follows that the
subject, uncompounded space, is a compounded
phenomenon because it is an established base,"[337]
etc. These neophytes at elementary logic and epistemology demonstrate many commonly proclaimed
points of damage [to such a position] and scornfully
laugh. However, how could this great scholar and
adept, who penetrated all of sūtra and tantra, not
know this little bit of reasoning? Though he said
such within hoping that, in dependence on his
words, [people would] have an effective way of
forming understanding of the meaning of dependent-arising, it appears that they have become examples of: "For persons pained by karma, even
medicine given becomes poison."

Speaking from the viewpoint that all phenomena have
"causes and conditions" in the sense of being designated in
dependence upon bases of designation and of being established in dependence upon an imputing consciousness,
Nor-sang-gya-tso made the profound statement that all phenomena are compounded. Jang-gya scolds those who, not
understanding his perspective, criticized him superficially
and scornfully by pointing out that if everything were compounded, then even uncompounded space would have to be
compounded. Nor-sang-gya-tso's point is that even uncompounded space is compounded *in this special sense* of being
designated in dependence upon a basis of designation and
of being established in dependence upon an imputing consciousness.

The above explanation of the meaning of the reasoning of dependent-arising is the unsurpassed thought of Chandrakīrti's etymological explanation of *pratītyasamutpāda*.

If you do not understand his etymology of dependent-arising, you cannot derive these three meanings. When you take *prati* as *prāpti* and *prati* + *i* (pratītya), as an indeclinable continuative meaning "having depended", like *prāpya*, and when you take *samutpāda* as meaning not just arising but also existing and established, then you can.

This is also indeed the final thought of the Foremost Great Being [Dzong-ka-ba], but since it appears that others have not explained it clearly, I have explained it a little.

21 The Centrality of Dependent-Arising

Now, I will say a little about the way that the two extremes are cleared away by this reasoning [of dependent-arising]. The main places for going wrong with respect to realizing the pure view here [according to the Consequentialist system] are of two types. One is the view of permanence, or the view of superimposition, that has a process of apprehension conceiving true existence, i.e., the conception that phenomena truly exist. The second is the view of annihilation, or deprecation, when the measure of the object of negation is not apprehended and, instead, is taken too far, whereby one is not able to induce ascertainment with respect to all the causes and effects of purification[338] and thorough affliction.

Here, with respect to the correct view, an extreme must be something non-existent. A conception of an extreme, that is to say, a consciousness holding an extreme, must exist, but the extreme that it holds must be non-existent. The extremes of behavior — indulgence and self-mortifying asceticism — exist, as do the extremes of meditation — excitement and laxity; however, with respect to the view, Buddhists are not steering a course between two existent things such as eating too much and eating too little, or health and disease. The two extremes are totally non-existent versions of the status of phenomena. Holding either of them is like falling into a chasm because such misapprehension induces suffering; this is why they are called extremes. The safe ground in the middle is where the actual fact is, where you will not hurt yourself; it is not a mixture of the two extremes.

Even in terms of behavior, the middle is a not a mixture of a little indulgence and a little mortifying asceticism. Similarly, the middle in meditation is not a mixture of a little excitement and a little laxity, but a state entirely devoid of those two.

In terms of the view of the status of phenomena, people usually either do not take the object of negation far enough or take it too far. In the first case, instead of taking their refutation through to refuting inherent existence as it is innately conceived, they refute only something coarser, still maintaining the superimposition of inherent existence. In the second case, they take the refutation too far, refuting the phenomena themselves, not allowing for the functionality of cause and effect, etc., thereby falling to an extreme of nihilism, a deprecation of what actually exists. Both cases are compared to falling into a chasm that brings suffering on oneself in that, with a view of superimposition, it is impossible to realize the correct status of phenomena and free oneself from cyclic existence and, with a view of deprecation, conviction in the cause and effect of karma is lost, resulting in tying the knot of cyclic existence even tighter.

> Both of these [extremes] can be refuted without residue in dependence on just this reasoning of dependent-arising. Through ascertaining the reason, one avoids the extreme of nihilism and finds ascertainment with regard to the dependent-arising of cause and effect, and through ascertaining the probandum, one avoids the extreme of permanence and

gains ascertainment with regard to absence of inherent existence.

In the syllogism, "The subject, I, am not inherently existent because of being a dependent-arising," ascertaining the reason means to understand that I am a dependent-arising. By understanding the dependent-arising of causes and effects, the extreme of nihilism, utter non-existence, is avoided. Ascertaining the probandum means to understand that I am not inherently existent. By understanding the absence of inherent existence, the extreme of superimposition or reification is avoided. Hence, through the one reasoning of dependent-arising, both extremes of nihilism and superimposition are avoided.

> With respect to gaining such ascertainment, that which has very strong force is just the reasoning of dependent imputation. Moreover, this is the incomparable lion's roar of the good explanations of the Foremost Lama [Dzong-ka-ba].

The syllogism is: The subject, I, am not inherently existent because of being *dependently imputed*. There is imputation in dependence on parts, in dependence upon basis of imputation, and in dependence upon an imputing consciousness. This third version of the meaning of dependent-arising is particularly powerful.

> Also, both extremes are avoided even through ascertainment of the reason and the thesis individually. Furthermore, in general, the extreme of existence is avoided through appearance, and the extreme of non-existence is avoided through emptiness. These are said to be distinguishing features[339] of the Middle Way Consequence School. In dependence upon secret essentials of the word of this Foremost One [Dzong-ka-ba], you should know that there is a distinctive way that these become distinguishing features of the Middle Way Consequence School that is not just what is explicitly

indicated. For, otherwise, even in each of the four schools of tenets, there are explanations that both the extreme of existence and the extreme of non-existence are avoided through appearance and that both extremes are also avoided through emptiness.

Within the reason — dependent-arising — itself, understanding that a phenomenon is dependent avoids the extreme of superimposition because it is being realized that the phenomenon does not exist in and of itself; understanding that it arises avoids the extreme of nihilism. Realization of the probandum, that a particular phenomenon is without inherent existence, avoids the extreme of reification because the very opposite of inherent existence is being understood, but also it can help avoid the extreme of deprecation because you have understood a strict delimiting of what is refuted — just inherent existence and not existence in general.

The more usual way is for ascertainment of appearance to keep one from an extreme of nihilism, deprecation, and for ascertainment of emptiness to keep one from an extreme of superimposition, reification. However, here through even ascertaining an appearance, the extreme of inherent existence can be avoided, and through ascertaining emptiness, the extreme of deprecation can be avoided.

The elimination of the extreme of existence by appearance and the elimination of the extreme of non-existence by emptiness seems unusual, but Jang-gya is saying that this style of avoiding the two extremes should work in any system. Thus, he is indicating that considerable reflection is needed to determine how this is a distinguishing feature of the Consequence School.

In general, there is the way that the two extremes are avoided with respect to things because they are dependent-arisings. In particular, there are ways that the two extremes are avoided, in dependence on reasoning, for the awareness of a person at the time of hearing and thinking about the texts of the Middle Way School, as well as ways that the two extremes are avoided for one's awareness when realization that arises from meditation has been generated — on the two levels of an ordinary being and a Superior. Furthermore, even among Superiors, due to the gradual increase of the force of mind of those on higher levels, there are many differences of subtlety in how, for one's mind, the two extremes are avoided as this becomes more[340] profound than on lower levels. For, Shāntideva says:[341]

> Even among yogis, at each level the higher
> Damage [the lower] through features of
>   their intelligence.

There are differences in understanding as you move from hearing to thinking to meditating and from ordinary being to Superior,·and then within that, as you advance higher and higher. Therefore, the Sa-gya scholar Dak-tsang[342] divides the teaching, and thus the learning, into three periods: (1) the non-analytical phase when one works on cause and effect and so forth, (2) the phase of slight analysis when one analyzes emptiness, and (3) the extremely analytical phase when one goes beyond empty and non-empty.

Jang-gya,[343] however, says that Dak-tsang has no Indian sources for this arrangement. For, the view Dak-tsang sets up in the first stage is destroyed in the second, and the one he sets up in the second is destroyed in the third. According to Jang-gya, Dak-tsang needs no opponent; he refutes himself. Still, Dak-tsang was a great scholar-yogi who, as even the Ge-luk-ba scholar Kensur Lekden reported, wrote a highly respected work on the Kālachakra system. Dak-tsang wants to prepare people for the dramatic experience of direct cognition of reality that is very different from how emptiness appears when one analyzes. When the mind ripens, a practitioner has something entirely different — a new phase.

"View" is very personal. Our view of emptiness should be changing as we study different systems. In a more abstract way, the view of emptiness never changes, but a particular person's view of emptiness changes right through to the end.

> Therefore, all the presentations of the two truths of the Middle Way Consequence School are taken from within the sphere of this reasoning of dependent-arising, and there are also many important reasons regarding many uncommon features at the time of path and fruit. Furthermore, these can be known well by persons who have complete understanding (1) that identifies the factor of emptiness by reason of having ascertained[344] the factor of appearance and (2) that induces ascertainment with respect to the factor of appearance through having taken the factor of emptiness as the reason. However, it is not possible that all these could be complete in the mode of initial dawning [of rough ideas to someone] who has not found well an understanding of the view. Moreover, these are seen to depend upon knowing well the meaning of how all presentations of cyclic existence and nirvana are only imputedly existent and, within that, knowing well what is eliminated and what is included within the term "mere nominality, only imputed existence".

Jang-gya will explain these points briefly in the next section.

Inspired because he has mentioned many profound points about the central teaching of dependent-arising, Jang-gya now offers a short poem before considering how all the reasonings proving emptiness derive from the reasoning of dependent-arising.

> Alas, I wonder whether this — endowed
>   with an array of ambrosia-lights
> Of Lo-sang-drak-ba's good explanations

> Which has come to the peak of the eastern
>   mountain of not low merit
> For the sake of generating manifest joy — is
>   glorious only for my own mind.

Jang-gya's presentation is endowed with the magnificence
of the good explanations provided by Dzong-ka-ba, whose
other name is Lo-sang-drak-ba. He is wondering whether
anyone will appreciate it.

> The form of a rainbow of the subtle body of
>   a hundred texts' good meanings,
> Written with the pen[345] of pure reasoning
> Through being reflected in the mirror of my
>   mind,
> Bestows joy through thousands of visions
>   and transformations.

If the light of this reasoning, reflected in the mirror of
Jang-gya's mind, can get to our minds, indeed it will bring
about thousands of changes in our attitudes, understanding, how we perceive ourselves, relate to others, and so
forth.

> That sage who, dwelling in the forest of
>   Nāgārjuna's ten million procedures,
> Is skilled at summoning the beautiful
>   woman of emptiness and
>   dependent-arising
> Through the messenger of the meditative
>   stabilization of stainless reasoning
> Is called a Proponent of the Middle Way
>   School.
>
> Those who have abandoned afar the bliss of
>   setting the mind in reality
> And who proceed crookedly with the pace
>   of explanation and debate of generalities
>   of words
> Speak from their mouths about

dependent-arising a hundred times
But such is empty of meaning like a butter
   lamp in a picture.[346]

If those who randomly study limited texts
   and, though lacking the force of mind
To discriminate what requires
   interpretation and what is definitive,
Nonetheless take up the burden of making
   "is" and "is not" all equal
Did not say anything, how could it not be
   nice!

Even though I have not experienced the
   supreme taste of realization arising from
   meditation,
Which is the fruit of laboring at the stainless
   texts,
How marvelous it is that the Foremost
   Father Lo-sang has caused to be born in
   me
The lot of propounding dependent-arising
   just as it is.

Those are stanzas between sections.

*How the Other Reasonings Derive from
Dependent-Arising*
The essentials of all the reasonings that prove selflessness and are cases of non-observation of something inextricably related [with inherent existence]
meet back to[347] just this reasoning of dependent-
arising. This is (1) because the main purpose of all
those reasonings is just to generate in the [mental]
continuum the view of the middle way upon simultaneously clearing away the two extremes, and just
this reasoning of dependent-arising explicitly
accomplishes this and (2) because those reasonings
also meet back to just this mode [of dependent-
arising] when followed out.

Inherent existence necessitates findability in at least one of the seven ways. Being inextricably related with such findability, if none of these seven is possible, inherent existence is impossible. The non-observation of these which are necessarily related with inherent existence, therefore, can serve as a means of proving, or as a sign of, the absence of inherent existence.

For example, whatever is a phenomenon is necessarily permanent or impermanent, and thus if something such as a cloak made of turtle hairs is neither permanent nor impermanent, then it is not a phenomenon and does not exist. Similarly, the inherently existent must be findable upon analysis in the seven ways, and something that is not findable in any of the seven ways does not inherently exist.

This non-finding of an object in any of the seven ways is a *non-observation* that serves as a sign of no inherent existence. The other way to prove emptiness is to *observe something contradictory* to inherent existence, such as dependent-arising. The observation that a house is a dependent-arising is sufficient to prove that it lacks inherent existence since inherent existence is impossible within dependent-arising. Here, Jang-gya is saying that all reasons that are non-observations of a related object meet back to, or derive from, the reasoning of dependent-arising, which is an observation of a contradictory object.

> As was established earlier, the main reasonings that this system uses for settling the two selflessnesses must be taken to be the two, the refutation of production from the four extremes and the sevenfold reasoning. The way that their essentials meet back to dependent-arising is set forth clearly in Chandrakīrti's *Supplement to (Nāgārjuna's) "Treatise on the Middle Way"* because (1) in that text [Chandrakīrti] clearly speaks of how the reasoning of the refutation of production from the four extremes meets back to the reasoning of dependent-arising:[348]

> Because things are not produced
> causelessly,
> Or from Īshvara and so forth as causes,
> Or from self, from other, or both,
> They are dependently produced.

And (2) in that same text [Chandrakīrti] clearly speaks of how the sevenfold reasoning meets back to dependent-arising:[349]

> That [chariot] is not established as [its own]
> suchness
> Or in the world in the seven ways,
> But without analysis, here in the world,
> Is imputed in dependence on its parts.

Moreover, when, having sought for the object imputed in the imputation of, for instance, the convention, "A sprout is growing," you find ascertainment that [a sprout] is not produced from self, from other, from both, or causelessly, this — through its own force — induces ascertainment that the growing of the sprout, etc., is just an imputation, and also when you find ascertainment that the convention "growing" [or "production"] is just an imputation, this — through its own force — induces ascertainment with respect to non-findability when the object imputed in the imputation of the convention of growing is sought. This way [in which understanding the one helps in understanding the other] is the way that the essentials of the reasoning refuting production from the four extremes meet back to dependent-arising. Dzong-ka-ba's *Essence of the Good Explanations* says:[350]

> Through [the reasoning that] external
> things, such as sprouts, and internal things,
> such as compositional activity, arise in de-
> pendence upon causes and conditions —

such as a seed and ignorance — their production and so forth are empty of an inherent nature in the sense of being established by way of their own character and are not produced from self, other, both, or causelessly. Since [Chandrakīrti] refutes [the four extreme types of production] in this way, [the object of negation] is refuted in a manner that meets back to just the reasoning of dependent-arising, the king of reasonings cutting all the nets of bad views.

This mainly is the reasoning of [things] being dependently produced, but when [considered] finely, it must also meet back to the reasoning that things are dependently imputed. This latter is more difficult to understand than the former.

Usually, when people see a dependent-arising, they immediately think that it must inherently exist. They feel that it is not like a snake imputed to a rope and has to be findable. Why? Because it was produced from a cause. "I didn't make this up!"

For instance, when we say, "Your child is growing up fast," or "The corn is growing," or "The flowers are growing," if we are not satisfied with these as mere nominalities and search to see if something is there in itself, something that you can point at, then we are looking for the object imputed in the imputation of those expressions. The world says that we should accept that these are findable phenomena without challenge; people will get angry if we poke around too much. They claim that when we say, "The corn is growing," we do not in any way intend to enter into such analysis. Of course, that is just the point: we accept the appearance of concrete objects non-analytically.

But are we being tied to something destructive by this lack of analysis? Does the lack of analysis bind us to something false? We have to notice our feelings of inherent existence when someone says, "The corn didn't grow much last week," and we say, "It grew a lot last week," or, when there is no rain and we say, "I'm so sorry that the corn didn't grow." We do not analyze these things, and usually it is upsetting to do so. Does it not go against the warp and woof of reality to analyze this way? However, opposing what we feel to be reality is not a sure sign of inappropriateness, for even calming the mind goes against our usual sense of the real. The mind is used to running everywhere; we are like drops being thrown around on top of the ocean with no idea that we are water. Yet it is said that the nature of the mind is to be at rest and concentrated.

The world does not think about whether an object is produced in these ways. This is why it is upsetting when such analysis is put forward. "What do you mean? It just grows!" We very much dislike limiting the possibilities to four. We have to be relaxed with ourselves. But why not take a different tack? Let the possibilities be five or six or ten or 100; bring on the possibilities. As many as we want. But, put a limit to them. Consider how many possibilities there really are. In fact, if it exists in a findable way, then it must be produced from self, other, both, or neither. After a while, the very perception of objects will be colored by understanding that they are not produced from self, other, both, or neither. This will crack, right then and there, our strong adherence to the object's inherent existence. Each thing will itself become a reason for its own absence of inherent existence.

In the previous chapters, we considered the entity of an object in terms of whole and parts, object designated and basis of designation. You may feel, "Well, even if I can't figure out the relationship between whole and parts, still General Motors did make my car, so there is no question about its concreteness." Production itself should tell us that the object is not inherently existent, but now just the opposite seems to be the case — production affirms the concrete appearance of objects. Therefore, our minds have to get inside production to the point where production is doubted, like the Zen Great Doubt. Did anyone at any time anywhere ever make anything? The Parthenon was built. The pyramids were built. The Sphinx was built. The slaves moved blocks of stone here and there; they made it. They produced it. How much wheat was produced in the U.S. and Russia last year? We have to get to the point where we doubt these things. Jesus was born. Buddha was born. Could you actually doubt that?

Are we doubting our understanding of production or the very existence of production? We have to come to the point where there is nothing we can point at that is the production of the Sphinx. At the time of analysis everything is doubted. In a sense, the doubt is always connected with inherent existence, the object of negation, but what does a non-findable Sphinx mean? Don't hold back. We do not want to lose cause and effect, but this very probing, if carried far enough, will help us understand cause and effect. Even though emptiness is a mere non-affirming negative, realization of it will induce greater realization of cause and effect — of dependent-arising — and, similarly, realization of dependent-arising will induce greater understanding of emptiness.

That a realization of emptiness induces ascertainment of dependent-arising does not mean that a consciousness realizing an emptiness of inherent existence either explicitly or implicitly understands dependent-arising. Emptiness is a non-affirming negative, and it is to be realized in space-like meditative equipoise with nothing appearing but a vacuity of inherent existence. Nevertheless, understanding emptiness assists in understanding dependent-arising, for emptiness means a lack of independence and therefore has the import of dependence.

While meditating on production, every now and then switch to dependent imputation. Realize that things are imputed in dependence on their parts and that they are not the collection of their parts, their parts individually, and so forth. Then, see if you had that same sense of no inherent existence when you were reflecting on their production. Try to bring the two together so that the reasoning of production will be just as strong as the reasoning of dependent imputation. It usually is not as strong because production, for us, seems to be a sign of inherent existence. However, when we examine the entity and cannot find it in the whole or the parts, we get a sense of an absence of inherent existence. See if you can force this into your understanding of production. Comparison of the two is a technique for seeing how deep our understanding of production is. Eventually, production should be just as powerful.

The way in which the essentials of the sevenfold reasoning meet back to dependent-arising is that (1) just the non-findability in seven ways induces ascertainment with respect to the person's being merely imputed in dependence upon the [mental and physical] aggregates and (2) just the realization [that the person is] only imputedly existent induces ascertainment with respect to the other [i.e., ascertainment that phenomena are not findable in these seven ways]. Dzong-ka-ba's *Essence of the Good Explanations* says:[351]

This also meets back to the reasoning of dependent-arising since the non-finding of the person as those seven due to being just imputed in dependence upon the aggregates is the meaning of the selflessness of persons.

If we cannot find something in these ways, we feel, "Get me out of here. Get me to something that is findable!" However, we must stay right with the sense of unfindability, for this very non-finding will help us to understand what dependent-arisings are. Eventually, we see that its unfindability necessitates its being merely imputedly existent. This is said to be very hard to comprehend.

Thus, even the other reasonings proving selflessness that are non-observations of related factors
contain all these features. Even each of those
reasonings refutes the view of permanence through
the conceptually isolatable function of the reasoning
itself, which is its negating findability at the end of
searching for the object imputed — this findability
being something that is necessarily related with inherent establishment, the object of negation. [Each
of those reasonings] also refutes the extreme of
annihilation through the conceptually isolatable
function of the fact that being merely dependently
imputed — the opposite of the object of negation,
inherent establishment — becomes the reason. You
should know that there are two imprints in dependence upon individual functions.

Non-findability has one imprint — refutation of the extreme of permanence, or inherent existence — and its counterpart, dependent imputation, has another imprint — refutation of the extreme of annihilation. Findability is something that is necessarily related with inherent existence
because if something inherently exists, it must be findable
in one of the seven ways, for instance. Therefore, not
finding something in the seven ways is called a reasoning
that is a non-observation of something that is necessarily
related with the object of negation, inherent existence. On
the other hand, being dependently imputed is opposite to
inherent existence, and thus when it is stated as a reason for
no inherent existence, it is called an observation of something opposite to the object of negation. Jang-gya is saying
that even those reasonings, such as not finding production
in the four ways or examining the object imputed and the
basis of imputation in seven ways, which are non-
observations of something necessarily related with inherent
existence, end up also involving an observation of something opposite to inherent existence becoming the reason.
This is because being dependently imputed also *becomes* the

reason even when only non-findability is explicitly stated. One imprint or result is the refutation of the extreme of permanence, and the other is the refutation of the extreme of annihilation.

Nevertheless, you also must differentiate well how, in the dependence on the way [the reason] is explicitly stated, it is an observation of what is opposite or a non-observation of what is necessarily related.

Even if a single reasoning has these two functions, in terms of its mode of *explicit* statement, it is either an observation of what is opposite to inherent existence or a non-observation of what is necessarily related with inherent existence.

The likes of the very great ability of this reasoning of dependent-arising explicitly to clear away the two extremes do not exist in other reasonings that state factors of emptiness [such as not being produced from self, from other, from both, or causelessly] as the reason. Also, within the reasoning of dependent-arising itself, just the reasoning of dependent imputation is very powerful.

[The Middle Way Autonomists] Bhāvaviveka and his spiritual son [Jñānagarbha] as well as Shāntarakṣhita and his spiritual son [Kamalashīla] also assert that the root of the reasonings refuting true existence meets back to having parts and that having parts is the meaning of dependent-arising. However, the way that these [Consequentialists] have the other reasonings meet back to dependent-arising is utterly different. Also, the way that the reasoning of dependent-arising explicitly eliminates the two extremes [in the Consequentialist system] is not like [what is asserted in] those systems. The masters of the Autonomy School and their students also say that emptiness and dependent-arising have the same import, but the way that they have the same import is not like this system of the [Consequence School]. Furthermore, just the Consequentialists mainly use the expression "king of reasonings" for this reasoning [of dependent-arising]. Dzong-ka-ba's *Great Exposition of the Stages of the Path to Enlightenment* says:

> When other sentient beings apprehend that [a phenomenon] is produced based on causes and conditions, in dependence on this they apprehend [that phenomenon] as having an inherent nature in the sense of existing by way of its own entityness, whereby they are bound [in cyclic existence]. The wise, in dependence on that sign [i.e., being a dependent-arising], refute that the phenomenon has inherent existence and induce ascertainment with respect to its absence of inherent existence, [thereby] cutting the bonds of views conceiving extremes. Therefore, this establishment of the absence of inherent existence through the sign of dependent-arising is a wondrous, great skillfulness in method.

And Dzong-ka-ba's *Praise of the Supramundane Buddha from the Point of View of Dependent-Arising* says:

> Just that which, through being
>   apprehended,
> Makes, for children, the bonds of extreme
>   conceptions more firm,
> For the wise is the door to cutting
> All the nets of elaboration [of the
>   conception of inherent existence].

His saying that just the reasoning of dependent-arising is, for the wise, the door to cutting all the bonds of extreme conceptions is in consideration that emptiness and dependent-arising come to have the same import.

Emptiness and dependent-arising come to have the same import for one who has understood them fully. We are always thinking, "What causes such and such?" But has this ever induced us to see things as without inherent existence? In meditation we see that a thing cannot be found, but then, when we come out of meditation, our minds become dull and stupid, and we forget what we have understood. We intentionally have to reflect on causation, as if this were somehow contradictory to the non-finding of things. However, when those who have properly trained in these reasonings wonder, "What are the causes of this?" "How will I do that?", "How big is this?" and so forth, these questions themselves induce ascertainment with respect to the unfindability of things. They can do the two at once. We are like angry little children: Either we get our way, or we go in the corner and refuse to do anything. Whatever sense of non-findability we have, we must make great effort to carry over to arising in dependence on causes and conditions.

Furthermore, that Nāgārjuna and his [spiritual] children as well as the Foremost Omniscient [Dzong-ka-ba] say that emptiness has the meaning of dependent-arising is not like positing that which is bulbous as the meaning of pot.

A particular definition (or defining characteristic) — such as that which has a bulbous belly, is flat-based, and can hold fluid — and what it defines, a pot, have the same import. Are emptiness and dependent-arising like this? They are not.

It also is not merely that a consciousness realizing one also realizes the other. Therefore, that emptiness comes to mean dependent-arising is not just for any person but is posited as so in the perspective of one who has already ascertained the pure view and has not forgotten it. Dzong-ka-ba's *Ocean of Reasoning, Explanation of (Nāgārjuna's) "Treatise on the Middle Way"* says:

> The meaning of emptiness coming to be the meaning of dependent-arising is for Proponents of the Middle Way School who have refuted inherent existence through valid cognition, not for others.

Therefore, even though some of our own [Ge-luk-ba] scholars assert that this is for persons ranging up from other parties [in a debate] whose continuums have been ripened [such that they are about ready to realize emptiness] and even though some others assert that it is for those whose analysis of the view is complete, I think just what was explained above is correct. The Foremost Omniscient [Dzong-ka-ba] says [in his *Three Principal Aspects of the Path*]:[352]

> When [the two realizations of appearance
>   and of emptiness exist] simultaneously
>   without alternation,
> And when from only seeing
>   dependent-arising as infallible,
> Ascertaining knowledge entirely destroys
>   the mode of apprehension [of inherently
>   existent objects],
> Then one has completed analysis of the
>   view.

And after that, he says:

> Further,[353] the extreme of [inherent]
>   existence is avoided by [knowledge of the
>   nature of] appearances [as existing as only
>   nominal designations],

And the extreme of [total] non-existence is
avoided by [knowledge of the nature of]
emptiness [as the absence of inherent
existence and not the absence of nominal
existence].
If, from within emptiness, you know the
mode of appearance of cause and effect,
Then you will not be captivated by extreme
views.

The third line could be interpreted as meaning, "If one
knows how an understanding of emptiness acts as a cause of
a better understanding of dependent-arising and how
understanding dependent-arising acts to bring about a better understanding of emptiness ..."

Through those statements [Dzong-ka-ba] clearly
speaks of how emptiness comes to have the import
of dependent-arising, but the meaning of those
statements is very difficult to realize. I do not think
that it would be correct to assert that the meaning of
the former passage is a mere ability to have a simultaneous appearance, with respect to one phenomenon, of its being a dependent-arising arisen
from causes and conditions and of its not being
inherently existent. The Foremost Ren-da-wa[354]
also says something quite similar to that statement:

When the two wisdoms of faith in
non-delusive cause and effect
And the realization that dependent-arisings
are empty
Are understood in inseparable union, then
one has entered
The path of the middle way free of
extremes.

And:

At the very time they appear, [phenomena]

are realized as empty
And when [355] emptiness is realized,
appearance is not refuted.
When ascertainment is found with respect
to the way that these two are unified,
Then the thought of the Conqueror has
been realized.

A Buddha's understanding of emptiness is such that it does not harm appreciation of dependent-arising, and a Buddha's understanding of dependent-arising is such that it does not harm appreciation of emptiness. The two are not seen as contradicting each other or making each other impossible.

Therefore, just as much as when one thoroughly analyzes with stainless reasoning, one generates greater ascertainment with respect to how these and those phenomena lack inherent existence, to that extent the inducement of ascertainment with respect to how those phenomena are merely dependent imputations develops in greater force. Also, just as much as the inducement of ascertainment with regard to the way that phenomena are only dependent imputations increases in greater force, to that extent the inducement of ascertainment with regard to the way the phenomena are empty of inherent existence increases in greater force.

Moreover, once an ascertaining consciousness — induced by inferential cognition that a sprout is without inherent existence through the sign of its being a dependent-arising — has been generated and does not deteriorate, it is evident that there are many different stages of levels of capacity with respect to how these two ascertaining consciousnesses assist each other due to gradual progress higher and higher.

This inferential cognition is based on the syllogism, "The

subject, a sprout, is not inherently existent because of being a dependent-arising." Whatever is a dependent-arising is necessarily not inherently existent. A sprout is a dependent-arising because of arising from its causes — seed, water, manure, and so forth. Therefore, a sprout is not inherently existent. That inferential realization induces a subsequent ascertaining consciousness, and from that point on, there are different levels of ability with respect to how the understanding of dependent-arising assists realization of emptiness and the understanding of emptiness assists realization of dependent-arising. Understanding of how these two work together changes as one progresses on the path.

In the Consequentialist system, the ascertaining consciousness that induces an inferential cognition is no longer an inference but is a direct perception[356] even though it is still conceptual. The reason why it is a direct perception is that it no longer relies on a reason; the first moment of cognition induces the next. Eventually, the conceptual direct perception turns into a non-conceptual direct perception, provided that it is teamed with powerful one-pointed concentration and then alternated with analytical meditation to the point where analysis induces more stability and stability induces more analysis; after this the imagistic, conceptual part of the cognition gradually disappears, resulting in non-conceptual direct cognition of emptiness.

> Since this topic [of how the two realizations assist each other] is extremely difficult to understand and, when understood, is amazing, the Protector Nāgārjuna says:
>
> > Relying on actions and effects
> > Within knowing this emptiness of phenomena
> > Is even more amazing than the amazing
> > And even more marvelous than the marvelous.
>
> And the Foremost Great Being [Dzong-ka-ba] says:

> What is more amazing
> And what is more marvelous
> Than that the two ascertainments —
> That all these are empty of inherent
>   existence
> And that this effect arises from that
>   [cause] —
> Assist each other without impediment!

To be a Proponent of the Middle Way School, this is the composite understanding that one has to create. Emptiness must remain a non-affirming negative, but realization of it must aid in the realization of dependent-arising, and vice versa.

Without valid cognition supporting the appearance of phenomena, how could this be something we would want to attain? Something beyond just ignorance is needed to support appearances. But do not fall into the trap of thinking that things will appear as they currently appear. Also, because of so much talk, in Ge-luk-ba texts, about valid cognition and about the importance of conceptual realization, you might think that the final aim is conceptual cognition; however, a Buddha has no conceptuality at all. Conceptual thought is helpful, but it leads to a point where you no longer need it.

> There are still many facets of the meaning of the sameness in import of emptiness and dependent-arising that should be understood in even more detail than what has been explained earlier. The likes of what appears in the Foremost Omniscient [Dzong-ka-ba's] scriptures — his "Great Exposition of Special Insight", "Middling Exposition of Special Insight", and *Great Commentary on (Nāgārjuna's) "Fundamental Treatise on the Middle Way Called 'Wisdom' "* — do not appear in any of the essays of instruction on the view composed by later scholars, [even though these are] renowned to be

very clear. Also, [what is found in Dzong-ka-ba's scriptures] does not appear in [others'] general presentations and critical analyscs of the texts, etc. Therefore, it is evident that when those scriptures of the Foremost Lama [Dzong-ka-ba] are explained by someone who knows how to explain them and heard by someone who knows how to listen, there are many sources that generate joy.

As has been evident throughout Jang-gya's presentation, he has great admiration for Dzong-ka-ba's works. Here he is warning that although there are many short texts that are renowned to be very clear and although the Ge-luk-ba monastic colleges all have their own textbooks on these topics, they do not match Dzong-ka-ba's actual works. The current Dalai Lama frequently makes the same point in public lectures, suggesting that Ge-luk-bas have turned away from their own roots and have become attached to popularized versions of philosophy and practice. Dzong-ka-ba's works are long and, at least initially, hard to read, but Jang-gya is saying that works, such as his own, that attempt to present the essence of Dzong-ka-ba's thought are no substitute for the original.

Jang-gya has finished his presentation of the reasonings proving emptiness with praise for Dzong-ka-ba's delineation of the compatability of dependent-arising and emptiness — that realization of the one mutually supports the other. It is clear that for him, the view of ultimate reality in the Middle Way School is neither agnostic nor nihilistic but a profound insight into the mutual dependence of an absence of over-concretization of objects and their effective, valid appearance. This combination of emptiness and appearance allows for a path of purification to a state of dynamic altruism, bringing about the welfare of others on an otherwise unimaginable scale. The foundation of the path is the recognition that emptiness negates not objects but an imagined status of objects. The realization of emptiness is not a vapid withdrawal from objects but eventually a dynamic, altruistically directed engagement with objects. Jang-gya beckons us to his vision of the harmony between an utter absence of inherent existence and the patterns of cause and effect.

Translation
Jang-gya's Text Without Commentary

The Harmony of Emptiness and Dependent-Arising in the
Middle Way Consequence School

Note numbers refer to those given earlier in the
commentary and thus are not necessarily sequential.

Outline of Jang-gya's Text
(The page numbers in this section are given first, followed by those in the commentary; the page numbers in parentheses refer to the Varanasi codex edition.)

BRIEF EXPRESSION OF THE SYSTEM OF THE
GLORIOUS MIDDLE WAY CONSEQUENCE
SCHOOL, SUPREME SUMMIT OF ALL SCHOOLS
OF TENETS, BEARING THE SUBDUER'S OWN
SYSTEM — 360-428, 36-354 (407.8-525.15)

I. Definition — 360-428, 36-354 (407.11-409.18)
II. Assertions of tenets — 364-428, 61-354 (409.18-525.15)
  A. How to settle the view of the bases — 364-428,
    61-354 (410.1-458.9)
    1. Explaining what is negated in relation to what
      bases — 364-372, 61-122 (410.3-416.16)
    2. Settling the selflessness that is the negative of the
      object negated — 373-428, 123-354 (416.16-
      458.9)
      a. An identification of the main reasonings re-
        futing the object of negation — 373-382, 123-
        155 (416.18-424.3)
        (1) Purpose of refuting the object of negation
            through reasoning — 373-380, 124-147
            (416.20-421.17)
        (2) Identification of the main reasonings —
            380-382, 148-155 (421.17-424.3)
      b. How those reasonings refute the object of
        negation, the two selves — 383-428, 156-354
        (424.3-458.9)

357

1 Definition of a Consequentialist

[The explanation of the Consequence School] is in two parts: definition and assertions of tenets.

DEFINITION OF A CONSEQUENTIALIST

The means of positing, or definition of, a Consequentialist is:

> a Proponent of the Middle Way School who asserts that it is not necessary to establish the modes of a reason from the viewpoint of the common appearance of the subject [of a debate] to non-mistaken valid cognitions of both disputants through the force of an objective mode of subsistence of things, but rather that an inferential consciousness cognizing selflessness is generated by a reason which has the three modes and which, leading only from the other party's assertions, is approved by that very other party.

360

Furthermore, in that way Chandrakīrti's *Clear Words*[106] gives, together with [showing its] correctness, the reason why a thesis is proven by a reason approved by the other party and why autonomous [syllogisms] should not be asserted:

> With regard to an inference for one's own purpose, [even you say that] just what is established for one-self is weightier at all [times], not what is established for both [oneself and an opponent, for in an inference for one's own purpose there is no opponent]. Therefore, expression of the definitions of logic [as they are renowned in the systems of the Autonomists and below][107] is not needed because the Buddhas help beings — trainees who do not know suchness — with reasoning as it is renowned to those [beings].

Chandrakīrti also indicates this with a worldly example; his *Clear Words* says:[109]

> It is just by a reason established for oneself, not by one established for the other [disputant], since such is seen in the world. In the world, sometimes [one party] prevails and [the other] is defeated by the word of a judge whom both take to be valid and sometimes by just one's own word, but victory or defeat is not by the other's word. Just as it is in the world, so it is also in logic because only the conventions of the world are appropriate in treatises of logic.

Positing the import of [being] a Consequentialist in that way is the flawless thought of [Chandrakīrti's] text. Dzong-ka-ba's *Great Exposition of the Stages of the Path to Enlightenment* says:

> Proving a thesis with a reason that is established for both parties with valid cognitions such as were explained previously is called an autonomous reason.

One who proves a thesis not that way, but through the three aspects [of a reason] approved by the other party is posited as a Consequentialist. It is very clear that this [explanation of the meaning of being a Consequentialist] is the thought of the master [Chandrakīrti].

In that case, a Consequentialist may also be defined as a Proponent of the Middle Way School who, without accepting autonomy, asserts that an inferring consciousness cognizing an absence of true existence is generated merely through what is approved by the other [party]. Moreover, it is suitable to give the definition of a Consequentialist as: a Proponent of the Middle Way School who does not accept, even conventionally, phenomena that are established by way of their own character.

Furthermore, the final root of the Consequentialists' many uncommon ways of positing the two truths is this non-assertion of establishment of objects by way of their own character even conventionally. Chandrakīrti's *Autocommentary on the "Supplement to (Nāgārjuna's) 'Treatise on the Middle Way' "*[110] says:[123]

> May scholars ascertain that, in terms of the doctrine of emptiness, the system which appears in this [treatise] — set out together with objections and answers to any [other] system — does not exist in other treatises.

He is saying that his own [Consequence School] system is not shared with commentaries by other Proponents of the Middle Way School [such as those by Autonomists, including Bhāvaviveka]. In explaining the meaning of that passage, the Foremost Great Being [Dzong-ka-ba] says in his *Essence of the Good Explanations:*[124]

> In the [Consequentialists'] own system, phenomena that are established by way of their own character are not asserted even conventionally, whereas those

[Proponents of True Existence] only posit [all phe-
nomena] in the context of that [establishment of
objects by way of their own character].

Earlier Tibetan scholars also used the term "Thoroughly
Non-Abiding Proponents of the Middle Way School" [for
the Consequentialists]. This appears to be based on a statement in the master Shūra's [i.e., Ashvaghosha's] *Essay
on the Stages of Cultivating the Ultimate Mind of
Enlightenment:*[126]

> Through synonyms such as emptiness, [suchness,
>   final reality] and so forth,
> Limitless examples such as likeness with a
>   magician's illusions, [dreams, mirages] and so
>   forth
> And the skillful means of a variety of vehicles,
> [Buddha] characterized the meaning of the middle
>   way not abiding [in any gross or subtle extremes].

Moreover, in reports of statements by the Foremost Elder
[Atīsha] this convention [of calling Consequentialists
"Thoroughly Non-Abiding Proponents of the Middle Way
School"] occurs, and it also does not appear that the Foremost Father [Dzong-ka-ba] and his spiritual sons [Gyel-tsap
and Kay-drup][127] refuted it. Although there are a couple [of
scholars] who say that Shūra's text was not written by the
master Shūra, such is exhausted as a mere thesis without
proof. It appears that all the great chariots [i.e., path-
blazing leaders] of the snowy land [Tibet] as well as all of
our own [Ge-luk-ba] scholars and adepts who appeared over
the years accepted it as valid.

A description of different internal divisions in the Middle
Way Consequence School, like those in the Autonomy
School, does not appear in other texts, and neither is there
seen an explanation of divisions of the Consequence School
by the Foremost Father and his spiritual sons. [Hence,
there are no significant subschools within the Consequence
School.]

2 Self

ASSERTIONS OF TENETS

This section has four parts: how to settle the view of the bases, the features of how, in dependence on that, a presentation of the two truths is made, how to progress on the path, and the fruits [of the paths. Only the first part is translated here.]

How to Settle the View of the Bases

This section has two parts: explaining what is negated in relation to what bases and settling the selflessness that is the negative of the object negated.

What is negated in relation to what. Proponents of Mind Only and of Autonomy assert that the two selves — through the negation of which in persons and phenomena the [two] selflessnesses are posited — are different and that the modes of conception of them also differ. Therefore, although one realized the subtle selflessness of persons [as presented by the Proponents of Mind Only and of Autonomy], it is not necessarily the case that one would also have cognized the subtle selflessness of phenomena. This being so, [the Proponents of Mind Only and of Autonomy] assert that it is not necessary to realize the subtle selflessness of phenomena in order merely to attain liberation.

This [Conscqucntialist] system asserts that it is necessary to cognize the subtle selflessness in order to achieve any of the three enlightenments [of a Hearer, Solitary Realizer, or Buddha]. For it is said in the Perfection of Wisdom Sūtras[137] that those who discriminate true existence[138] are not liberated. Shāntideva says,[139] "Scripture says that without this path there is no enlightenment."

Therefore, the two selflessnesses are differentiated by way of the bases that have the attribute [of selflessness], persons and [other] phenomena such as the [mental and physical] aggregates. It is not asserted that they are differentiated from the viewpoint of two different non-existent selves. Just as an emptiness of true existence of a phenomenon such as a [mental or physical] aggregate is posited as a selflessness of a phenomenon, so also must an emptiness of true existence of a person be posited as a selflessness of a person. For the reason [to do so in both instances] is the same. That is the thought [of the Consequence School]. Therefore, Chandrakīrti's *Supplement to (Nāgārjuna's) "Treatise on the Middle Way"* says:[143]

> In order to release transmigrators [from the afflictive obstructions and the obstructions to omniscience], this selflessness was set forth in two aspects by way of a division into phenomena and persons.

What is the self to be negated in terms of persons and [other] phenomena? Chandrakīrti's *Commentary on (Āryadeva's) "Four Hundred"* says:

> Here, 'self' is an inherent nature[146] of phenomena, that is, a non-dependence on another. The non-existence of this is selflessness. Selflessness is realized as twofold through a division into phenomena and persons — a selflessness of phenomena and a selflessness of persons.

Thus, whether the base is a person or a phenomenon, the innate mode of conception of self is to conceive that it exists objectively through its own entity and is not posited through the force of conceptuality. The conceived object of that conception is the self to be negated on this occasion and is the hypothetical measure of true existence.

The Proponents of the Middle Way Autonomy School make the distinction of refuting the three — true existence, ultimate existence, and existing as its own reality[150] — but not refuting the three — inherent existent, existence by way of its own character, or existence by way of its own entity.[151] However, in this [Consequence] system, true existence, etc., and existence by way of its own character, etc., are asserted as having the same meaning.

Therefore, Dzong-ka-ba's *Differentiation of the Interpretable and the Definitive* [also called the *Essence of the Good Explanations*] says, "The existence of an objective mode of subsistence [means] a self-powered entity." Since it is asserted that autonomous[153] and self-powered[154] are synonyms, when the Middle Way Autonomists maintain that the three modes [of a reason][155] are established from their own side, this has the full meaning of true existence in this system [of the Consequence School]. Āryadeva's *Four Hundred* says,[156] "All these are not self-powered; hence, there is no self [inherent existence]." Also, Chandrakīrti's *Commentary on (Āryadeva's) "Four Hundred"* states these as having the same meaning: "own entity, inherent existence, self-powered, and non-reliance on another".[157]

Question: Since the self refuted on this occasion is [a thing's] existing by way of a mode of subsistence that is not posited through the force of conceptuality, in "posited through the force of conceptuality" to what does "conceptuality" refer? How are things posited through its force? What is the difference between this and the Autonomy School's assertion that a mode of subsistence not posited through the force of an awareness does not exist?

Answer: With regard to the way in which things are

posited through the force of conceptuality, Āryadeva's *Four Hundred* says:[160]

> Without [imputation by] conceptuality [like the imputation of a snake to a rope], there is no [finding of] the existence of desire and so forth. If so, who with intelligence would maintain that a real object is produced [dependent on] conceptuality? [For, being imputed by conceptuality and existing as its own reality are contradictory.]

Chandrakīrti's commentary on this passage says:[161]

> There is no question that what exists merely due to the existence of conceptuality and does not exist without the existence of conceptuality is, like a snake imputed to a coiled rope, to be ascertained as not established by way of its own entity.

Therefore, conceptuality [here refers to] this ordinary, innate awareness which makes designations of forms and so forth through having become accustomed again and again since beginningless time to thinking, "This is a form," "This is a feeling," and so forth.

[The example of a rope-snake illustrates] how things are posited through the force of [ordinary innate conceptuality]. When darkness has fallen on a rope, it is thought to be a snake since the variegated colors of the rope and the way in which it is coiled are like a snake and it is seen in a dim place. At that time, neither the color of the rope, its shape, its other parts, nor the collection of those parts may be posited as something that is a snake.[167] The snake of this occasion is only a mere designation by conceptuality in dependence upon the rope.

Similarly, when the thought "I" arises in terms of the five [mental and physical] aggregates that are its bases of designation, neither the individual aggregates, the collection, their continuum, nor their parts can be posited as something that is I.[168] Furthermore, there is not in the least any phenomenon that is a separate entity from those [mental and physical aggregates] and can be apprehended as something that is I. The I is merely posited by conceptuality in dependence upon the aggregates.

Although the way in which all phenomena are imputed by conceptuality is, in this way, like the imputing of a snake to a rope, a rope-snake and phenomena such as forms are not the same with respect to whether or not they conventionally exist. For they are dissimilar in terms of whether or not conventional valid cognition damages an assertion [made] in accordance with what is being imputed.

Furthermore, with respect to how [phenomena] are mere nominal imputations, one engages in adopting [virtues] and discarding [non-virtues] in dependence on mere nominalities which are conventions designated to these phenomena such as forms, "This is a form," "This is a feeling," and so forth, and through this, desired aims are accomplished. Also, within the context of mere nominality, all affirmations and negations of correctness and incorrectness, etc., as well as all agents, actions, and objects are possible. However, if one is not satisfied with mere nominalities and enters into searching to find the object imputed in the expression "form", [trying to discover] whether it can be taken as color, shape, some other factor, or the collection of all these, and so forth, one will not find anything, and all presentations [of phenomena] will become impossible.

Making presentations of what is and is not correct in the context of mere nominalities is most feasible. For example, there were two villagers who went to a city to see the sights. They went into a temple and began to look at the paintings, whereupon one of them said, "That one holding a trident in his hand is Nārāyaṇa; the other holding a wheel in his hand is Maheshvara." The other villager said, "You are mistaken; the one holding a trident is Maheshvara, and the one holding a wheel is Nārāyaṇa." And thus they disputed.

A wandering holy man was nearby. They went up to him, and each spoke his thought. The wanderer thought, "Being murals on a wall, these are neither Maheshvara nor Nārā-yaṇa." Although he knew that, still he did not say, "These are not gods, but paintings." Instead, in conformity with the conventions of the world, he told the two villagers that one of them was right and the other wrong. Through his speaking thus, the wishes of the two villagers were fulfilled, and the wanderer also did not incur the fault of telling a lie.

Likewise, although all phenomena do not have objective establishment, presentations such as, "This is correct, and that is incorrect," are feasible within the context of mere nominalities. Although the Supramundane Victor [Buddha] sees that all phenomena do not truly exist, even he teaches the adopting [of virtues] and discarding [of non-virtues] using terminology as the world does, thereby bringing about the welfare of transmigrators.

This way [of presenting nominalities] was taught by Bud-dhapālita, a great master who had attained yogic feats, in his commentary on the eighteenth chapter of Nāgārjuna's *Treatise on the Middle Way*. The honorable Chandrakīrti and the revered Shāntideva also, through many examples and reasonings, explain still other ways in which agent, object, and action are feasible within the context of mere nominalities. I will not elaborate more on the topic here.

This presentation of conventions is the uncommon way in which the three masters [Buddhapālita, Chandrakīrti, and Shāntideva] comment on the thought of the Superior [Nāgārjuna]. The Foremost Omniscient Father [Dzong-ka-ba] and his spiritual sons [Gyel-tsap and Kay-drup] fre-quently advised that just this is the final difficult point of the Middle Way School view.

About this way [of presenting conventionalities], the *Questions of Upāli Sūtra* says:[170]

These alluring blossoming flowers of various colors
And these fascinating brilliant mansions of gold
Are without any [inherently existent] maker here.
They are posited through the power of
  conceptuality,

The world is imputed through the power of
conceptuality.

And the *King of Meditative Stabilizations Sūtra* says:[171]

Nirvana is not found
In the way nirvana is taught
By words to be profound.
The words also are not found ...

And a *Perfection of Wisdom Sūtra* says:

It is this way: this "Bodhisattva" is only a name. It
is this way: this "enlightenment" is only a name. It
is this way: this "perfection of wisdom" is only a
name ...

And the Superior Nāgārjuna's *Precious Garland* says that
name-only does not exist ultimately:[172]

Because the phenomena of forms are
Only names, space too is only a name.
Without the elements, how could forms
     [inherently] exist?
Therefore even "name-only" does not [inherently]
     exist.

And Nāgārjuna's *Precious Garland of Advice*[173] also says
that, except for what is merely posited by the power of
nominal designations, nothing at all exists:

Other than as a convention
What world is there in fact
Which would be "[inherently] existent" or
     "[inherently] not existent"?

Based on not understanding those reasons, Middle Way
Autonomists and below [i.e., Proponents of Mind Only,
Proponents of Sūtra, and Proponents of the Great Exposi-
tion] maintain that when the expression, "This person did
this deed," is imputed, an accumulator of deeds[174] and so
forth can be posited [only] if there comes to be something

that is posited as the person upon finding it — for instance, a part, the collection [of parts], or the continuum from among the bases of designation [of that person]. If nothing is found, [an accumulator of deeds] cannot be posited. It is the same also for the Sūtra School's positing as space the non-affirming negative that is a mere elimination of any obstructive tangibility and is the same also for [the presentations in] higher [systems but not the Consequence School].

In this system [of the Consequence School], it is admissible, without having in that way to search for and find the object designated, to posit all agents and actions, as in the case of a person as an accumulator of deeds *(karma)*. This is a marvelous distinctive feature [of the Consequence School].

The Autonomists maintain that in [the phrase] "a mode of subsistence not posited through the force of an awareness is to be taken as the object negated [in the view of selflessness]", the word "awareness" refers to an unmistaken nondefective consciousness. However, in the Consequentialists' [assertion of phenomena] as being posited through the force of conceptuality, conceptuality is asserted to be a mistaken consciousness. Hence, they differ.

Therefore, the Consequentialists even posit the mere I or mere person as the object of observation of the innate [false] view of the transitory collection[175] [as an inherently existent self]; they do not posit the [mental and physical] aggregates, etc., [as its object of observation]. The object of observation of an innate [false] view of the transitory collection that [mis]conceives mine is mine itself. A consciousness conceiving persons of other continuums to be established by way of their own character is not an innate [false] view of the transitory collection but is an innate conception of a self of persons.

The objects of the innate conception of a self of phenomena are the aggregates of forms and so forth, either those included in [your own] continuum or not. Although in that way the objects of observation of a consciousness conceiving a self of persons and of a consciousness conceiving a self of phenomena are different, their subjective aspects are the same in that they [both] conceive that the object is established by way of its own character. Hence, there is no fallacy of its [absurdly] following that there are two discordant modes of conception that are roots of cyclic existence.

The way in which an innate consciousness conceiving true existence conceives an inherently existent person in the context of the aggregates of form and so forth is not to conceive such upon having analyzed [whether the person and the mental and physical aggregates] are one or different. Rather, it conceives such through the force of ordinary familiarity, without any reasons at all. [This] innate consciousness has no mode in which it conceives of oneness, difference, and so forth [of the person and the mental and physical aggregates]. Therefore, the Foremost Omniscient [Dzong-ka-ba] spoke even of the *non-analytical* innate conception of true existence.

Although even a consciousness conceiving true existence is posited as an object to be refuted through reasoning, the main [object to be refuted through reasoning] is the conceived object itself [inherent existence].

In order to distinguish the fine points of these presentations, it is necessary to rely on many causal collections — training in detail in the great texts as well as relying for a long time on a wise spiritual guide who has thoroughly penetrated the instructions in the teaching of the Foremost Father [Dzong-ka-ba] and his spiritual sons [Gyel-tsap and Kay-drup], and so forth. These topics are not in the province of either those professors of vanity who are biased toward foolish meditations or of those professors of public speaking who meditate on wasting their human life with criticism directed outside as if such were the supreme state.

3 Purpose of Reasoning

SETTLING THE SELFLESSNESS THAT IS THE NEGATIVE OF THE OBJECT OF NEGATION

This section has two parts: an identification of the main reasonings refuting the object of negation and how those reasonings refute the object of negation, the two selves.

IDENTIFICATION OF THE MAIN REASONINGS REFUTING THE OBJECT OF NEGATION

This section has two parts: the purpose of refuting the object of negation through reasoning and an identification of the main reasonings.

Purpose of Refuting the Object of Negation

Concerning that, the honorable Superior Nāgārjuna made commentary on the thought of the definitive sūtras, and two who made clear commentary on those in exact accordance with [his] meaning are Buddhapālita and Chandrakīrti. Also, the great master Shāntideva expounded in agreement with these two. According to the assertions of these three great chariots [i.e., great leaders], it is the thought of the sūtras of the perfection of wisdom class that, without even considering omniscience, in order merely to attain[182] release from cyclic existence, one must necessarily realize the suchness of persons and phenomena. For, passages in Perfection of Wisdom Sūtras say (1) that those who have discrimination of true existence[183] are not liberated, (2) that the completely perfect Buddhas of the past, present, and future as well as even all from Stream Enterers through to Solitary Realizers attain [their respective levels] in dependence upon this perfection of wisdom, and (3) that "even those who wish to train in the grounds of the Hearers should train in this perfection of wisdom," etc. This is also the thought of the Superior Nāgārjuna, for his *Sixty Stanzas of Reasoning*[184] teaches that there is no release for those who have fallen to the extremes of [inherent] existence or [utter] non-existence:

> Through [the view of inherent] existence one is not
>   released;
> Through [the view of] no [nominal] existence there
>   is nothing but cyclic existence.

And then, [Nāgārjuna's *Sixty Stanzas of Reasoning*] says that Superiors are liberated from cyclic existence through unerring knowledge of the suchness of things and non-things:

> Through thorough knowledge of things and
>   non-things,
> A great being is liberated.

And also Nāgārjuna's *Precious Garland of Advice for the King* establishes that the means for achieving high status[185] [as a human or god] is the faith of conviction, and that with such faith as a precursor one becomes a vessel for wisdom, which is the means for achieving the definite goodness[186] [of liberation and omniscience]. He says that wisdom is the knowledge that the two — I and mine — do not ultimately exist. And, based on this [reason], he says that when one knows that the [mental and physical] aggregates do not truly exist, the conception of [a truly existent] I is extinguished.

Also, he says that until the conception of the aggregates as truly existent is extinguished, cyclic existence is not overcome and that when [this conception] is extinguished, cyclic existence is overcome. Also, he says that through the view of [utter] non-existence, one cycles in bad transmigrations and that through the view of [inherent] existence, one cycles in happy transmigrations and, therefore, in order to be free from these two [types of transmigrations], one must understand the reality that is not based on the two extremes of [inherent] existence and no [nominal] existence. Nāgārjuna's *Precious Garland* says:[187]

As long as a [mis]conception of the aggregates exists,
So long, therefore, does a [mis]conception of I exist.
Further, when the [mis]conception of I exists,
There is action, and from that there is birth.

And Nāgārjuna's *Praise of the Supramundane* says:

You [Buddha] taught that without realizing
Signlessness there is no liberation.

And so on. [These passages from] the *Precious Garland* and the *Sixty Stanzas* mainly prove that realization of the subtle emptiness is definitely necessary for a path releasing one from cyclic existence. For, Dzong-ka-ba's *Ocean of Reasoning, Explanation of (Nāgārjuna's) "Treatise on the Middle Way"* says:

In this [*Praise of the Supramundane*] and also in the former two [the *Sixty Stanzas on Reasoning* and *Precious Garland of Advice for the King*] there are indeed many teachings on the suchness of dependent-arising, which is the negation of inherent existence in persons and phenomena. However, they appear as branches proving the chief [assertion] — that understanding the meaning of the reality that is not based on the two extremes is definitely necessary for a path releasing one from cyclic existence.

Moreover, it is necessary to realize suchness with [a mind] that eradicates the mode of apprehension of an innate consciousness conceiving self. Through merely not engaging the mind in the two selves [i.e., the inherent existence of persons and the inherent existence of other phenomena] or merely stopping the mind from moving to other objects, it cannot be posited that one has realized emptiness. For, otherwise, it would [absurdly] follow that even [such minds as] sleep and fainting, etc., would realize suchness.

All the chariots [i.e., great leaders] of the Great Vehicle speak — with one voice and one thought — of [the necessity for analytically refuting inherent existence]. Āryadeva says:

When selflessness is seen in objects
The seeds of cyclic existence are destroyed.

And the honorable Chandrakīrti says:[196]

[Extreme] conceptions arise with [a consciousness conceiving inherently existent] things.
It has been thoroughly analyzed how phenomena do not [inherently] exist.

And the master Bhāvaviveka says:

With the mind in meditative equipoise
Wisdom analyzes in this way
The entities of these phenomena
That are apprehended conventionally.

And the venerable Shāntideva also says:

When [these things] are sought as realities
Who is attached and to what is there attachment?

Etc. And the glorious Dharmakīrti also says:

Without disbelieving the object of this [misconception]
It is impossible to abandon [misconceiving it].

Etc. Therefore, one must analyze well what that which is

conceived by consciousnesses erroneously conceiving [persons and phenomena] as the two selves is. After analyzing that, it is necessary to bring about the collapse of the false edifice of mistake by way of inducing conviction through pure scripture and reasoning that [things] do not exist as they are conceived by this [erroneous consciousness]. That this is needed is an indispensable excellent essential [of the path]. Hence, it is important to analyze again and again with the wisdom of individual investigation.

In that way the *Superior Sūtra of the Sport of Mañjushrī* also says:[198]

> "O daughter, how is a Bodhisattva victorious in battle?"
> "Mañjushrī, when analyzed, all phenomena are unobservable."

And the *Superior Sūtra of the King of Meditative Stabilizations* says:[199]

> If the selflessness of phenomena is analyzed
> And if this analysis is cultivated in meditation,
> It causes the effect of attaining nirvana.
> Through no other cause does one come to peace.

And the *Superior Sūtra of the Cloud of Jewels* says,[200] "To analyze with special insight and thereupon realize the lack of inherent entityness is to enter into signlessness." And the *Questions of Brahmā Sūtra* says,[201] "Those who properly investigate phenomena individually are the intelligent."

Therefore, in general, the great chariots have set forth — through refutations and proofs — many paths of reasoning that differentiate, among the word of the Conqueror, what is definitive and what requires interpretation. In particular, the statements of many forms of reasonings for delineating suchness were made only for the sake of illuminating for the fortunate the path to liberation. They were not made for the sake of becoming intent on debate. The Buddhapālita Commentary on (Nāgārjuna's) "Treatise on the Middle Way" says:[202]

What purpose is there in teaching dependent-arising? The master [Nāgārjuna], whose nature is compassion, saw that sentient beings are oppressed by various sufferings; in order to release them, he assumed the task of teaching the reality of things, just as it is; hence, he began the teaching of dependent-arising.

And Chandrakīrti's *Supplement* says:[203]

> The analyses done in [Nāgārjuna's] *Treatise* are not for attachment
> To disputation but for liberation; they teach suchness.

And the Foremost Great Being [Dzong-ka-ba] says:

> All of the various, reasoned analyses set forth in Nāgārjuna's *Treatise on the Middle Way* are only for the sake of sentient beings' attaining release.

One must understand well what is excluded by the words "not for attachment to disputation" in the former quote and by the word "only" in the latter quote.

In general, analysis of individual investigation that takes valid scripture and reasoning as the means of attestation[204] is important whether you are hearing, thinking, or meditating. Moreover, if [your practice] is conjoined with the special causal and continual motivations that involve directing these analyses as means of yourself and others attaining liberation and omniscience, you come into accord with the meaning of what both the unsurpassed Teacher [Buddha] himself and the great chariots taught with such striving. Therefore, it is right for those who want goodness to strive in this way.

Most of the hearing,[207] thinking, and meditating as well as explaining, debating, and writing done by those who boast of practicing religion and boast of helping [Buddha's] teaching is not only not helpful to themselves and others, but also pollutes their mental continuums with many ill deeds related with the doctrine. It should be understood that in the end those who think that they are maintaining the teaching through fighting, quarrelling, heaving [stones, etc.][208] and [wielding] weaponry and clubs are, due to impure motivation, only [like] medicine that has become poison and deities who have become demons.

Therefore Āryadeva says that one makes the suffering of cyclic existence more distant even through having doubt tending to the fact with regard to the profound nature of phenomena:[209]

> Those whose merit is small
> Have no doubts about this doctrine.
> Even through merely having doubt
> Cyclic existence is torn to tatters.

And in particular, the glorious Chandrakīrti says[211] that at this time of the end of [Buddha's] teaching, it is very good fortune merely to take interest — for even a moment — in this very profound topic. He says:

> In this tumultuous age when Buddhism is deprived of the essential meanings taught by the Omniscient One, anyone who can clear away two-mindedness for even a moment and cognize emptiness is fortunate.

And the *Taming Demons Chapter*[212] and the *Ajātashatru Sūtra*[213] say that since taking an interest in this profound nature of phenomena purifies even the karmic obstructions that lead to immediate rebirth in a hell,[214] what need is there to mention [its purifying] minor [infractions of] rites and ethics?

Having gained conviction well in such, you should strive at means to expand [in your own continuum] the potential of this type of doctrine. For, the Foremost Great Being [Dzong-ka-ba] says:

> Therefore, you should plant wishes for hearing the texts, memorizing them, and thinking and meditat-

ing on their meaning, as well as having faithful interest [in the profound emptiness] in all lives within not damaging conviction in the dependent-arising of causes and effects.

IDENTIFICATION OF THE MAIN REASONINGS

In general, the countless forms of reasonings for ascertaining selflessness that are set forth in the texts of the Middle Way are included within two types, reasonings for ascertaining the selflessness of persons and reasonings for ascertaining the selflessness of phenomena. This is because the bases of adherence to the two selves — which are the chief of those things that bind one in cyclic existence — are persons and phenomena and, therefore, the main bases with respect to which selflessness is ascertained must also be persons and phenomena. In that way Dzong-ka-ba's *Differentiation of the Interpretable and the Definitive* says:[215]

> The principal fetters [that bind one in cyclic existence] are adherence to the two selves (1) with regard to the person, which is the object of observation that generates the thought "I", and (2) with regard to the phenomena of that person's continuum. Therefore, these two are also the principal bases with respect to which the conception of self is refuted through reasoning. Consequently, the reasonings also are included in the refutations of the two selves.

Furthermore, among them, the main reasoning for settling the selflessness of phenomena is just the reasoning refuting production from the four extremes. For, when the Superior Nāgārjuna explained the thought of the statement in the *Sūtra on the Ten Grounds*[216] where it says that a Bodhisattva enters onto the sixth ground through the ten samenesses, he considered that through only demonstrating with reasoning that all phenomena are the same in being without [inherently existent] production, the other samenesses would be easily demonstrated. And thus, at the beginning of the *Treatise on the Middle Way* Nāgārjuna says:[217]

> There is never production
> Anywhere, of any thing
> From itself, from others,
> From both, or causelessly.

And in the glorious Chandrakīrti's *Supplement to (Nāgārjuna's) "Treatise on the Middle Way"* the demonstration of the reasoning for settling the selflessness of phenomena is seen to be only the reasoning refuting production of the four extreme types — "It does not arise from itself; how could it arise from others? ... Those who analyze will quickly be released."[218] Therefore, Dzong-ka-ba's *Differentiation of the Interpretable and the Definitive* says,[219] "The principal reasoning proving the selflessness of phenomena is the reasoning refuting production from the four extremes."

The main reasoning for settling the selflessness of persons is the sevenfold reasoning (1) because Chandrakīrti's *Supplement to (Nāgārjuna's) "Treatise on the Middle Way"* says that just as a chariot is not found through searching in the seven ways but is posited as imputedly existent — imputed in dependence upon its own branches [i.e., parts] — so a person also is to be posited that way, and it says that just this is a method for easily finding the profound view:[220]

> How could what does not exist in these seven ways
>   be said to exist [inherently]?
> Yogis do not find the [inherent] existence of this
>   [chariot].
> Since through that [way yogis] easily enter also into
>   suchness,
> The establishment of [a chariot] also should be
>   accepted in that way.

And (2) because in that treatise [i.e., Chandrakīrti's *Supple-*

ment] ascertainment of the selflessness of persons is done only through the sevenfold reasoning, and (3) because this reasoning is said also in Dzong-ka-ba's *Differentiation of the Interpretable and the Definitive* to be the principal one.[221]

The reason of dependent-arising is the main of all reasonings in this system. All these former reasonings derive from just that of dependent-arising. In this way, moreover, the honorable Chandrakīrti says:[222]

> Since things are dependently arisen,
> They cannot sustain these conceptions [of being
>   produced from self, other, and so forth].
> Therefore, this reasoning of dependent-arising
> Cuts through all the nets of bad views.

It is very difficult to realize how all the other reasonings must derive from this [reasoning of dependent-arising] and do not have such an exceptional ability to cut through the nets of bad views as this does. Therefore, the Foremost Father [Dzong-ka-ba] and his spiritual sons [Gyel-tsap and Kay-drup] praise it, saying that the reason of dependent-arising is the king of reasonings.

The refutation of production of the existent and non-existent and the refutation of production of the four alternatives are reasonings for settling the selflessness of phenomena. The lack of being one or many is applied to both selflessnesses. The extensive teaching of the reasoning that is the lack of being one or many by way of an analysis of four essentials set forth in Dzong-ka-ba's *Small Exposition of the Stages of the Path*[223] is based on the eighteenth chapter of Nāgārjuna's *Treatise on the Middle Way*. It is said that this chapter teaches the meanings of all the other twenty-six chapters of Nāgārjuna's *Treatise on the Middle Way*, arranged in stages of practice; hence, [Dzong-ka-ba's teaching of the four essentials] in this way is very important. There are many reasons for this, but I will leave them for the time being.

4 Refuting a Self of Phenomena

The presentation of how those reasonings refute the objects of negation, the two selves, has three parts: (1) reasonings refuting a self of phenomena, (2) reasoning refuting a self of persons, and (3) the king of reasonings, the reason of dependent-arising, refuting self with respect to both persons and phcnomena.[224]

REASONINGS REFUTING A SELF OF PHENOMENA

EXPLAINING THE REASONING OF THE DIAMOND FRAGMENTS REFUTING PRODUCTION OF THE FOUR EXTREME TYPES[225]

Nāgārjuna's *Treatise on the Middle Way* presents four theses of non-production from the four extremes:[226]

> There is never production
> Anywhere of any thing
> From itself, from others,
> From both, or causelessly.

Furthermore, these theses are merely non-affirming negatives, not implying any other positive phenomenon.

383

Question: Why are only four theses stated?

Answer: If things were inherently produced, then [this production] would necessarily be one of the four extreme types of production. Due to that, if these four theses are established, it is easily established that there is no inherently existent production. Therefore, the reasoning refuting the four extremes is a decisive reasoning.

Objection: If, when production of the four extreme types is refuted, a negation of inherent production is implicitly established, then it follows that these theses are not non-affirming negatives.

Answer: There is no such fallacy. For something to be an affirming negative it must prove or imply another *positive* phenomenon.

The reason why, if there were inherently existent production, it would necessarily be one of the four extreme types of production, is that it is certain that production is either caused or causeless, and if it is caused, it is limited to three types — production of an effect (1) that is the same entity as the causes, (2) that is a different entity from the causes, and (3) that is a composite of being the same entity as and a different entity from the causes. The Foremost Omniscient [Dzong-ka-ba's] saying this in both of his *Great Explanations* — of Nāgārjuna's *Treatise on the Middle Way* and Chandrakīrti's *Supplement* — is a very important, good explanation of the great texts from his experience. However, it seems that most of those who write on the Middle Way School put this in a category of minor importance. In any case, they discuss it very briefly.

Refutation of Production from Self

The refutation of the production [of an effect] from a cause that is the same entity [as that effect] is this: If a sprout that is being produced were produced again from its own entity, that production would be senseless. For, the sprout's own entity would have already attained existence earlier at the time of its causes. There is entailment because production is for the sake of [an effect's] attaining its own entity.

Objection: It is not contradictory for something to have already attained its own entity but to be produced again.

Answer: If that were the case, then continuations similar to the effects — such as sprouts — would never be produced and the causes' similar continuations — such as seeds — would be produced without interruption until the end of cyclic existence. For, just that which was already produced would have to be produced in duplicate again and again. Chandrakīrti's *Supplement to (Nāgārjuna's) "Treatise on the Middle Way"* says:[228]

> There is no point in the production of something
> from itself.
> Also, the production again of what has been
> produced is just not feasible.
> If it is thought that the already produced is
> produced again,
> One would not find the production of such things as
> sprouts here [in the world],
> And a seed would just be produced to the end of
> cyclic existence.

Concerning this, since the Sāṃkhyas assert that seed and sprout are mutually different, they do not assert that a sprout[230] is produced from a sprout; however, they assert that the nature of the sprout and the nature of the seed are one and that their natures are mutually each other. Therefore, the previously explained fallacies apply [to their position].

The [Sāṃkhyas] themselves do not assert such, but because the two, seed and sprout, are [for them] one by inherent nature, their being one becomes the mode of subsistence of seed and sprout, whereby they would be undifferentiable. [The Sāṃkhyas] are logically forced [into this position] whereupon the fallacy is demonstrated.

[When production from self] is refuted in Chandrakīrti's *Supplement* and in his commentary on it, the reasonings used are those that he makes in commentary as well as [other] reasonings [cited] from Nāgārjuna's *Treatise on the Middle Way*. [The first are:]

1. If cause and effect were one entity, it would [absurdly] follow that seed and sprout would not differ with respect to shape, color, taste, and capacity.
2. It would [absurdly] follow that when its former state [as a seed] was given up, the single nature of seed and sprout would be lost.
3. It would [absurdly] follow that during each of the states of seed and sprout, both seed and sprout would be equally apprehendable or not.
4. Worldly renown damages [the position] that seed and sprout are of one nature.

In refuting production from self, [Chandrakīrti] also uses the reasonings in Nāgārjuna's *Treatise on the Middle Way* that it would [absurdly] follow that the producer and the produced would be one and that the three — action, agent, and object — would be one.[234]

Refutation of Production from Other

"Other" in "production from other" is not merely other; it is other that is established by way of its own character. Moreover, those who propound production from other assert that in the same way that a rice seed is established by way of its own character as other than the sprout of rice that is its own effect, so such things as fire and charcoal also are established by way of their own character as other than the sprout of rice. If those two modes of being other are asserted to be similar, then thick darkness which [is supposed to be] cleared away [by light] would [absurdly] arise even from a blazing flame that [is supposed to] clear away [darkness], and anything would come from anything else, whether they are cause and effect or not. For, they would all equally have otherness that is established by way of its own character. This is the reasoning taught in the twentieth chapter of Nāgārjuna's *Treatise on the Middle Way:*[237]

> If cause and effect had otherness,
> Cause and non-cause would become equal.

This reasoning is also taught in Buddhapālita's commentary on this point and by the glorious Chandrakīrti who says:[238]

> If, depending on others, another were to arise,
> Then thick darkness would arise even from a
>   tongue of flame
> And all would be produced from all
> Because even all non-producers would equally have
>   otherness. ...

Objection: Things are not posited as cause and effect merely because they are others that are established by way of their own character. Things are posited as cause and effect only because they are a special kind of others — [the cause] having the ability to bring about the effect and so forth. Thus, the determination of causes and non-causes [with respect to a particular effect] is feasible.

Answer: That also is incorrect, for once things are established by way of their own character as other, being other must be their mode of subsistence. Once that is the case, they must be other factualities that are utterly devoid of any relation with each other. Thus, it would be utterly impossible for a rice seed and a barley seed to differ with regard to having or not having the ability to produce a rice sprout and so forth.

Furthermore, if production from other existed by way of its own entity, the effect would have to exist before it was produced. For once production is asserted, the two — the ceasing of the cause and the nearing to production of the effect — must be simultaneous, and in that case the two actions of production and cessation also would have to be simultaneous, whereby cause and effect would also have to be simultaneous. The reason for [the consequent simultaneity of cause and effect] is that an action of nearing production has to depend on something, such as a sprout, that is the agent in the expression, "This effect is growing." Therefore, they are supporter and supported. If such a supporter and supported were established by way of their own character, then whenever the activity of growing existed, the sprout would have to exist. For, its nature could not possibly change. Therefore, Chandrakīrti's *Supplement to (Nāgārjuna's) "Treatise on the Middle Way"* says,[239] "Without an agent, this growing is also not a feasible entity."

In terms of nominally existent production, if things become supporter and supported at some time, it is not necessary that they be so at all times. Therefore, [mere, conventional production] does not have these fallacies. The Foremost Omniscient [Dzong-ka-ba] maintains that this is a subtle[240] and very meaningful reasoning in this system that refutes production from other.

Not only is production from other not asserted even conventionally by this system, but also it is asserted that no innate consciousness conceives causes and effects as others that are different by way of their own character. Chandrakīrti's *Supplement* says,[241] "There is no production from other even in the world."

Refutation of Production From Both Self and Other
That part which is production from self is refuted by the reasoning refuting production from self; that part which is production from other is refuted by the reasoning refuting production from other. Chandrakīrti's *Supplement* says:[243]

> Production from both is also not an admissible entity
> Because the fallacies already explained are incurred.

Refutation of Causeless Production
If [things] were produced causelessly, there would be no

causes for production at a certain place and time and of a certain nature. Therefore, something produced from one thing would be produced from all things, and all work would be just senseless. [Chandrakīrti] says:[245]

> If it is viewed that [things] are only produced
>   causelessly,
> Then everything would always be produced from
>   even everything,
> And this world also would not gather in so many
>   ways
> Such things as seeds for the sake of their effects.

Through refuting production of the four extreme types in this way, production that is established by way of its own character is negated. However, the refutation of production of the four extreme types does not refute merely conventional production. For, merely conventional production does not have to be any of the four extreme types of production. Not only that, but also dependent production itself establishes that things are not produced from the four extremes. Dzong-ka-ba's *Great Commentary on (Nāgārjuna's) "Treatise on the Middle Way"* says:

> Therefore, that, by the very necessity of accepting that a sprout is produced in dependence on a seed, one is able to refute these four [extreme types of production] is a distinguishing feature of the reasoning of dependent-arising, the king of reasonings.

Furthermore, the master Buddhapālita, who attained yogic feats, says:

> Here [an objector] says, "Show how this which is called production is only a convention."
> *Answer:* This is shown initially [in the first stanza of the first chapter of Nāgārjuna's *Treatise on the Middle Way*]:[250]
>
>> There is never production

Anywhere of any thing
From itself, from others,
From both, or causelessly.

Also, the *Buddhapālita Commentary* says, "Hence, because there is no [inherently existent] production, this which is called production is only a convention."

REFUTATION OF PRODUCTION OF THE FOUR ALTERNATIVES

[Some of] our own recent scholars apply the reasonings explained in the basic text and commentary of [the Middle Way Autonomist] Jñānagarbha's *Discrimination of the Two Truths* here [in the Middle Way Consequence School. However] most texts concerning the Consequence School describe just the reasons of the diamond fragments as a refutation of the four alternatives. Except for this, it does not appear that what Jñānagarbha explains in the *Discrimination of the Two Truths* is set forth with much emphasis in the Consequence School.

REASONING REFUTING PRODUCTION OF THE EXISTENT AND NON-EXISTENT

Causes do not produce inherently existent effects, for the inherently existent has no need for causes.[255] Non-existent effects also are not produced, because causes could not do anything for the non-existent. Effects that are both existent and non-existent also are not produced, because a composite of these two does not occur. Also, causes do not produce effects that are neither existent nor non-existent, for something that is neither of these two does not occur. This [reasoning] is explained in the basic text and commentary of Chandrakīrti's *Supplement*, in Shāntideva's *Engaging in the Bodhisattva Deeds*, and also in Atīsha's *Lamp for the Path to Enlightenment*.[256]

One can understand [the reasoning of] the lack of being one or many through the explanation of the sevenfold reasoning.

5 Refuting a Self of Persons

The presentation of the reasoning for ascertaining the self-lessness of persons has three parts: (1) ascertaining the self as not inherently existent, (2) showing that this also establishes the mine as not inherently existent, (3) how this reasoning is applied to other [phenomena].

ASCERTAINING THE SELF AS NOT INHERENTLY EXISTENT

Nāgārjuna's *Treatise on the Middle Way* describes a fivefold reasoning:[261]

> The One Gone Thus is not the aggregates, nor is he
> other than the aggregates.
> The aggregates are not in him, nor is he in them.
> The One Gone Thus does not possess the
> aggregates.
> What One Gone Thus is there?

Three positions, the two of mutual dependence and the one of possession, are included in the two positions of sameness and difference; however, in consideration of the modes of conception in which the [false] view of the transitory collection operates, five positions are set out in the tenth and

391

twenty-second chapters [of Nāgārjuna's *Treatise on the Middle Way*].

Objection: [Buddha] says in sūtra that (1) forms are not the self, (2) the self does not possess forms, (3) the self is not in forms, (4) nor are forms in the self, and he spoke similarly with respect to the remaining four aggregates. In this way, he taught antidotes to the twenty parts of the [false] view of the transitory collection. Hence, would a fourfold analysis not be appropriate? Why is it explained as having five aspects?

Answer: [Buddha] spoke this way in sūtra because the [false] view of the transitory collection is unable to conceive of self without there being first an apprehension of the aggregates and, hence, within observing the aggregates in these four ways, it engages in [the conception of] self [inherent existence]. Therefore, a fifth base of the apprehension of self as something other, beyond the aggregates, does not occur except in [the philosophies of the non-Buddhist] Forders.[264] This is the reason why [Buddha] did not speak of a fifth position.

Nāgārjuna spoke of a fifth position in the *Treatise on the Middle Way* because he wanted to refute the systems of the Forders as well. Furthermore, one should understand [the refutation of the Forders' systems] as a branch of the process of coming to a decisive conclusion when refuting the innate self within settling selflessness in one's own continuum.

The honorable, glorious Chandrakīrti made a sevenfold reasoning, adding two more to those negations: that the mere collection [of the bases of designation] is the self and that the shape [of the body] is the self. [Chandrakīrti] added [these two refutations] in order to refute the Buddhist schools of tenets that propound true existence and certain Autonomists who posit the mind as the self or who posit some attribute of a person such as the collection of the aggregates or their shape [to be the self].

Furthermore, sūtra teaches that the conventionalities of self and chariot are posited similarly:

"Self" is a devilish mind.
You are under the control of a [bad] view.
These conditioned aggregates are empty.
There is no sentient being here.

Just as a chariot is designated
In dependence upon collections of parts,
So, conventionally, a sentient being
[Is designated] in dependence upon the aggregates.

Moreover, Chandrakīrti sets forth the sevenfold reasoning to clarify that [the Consequence School] has a special mode of positing the similarity [between a chariot and a person] that is not shared with the Autonomists or the other lower [systems of tenets]. This can be understood in detail from one who has become skilled in the word of the Foremost [Dzong-ka-ba].

Thus the sevenfold reasoning is neither too extensive nor too brief and has many features. Dzong-ka-ba's *Great Exposition of the Stages of the Path to Enlightenment* says:

This presentation, as explained earlier, starting from [examining] a chariot, has, in brief, three features: (1) the feature of easily refuting the view of permanence which is the superimposition of inherent existence on phenomena, (2) the feature of easily refuting the view of annihilation which is to think that dependent-arisings are not feasible in the context of no inherent existence, and (3) the stages of a yogi's analysis, through the practice of which the first two features are achieved.

The third is explained to be the feature of easily gaining conviction about illusory-like dependent-arisings when one analyzes with this mode of analysis.

Now I will explain the sevenfold reasoning itself. The explanation is in two parts: stating the example and applying it to the meaning.

Stating the Example

Chandrakīrti's *Supplement* says that although upon analyzing a chariot in the seven ways — whether it is one with its own parts, different from them, and so forth — it is not found, it is permissible for valid cognition to posit, without invalidation, a chariot designated in dependence upon the parts of the chariot, and that likewise the self, the aggregates, and so forth are posited in a similar manner. The *Supplement* says:

> A chariot is not asserted to be other than its parts,
> Nor non-other. It also does not possess them.
> It is not in the parts, nor are the parts in it.
> It is not the mere collection [of its parts], nor is it
> [their] shape.
> [The self and the aggregates are] similar.

Concerning this, the subject, a chariot, is not inherently the same as its parts — axles, wheels, nails, and so forth — because, if it were, there would be the fallacies that (1) just as there are many parts, so there also would be many chariots, (2) or in another way, just as the chariot is one, so the parts also would be one, and (3) agent and object would be one, etc.

The subject, a chariot, is not inherently different from its parts because otherwise they would be different entities and whatever are different entities and simultaneous must be unrelated other factualities; hence, like a horse and an ox, a chariot would have to be observed separately from its parts but it is not.

With regard to a chariot, the subject, the two positions of dependence — that a chariot inherently depends on its parts or that its parts inherently depend on it — also are not feasible. For, if [either of] these two [positions] were the case, [the chariot and its parts] would have to be inherently different, whereas this has already been explained as not feasible.

With regard to a chariot, the subject, either way in which the chariot could inherently possess its parts — in the sense that, for instance, Devadatta possesses an ox or in the sense that Devadatta possesses ears — also is not feasible. For, according to the former mode of possession, they would be inherently established as different entities, and, according to the latter, they would be inherently established as one entity, and both of these have already been refuted.

With regard to a chariot, the subject, it is not feasible to posit the mere collection of its parts as it, because in that case it would [absurdly] follow that once all the parts of the chariot — wheels, axles, etc. — without anything missing were piled unassembled, in one place, there would be a chariot even in that mere collection. Our own [Buddhist] Proponents of True Existence [that is, Great Exposition School, Sūtra School, and Mind Only School] maintain that although there is no whole,[267] there is a mere composite[268] of the parts. However, even this [composite] is not feasible [as a chariot] because [according to them] the whole does not exist and, therefore, the parts also would not exist.

With regard to the subject, a chariot, it is also not admissible to posit the special shape of its parts to be it. For, it is not feasible for the shapes of the individual parts to be the chariot, nor is it feasible for the shape of the collection of the parts to be the chariot. The first [reasoning, that it is not feasible for the shapes of the individual parts to be the chariot] is established because it is not feasible for shapes that are not different from the shapes of the parts before they were assembled to be a chariot, nor is it feasible for some other shapes that are unlike the shapes previous [to their being assembled] to be a chariot. The first [reason, that it is not feasible for shapes that are not different from the shapes of the parts before they were assembled to be a chariot] is established because, otherwise, since there is no difference in the shapes of the wheels and so forth before being assembled and afterwards, just as there was no chariot before [the parts] were assembled, so there would be no chariot even after [the parts] are assembled. The second [reason, that it is not feasible for some other shapes that are unlike the shapes previous to their being assembled to be a chariot] is established because if the wheels, axles, and so forth have some other, different shapes after they have been assembled that they did not have before they were assembled, this would have to be observed, but it is not.

The second part of the earlier reason — that the shape of the collection of its parts cannot be posited as the chariot — is so because in the systems of the Proponents of True Existence the collection is not substantially established, and, therefore, it is not feasible for the shape of that [collection] to be substantially established, whereas they assert that a chariot is substantially established. Moreover, it is the case [that they assert a substantially existent chariot] because those systems maintain that the bases of designation of all imputed existents are substantially existent. Furthermore, in our own system, in which the basis of designation of an imputed existent is not asserted to be substantially existent, the shape of the collection of parts is the basis of designation of a chariot, not a chariot.

Objection: When sought thus in these seven ways, a chariot is not found, and, therefore, a chariot does not exist. However, this is not feasible, for such [expressions as] "Bring the chariot!" "Buy a chariot!" and "Prepare the chariot!" are renowned in the conventions of the world.

Answer: There is no such fallacy. In our system, when a chariot is analyzed in these seven ways, it is not found, and it is not found either as an ultimate truth or as a conventional truth, but this does not make a chariot non-existent. For, (1) the assertion of a chariot is not made due to [the chariot's] being established by reasoning analyzing whether it inherently exists or not, but is established by only a non-defective, ordinary, worldly — that is, conventional — consciousness without any analysis that searches for the object designated, and (2) moreover, the way in which [a chariot] *is* posited is that it is established as only existing imputedly in the sense of being designated in dependence upon its parts, wheels and so forth. Chandrakīrti's *Supplement* says:[269]

That [chariot] is not established in these seven ways
Either as [its own] suchness or in the world,
But without analysis it is designated here
From [the viewpoint of] the world in dependence
    upon its parts.

Chandrakīrti's *Autocommentary on the "Supplement to (Nāgārjuna's) 'Treatise on the Middle Way'"* clearly speaks of how [phenomena] are established in a nominal way:

Not only does this position just very clearly establish the designation of the convention, chariot, from the viewpoint of what is renowned in the world, but also these nominalities should be asserted from the viewpoint of worldly renown without analysis.

The Autonomists and the other lower tenet systems — having seen that if the collection of parts, etc., were not posited as an illustration of a whole, etc., [no phenomenon could be posited at all since] there is no whole, etc., which is a separate entity from those — assert that [something] from within[270] the bases of designation is posited as this and that phenomenon. They do not know how to posit a phenomenon if an object that is designated as that phenomenon is not found when sought. Therefore, because they do not accept that chariots and so forth are mere nominal designations, they assert that chariots and so forth conventionally are established by way of their own character.

Although this supreme system does not hold that anything such as the collection of parts or something within it is an illustration of the whole and so forth, it is able to present well all actions and agents within the context of mere nominal designation of whole, etc. The Foremost Omniscient [Dzong-ka-ba] advised that since this mode of commenting on the meaning of the scriptures is the Subduer [Buddha's] own uncommon thought, those who are discriminating should train in this system of interpreting Buddha's thought. It appears that this way [of positing phenomena within the context of mere nominal designation] is a supremely difficult point that was not in the province of mind of many who were famed as great pandits in the land of the Superiors [India], and except for the Omniscient Father [Dzong-ka-ba] and his spiritual sons [Gyel-tsap and Kay-drup] most of the scholars and adepts in snowy Tibet also were unable to see even a part of this.

This mode of analysis is a profound means of quickly finding the view of emptiness. Chandrakīrti's *Autocommentary on the "Supplement to (Nāgārjuna's) 'Treatise on the Middle Way' "* says:[272]

> Because these worldly conventionalities do not exist when investigated in this way but do exist by way of non-analytical renown, yogis, when they analyze these in these stages, will penetrate very quickly to the depths of suchness.

Applying the Example to the Meaning
One should consider whether this so-called person or self which is the basis of the conception thinking "I" is the same as one's own [mental and physical] aggregates or different from them because, if it exists, it must be one of those two. For, in general, it is seen in the world that if something is affirmed by the mind to have a counterpart, it is excluded from being without a counterpart; and, if something is affirmed as not having a counterpart, it is excluded from having a counterpart. Therefore, oneness and otherness are a mutually exclusive dichotomy.

[Refutation of Oneness]
If the self and the aggregates were one, there would be three fallacies:

(1) asserting a self would be senseless;
(2) there would be many selves;

(3) the self would have production and disintegration.

(1) If the self and the aggregates were inherently one, asserting a self would be senseless because "self" would merely be a synonym of "aggregates", like "moon" and "rabbit-bearer". Nāgārjuna's *Treatise on the Middle Way, Called "Wisdom"* says:[278]

> When it is taken that there is no self
> Except for the appropriated [aggregates],
> Then just the appropriated [aggregates] are the self,
> In which case your self is non-existent.

(2) If the self and the aggregates were inherently one, then just as there are many aggregates, so there would be many selves. Chandrakīrti's *Supplement to (Nāgārjuna's) "Treatise on the Middle Way"* says:[279]

> If the self were the aggregates, then,
> Since they are many, those selves would also be
>   many.

(3) If the self and the aggregates were one, it would [absurdly] follow that the self would be subject to production and disintegration. For, the aggregates are subject to production and disintegration. Nāgārjuna's *Treatise on the Middle Way* says:[280]

> If the self were the aggregates,
> It would have production and disintegration.

Objection: What fallacy is there in the self's having production and disintegration?

Answer: If production and disintegration are only conventions, there is no fallacy. However, if the self has production and disintegration that are established by way of their own character, there would be three fallacies: (a) remembering [former] births would be impossible; (b) actions done would be wasted; (c) one would meet with [the effects of] actions not performed [by oneself]. Moreover, those three fallacies arise due to [the consequence that] if the selves of former and later births were individuals that are established by way of their own character, they would be unrelated other factualities.

Objection: There is no fallacy. For, although [former and later births] are individuals that are established by way of their own character, they are of one continuum.

Answer: That also is not feasible because if [former and later lives] were different by way of their own entities, they could not be one continuum just as, for example, with Maitreya and Upagupta are not. Chandrakīrti's *Supplement* says:[281]

> The phenomena dependent on Maitreya and
> Upagupta
> Are just other and thus do not belong to one
> continuum.
> It is inadmissible for things that are individual
> By way of their own character to belong to one
> continuum.

Refutation of the Position That the Self and the Aggregates Are Different

If the self were established by way of its own character as different from the [mental and physical] aggregates, it would not have the character of the aggregates: production, abiding, and disintegration. For, [the self] would be an other factuality unrelated to the aggregates. It is like, for example, a horse, which, since it is different from an ox, does not have [the specific characteristics of an ox, which are] a hump [on the shoulders] and so forth. If this were the case, [the mental and physical aggregates] would not exist as the basis for the designation of the convention of a self, nor would they exist as an object of a [consciousness] conceiving self. For, the self would be uncompounded, like a sky-flower. Chandrakīrti sets this forth in his *Clear Words* in the form of an other-renowned syllogism.

Moreover, if the self and the aggregates were inherently different, [the self] would have to be observed as a different factuality from the characteristics of the aggregates, such as being suitable [to be called] form, just as form and consciousness, for example, are observed as different.

The former reasoning is taught in the eighteenth chapter [of Nāgārjuna's *Treatise on the Middle Way*] with:[283]

> If [the self] were other than the aggregates,
> It would not have the character of the aggregates.

The latter reasoning is taught in the twenty-seventh chapter [of Nāgārjuna's *Treatise on the Middle Way*] with:[284]

> If [the self] is other, then it should be apprehended
> Without the appropriation; but it is not [so]
> apprehended.

There are a great many difficult points to be explained with regard to these reasonings refuting oneness and difference, but I will not elaborate on them here.

How the Remaining Positions Are Refuted by These Reasonings

Through having refuted those two [positions of] oneness and difference of entity, the two positions of dependence — that the self exists in dependence on the aggregates and that the aggregates exist in dependence on the self — also are refuted. For, although these two [positions of dependence] would be feasible if [the self and the aggregates] were different entities, the position that they are different entities has already been refuted.

The position that the self possesses the aggregates is also not feasible. For, as was explained at the time of the chariot, the two modes of possession do not pass beyond the positions of oneness and difference.

Moreover, it is also not feasible that the mere collection of the aggregates is the self. For since it is said that the self is designated in dependence upon the five aggregates, the five aggregates are the basis of designation and the person is the phenomenon designated, and it is not feasible that the basis of designation be the phenomenon designated. The thrust of this reasoning [that the basis of designation cannot be the phenomenon designated] is slightly difficult to realize. Moreover, this should be understood from (1) the [Consequence School's] uncommon way of interpreting the force of the words in the previously quoted sūtra:

> Just as a chariot is designated
> In dependence upon collections of parts,
> So conventionally a sentient being
> [Is designated] in dependence upon the aggregates.

and (2) from detailed[285] realization of the essentials of reasoning in Chandrakīrti's *Autocommentary on the "Supplement to (Nāgārjuna's) 'Treatise on the Middle Way'"* that illuminate this reasoning through proof statements.

Moreover, if the collection [of the aggregates] is the self, there is also the fallacy that agent and object would be one. This also refutes the assertion made by some of our own [Buddhist] schools of tenets that the self is the continuum of the aggregates.

It is also not feasible to assert that the shape of the aggregates is the self. For, shape exists only in physical things, and, therefore, [if the self were shape] the self could not be posited [in dependence] upon mind and so forth.

The non-finding of a self anywhere, when analyzed thus with reasoning in these seven ways, is the meaning of the absence of inherent existence of the self. Since this fact is similar in terms of both of the two truths, there is no self established by way of its own character even conventionally. Nevertheless, when there is no analysis seeking the object designated, the self or person is established by valid cognition, with no possibility of denial, as being able to perform activities. Therefore, persons exist conventionally.

Moreover, when an awareness thinking, "I," is produced, it is produced in dependence on having taken the five aggregates in one's own continuum as a basis. Therefore, [the I] exists as a mere designation in dependence upon the five aggregates. Moreover, these [points] are the thought of the root text and autocommentary of Chandra-kīrti's *Supplement* quoted earlier:[287]

> That [chariot] is not established in these seven ways
> Either as [its own] suchness or in the world,
> But without analysis it is designated here
> From [the viewpoint of] the world in dependence
>   upon its parts.

Chandrakīrti's *Commentary on (Āryadeva's) "Four Hundred"* says that something illusory must be left over as a remainder:

> For that reason, when analyzed thus, the inherent existence of things is not established. Hence, just an illusory-like nature is left over as a remainder with respect to things individually.

The Foremost Omniscient [Dzong-ka-ba] says:

> This combination of the following two [factors] barely occurs — (1) refuting, without residue, the object of negation [inherent existence] through reasoned analysis and (2) the feasibility of positing, as left after the negation, without losing anything, all the functionalities of dependently arisen causes and effects as like illusions. Therefore, it is very difficult to gain the view of the Middle Way.

Regarding that, all proponents of tenets among our own schools of the high and low vehicles, present their own systems as systems that are free from the extremes. And, in particular, the other [i.e., non-Consequentialist] great chariots of the Mind Only and Middle Way Schools have ways of presenting the meaning of the middle free from extremes and of presenting illusory-like [appearances]. If you understand well how assertions on these by the higher schools of tenets are more to the point[288] and more difficult to realize than those of the lower systems of tenets and that nevertheless all of those [non-Consequentialist schools] do not contain the essentials of being free from all extremes as in the presentation of the two truths in this supreme system and if you understand well how only this system avoids all the very subtle extremes and how it also has profound features totally unlike the other systems in its positing illusory-like [appearances], you will develop firm and genuine faith, induced through the path of reasoning, in general in the texts of the father [Nāgārjuna] and his spiritual sons and in particular in the texts of the great lords of adepts who properly expounded the Consequentialist system as well as in the high sayings of the father, the Foremost Great Being [Dzong-ka-ba] and his spiritual sons [Gyel-tsap and Kay-drup].

You must understand, just as they are, the essentials of the reasonings explained previously and the essentials of the presentation [of appearances] as like illusions, and you must also understand the stages in which these are properly taken to mind as well as the subtle distinctions in generating experience of them. These understandings come (1) through penetrating well in depth, not just superficially, the scriptures of the Foremost [Dzong-ka-ba] in general and his great and small *Expositions of the Stages of the Path to Enlightenment* in particular; (2) through properly relying on excellent spiritual friends who, along with meeting [exalted beings in meditative vision], have obtained certain subtle and secret essentials of the speech of the Foremost Great Being [Dzong-ka-ba] which were given orally to the excellent among his spiritual children, great Bodhisattvas abiding on the grounds, transmitted in stages and put down in writing by the scholars and adepts of this system; (3) through taking to mind the meaning of these texts again and again by means of properly thought out reasoning; and moreover (4) through engendering unusually great effort in the many external and internal causal collections. Moreover, it is very right to strive in this way. For the omniscient Gyel-tsap says:[289]

Until I found the Foremost Holy [Dzong-ka-ba],
I had not even partially realized
Dependent-arising, the middle free from extremes
The path severing the root of cyclic existence.

Even [Gyel-tsap] the Great Lord of Reasoning who rivals the likes of the six ornaments[290] of Jambudvīpa, the land of Superiors [India], did not realize even a portion of this view of the Middle Way free from extremes, prior to meeting the Foremost Great Being [Dzong-ka-ba].

Also, [Gyel-tsap] says that he realized the meaning of the middle free from extremes through the kindness of the Foremost Omniscient [Dzong-ka-ba]:[291]

In the good explanations of the excellent spiritual
    friend
Is explained, just as it is, the meaning of
    dependent-arising, the middle free from extremes
Which is just as asserted by the protector Nāgārjuna,
And is the single thought of Buddhapālita,
    Chandrakīrti, and Shāntideva.

[Gyel-tsap] also says that it is necessary to work hard at this[292] way because it is the excellent life of the path of liberation and omniscience:[293]

Without realizing the principle of the middle free
    from the extremes,
One cannot reach the levels[294] of the supreme
    Superiors.
Therefore, having concluded that emptiness means
    dependent-arising,
Make effort at practice, striving in the proper way.

[Gyel-tsap] also says that upon understanding that this supreme system is difficult to find and that in not very long it will disappear, discriminating people should generate effort quickly, quickly:[295]

Since proponents of the two truths of Nāgārjuna's

good system,
Difficult to find in even a billion eons,
In not long will disappear from this world,
The discriminating should quickly generate effort.

These points are very important, appearing to be advice of the utmost profundity. Since I wish to explain about the Consequence School[296] only briefly here, you should understand the essentials of the tenets of this system at length from other [texts].

SHOWING THAT THIS [ASCERTAINMENT OF PERSONS AS NOT INHERENTLY EXISTENT] ALSO ESTABLISHES THE MINE AS NOT INHERENTLY EXISTENT

When the self is sought in this way by means of reasoning that examines whether or not it is inherently existent, it is not found to be any of these seven, whereby inherent existence is negated with respect to the self. At this point, that the mine is established by way of its own character is also easily negated. Nāgārjuna's *Fundamental Text Called "Wisdom"* says:[297]

If [an inherently existent] self does not exist,
How could [inherently existent] mine exist?

Moreover, although just an awareness that realizes the I to be without inherent existence does not explicitly apprehend the mine to be without inherent existence, when the mind turns to the mine in a manner of analyzing whether inherent existence exists or not, based on the functioning of the former awareness, [the mine] is easily established as without inherent existence. Because [this mind] does not consider another proof, no separate reasoning [for refuting the inherent existence of the mine] is set forth in the great texts.

Two different ways of asserting [mine] appear. [One system explains that] the eyes, ears, and so forth included in one's own continuum are illustrations of mine but are not objects of observation of an innate [false] view of the transitory collection that conceives [inherently existent] mine. They explain that this is the thought of the Foremost Father [Dzong-ka-ba] and his spiritual sons [Gyel-tsap and Kay-drup].

[Another system explains that] the eyes, ears, and so forth are the bases of designation[300] of the mine but are not illustrations[301] of mine because it is not feasible for a basis of designation to be the phenomenon designated. [Jam-yang-shay-ba says that] the explanation in Kay-drup's *Opening the Eyes of the Fortunate* that eyes, ears, and so forth are illustrations of mine merely indicates that these are illustrations of things taken as mine; it does not indicate they are mine itself.[302] [Jam-yang-shay-ba says that] this way of explaining [mine] is the thought of Dzong-ka-ba's *Great Commentary on (Nāgārjuna's) "Fundamental Text Called 'Wisdom' "*.[303] Although there appears to be much to be investigated in both these assertions, I wish to elaborate on them elsewhere.

HOW THIS REASONING IS APPLIED TO OTHER PHENOMENA

Chandrakīrti's *Supplement to (Nāgārjuna's) "Treatise on the Middle Way"* says that all these phenomena, renowned in the world, do not exist when sought in the seven ways and that they are posited as existent for a non-analytical, conventional consciousness:[304]

> Parts, qualities, passion, definition, fuel, and so forth
> As well as whole, qualificand, the impassioned,[305] illustration,[306] fire, and so forth —
> These do not exist in the seven ways when subjected to the analysis of the chariot;
> They exist through worldly renown which is other than that.

In the *Chapter Showing the Three Vows Sūtra* [Buddha] says that what is renowned in the world is not refuted by reasoning:

> The world argues with me, I do not argue with the world. Whatever is accepted in the world as existent and non-existent, that I also accept in that way.

6 Dependent-Arising

The presentation of the king of reasonings, the reason of dependent-arising, has two parts: the actual explanation and how the other reasonings derive from this.

ACTUAL EXPLANATION OF DEPENDENT-ARISING

The *Questions of Sāgaramati Sūtra*[308] says that inherent establishment is refuted through the reasoning of dependent-arising:

> Those which arise dependently
> Are free of inherent existence.

And the *Questions of Anavatapta, the King of Nāgas, Sūtra* says:

> Those which are produced from conditions are not
>   produced.
> They do not have an inherent nature of production.
> Those which depend on conditions are said to be
>   empty.
> One who knows emptiness is aware.

In that, production from conditions is the reason. No production is the probandum. The meaning of not being produced is indicated by the second line. It is not that mere production is being eliminated; inherently established production is being eliminated. Moreover, in the *Descent into Laṅkā Sūtra*, the Teacher [Buddha] himself clarifies his thought:

> O Mahāmati, thinking of no *inherently existent* production, I said that all phenomena are not produced.

[In the passage from the *Questions of Anavatapta Sūtra*,] through the relating of [the relative] "which" and [the correlative] "those", the subjects that are the substrata [of an absence of inherently existent production] are indicated. They are external things such as sprouts and internal things such as compositional activity. The third line means that just dependence and reliance on conditions is the meaning of [being] empty of inherent existence. This statement indicates that an emptiness of inherent existence is the meaning of dependent-arising. It does not indicate an emptiness that is the absence of the capacity to perform functions — that is, a negative of mere production.

Seeing that just this teaching of this reasoning as refuting all extremes is an unsurpassed distinctive feature elevating his teacher, the Supramundane Victor, above all other teachers, Nāgārjuna's mind was captivated by this mode [of dependent-arising], whereupon the glorious protector, the Superior Nāgārjuna — in his *Fundamental Text Called "Wisdom"*, *Sixty Stanzas of Reasoning*, his Collection of Praises, and so forth — praised the Supramundane Victor from the viewpoint of just his speaking of dependent-arising. Also, our own excellent leader, the Foremost Great Being [Dzong-ka-ba] says:[309]

> Homage to the Conqueror who perceived
> And gave instruction on dependent-arising.
> Through perceiving and setting forth such
> He has unsurpassed wisdom and is the unsurpassed

teacher.

And so on. Praising Buddha in this way is pure speech of praise induced by genuine faith induced by the path of reasoning; therefore, these are not artificial words or words of flattery.

The Sanskrit original of dependent-arising is *pratītya-samutpādaḥ*.[311] Most earlier masters said that *prati* is a distributive, [meaning] diversely, and that *i*, [the verbal root meaning] going, is used [to mean] departing and disintegrating. Through adding the affix *ya* to that [verbal root *i*], *itya* is taken as a secondary derivative noun, which comes to mean "that which goes". Hence, they say that [*pratītya-samutpāda* means] the arising of what possess going and disintegration diversely.

In that case, except for the general dependent-arising, which is the arising of effects from causes, when each particular case is specified such as in "A consciousness arises in dependence upon an eye [sense power]," [the etymology] is not suitable because within one thing there is no way to explain the term "diversely". Taking it as a secondary derivative noun is not feasible also because, in that case, it would be wrong [for the text] to read, "Having depended on an eye sense power and forms" (*cakṣuḥ pra-tītya rūpāṇi ca*) and would instead have to read on all occasions, "A consciousness which departs to an eye [sense power] and forms" (*cakṣuḥ pratītyaṃ vijñānaṃ rūpāṇi ca*) [and it is obvious to anyone who has seen the text that it is not written that way]. Since no case ending is to be seen [with *pratītya*],[314] it is suitable only to be a continuative with an indeclinable ending.

Also, the master Bhāvaviveka does not make individual explanations of the meanings of *prati*, and so forth. He explains it only as a term used to mean that "When this is, that arises," or "Due to having this condition, that arises," like [the term] wild sesame. For Chandrakīrti's *Clear Words* says:

Such is said [by Bhāvaviveka] having asserted *pra-*

tītyasamutpāda to be a conventional term [not necessarily following its etymological meaning] like
araṇyetilaka, etc.

That also is not feasible because the master, the Superior
Nāgārjuna spoke within dividing [the term] into its individual components, *pratītya (brten pa)* and *samutpāda
('byung ba)* [in his *Sixty Stanzas of Reasoning*]:[316]

That which is produced having met this and that
[collection of causes and conditions]
Is not inherently produced.
(*Tat tat prāpya yad utpannaṃ notpannaṃ tat
svabhāvataḥ.*)[317]

Even if [Bhāvaviveka] wants to set forth [this position] as
the meaning of the passage in Nāgārjuna's *Precious
Garland*,[318] "When this[319] is, that arises, like long when
there is short," he has to explain [*pratītya*] as having the
meaning of "meeting" (*'phrad pa, prāpya/prāpti*). This is
because[320] he has to assert just that long comes to be having
met short and having depended on short, or in reliance
upon short.

Therefore, the honorable master Chandrakīrti's own system is: Because *prati* is used for "meeting" and *i* is used for
"going", *pratītya* — which has the continuative affix *[ya]*[323]
on that [*i* base] — through being modified by the modifier
[*prati*], is used for "meeting", that is to say, "depending"
or "relying". [The verbal root] *i* alone is generally used for
"going", *pratītya* — which has the continuative affix *ya*[323]
mean "meeting" and so forth. That this is so is like, for
example, the fact that the water of the Ganges is extremely
sweet, but when it mixes with the ocean, it comes to have a
salty taste. Moreover, in that way, Chandrakīrti's *Clear
Words* says:

In that, *prati* has the meaning of meeting (*'phrad pa,
prāpti*). [The verbal root] *i* has the meaning of
going. The term *pratītya*, a continuative, is used for

"meeting" — that is, "relying" — because the root is completely modified by a modifier [i.e., the prefix *prati*]. It is explained:

Through the force of a modifier
The meaning of the verbal root is
completely changed.
Just as, though the water of the Ganges is
sweet,
[It is completely changed] by the water of
the ocean.

The term *pāda*, which has *samut* preceding it, is used for "arising". It is also suitable to be explained as "existing" (*yod pa, sat*) and "established" (*grub pa, siddha*).

Therefore, in brief, our own system is this: The meaning of *pratītyasamutpāda* is the existence, establishment, or arising of things in dependence upon causes and conditions. Chandrakīrti's *Clear Words* says, "Hence, the meaning of *pratītyasamutpāda*[325] is the arising of things in reliance upon causes and conditions." In that way, it is very important to know well the many different ways that [those great scholars, called] great chariots, etymologized *pratītyasamutpāda* because, in dependence upon their etymologies, there are many essential points of the different ways of generating ascertainment about the extent of the meaning of dependent-arising and about the depth of penetration of suchness.

Furthermore, since I wish to explain this extensively elsewhere, I will express [here] just a little about the assertions of the glorious Chandrakīrti. In that way, the meaning of dependent-arising is explained as meeting, relying, and depending. The reason for this is as follows. In general, meet, rely, and depend are said even to be synonymous. However, if we separate them in order to facilitate understanding, "meeting" as a reason [for the absence of inherent existence of things] bears within it the sense of dependent-arising as the production of things from their own causes.

This is [an assertion held in] common also with lower tenet systems. Moreover, since [the Middle Way School and the lower tenet systems] are similar in their assertions of the meaning of dependent-arising just to that point, this is said to be "common". However [Proponents of the Middle Way School] do not [assert] the truly existent dependent-arising that those [of the lower systems] assert; also, [in lower tenet systems] they do not assert that the absence of true existence is what is proved [by dependent-arising].

"Meeting" refers to the meeting of the actions of production of the effect and cessation of the cause. It is not that cause and effect meet.

"Relying" indicates a reason [for the absence of inherent existence of phenomena] that is the attainment by compounded and uncompounded phenomena of their own entities in reliance upon their own parts. This is in terms of explaining *samutpāda* as [meaning] "established".[327] [Here the meaning of dependent-arising] has a wider application than the former [because it applies to all phenomena, both the permanent and impermanent]. The mere meaning that is explicitly indicated [in "establishment-in-reliance"] is in common with other Proponents of the Middle Way School.

"Dependence" indicates a reason [for the absence of inherent existence of things] that is the dependent designation of all phenomena — their being established as mere designations in dependence upon their own bases of designation. This is a feature of only this supreme system; it is not common to Autonomists and below.

Accordingly, if you take the meaning of arising in the phrase "arising of things" from that passage in Chandrakīrti's *Clear Words* to be mere production, it then indicates the first reason, and if you take it as establishment or existence, then it also indicates the two latter reasons. If you take "causes and conditions" as merely the seed that is the substantial cause of a sprout and the water, manure, and so forth that are its contributing conditions, then it indicates the former reason. If you take "causes and conditions" to

mean the cause for something's achieving its own entity —
its basis of imputation or parts — then it indicates the
middle reason. If you take "causes and conditions" to be
the respective conceptual consciousnesses that impute phenomena, then it indicates the last reason.

Therefore, the "causes and conditions" in Chandrakīrti's
phrase "in reliance upon causes and conditions" should not
be taken as only the causes and conditions of compounded
phenomena such as seeds, water, manure, and so forth.
That it must also refer to the imputing conceptual consciousness is the special thought of the glorious Chandrakīrti and the Foremost Great Being [Dzong-ka-ba]. Nevertheless, most of those discriminating persons whose heads are
adorned with paṇḍita hats with very sharp points have still
not drawn out[328] [this topic]. There also is a mode of
explanation — that others have not drawn out[329] — in
which meeting, relying, and depending [are taken as in-
dicating] only the third reason from the viewpoint of treating them as synonyms. I will not elaborate on this here.

Also, regarding those, the Foremost Great Being [Dzong-
ka-ba] says in his *Small Exposition of the Stages of the Path
To Enlightenment*:

> Therefore, external things, such as sprouts, and
> internal things, such as compositional activity, arise
> in dependence upon, respectively, seeds, etc., and
> ignorance, etc.

This indicates the first reason. Also, that same work says:

> [Whatever is established by way of its own entity-
> ness] must be inherently established, that is, be able
> to set itself up under its own power, whereby it is
> contradictory for it to rely on causes and conditions.

This indicates the middle reason. Also, that work says:

> Through this, you should understand that persons,
> pots, and so forth are without inherent establish-
> ment because of being imputed in dependence on

their own collections [of parts].

This indicates the third reason. However, [Dzong-ka-ba,] collecting them all into the common and the uncommon, says in that same work, "Those are the two presentations of the reasoning of dependent-arising."

Not only that, but also Dzong-ka-ba's *Great Explanation of (Chandrakīrti's) "Supplement to (Nāgārjuna's) 'Treatise on the Middle Way'"* says:

> The Supramundane Victor said, "The essence of phenomena is this: When this is, that arises; because this is produced, that is produced. Through the condition of ignorance, there are compositional activities," and so forth. And Nāgārjuna's *Precious Garland* says:[333]

>> When this is, that arises,
>> Like short when there is long.
>> When this is produced, that is produced,
>> Like light from the arising of a flame.

> And Nāgārjuna's *Fundamental Text Called "Wisdom"* also says:[334]

>> A doer arises in dependence on a doing
>> And a doing arises in dependence upon just
>>   that doer.
>> Except for that, we do not see
>> Another cause for their establishment.

Even each of these three passages which [Dzong-ka-ba] cites in series are suitable to indicate all three presentations [of the meaning of dependent-arising], but in terms of what they mainly indicate and in terms of sequence, they set forth the three different presentations of the reasoning [of dependent-arising].

This [threefold interpretation of dependent-arising] is also the assertion of the glorious Chandrakīrti. Chandrakīrti's *Commentary on (Āryadeva's) "Four Hundred"* says:[335]

Here, that which has its own intrinsic existence, has inherent existence, has its own power, or has no dependence on others would be self-established; therefore, it would not have a dependent arising. However, all compounded things are dependent-arisings. In that way, things that have dependent arising are not self-powered because they are produced in dependence upon causes and conditions. All these [phenomena] are not self-powered; therefore, no things have self, inherent existence.

If you know in detail [Dzong-ka-ba's] mode of interpretation of the meaning of this citation [as set forth] in his *Great Exposition of Special Insight,* you will understand [how the passage indicates the threefold interpretation of dependent-arising].

In dependence on certain such special points, the definitive great scholar Nor-sang-gya-tso[336] is renowned to have said, "Whatever is an established base [i.e., whatever exists] is a compounded phenomenon." About this, many skilled and unskilled people have said, "It [absurdly] follows that the subject, uncompounded space, is a compounded phenomenon because it is an established base,"[337] etc. These neophytes at elementary logic and epistemology demonstrate many commonly proclaimed points of damage [to such a position] and scornfully laugh. However, how could this great scholar and adept, who penetrated all of sūtra and tantra, not know this little bit of reasoning? Though he said such within hoping that, in dependence on his words, [people would] have an effective way of forming understanding of the meaning of dependent-arising, it appears that they have become examples of: "For persons pained by karma, even medicine given becomes poison."

The above explanation of the meaning of the reasoning of dependent-arising is the unsurpassed thought of Chandrakīrti's etymological explanation of *pratītyasamutpāda.* This is also indeed the final thought of the Foremost Great Being [Dzong-ka-ba], but since it appears that others have not explained it clearly, I have explained it a little.

Now, I will say a little about the way that the two extremes are cleared away by this reasoning [of dependent-arising]. The main places for going wrong with respect to realizing the pure view here [according to the Consequentialist system] are of two types. One is the view of permanence, or the view of superimposition, that has a process of apprehension conceiving true existence, i.e., the conception that phenomena truly exist. The second is the view of annihilation, or deprecation, when the measure of the object of negation is not apprehended and, instead, is taken too far, whereby one is not able to induce ascertainment with respect to all the causes and effects of purification[338] and thorough affliction. Both of these [extremes] can be refuted without residue in dependence on just this reasoning of dependent-arising. Through ascertaining the reason, one avoids the extreme of nihilism and finds ascertainment with regard to the dependent-arising of cause and effect, and through ascertaining the probandum, one avoids the extreme of permanence and gains ascertainment with regard to absence of inherent existence.

With respect to gaining such ascertainment, that which has very strong force is just the reasoning of dependent imputation. Moreover, this is the incomparable lion's roar of the good explanations of the Foremost Lama [Dzong-ka-ba]. Also, both extremes are avoided even through ascertainment of the reason and the thesis individually. Furthermore, in general, the extreme of existence is avoided through appearance, and the extreme of non-existence is avoided through emptiness. These are said to be distinguishing features[339] of the Middle Way Consequence School.

In dependence upon secret essentials of the word of this Foremost One [Dzong-ka-ba], you should know that there is a distinctive way that these become distinguishing features of the Middle Way Consequence School that is not just what is explicitly indicated. For, otherwise, even in each of the four schools of tenets, there are explanations that both the extreme of existence and the extreme of non-existence are avoided through appearance and that both extremes are also avoided through emptiness.

In general, there is the way that the two extremes are avoided with respect to things because they are dependent-arisings. In particular, there are ways that the two extremes are avoided, in dependence on reasoning, for the awareness of a person at the time of hearing and thinking about the texts of the Middle Way School, as well as ways that the two extremes are avoided for one's awareness when realization that arises from meditation has been generated — on the two levels of an ordinary being and a Superior. Furthermore, even among Superiors, due to the gradual increase of the force of mind of those on higher levels, there are many differences of subtlety in how, for one's mind, the two extremes are avoided as this becomes more[340] profound than on lower levels. For, Shāntideva says:[341]

> Even among yogis, at each level the higher
> Damage [the lower] through features of their
> intelligence.

Therefore, all the presentations of the two truths of the Middle Way Consequence School are taken from within the sphere of this reasoning of dependent-arising, and there are also many important reasons regarding many uncommon features at the time of path and fruit. Furthermore, these can be known well by persons who have complete understanding (1) that identifies the factor of emptiness by reason of having ascertained[344] the factor of appearance and (2) that induces ascertainment with respect to the factor of appearance through having taken the factor of emptiness as the reason. However, it is not possible that all these could be complete in the mode of initial dawning [of rough ideas to someone] who has not found well an understanding of the view. Moreover, these are seen to depend upon knowing well the meaning of how all presentations of cyclic existence and nirvana are only imputedly existent and, within that, knowing well what is eliminated and what is included within the term "mere nominality, only imputed existence".

Alas, I wonder whether this — endowed with an
  array of ambrosia-lights
Of Lo-sang-drak-ba's good explanations
Which has come to the peak of the eastern
  mountain of not low merit
For the sake of generating manifest joy — is
  glorious only for my own mind.

The form of a rainbow of the subtle body of a
  hundred texts' good meanings,
Written with the pen[345] of pure reasoning
Through being reflected in the mirror of my mind,
Bestows joy through thousands of visions and
  transformations.

That sage who, dwelling in the forest of
  Nāgārjuna's ten million procedures,
Is skilled at summoning the beautiful woman of
  emptiness and dependent-arising
Through the messenger of the meditative
  stabilization of stainless reasoning
Is called a Proponent of the Middle Way School.

Those who have abandoned afar the bliss of setting
  the mind in reality
And who proceed crookedly with the pace of
  explanation and debate of generalities of words
Speak from their mouths about dependent-arising a
  hundred times
But such is empty of meaning like a butter lamp in a
  picture.[346]

If those who randomly study limited texts and,
  though lacking the force of mind
To discriminate what requires interpretation and
  what is definitive,

Nonetheless take up the burden of making "is" and
"is not" all equal
Did not say anything, how could it not be nice!
Even though I have not experienced the supreme
taste of realization arising from meditation,
Which is the fruit of laboring at the stainless texts,
How marvelous it is that the Foremost Father
Lo-sang has caused to be born in me
The lot of propounding dependent-arising just as it
is.

Those are stanzas between sections.

HOW THE OTHER REASONINGS DERIVE FROM DEPENDENT-ARISING

The essentials of all the reasonings that prove selflessness and are cases of non-observation of something inextricably related [with inherent existence] meet back to[347] just this reasoning of dependent-arising. This is (1) because the main purpose of all those reasonings is just to generate in the [mental] continuum the view of the middle way upon simultaneously clearing away the two extremes, and just this reasoning of dependent-arising explicitly accomplishes this and (2) because those reasonings also meet back to just this mode [of dependent-arising] when followed out.

As was established earlier, the main reasonings that this system uses for settling the two selflessnesses must be taken to be the two, the refutation of production from the four extremes and the sevenfold reasoning. The way that their essentials meet back to dependent-arising is set forth clearly in Chandrakīrti's *Supplement to (Nāgārjuna's) "Treatise on the Middle Way"* because (1) in that text [Chandrakīrti] clearly speaks of how the reasoning of the refutation of production from the four extremes meets back to the reasoning of dependent-arising:[348]

Because things are not produced causelessly,

Or from Īshvara and so forth as causes,
Or from self, from other, or both,
They are dependently produced.

And (2) in that same text [Chandrakīrti] clearly speaks of
how the sevenfold reasoning meets back to dependent-
arising:[349]

> That [chariot] is not established as [its own]
>   suchness
> Or in the world in the seven ways,
> But without analysis, here in the world,
> Is imputed in dependence on its parts.

Moreover, when, having sought for the object imputed in
the imputation of, for instance, the convention, "A sprout
is growing," you find ascertainment that [a sprout] is not
produced from self, from other, from both, or causelessly,
this — through its own force — induces ascertainment that
the growing of the sprout, etc., is just an imputation, and
also when you find ascertainment that the convention
"growing" [or "production"] is just an imputation, this —
through its own force — induces ascertainment with respect
to non-findability when the object imputed in the imputation of the convention of growing is sought.

This way [in which understanding the one helps in
understanding the other] is the way that the essentials of the
reasoning refuting production from the four extremes meet
back to dependent-arising. Dzong-ka-ba's *Essence of the
Good Explanations* says:[350]

> Through [the reasoning that] external things, such
> as sprouts, and internal things, such as composi-
> tional activity, arise in dependence upon causes and
> conditions — such as a seed and ignorance — their
> production and so forth are empty of an inherent
> nature in the sense of being established by way of
> their own character and are not produced from self,
> other, both or causelessly. Since [Chandrakīrti] re-

futes [the four extreme types of production] in this way, [the object of negation] is refuted in a manner that meets back to just the reasoning of dependent-arising, the king of reasonings cutting all the nets of bad views.

This mainly is the reasoning of [things] being dependently produced, but when [considered] finely, it must also meet back to the reasoning that things are dependently imputed. This latter is more difficult to understand than the former.

The way in which the essentials of the sevenfold reasoning meet back to dependent-arising is that (1) just the non-findability in seven ways induces ascertainment with respect to the person's being merely imputed in dependence upon the [mental and physical] aggregates and (2) just the realization [that the person is] only imputedly existent induces ascertainment with respect to the other [i.e., ascertainment that phenomena are not findable in these seven ways]. Dzong-ka-ba's *Essence of the Good Explanations* says:[351]

> This also meets back to the reasoning of dependent-arising since the non-finding of the person as those seven due to being just imputed in dependence upon the aggregates is the meaning of the selflessness of persons.

Thus, even the other reasonings proving selflessness that are non-observations of related factors contain all these features.

Even each of those reasonings refutes the view of permanence through the conceptually isolatable function of the reasoning itself, which is its negating findability at the end of searching for the object imputed — this findability being something that is necessarily related with inherent establishment, the object of negation. [Each of those reasonings] also refutes the extreme of annihilation through the conceptually isolatable function of the fact that being merely dependently imputed — the opposite of the object of negation, inherent establishment — becomes the reason. You should know that there are two imprints in dependence upon individual functions. Nevertheless, you also must differentiate well how, in dependence on the way [the reason] is explicitly stated, it is an observation of what is opposite or a non-observation of what is necessarily related.

The likes of the very great ability of this reasoning of dependent-arising explicitly to clear away the two extremes do not exist in other reasonings that state factors of emptiness [such as not being produced from self, from other, from both, or causelessly] as the reason. Also, within the reasoning of dependent-arising itself, just the reasoning of dependent imputation is very powerful.

[The Middle Way Autonomists] Bhāvaviveka and his spiritual son [Jñānagarbha] as well as Shāntarakṣhita and his spiritual son [Kamalashīla] also assert that the root of the reasonings refuting true existence meets back to having parts and that having parts is the meaning of dependent-arising. However, the way that these [Consequentialists] have the other reasonings meet back to dependent-arising is utterly different. Also, the way that the reasoning of dependent-arising explicitly eliminates the two extremes [in the Consequentialist system] is not like [what is asserted in] those systems. The masters of the Autonomy School and their students also say that emptiness and dependent-arising have the same import, but the way that they have the same import is not like this system of the [Consequence School]. Furthermore, just the Consequentialists mainly use the expression "king of reasonings" for this reasoning [of dependent-arising]. Dzong-ka-ba's *Great Exposition of the Stages of the Path to Enlightenment* says:

> When other sentient beings apprehend that [a phenomenon] is produced in dependence on causes and conditions, based on this they apprehend [that phenomenon] as having an inherent nature in the sense of existing by way of its own entityness, whereby they are bound [in cyclic existence]. The wise, in

dependence on that sign [i.e., being a dependent-arising], refute that the phenomenon has inherent existence and induce ascertainment with respect to its absence of inherent existence, [thereby] cutting the bonds of views conceiving extremes. Therefore, this establishment of the absence of inherent existence through the sign of dependent-arising is a wondrous, great skillfulness in method.

And Dzong-ka-ba's *Praise of the Supramundane Buddha from the Point of View of Dependent-Arising* says:

> Just that which, through being apprehended,
> Makes, for children, the bonds of extreme
>   conceptions more firm,
> For the wise is the door to cutting
> All the nets of elaboration [of the conception of
>   inherent existence].

His saying that just the reasoning of dependent-arising is, for the wise, the door to cutting all the bonds of extreme conceptions is in consideration that emptiness and dependent-arising come to have the same import.

Furthermore, that Nāgārjuna and his [spiritual] children as well as the Foremost Omniscient [Dzong-ka-ba] say that emptiness has the meaning of dependent-arising is not like positing that which is bulbous as the meaning of pot. It also is not merely that a consciousness realizing one also realizes the other. Therefore, that emptiness comes to mean dependent-arising is not just for any person but is posited as so in the perspective of one who has already ascertained the pure view and has not forgotten it. Dzong-ka-ba's *Ocean of Reasoning, Explanation of (Nāgārjuna's) "Treatise on the Middle Way"* says:

> The meaning of emptiness coming to be the meaning of dependent-arising is for Proponents of the Middle Way School who have refuted inherent existence through valid cognition, not for others.

Therefore, even though some of our own [Ge-luk-ba] scholars assert that this is for persons ranging up from other parties [in a debate] whose continuums have been ripened [such that they are about ready to realize emptiness] and even though some others assert that it is for those whose analysis of the view is complete, I think just what was explained above is correct.

The Foremost Omniscient [Dzong-ka-ba] says [in his *Three Principal Aspects of the Path*]:[352]

> When [the two realizations of appearance and of
>   emptiness exist] simultaneously without
>   alternation,
> And when from only seeing dependent-arising as
>   infallible,
> Ascertaining knowledge entirely destroys the mode
>   of apprehension [of inherently existent objects],
> Then one has completed analysis of the view.

And after that, he says:

> Further,[353] the extreme of [inherent] existence is
>   avoided by [knowledge of the nature of]
>   appearances [as existing as only nominal
>   designations],
> And the extreme of [total] non-existence is avoided
>   by [knowledge of the nature of] emptiness [as the
>   absence of inherent existence and not the absence
>   of nominal existence].
> If, from within emptiness, you know the mode of
>   appearance of cause and effect,
> Then you will not be captivated by extreme views.

Through those statements [Dzong-ka-ba] clearly speaks of how emptiness comes to have the import of dependent-arising, but the meaning of those statements is very difficult to realize. I do not think that it would be correct to assert that the meaning of the former passage is a mere ability to have a simultaneous appearance, with respect to one phenomenon, of its being a dependent-arising arisen from causes and conditions and of its not being inherently existent.

The Foremost Ren-da-wa[354] also says something quite similar to that statement:

> When the two wisdoms of faith in non-delusive
> cause and effect
> And the realization that dependent-arisings are
> empty
> Are understood in inseparable union, then one has
> entered
> The path of the middle way free of extremes.

And:

> At the very time they appear, [phenomena] are
> realized as empty
> And when[355] emptiness is realized, appearance is
> not refuted.
> When ascertainment is found with respect to the
> way that these two are unified,
> Then the thought of the Conqueror has been
> realized.

Therefore, just as much as when one thoroughly analyzes with stainless reasoning, one generates greater ascertainment with respect to how these and those phenomena lack inherent existence, to that extent the inducement of ascertainment with respect to how those phenomena are merely dependent imputations develops in greater force. Also, just as much as the inducement of ascertainment with regard to the way that phenomena are only dependent imputations increases in greater force, to that extent the inducement of ascertainment with regard to the way the phenomena are empty of inherent existence increases in greater force.

Moreover, once an ascertaining consciousness — induced by inferential cognition that a sprout is without inherent existence through the sign of its being a dependent-arising

— has been generated and does not deteriorate, it is evident that there are many different stages of levels of capacity with respect to how these two ascertaining consciousnesses assist each other due to gradual progress higher and higher.

Since this topic [of how the two realizations assist each other] is extremely difficult to understand and, when understood, is amazing, the Protector Nāgārjuna says:

> Relying on actions and effects
> Within knowing this emptiness of phenomena
> Is even more amazing than the amazing
> And even more marvelous than the marvelous.

And the Foremost Great Being [Dzong-ka-ba] says:

> What is more amazing
> And what is more marvelous
> Than that the two ascertainments —
> That all these are empty of inherent existence
> And that this effect arises from that [cause] —
> Assist each other without impediment!

There are still many facets of the meaning of the sameness in import of emptiness and dependent-arising that should be understood in even more detail than what has been explained earlier. The likes of what appears in the Foremost Omniscient [Dzong-ka-ba's] scriptures — his "Great Exposition of Special Insight", "Middling Exposition of Special Insight", and *Great Commentary on (Nāgārjuna's) "Fundamental Treatise on the Middle Way Called 'Wisdom' "* — do not appear in any of the essays of instruction on the view composed by later scholars, [even though these are] renowned to be very clear. Also, [what is found in Dzong-ka-ba's scriptures] does not appear in [others'] general presentations and critical analyses of the texts, etc. Therefore, it is evident that when those scriptures of the Foremost Lama [Dzong-ka-ba] are explained by someone who knows how to explain them and heard by someone who knows how to listen, there are many sources that generate joy.

Appendix: PAGE CORRELATIONS, TIBETAN TO
ENGLISH
(Varanasi codex edition, 407.8 — 458.9)

Tibetan Page	Commentary Page	Translation Page
407.8	36.1	360.1
408	50.32	361.16
409	53.5	362.19
410	61.4	364.5
411	82.6	365.32
412	90.21	367.1
413	98.5	368.11
414	100.4	369.7
415	103.6	370.14
416	115.1	371.34
417	124.6	373.13
418	127.9	375.16
419	137.24	376.bottom
420	140.33	377.bottom
421	145.31	379.4
422	148.8	380.10
423	151.23	381.29
424	154.22	382.25
425	159.34	384.22
426	167.34	385.31
427	175.24	387.10
428	178.27	388.18
429	184.26	389.29
430	212.19	391.14
431	221.16	392.bottom
432	224.bottom	394.16
433	238.27	395.14
434	243.12	396.17
435	246.17	397.22
436	263.8	398.23
437	267.18	399.bottom
438	273.4	401.15
439	282.1	402.24

440	288.12	404.3
441	290.15	405.4
442	293.8	406.16
443	299.11	407.bottom
444	305.5	410.17
445	309.13	411.20
446	312.19	412.28
447	315.14	413.33
448	319.15	415.5
449	323.10	416.12
450	328.15	417.25
451	332.26	418.27
452	335.21	419.34
453	337.29	421.18
454	339.30	422.26
455	345.8	424.6
456	346.33	425.16
457	349.24	427.4
458	352.7	428.18

Bibliography of Works Cited

Sūtras and tantras are listed alphabetically by English title in the first section. Indian and Tibetan treatises are listed alphabetically by author in the second section; other works are listed alphabetically by author in the third section.

"P", standing for "Peking edition", refers to the *Tibetan Tripiṭaka* (Tokyo-Kyoto: Tibetan Tripiṭaka Research Foundation, 1956).

1. Sūtras and Tantras

Ajātashatru Sūtra/ The Superior Great Vehicle Sūtra Called "Removing the Regret of Ajātashatru"
āryājātaśatrukarukṛtyavinodanānāmamahāyānasūtra
'phags pa ma skyes dgra'i 'gyod pa bsal ba zhes bya ba theg pa chen po'i mdo
P882, vol. 35

Chapter Showing the Three Vows Sūtra
trisambaranirdeśaparivartasūtra
sdom pa gsum bstan pa'i le'u'i mdo
P760.1, vol. 22

Descent Into Laṅkā Sūtra
laṅkāvatārasūtra
lang kar gshegs pa'i mdo

P775, vol. 29
Sanskrit: *Saddharmalaṅkāvatārasūtram*. P.L. Vaidya, ed.
Buddhist Sanskrit Texts No. 3. Darbhanga: Mithila Insti-
tute, 1963; also: Bunyiu Nanjio, ed. Bibl. Otaniensis, vol. I.
Kyoto: Otani University Press, 1923
English translation: D.T. Suzuki. *The Lankavatara Sutra*.
London: Routledge and Kegan Paul, 1932
King of Meditative Stabilizations Sūtra
samādhirājasūtra/ sarvadharmasvabhāvasamatāvipañcatasa-
mādhirājasūtra
ting nge 'dzin rgyal po'i mdo/ chos thams cad kyi rang bzhin
mnyam pa nyid rnam par spros pa ting nge 'dzin gyi rgyal
po'i mdo
P795, vol. 31-2; Toh 127, Dharma vol. 20
Sanskrit: *Samādhirājasūtram*. P.L. Vaidya, ed. Buddhist Sanskrit Texts, No. 2. Darbhanga: Mithila Institute, 1961
Partial English translation (of chapters eight, nineteen, and
twenty-two): K. Regamey. *Three Chapters from the Samādhi-
rājasūtra*. Warsaw: Publications of the Oriental Commission,
1938
Questions of Anavatapta, the King of Nāgas, Sūtra
anavataptanāgarājaparipṛcchāsūtra
klu'i rgyal po ma dros pas zhus pa'i mdo
P823, vol. 33
Questions of Brahmā Sūtra
brahmāparipṛcchāsūtra
tshangs pas zhus pa'i mdo
P825, vol. 33
Questions of Sāgaramati Sūtra
sāgaramatiparipṛcchāsūtra
blo gros rgya mtshos zhus pa'i mdo
P819, vol. 33
Questions of Upāli Sūtra
upāliparipṛcchā
nye bar 'khor gyis zhus pa
[?]
Superior Sūtra of the Cloud of Jewels
ratnameghasūtra
dkon mchog sprin gyi mdo
P879, vol. 35

Superior Sūtra of the Sport of Mañjushrī
mañjuśrīvikrīḍitasūtra
'jam dpal rnam par rol pa'i mdo
P764, vol. 27
Sūtra on the Ten Grounds
daśabhūmikasūtra
mdo sde sa bcu pa
P761.31, vol. 25
Sanskrit: *Daśabhūmikasūtram.* P.L. Vaidya, ed. Buddhist Sanskrit Texts No. 7. Darbhanga: Mithila Institute, 1967
English translation: M. Honda. "An Annotated Translation of the 'Daśabhūmika' ". in D. Sinor, ed., *Studies in Southeast and Central Asia,* Śatapiṭaka Series 74. New Delhi: 1968, pp. 115-276
Taming Demons Chapter
bdud 'dul ba'i le'u
[?]

2. Sanskrit and Tibetan Works

Āryadeva (*'phags pa lha,* second to third century, C.E.)
Four Hundred/Treatise of Four Hundred Stanzas
catuḥśatakaśāstrakārikā
bstan bcos bzhi brgya pa zhes bya ba'i tshig le'ur byas pa
P5246, vol. 95
Edited Tibetan and Sanskrit fragments along with English translation: Karen Lang. "Aryadeva on the Bodhisattva's Cultivation of Merit and Knowledge". Ann Arbor: University Microfilms, 1983
Italian translation of the last half from the Chinese: Giuseppe Tucci, "La versione cinese del Catuḥśataka di Aryadeva, confronta col testo sanscrito et la traduzione tibetana". *Rivista degli Studi Orientalia* 10 (1925), pp. 521-567
Length of a Forearm
hastavālaprakaraṇakārikā
rab tu byed pa lag pa'i tshad kyi tshig le'ur byas pa
P5248, vol. 95; P5244, vol. 95
Avalokitavrata (*spyan ras gzigs brtul zhugs,* seventh or eighth century)

Explanatory Commentary on (Bhāvaviveka's) "Lamp for (Nāgār-juna's) 'Wisdom'"
prajñāpradīpaṭīkā
shes rab sgron ma'i rgya cher 'grel pa
P5259, vol. 96-7
Bhāvaviveka (*legs ldan 'byed*, c.500-570?)
Heart of the Middle Way
madhyamakahṛdayakārikā
dbu ma'i snying po'i tshig le'ur byas pa
P5255, vol. 96
Partial English translation (chap. III. 1-136): S. Iida. *Reason and Emptiness*. Tokyo: Hokuseido, 1980
Buddhapālita (*sangs rgyas bskyangs*, c.470-540?)
Buddhapālita Commentary on (Nāgārjuna's) "Treatise on the Middle Way"
buddhapālitamūlamadhyamakavṛtti
dbu ma rtsa ba'i 'grel pa buddha pā li ta
P5254, vol. 95; Toh 3842, Tokyo *sde dge* vol. 1
Edited Tibetan edition: (Ch.1-12): Max Walleser. Bibliotheca Buddhica XVI. Osnabrück: Biblio Verlag, 1970
English translation of Ch.1: Judit Fehér. in Louis Ligeti, ed., *Tibetan and Buddhist Studies Commemorating the 200th Anniversary of the Birth of Alexander Csoma de Körös*, vol. 1. Budapest: Akadémiai Kiado, 1984, pp. 211-240
English translation of Ch.18: Chr. Lindtner. in *Indo-Iranian Journal* 23 (1981), pp. 187-217.
Chandrakīrti (*zla ba grags pa*, seventh century)
Autocommentary on the "Supplement to (Nāgārjuna's) 'Treatise on the Middle Way'"
madhyamakāvatārabhāṣya
dbu ma la 'jug pa'i bshad pa/dbu ma la 'jug pa'i rang 'grel
P5263, vol. 98
Also: Dharmsala: Council of Religious and Cultural Affairs, 1968
Edited Tibetan: Louis de la Vallée Poussin. *Madhyamakāvatāra par Candrakīrti*. Bibliotheca Buddhica IX. Osnabrück: Biblio Verlag, 1970
French translation (up to VI.165): Louis de la Vallée Poussin. *Muséon* 8 (1907), pp. 249-317; *Muséon* 11 (1910), pp. 271-358; and *Muséon* 12 (1911), pp. 235-328.

German translation (VI.166-226): Helmut Tauscher. *Candrakīrti-Madhyamakāvatāraḥ und Madhyamakāvatārabhāṣyam*. Wien: Wiener Studien zur Tibetologie und Buddhismuskunde, 1981

Clear Words, Commentary on (Nāgārjuna's) "Treatise on the Middle Way"
mūlamadhyamakavṛttiprasannapadā
dbu ma rtsa ba'i 'grel pa tshig gsal ba
P5260, vol. 98
Also: Dharmsala: Tibetan Publishing House, 1968
Sanskrit: *Mūlamadhyamakakārikās de Nāgārjuna avec la Prasannapadā Commentaire de Candrakīrti*. Louis de la Vallée Poussin, ed. Bibliotheca Buddhica IV. Osnabrück: Biblio Verlag, 1970
English translation (Ch.I, XXV): T. Stcherbatsky. *Conception of Buddhist Nirvāṇa*. Leningrad: Office of the Academy of Sciences of the USSR, 1927; revised rpt. Delhi: Motilal Banarsidass, 1978, pp. 77-222
English translation (Ch.II): Jeffrey Hopkins. "Analysis of Coming and Going". Dharmsala: Library of Tibetan Works and Archives, 1974
Partial English translation: Mervyn Sprung. *Lucid Exposition of the Middle Way, the Essential Chapters from the Prasannapadā of Candrakīrti translated from the Sanskrit*. London: Routledge, 1979, and Boulder: Prajñā Press, 1979
French translation (Ch.II-IV, VI-IX, XI, XXIII, XXIV, XXVI, XXVII): Jacques May. *Prasannapadā Madhyamaka-vṛtti, douze chapitres traduits du sanscrit et du tibétain*. Paris: Adrien-Maisonneuve, 1959
French translation (Ch.XVIII-XXII): J.W. de Jong. *Cinq chapitres de la Prasannapadā*. Paris: Geuthner, 1949
French translation (Ch.XVII): É. Lamotte. "Le Traité de l'acte de Vasubandhu, Karmasiddhiprakaraṇa", *MCB* 4 (1936), 265-288
German translation (Ch.V and XII-XVI): St. Schayer. *Ausgewählte Kapitel aus der Prasannapadā*. Krakow: Naktadem Polskiej Akademji Umiejetnosci, 1931
German translation (Ch.X): St. Schayer. "Feuer und Brennstoff". *Rocznik Orjentalistyczny* 7 (1931), pp. 26-52
Commentary on (Āryadeva's) "Four Hundred Stanzas on the

Yogic Deeds of Bodhisattvas"
bodhisattvayogacaryācatuḥśatakaṭīkā
byang chub sems dpa'i rnal 'byor spyod pa gzhi brgya pa'i
rgya cher 'grel pa
P5266, vol. 98; Toh 3865, Tokyo *sde dge* vol. 8
Edited Sanskrit fragments: Haraprasād Shāstri, ed. "Ca-
tuḥśatika of Ārya Deva," Memoirs of the Asiatic Society
of Bengal, III no 8 (1914), pp. 449-514
Also (Ch.8-16): Vidhusekhara Bhattacarya, ed. *The Catuḥśataka of Āryadeva: Sanskrit and Tibetan texts with copious extracts from the commentary of Candrakīrtti*, Part II.
Calcutta: Visva-Bharati Bookshop, 1931
Supplement to (Nāgārjuna's) "Treatise on the Middle Way"
madhyamakāvatāra
dbu ma la 'jug pa
P5261, P5262, vol. 98
Edited Tibetan: Louis de la Vallée Poussin. *Madhyamakāvatāra par Candrakīrti*. Bibliotheca Buddhica IX. Osnabrück: Biblio Verlag, 1970
English translation (Ch.I-V): Jeffrey Hopkins. in *Compassion
in Tibetan Buddhism*. Valois, NY: Gabriel Snow Lion,
1980
English translation (Ch.VI): Stephen Batchelor, trans. in
Geshé Rabten's *Echoes of Voidness*. London: Wisdom,
1983, pp. 47-92
See also references under Chandrakīrti's *Autocommentary on
the "Supplement"*
Chö-ğyi-gyel-tsen, Jay-ɗzun *(rje btsun chos kyi rgyal mtshan*, 1469-
1546
*A Good Explanation Adorning the Throats of the Fortunate: A
General Meaning Commentary Clarifying Difficult Points in
(Ḏzong-ka-ɓa's) "Illumination of the Thought: An Explanation
of (Chandrakīrti's) "Supplement to (Nāgārjuna's) 'Treatise on
the Middle Way' "*
bstan bcos dbu ma la 'jug pa'i rnam bshad dgongs pa rab gsal
gyi dka' gnad gsal bar byed pa'i spyi don legs bshad skal
bzang mgul rgyan
Collected Works, vol. ma. n.p.d. [Se-ra Jay College publication in India in early 1980's]
Presentation of Tenets

grub mtha'i rnam gzhag
Bylakuppe: Se-ra Byes Grwa-tshaṅ, 1977
Ḍak-tsang Shay-rap-rin-chen (*stag tshang lo tsā ba shes rab rin chen,* born 1405)
Ocean of Good Explanations, Explanation of "Freedom From Extremes Through Understanding All Tenets"
grub mtha' kun shes nas mtha' bral grub pa zhes bya ba'i
    bstan bcos rnam par bshad pa legs bshad kyi rgya mtsho
Thim-phu: Kun-bzang-stobs-rgyal, 1976
Dharmakīrti (*chos kyi grags pa,* seventh century)
Commentary on (Dignāga's) "Compendium on Prime Cognition"
pramāṇavārttikakārikā
tshad ma rnam 'grel gyi tshig le'ur byas pa
P5709, vol. 130
Also: Sarnath, India: Pleasure of Elegant Sayings Press, 1974
Sanskrit: *Pramāṇavārttika of Acharya Dharmakīrtti.* Swami
    Dwarikadas Shastri, ed. Varanasi: Bauddha Bharati, 1968
Ḍrak-ba-shay-drup (*grags pa bshad sgrub,* co no ba, 1675 1748)
Condensed Essence of All Tenets
grub mtha' thams cad kyi snying po bsdus pa
Delhi: Mey College of Sera, 1969
Ḍzong-ka-ba (*tsong kha pa,* 1357-1419)
Four Interwoven Annotations on (Ḍzong-ka-ba's) "Great Exposition of the Stages of the Path"
The Lam rim chen mo of the incomparable Tsong-kha-pa, ...
New Delhi: Chos-'phel-legs-ldan, 1972
Essence of the Good Explanations, Treatise Differentiating the Interpretable and the Definitive
drang ba dang nges pa'i don rnam par phye ba'i bstan bcos
    legs bshad snying po
P6142, vol. 153
Sarnath: Pleasure of Elegant Sayings Press, 1973 [on the
    cover in roman letters is *Dan-ne-leg-shed nying-po*]
English translation: Robert Thurman. *Tsong Khapa's Speech of Gold in the Essence of True Eloquence.* Princeton: Princeton University Press, 1984.
Great Exposition of the Stages of the Path/ Stages of the Path to Enlightenment Thoroughly Teaching All the Stages of Practice of the Three Types of Beings
lam rim chen mo/ skyes bu gsum gyi rnyams su blang ba'i

rim pa thams cad tshang bar ston pa'i byang chub lam gyi
rim pa
P6001, vol. 152
Also: Dharmsala: Shes rig par khang, 1964
Also: Delhi: Ngawang Gelek, 1975-
English translation of the parts on calm abiding and special
insight by Alex Wayman in *Calming the Mind and Discerning the Real*. New York: Columbia University Press, 1978;
reprint New Delhi: Motilal Banarsidass, 1979
Illumination of the Thought, Extensive Explanation of (Chandrakīrti's) "Supplement to (Nāgārjuna's) 'Treatise on the Middle Way' "
dbu ma la 'jug pa'i rgya cher bshad pa dgongs pa rab gsal
P6143, vol. 154
Also: Sarnath, India: Pleasure of Elegant Sayings Press, 1973
English translation (first five chapters): Jeffrey Hopkins. in
Compassion in Tibetan Buddhism. Valois, New York: Snow
Lion, 1980
Middling Exposition of the Stages of the Path/ Small Exposition of the Stages of the Path To Enlightenment
lam rim 'bring/ lam rim chung ngu
P6002, vol. 152-3
Also: Dharmsala: Shes rig par khang, 1968
Also: Mundgod: Ganden Shardzay, n.d., (edition including
outline of topics by Trijang Rinbochay)
English translation of the section on special insight by
Robert Thurman, "The Middle Transcendent Insight" in
Life and Teachings of Tsong Khapa. Dharmasala: Library
of Tibetan Works and Archives, 1982, pp. 108-85; and by
Jeffrey Hopkins, "Special Insight: From Dzong-ka-ba's
Middling Exposition of the Stages of the Path to Enlightenment Practiced by Persons of Three Capacities with supplementary headings by Trijang Rinbochay", unpublished
manuscript
Ocean of Reasoning, Explanation of (Nāgārjuna's) "Treatise on the Middle Way"/Great Commentary on (Nāgārjuna's) "Treatise on the Middle Way"
dbu ma rtsa ba'i tshig le'ur byas pa shes rab ces bya ba'i rnam
bshad rigs pa'i rgya mtsho
P6153, vol. 156

Also: Sarnath, India: Pleasure of Elegant Sayings Printing Press, no date

Also: in *rje tsong kha pa'i gsung dbu ma'i lta ba'i skor*, vol. 1 and 2, Sarnath, India: Pleasure of Elegant Sayings Press, 1975

Praise of Dependent-Arising/ Praise of the Supramundane Victor Buddha from the Approach of His Teaching the Profound Dependent-Arising, Essence of the Good Explanations

rten 'brel bstod pa/sang rgyas bcom ldan 'das la zab mo rten cing 'brel bar 'byung ba gsung ba'i sgo nas bstod pa legs par bshad pa'i snying po

P6016, vol. 153

English translation: Geshe Wangyal. in *The Door of Liberation*. New York: Lotsawa, 1978, pp. 117-25. Also: Robert Thurman. in *Life and Teachings of Tsong Khapa*. Dharmsala: Library of Tibetan Works and Archives, 1982, pp. 99-107

The Three Principal Aspects of the Path

lam gtso rnam gsum/ tsha kho dpon po ngag dbang grags pa la gdams pa

P6087, vol. 153

English translation: Geshe Wangyal. in *The Door of Liberation*. New York: Lotsawa, 1978, pp. 126-60. Also: Geshe Sopa and Jeffrey Hopkins. in *Practice and Theory of Tibetan Buddhism*. New York: Grove Press, 1976, pp. 1-47. Also: Jeffrey Hopkins. Including commentary from the Dalai Lama, in Tenzin Gyatso's *Kindness, Clarity, and Insight*. Ithaca, N.Y.: Snow Lion, 1984, pp. 118-56. Also: Robert Thurman. in *Life and Teachings of Tsong Khapa*. Dharmsala, Library of Tibetan Works and Archives, 1982, pp. 57-8

Ge-dun-gya-tso, Second Dalai Lama (*dge 'dun rgya mtsho*, 1476-1542)

Ship For Entering the Ocean of Tenets

grub mtha' rgya mtshor 'jug pa'i gru rdzings

Vāraṇāsi: Ye shes stobs ldan, 1969

Gön-chok-jik-may-wang-bo (*dkon mchog 'jigs med dbang po*, 1728-91)

Precious Garland of Tenets/Presentation of Tenets, A Precious Garland

grub pa'i mtha'i rnam par bzhag pa rin po che'i phreng ba
Dharmsala: Shes rig par khang, 1969
English translation: Sopa and Hopkins. in *Practice and Theory of Tibetan Buddhism*. New York: Grove, 1976, pp. 48-145. Also: H.V. Guenther. in *Buddhist Philosophy in Theory and Practice*. Baltimore: Penguin, 1972
Gyel-tsap, (*rgyal tshab*, 1364-1432)
   Explanation of (Shāntideva's) "Engaging in the Bodhisattva Deeds": Entrance of Conqueror Children
   byang chub sems dpa'i spyod pa la 'jug pa'i rnam bshad rgyal sras 'jug ngogs
   Varanasi: 1973
Jam-ȳang-shay-b̄a (*'jam dbyangs bzhad pa*, 1648-1721)
   Great Exposition of Tenets/ Explanation of 'Tenets', Sun of the Land of Samantabhadra Brilliantly Illuminating All of Our Own and Others' Tenets and the Meaning of the Profound [Emptiness], Ocean of Scripture and Reasoning Fulfilling All Hopes of All Beings
   grub mtha' chen mo/ grub mtha'i rnam bshad rang gzhan grub mtha' kun dang zab don mchog tu gsal ba kun bzang zhing gi nyi ma lung rigs rgya mtsho skye dgu'i re ba kun skong
   Musoorie: Dalama, 1962
   English translation (beginning of the Prāsaṅgika chapter): Jeffrey Hopkins. in *Meditation on Emptiness*. London: Wisdom, 1983.
   Great Exposition of the Middle Way/ Analysis of (Chandrakīrti's) "Supplement to (Nāgārjuna's) 'Treatise on the Middle Way' ", Treasury of Scripture and Reasoning, Thoroughly Illuminating the Profound Meaning [of Emptiness], Entrance for the Fortunate
   dbu ma chen mo/ dbu ma 'jug pa'i mtha' dpyod lung rigs gter mdzod zab don kun gsal skal bzang 'jug ngogs
   Buxaduor: Gomang, 1967
Jang-ḡya Rol-b̄ay-dor-jay (*lcang skya rol pa'i rdo rje*, 1717-86)
   Presentation of Tenets/ Clear Exposition of the Presentations of Tenets, Beautiful Ornament for the Meru of the Subduer's Teaching
   grub mtha'i rnam bzhag/ grub pa'i mtha'i rnam par bzhag pa

gsal bar bshad pa thub bstan lhun po'i mdzes rgyan
Varanasi: Pleasure of Elegant Sayings Printing Press, 1970
Also: an edition published by gam bcar phan bde legs bshad
gling grva tshang dang rgyud rnying slar gso tshogs pa, in
the royal year 2109 [n.d.]
Also: *Buddhist Philosophical Systems of Lcan-skya Rol-pahi
Rdo-rje*. Edited by Lokesh Chandra. Śata-piṭaka Series
(Indo-Asian Literatures), v. 233. New Delhi, 1977
Sautrāntika chapter translated by Anne C. Klein in *"Mind
and Liberation: The Sautrāntika Tenet System in Tibet"*. Ann
Arbor: University Microfilms, 1981.
Svātantrika chapter translated by Donald S. Lopez jr. in *A
Study of Svātantrika*. Ithaca: Snow Lion, 1987
Kay-drup Ge-lek-bel-sang-bo (*mkhas sgrub dge legs dpal bzang po*,
1385-1438)
*Thousand Dosages/ Opening the Eyes of the Fortunate, Treatise
Brilliantly Clarifying the Profound Emptiness*
stong thun chen mo/zab mo stong pa nyid rab tu gsal bar
byed pa'i bstan bcos skal bzang mig 'byed
The Collected Works of the Lord Mkhas-grub rje dge-legs-
dpal-bzan-po, vol. 1, 179-702
New Delhi: Mongolian Lama Gurudeva, 1980
Long-chen-rap-jam (*klong chen rab 'byams/ klong chen dri med 'od
zer*, 1308-1363)
Treasury of Tenets, Illuminating the Meaning of All Vehicles
theg pa mtha' dag gi don gsal bar byed pa grub pa'i mtha' rin
po che'i mdzod
Gangtok, Dodrup Chen Rinpoche, 1969[?]
Precious Treasury of the Supreme Vehicle
theg pa'i mchog rin po che'i mdzod
Gangtok, Dodrup Chen Rinpoche, 1969[?]
Nāgārjuna (*klu sgrub*, first to second century, C.E.)
Praise of the Supramundane [Buddha]
lokātītastava
'jig rten las 'das par bstod pa
P2012, vol. 46
Edited Tibetan and Sanskrit along with English translation:
Chr. Lindtner in *Nagarjuniana*. Indiske Studier 4, pp.
121-38. Copenhagen: Akademisk Forlag, 1982

442   *Emptiness Yoga*

Precious Garland of Advice for the King
rājaparikathāratnāvalī
rgyal po la gtam bya ba rin po che'i phreng ba
P5658, vol. 129
Edited Sanskrit, Tibetan, and Chinese: *Nāgārjuna's Ratnā-
valī, Vol. 1, The Basic Texts (Sanskrit, Tibetan, and
Chinese).* Michael Hahn, ed. Bonn: Indica et Tibetica
Verlag, 1982
English translation: Jeffrey Hopkins in Nāgārjuna and the
Seventh Dalai Lama, *The Precious Garland and the Song of
the Four Mindfulnesses.* New York: Harper and Row, 1975
Sixty Stanzas of Reasoning
yuktiṣaṣṭikākārikā
rigs pa drug cu pa'i tshig le'ur byas pa
P5225, vol. 95; Toh 3825, Tokyo *sde dge* vol. 1
Edited Tibetan with Sanskrit fragments and English translation: Chr. Lindtner in *Nagarjuniana.* Indiske Studier 4,
pp. 100-119. Copenhagen: Akademisk Forlag, 1982
*Treatise on the Middle Way/ Fundamental Treatise on the Middle
Way, Called "Wisdom"*
madhyamakaśāstra/prajñānāmamūlamadhyamakakārikā
dbu ma'i bstan bcos/dbu ma rtsa ba'i tshig le'ur byas pa shes
rab ces bya ba
P5224, vol. 95
Edited Sanskrit: *Nāgārjuna, Mūlamadhyamakakārikāḥ.* J.W.
de Jong, ed. Adyar: Adyar Library and Research Centre,
1977. Also: Chr. Lindtner in *Nāgārjuna's Filosofiske Vaer-
ker.* Indiske Studier 2, pp. 177-215. Copenhagen:
Akademisk Forlag, 1982
English translation: Frederick Streng. *Emptiness: A Study in
Religious Meaning.* Nashville, New York: Abingdon Press,
1967. Also: Kenneth Inada. *Nāgārjuna: A Translation of
his Mūlamadhyamakakārikā.* Tokyo, The Hokuseido
Press, 1970. Also David J. Kalupahana. *Nāgārjuna: The
Philosophy of the Middle Way.* Albany: State University
Press of New York, 1986
Italian translation: R. Gnoli. *Nāgārjuna: Madhyamaka Kāri-
kā, Le stanze del cammino di mezzo.* Enciclopedia di autori
classici 61. Turin: P. Boringhieri, 1961

Bibliography 443

Danish translation: Chr. Lindtner in *Nāgārjuna's Filosofiske Vaerker*. Indiske Studier 2, pp. 67-135. Copenhagen: Akademisk Forlag, 1982
Nga-w̄ang-b̄el-den (*ngag dbang dpal ldan*, b.1797)
Annotations for (Jam-ȳang-shay-b̄a's) "Great Exposition of Tenets", Freeing the Knots of the Difficult Points, Precious Jewel of Clear Thought
grub mtha' chen mo'i mchan 'grel dka' gnad mdud grol blo gsal gces nor
Sarnath: Pleasure of Elegant Sayings Press, 1964
Stating the Mode of Explanation in the Textbooks on the Middle Way and the Perfection of Wisdom In the Lo-s̄el-l̄ing and Go-mang Colleges: Festival For Those of Clear Intelligence
blo gsal gling dang bkra shis sgo mang grva tshang gi dbu .
phar gyi yig cha'i bshad tshul bkod pa blo gsal dga' ston
Collected Works, vol. ga
New Delhi: Guru Deva, 1983
Nga-w̄ang-l̄o-sang-gya-tso (*ngag dbang blo bzang rgya mtsho*, Fifth Dalai Lama, 1617-1682)
Sacred Word of Mañjushrī, Instructions on the Stages of the Path to Enlightenment
byang chub lam gyi rim pa'i 'khrid yig 'jam pa'i dbyangs kyi zhal lung
Thimphu, Bhutan: kun bzang stobs rgyal, 1976
English translation of the "Perfection of Wisdom Chapter": Jeffrey Hopkins. in "Practice of Emptiness". Dharmsala: Library of Tibetan Works and Archives, 1974
Rabten, Geshe
Annotations For the Difficult Points of (Dzong-ka-b̄a's) "Essence of the Good Explanations", Joyous Festival For The Unbiased With Clear Awareness
drang nges rnam 'byed legs bshad snying po dka' gnad rnams mchan bur bkod pa gzur gnas blo gsal dga' ston
n.p.d. [edition in India in the early 1970's]
Shāntideva (*zhi ba lha*, eighth century)
Engaging in the Bodhisattva Deeds
bodhisattvacaryāvatāra
byang chub sems dpa'i spyod pa la 'jug pa
P5272, vol. 99
Sanskrit and Tibetan edition: *Bodhicaryāvatāra.*

Vidhushekhara Bhattacharya, ed. Calcutta: The Asiatic
Society, 1960
English translation: Stephen Batchelor. *A Guide to the Bodhi-
sattva's Way of Life*. Dharmsala: LTWA, 1979. Also: Ma-
rion Matics. *Entering the Path of Enlightenment*. New
York: Macmillan Co, 1970.
Contemporary commentary: Geshe Kelsang Gyatso.
Meaningful to Behold. London: Wisdom, 1980

Shūra/ Ashvaghoṣha (*dpa' bo/ rta dbyangs*, third or fourth century)
*Cultivation of the Ultimate Mind of Enlightenment/ Essay on the
Stages of Cultivating the Ultimate Mind of Enlightenment*
paramārthabodhicittabhāvanākramavarṇasaṃgraha
don dam pa byang chub kyi sems bsgom pa'i rim pa yi ger
bris pa
P5431, vol. 103

Tu- gen-lo-sang-chö-ḡyi-nyi-ma (*thu'u bkvan blo bzang chos kyi nyi
ma*, 1737-1802)
*Mirror of the Good Explanations Showing the Sources and Asser-
tions of All Systems of Tenets*
grub mtha' thams cad kyi khungs dang 'dod tshul ston pa
legs bshad shel gyi me long
Sarnath: Chhos Je Lama, 1963

3. Other Works

Avedon, John F. *In Exile From the Land of Snows*. New York:
Knopf, 1984.

Bhattacharya, Vidhushekhara, ed. *Bodhicaryāvatāra*. Bibliotheca
Indica, vol. 280. Calcutta: The Asiatic Society, 1960.

Chandra, Lokesh, ed. *Materials for a History of Tibetan Literature*.
Śata-piṭaka series, vol. 28-30. New Delhi: International
Academy of Indian Culture, 1963.

Clark, Walter Eugen. *Two Lamaistic Pantheons*, vol. I and II.
Cambridge, Mass., 1937.

Fifth Dalai Lama. "Practice of Emptiness" (the "Perfection of
Wisdom Chapter" of the *Sacred Word of Mañjushrī* [*dpal
zhal lung*]). Jeffrey Hopkins, translator. Dharmsala: Library of
Tibetan Works and Archives, 1974.

Grupper, Samuel M. "Manchu Patronage And Tibetan Buddhism During the First Half of the Ch'ing Dynasty". *The Journal of the Tibet Society*, vol. 4, 1984, pp. 47-75.

Gyatso, Tenzin, The Fourteenth Dalai Lama. *The Buddhism of Tibet and The Key to the Middle Way*. London: George Allen and Unwin, 1975. Translated by Jeffrey Hopkins. Reprinted in a combined volume, *The Buddhism of Tibet*. London: George Allen and Unwin, 1983.

──────. *The Kālachakra Tantra: Rite of Initiation for the Stage of Generation*. Translated and introduced by Jeffrey Hopkins. London: Wisdom Publications, 1985.

──────. *Kindness, Clarity, and Insight*. Trans. and edited by Jeffrey Hopkins, coedited by Elizabeth Napper. Ithaca: Snow Lion, 1984.

Hopkins, Jeffrey, trans. "Analysis of Going and Coming", by Chandrakīrti. Dharamsala: Library of Tibetan Works and Archives, 1976.

──────, trans. *Compassion in Tibetan Buddhism*. London: Rider and Co., 1980

──────. *Meditation on Emptiness*. London: Wisdom, 1983.

──────, trans. *Practice of Emptiness*. Dharmsala: Library of Tibetan Works and Archives, 1974.

──────, trans. Nāgārjuna and the Seventh Dalai Lama, *The Precious Garland and the Song of the Four Mindfulnesses*. New York: Harper and Row, 1975.

──────, trans. Tsong-ka-ba, *Tantra in Tibet*. London: George Allen & Unwin, 1977.

──────, trans. Tsong-ka-ba, *Yoga of Tibet*. London: George Allen & Unwin, 1981.

Jong, Jan W. de. "La Madhyamakaśāstrastuti de Candrakīrti" in *Oriens Extremus*, Jahrg. 9, 1962, pp. 47-56. Reprinted in *J.W. De Jong Buddhist Studies*, pp. 541-50. Rep. of China: Asian Humanities Press, 1979.

──────. "Textcritical Notes on the Prasannapadā". *Indo-Iranian Journal* 20 (1978), pp. 25-59 and 217-52.

Kalupahana, David J. *Nāgārjuna: The Philosophy of the Middle Way*. Albany: State University Press of New York, 1986.

Kämpfe, Hans-Rainer. *Ñi ma'i 'od zer/Naran-u gerel: Die Biographie des 2. Pekinger Lčaṅ skya-Qutuqtu Rol pa'i rdo rje (1717-1786)*, Monumenta Tibetica Historica, Abt. II, Bd. 1. Wissenschaftsverlag, Sankt Augustin, 1976.

Klein, Anne C. *"Mind and Liberation: The Sautrāntika Tenet System in Tibet"*. Ann Arbor: University Microfilms, 1981.

La Vallée Poussin, Louis de, trans. *Madhyamakāvatāra. Muséon* 8 (1907), pp. 249-317; 11 (1910), pp. 271-358; and 12 (1911), pp. 235-328.

————, ed. *Mūlamadhyamakakārikās de Nāgārjuna avec la Prasannapadā Commentaire de Candrakīrti.* Bibliotheca Buddhica IV. Osnabrück: Biblio Verlag, 1970

Lang, Karen. "Aryadeva on the Bodhisattva's Cultivation of Merit and Knowledge". Ann Arbor: University Microfilms, 1983.

Lati Rinbochay. *Mind in Tibetan Buddhism.* Elizabeth Napper, trans. and ed. Valois, New York: Snow Lion, 1980.

Lessing, Ferdinand D. *Yung-Ho-Kung; an iconography of the Lamaist cathedral in Peking.* Stockholm, 1942.

Lindtner, Christian. *Nagarjuniana.* Indiske Studier 4. Copenhagen: Akademisk Forlag, 1982.

Lopez, Donald S. *A Study of Svātantrika.* Ithaca: Snow Lion, 1987.

Nāgārjuna and Kaysang Gyatso. *Precious Garland and the Song of the Four Mindfulnesses.* London: George Allen and Unwin, 1975.

Napper, Elizabeth. "Dependent-Arising and Emptiness: A Tibetan Buddhist Interpretation of Mādhyamika Philosophy Emphasizing the Compatibility of Emptiness and Conventional Phenomena". Ann Arbor: University Microfilms, 1985.

Perdue, Daniel. "Practice and Theory of Philosophical Debate in Tibetan Buddhist Education". Ann Arbor: University Microfilms, 1983.

Ruegg, David Seyfort. *The Literature of the Madhyamaka School of Philosophy in India.* Wiesbaden: Otto Harrassowitz, 1981.

Schubert, Johannes. *Tibetische Nationalgrammatik, Das Sum.cu.-pa und Rtags.kyi. 'jug.pa des Grosslamas von Peking Rol.pai. rdo.rje.* Leipzig: 1937.

Shakabpa, Tsepon W.D. *Tibet: A Political History.* Repr. New York: Potala Corp., 1984.

Smith, E. Gene. Introduction to N. Gelek Demo, Collected Works of Thu'u-bkwan Blo-bzang-chos-kyi-nyi-ma, vol. 1. Delhi, 1969.

Snellgrove, David L., trans. *Hevajra Tantra*, Parts I and II. London: Oxford University Press, 1959.

Snellgrove, David L., and Richardson, Hugh, *A Cultural History of Tibet*. New York: Praeger, 1968.

Sopa, Geshe Lhundup, and Hopkins, Jeffrey. *Practice and Theory of Tibetan Buddhism*. London: Rider and Co., 1976.

Suzuki, Daisetz T. *The Lankavatara Sutra*. London: Routledge and Kegan Paul, 1932.

Tenzin Gyatso, Dalai Lama XIV. *The Buddhism of Tibet and the Key to the Middle Way*. Jeffrey Hopkins, trans. London: George Allen & Unwin, 1975.

———— and Jeffrey Hopkins. *The Kālachakra Tantra: Rite of Initiation*. London: Wisdom, 1985.

————. *Kindness, Clarity, and Insight*. Jeffrey Hopkins, trans. and ed.; Elizabeth Napper, co-editor. Ithaca, N.Y.: Snow Lion Publications, 1984.

Thurman, Robert, ed. *The Life & Teachings of Tsong Khapa*. Dharamsala: Library of Tibetan Works and Archives, 1982.

————. *Tsong Khapa's Speech of Gold in the Essence of True Eloquence*. Princeton: Princeton University Press, 1984.

Tsong-ka-pa. *Tantra in Tibet*. Translated and edited by Jeffrey Hopkins. London: George Allen & Unwin, 1977.

Wangyal, Geshe. *Door of Liberation*. New York: Maurice Girodius, 1973; reprint, New York: Lotsawa, 1978.

Notes

1. *lcang skya rol pa'i rdo rje.* The biographical material is drawn from E. Gene Smith's introduction to N. Gelek Demo, Collected Works of Thu'u-bkwan Blo-bzang-chos-kyi-nyi-ma (Delhi, 1969), vol. 1, pp. 2-12, and from a brief biography put together at my request by Geshe Thupten Gyatso of the Tibetan Buddhist Learning Center in New Jersey. The material was further amplified and explained by Khetsun Sangpo Rinbochay, who was visiting the University of Virginia under the auspices of the Center for South Asian Studies. Both Gene Smith and Geshe Thupten Gyatso are condensing Tu-gen-lo-sang-chö-gyi-nyi-ma's long biography of Jang-gya, found in the first volume of his Collected Works, which is 414 pages (827 sides) in length and is divided into twenty-five chapters. It need not be mentioned that the biography does not provide unbiased evidence for the events of this period and that it certainly is written with the intent of glorifying Jang-gya's life; nevertheless, there is no denying his tremendous accomplishments at the Chinese court.

    Another biography of Jang-gya, authored by his younger brother Chu-sang Nga-wang-tup-den-wang-chuk (*chu bzang ngag dbang thub bstan dbang phyug,* born 1736) in 1787, found at the beginning of the supplementary volume of the Peking edition of Jang-gya's Collected Works, has been translated by Hans-Rainer Kämpfe in *Ñi ma'i 'od zer/Naran-u gerel: Die Biographie des 2. Pekinger Lčan skya-Qutuqtu Rol pa'i rdo rje (1717-1786),*

448

Monumenta Tibetica Historica, Abt. II, Bd. 1, Wissenschaftsverlag, Sankt Augustin, 1976. For an illuminating review article of
this, see Samuel M. Grupper, "Manchu Patronage And Tibetan
Buddhism During the First Half of the Ch'ing Dynasty", *The
Journal of the Tibet Society*, vol. 4, 1984, pp. 47-75. Grupper
presents the view that the Manchu allegiance to Tibetan Buddhism during the first half of the Ch'ing dynasty was genuine and
not just a technique for holding the loyalty of the Mongolian
nobility. Among evidence (see pp. 58-59) not included in this
chapter is the fact that an image of the Yung-cheng Emperor,
depicted as a lama, was installed at the Sung chu Temple, the
Jang-ḡya residence in Beijing. For additional reading about the
inception of Manchu influence, see Tsepon W.D. Shakabpa,
Tibet: A Political History (rep. New York: Potala Corp., 1984),
pp. 140-152.

2. *ye shes bstan pa'i sgron me.*

3. According to one traditional system of dating, his birth is
calculated as being 2632 years after Shākyamuni Buddha's death,
which, by that system of calculation, would mean that Shākyamuni's death occurred in 915 B.C., instead of around 483 B.C. as is
usually given in accordance with Southern Buddhist calculations.

4. The first month of the Tibeto-Mongolian calendar, which
falls in February or March of the Western calendar.

5. *nub pad mo'i sde.* Khetsun Sangpo pointed out that the
district name is clearly Tibetan (by way of Sanskrit for *padmo*)
even though *lang gru'u* is Chinese.

6. *lang gru'u sde bzhi*, in the Ba-ri (*dpa' ri*) region of the Am-do
Province of Tibet which the Chinese presently include in Qinghai
Province. *lang gru'u* is not to be confused, as Gene Smith (p. 3)
has done, with *lan gru*, present-day Lanzhou in Gansu Province,
China. Many thanks to Geshe Thupten Gyatso for identifying
this.

7. *a mdo.*

8. *tsong kha*, a region that includes the birthplace of Dzong-ka-
ba (*tsong kha pa*, 1357-1419), the founder of the Ge-luk-ba order
of which Jang-ḡya was a prominent lama.

9. *guru bstan 'dzin.*

10. *chi kya dpon po.*

11. *chi kya tshangs pa*, the latter being a dialectical form for
sngags pa.

12. *bu skyid.*
13. *dgon lung byams pa gling.*
14. *lcang skya ngag dbang blo bzang chos ldan,* 1642-1714.
15. *grags pa bsod nams.*
16. *thu'u bkvan blo bzang chos kyi nyi ma,* 1737-1802.
17. *chu bzang blo bzang bstan pa'i rgyal mtshan.*
18. *ngag dbang chos kyi grag pa bstan pa'i rgyal mtshan.*
19. *bstan 'dzin ching wang.*
20. P. 3.
21. I am using my system of "phonetic" spelling rather than Gene Smith's transliteration which is "Lcang-skya".
22. *ngag dbang chos kyi rgya mtsho,* 1680-1736. For the third Tu-ḡen, see n. 1.
23. *bsam yas.* References for the debate are, as cited in Elizabeth Napper, "Dependent-Arising and Emptiness: A Tibetan Buddhist Interpretation of Mādhyamika Philosophy Emphasizing the Compatibility of Emptiness and Conventional Phenomena", (Ann Arbor: University Microfilms, 1981), n. 40, p. 808:

> Paul Demiéville, *Le concile de Lhasa: une controverse sur le quiétisme entre bouddhiste de l'Inde et de la Chine au VIIIe siècle de l'ère chrétienne,* Bibliothèque de l'Institut des Hautes Etudes Chinoises, VII (Paris: Imprimerie Nationale de France, 1952); Giuseppe Tucci, *First Bhā-vanākrama of Kamalaśīla,* Minor Buddhist texts, II, Serie Orientale Roma IX, 2 (Rome: IS.M.E.O., 1958; G.W. Huston, *Sources for a History of the bSam yas Debate* (Sankt Augustin: VGH Wissenschaftsverlag, 1980); Yanagida Seizan's "The *Li-tai fa-pao chi* and the Ch'an Doctrine of Sudden Awakening" in Lai and Lancaster, ed, *Early Ch'an in China and Tibet,* Berkeley Buddhist Studies Series 5 (Berkeley: 1983); and Luis Gomez' "Indian Materials on the Doctrine of Sudden Enlightenment" in *Early Ch'an in China and Tibet,* op. cit., as well as his "The Direct and the Gradual Approaches of Zen Master Mahāyāna: Fragments of the Teachings of Mo-ho-yen" in Gimello and Gregory, ed, *Studies in Ch'an and Hua-yen* (Honolulu: University of Hawaii Press, 1983). See Alex Wayman's chapter, "Discursive Thought and the bSam-yas Debate", pp. 44-58, in his *Calming the*

Mind and Discerning the Real for interesting disagreements with opinions set forth by Demiéville and Tucci.

24. *zhi byed pa.*

25. *pha dam pa sangs rgyas.*

26. Gene Smith (p. 4) describes this identification as "a strange flower produced from Lcang-skya's fertile mind".

27. *khri chen blo bzang bstan pa'i nyi ma,* 1689-1746.

28. *skal bzang rgya mtsho.*

29. *mgar thar.*

30. This section on the political situation of the period preceding Ĵang-ĝya's mission is drawn from Snellgrove and Richardson, *Cultural History of Tibet,* (New York: Praeger, 1968), pp. 204-220.

31. *lha bzang.*

32. *li thang.*

33. *sku 'bum.*

34. *pho lha bsod nams stobs rgyas,* 1689-1747. For an account of his life, see K. Dondup, *The Water-Horse and Other Years: a history of 17th and 18th Century Tibet,* (Dharmsala: Library of Tibetan Works and Archives, 1984), pp. 73-100.

35. p. 219.

36. Snellgrove and Richardson, *Cultural History of Tibet,* p. 220.

37. *bkra shis lhun po.*

38. *blo bzang ye shes,* born 1663.

39. *tham ka bla ma.*

40. *bstan 'gyur.*

41. *bka' 'gyur.*

42. *dag yig mkhas pa'i byung gnas.*

43. *dga' ldan byin chags gling.* For a description of this institution, see F.D. Lessing, *Yung-Ho-Kung; an iconography of the Lamaist cathedral in Peking,* (Stockholm, 1942).

44. *rta tshag rje drung blo bzang dpal ldan.*

45. *'phags pa,* 1235-1280.

46. See David L. Snellgrove's translation of this tantra in *Hevajra Tantra,* Parts I and II, (London: Oxford University Press, 1959).

47. On the surface, it seems that Tibetan biographers frequently insist on not recognizing individual initiative for change and instead resort to explanations that make a good deal of human

history a drama of the descent and intervention of the divine. Divine origins give more authority to institutions, but such exaggeration also seems to pervert the basic Buddhist notion of individual effort. Nevertheless, through a biographer's assumption of manifold perspectives, there remains a strong emphasis on individual effort by highly motivated beings. The extraordinary emphasis on divine intervention may reflect the fecundity of deity yoga, in which meditators rise from a state of dissolution into emptiness as whatever deity they wish. Such play seems present in the ready willingness to identify great personages as incarnations of deities.

48. *sku 'bum*.

49. *btsan po dgon*.

50. *dkon mchog 'jigs med dbang po*, 1728-1791.

51. *skal bzang tshe dbang*.

52. *rin chen lhun grub*.

53. *hu thog thu*.

54. *me gro ru thog*.

55. *phur bu lcog byams pa rin po che*.

56. *dpal ldan ye shes*, born 1737.

57. *gtsang*.

58. The biography is called the *Fruit Clusters of Wish-Granting Jewels (dpag bsam rin po che'i snye ma)*.

59. *rje btsun dam pa*, 1758-1773.

60. *ye shes bstan pa'i nyi ma*.

61. *khri chen ngag dbang mchog ldan*.

62. *'jam dpal zhal lung*.

63. *tshad ma rnam 'grel, pramāṇavarttika*.

64. *rje btsun chos kyi rgyal mtshan*.

65. *dben sa pa*.

66. *lta ba'i gsung mgur*.

67. *rim lnga gsal sgron*.

68. *bra sti dge bshes*.

69. *ke'u tshang*.

70. *ri bo rtse lnga*.

71. "Manchu Patronage And Tibetan Buddhism During the First Half of the Ch'ing Dynasty", n. 37, p. 74. In an inscription at the so-called Lama Temple in Beijing, the Ch'ien-lung Emperor, late in his life, defensively explains his patronage of the Ge-luk-ba church, largely in terms of the need to control the

Mongols, against criticism that he "over-patronized the Yellow Church". The tone and character of the inscription contrasts sharply with an earlier inscription from the time of the dedication of the temple. As Ferdinand Lessing says:

A world separates this self-justification and philippic against Lamaism from the dedicatory inscription in front of Hall I; there the filial son, the pious friend of the priests, a Chinese *Açoka Dharmarāja* speaks, here a disappointed monarch perorates, an old man, full of acrimony and acerbity. Nearly half a century has elapsed between the composition of the two documents, almost sixty years of open, and covert warfare, a struggle for power, analogous to that which filled the middle ages in Europe, when emperor and pope fought for supremacy. The Chinese Emperor, in his self-defence, gives us glimpses into that world of ruse and intrigue which, as he supposed, menaced his temporal sway. At last, he thinks, he has won the game: By repulsing the *Gurkhas* he now enjoys his final triumph, feeling himself to be the saviour of the Yellow Church and simultaneously a good father to all his subjects. He makes an effort to prove that he is not, as his Chinese critics have asserted, a bigotted tool in the hands of the lamas. Far from that, he has acted as a sovereign arbiter who, by his Imperial authority, has put an end to all those sinister intrigues and glaring malpractices, pillorying the names of the conspirators by having them chiselled in stone and preserving them in the very Cathedral of Lamaism in Peking, as a warning to future generations. While the first inscription is permeated by religious aspiration and couched in poetical diction, this document is conceived in the sober style of the Imperial Chancery.

Undoubtedly, the situation was very complex. See F.D. Lessing, *Yung-Ho-Kung; an iconography of the Lamaist cathedral in Peking*, pp. 61-62.

72. For these, see Gene Smith, Appendix II, pp. 3-7; for a list of Ĵang-ḡya's fourteen previous incarnations which includes Še-ra Jay-dzun Chö-ḡyi-gyel-tsen (*se ra rje btsun chos kyi rgyal mtshan*, 1469-1546), as well as an additional list of three including Mar-ba

Chö-ḡyi-Ío-drö (*mar pa chos kyi blo gros*, 1012-1097), see Appendix I of the same, pp. 1-2. The third Paṇ-chen Lama wrote a prayer-petition to the fourteen incarnations, and Ḡön-chok-jik-may-ẅang-bo gave short accounts of them in his *ngo mtshar dad pa'i ljon shing*.

73. For a complete listing, see Lokesh Chandra, ed., *Materials for a History of Tibetan Literature*, New Delhi: International Academy of Indian Culture, 1963), Part One, pp. 192-199. One of the eight volumes is a volume of secret works; see p. 199 of the aforementioned work. The following description of Jang-ḡya's writings is drawn from the same as well as pp. 38-45.

74. See Johannes Schubert, *Tibetische Nationalgrammatik, Das Sum.cu.pa und Rtags.kyi. 'jug.pa des Grosslamas von Peking Rol. pai.rdo.rje* (Leipzig: 1937).

75. Lokesh Chandra (p. 39) reports that the large dictionary was composed in a year by a large staff, being completed by the end of 1742 and that the enumeration of the staff is reported in "Heissig, *Blockdrucke*, 99 p. 87".

76. As Lokesh Chandra reports (p. 39), the former is repro-duced by Sergei Fedorovich Oldenburg in *Bibliotheca Buddhica* V (St. Petersburg, 1903), and the latter is reproduced by Walter Eugen Clark in *Two Lamaistic Pantheons*, vol. I and II (Cam-bridge, Mass., 1937).

77. The book is called *tshad ma'i lam rim* or *gnyid mo che'i rmi lam gyi rol mtshor shar ba'i bstan bcos ngo mtshar zla ba'i snang brnyan*, which Tu-ḡen reproduces on pp. 679-696 of the biography.

78. *grub pa'i mtha'i rnam par bzhag pa gsal bar bshad pa thub bstan lhun po'i mdzes rgyan*. "Meru" is the mountain at the center of this world system in Buddhist cosmology. Three editions have been used:

1 Varanasi: Pleasure of Elegant Sayings Printing Press, 1970; in the notes, this will be called the "Varanasi codex edition".

2 an edition published under the sponsorship of *gam bcar phan bde legs bshad gling grva tshang dang rgyud rnying slar gso tshogs pa*, in the royal year 2109 [n.d.]; since the first sponsor is the Nam-gyel College presently in Dharmsala, India, in the notes it will be called the "Nam-gyel edition".

3 *Buddhist Philosophical Systems of Lcan-skya Rol-pahi Rdo-rje,*

edited by Lokesh Chandra, Śata-piṭaka Series (Indo-Asian Literatures), v. 233, (New Delhi, 1977); in the notes, this will be called the "Lokesh Chandra edition".

The first in the list above has been used as the basic edition simply because of its readibility. It has been checked primarily against the second in the list and emended as indicated in the notes.

The chapter on the Sūtra School has been translated by Anne C. Klein in "*Mind and Liberation: The Sautrāntika Tenet System in Tibet*", (Ann Arbor: University Microfilms, 1981), and the chapter on the Autonomy School has been translated by Donald S. Lopez jr. in *A Study of Svatantrika*, (Ithaca: Snow Lion, 1987).

79. *grub mtha'i rnam bzhag.*

80. P. 6.

81. *grub mtha' chen mo*, the longer title of which is *Explanation of "Tenets", Sun of the Land of Samantabhadra Brilliantly Illuminating All of Our Own and Others' Tenets and the Meaning of the Profound [Emptiness], Ocean of Scripture and Reasoning Fulfilling All Hopes of All Beings (grub mtha'i rnam bshad rang gzhan grub mtha' kun dang zab don mchog tu gsal ba kun bzang zhing gi nyi ma lung rigs rgya mtsho skye dgu'i re ba kun skong)*, (Musoorie: Dalama, 1962). The section on the Consequence School in Jam-ȳang-shay-b̄a's text that corresponds to that of Jang-ḡya offered in this book is found in my *Meditation on Emptiness*, (London: Wisdom Publications, 1983), pp. 583-697.

82. *rje* is often used as a translation equivalent for *svāmi*. Just as in *rdo rje*, *rje* means the *foremost* of stones, i.e., a diamond, so here *rje* refers to a "foremost being", someone at the forefront of all beings.

83. As in *rje yab sras* "the Foremost Father and [Spiritual] Sons".

84. *rje bdag nyid chen po.*

85. *rje bla ma.*

86. *rje thams cad mkhyen pa.*

87. As in *rje thams cad mkhyen pa yab sras* "the Foremost Omniscient Father and Sons".

88. As in *thams cad mkhyen pa yab sras* "the Omniscient Father and Sons".

89. In the section translated in this book, Jang-ğya cites, among Dzong-ka-ba's works, his:

1 *Differentiation of the Interpretable and the Definitive*, also called *Essence of the Good Explanations*, five quotations
2 *Great Commentary on (Nāgārjuna's) "Treatise on the Middle Way"*, also called *Ocean of Reasoning, Explanation of (Nāgārjuna's) "Treatise on the Middle Way"*, five quotations
3 *Great Exposition of the Stages of the Path to Enlightenment*, three quotations.
4 *Praise of the Supramundane Buddha from the Point of View of Dependent-Arising*, three quotations.
5 *Great Explanation of (Chandrakīrti's) "Supplement to (Nāgārjuna's) 'Treatise on the Middle Way' "/ Illumination of the Thought*, three quotations
6 *Small Exposition of the Stages of the Path To Enlightenment*, two quotations
7 *Three Principal Aspects of the Path*, two quotations.

For the complete Tibetan titles, see the Bibliography. For a complete list of the texts that Jam-yang-shay-ba cites in the corresponding part of his *Great Exposition of Tenets*, see *Meditation on Emptiness*, pp. 569-572.

90. The corresponding section in Jam-yang-shay-ba's presentation has 209 quotations (for a listing, see *Meditation on Emptiness*, pp. 569-572) whereas Jang-ğya, as follows, has 111 (including a few references that are not actual quotations):

1 Chandrakīrti's *Supplement to (Nāgārjuna's) "Treatise on the Middle Way"*, twenty-one quotations
2 Nāgārjuna's *Treatise on the Middle Way/ Fundamental Text Called "Wisdom"*, thirteen quotations
3 Nāgārjuna's *Precious Garland*, six quotations
4 Chandrakīrti's *Clear Words*, five quotations
4 Chandrakīrti's *Commentary on (Āryadeva's) "Four Hundred"*, five quotations
4 Dzong-ka-ba's *Differentiation of the Interpretable and the Definitive/ Essence of the Good Explanations*, five quotations
4 Dzong-ka-ba's *Ocean of Reasoning, Explanation of (Nāgārjuna's) "Treatise on the Middle Way"/ Great Commentary on (Nāgārjuna's) "Treatise on the Middle Way"*, five quotations
5 Aryadeva's *Four Hundred*, four quotations

5 *Buddhapālita Commentary on (Nāgārjuna's) "Treatise on the Middle Way"*, four quotations
6 Chandrakīrti's *Autocommentary on the "Supplement to (Nāgārjuna's) 'Treatise on the Middle Way' "*, three quotations
6 Dzong-ka-ba's *Great Exposition of the Stages of the Path to Enlightenment*, three quotations
6 Dzong-ka-ba's *Great Explanation of (Chandrakīrti's) "Supplement to (Nāgārjuna's) 'Treatise on the Middle Way' "/ Illumination of the Thought*, three quotations
6 Dzong-ka-ba's *Praise of the Supramundane Buddha from the Point of View of Dependent-Arising*, three quotations
7 Dzong-ka-ba's *Small Exposition of the Stages of the Path*, two quotations
7 Nāgārjuna's *Sixty Stanzas of Reasoning*, two quotations
7 Shāntideva's *Engaging in the Bodhisattva Deeds*, two quotations
7 *Superior Sūtra of the King of Meditative Stabilizations*, two quotations
7 Dzong-ka-ba's *Three Principal Aspects of the Path*, two quotations
8 one quotation each:
   Bhāvaviveka's *Heart of the Middle Way*
   Dharmakīrti's *Commentary on (Dignāga's) "Compendium of [Teachings on] Valid Cognition"*
   Gyel-tsap's, *Explanation of (Shāntideva's) "Engaging in the Bodhisattva Deeds": Entrance of Conqueror Children*
   Kay-drup's *Opening the Eyes of the Fortunate*
   Nāgārjuna's *Praise of the Supramundane*
   Nor-sang-gya-tso
   Ren-da-wa
   Shūra's (i.e., Ashvaghoṣha's) *Essay on the Stages of Cultivating the Ultimate Mind of Enlightenment*
   Chapter Showing the Three Vows Sūtra
   Superior Sūtra of the Sport of Mañjushrī
   Superior Sūtra of the Cloud of Jewels
   Questions of Brahmā Sūtra
   Questions of Upāli Sūtra
   Perfection of Wisdom Sūtra
   Taming Demons Chapter
   Ajātashatru Sūtra
   Sūtra on the Ten Grounds

unidentified sūtra
Questions of Sāgaramati Sūtra
Questions of Anavatapta, the King of Nāgas, Sūtra
Descent into Laṅkā Sūtra.

The authors in order of frequency of quotation are:

1 Chandrakīrti, thirty-four quotations
2 Nāgārjuna, twenty-three quotations
3 Dzong-ka-ba, twenty-three quotations
4 Buddha (sūtra), fifteen quotations
5 Āryadeva, four quotations
5 Buddhapālita, four quotations
6 Shāntideva, two quotations
7 Bhāvaviveka, Dharmakīrti, Gyel-tsap, Kay-drup, Ren-da-wa, and Shūra (i.e., Ashvaghoṣha), one quotation each.

Both Jam-ȳang-shay-ba and Jang-ḡya cite Chandrakīrti most frequently, thereby indicating the central importance of Chandrakīrti in interpreting Nāgārjuna's thought. Jam-ȳang-shay-ba, however, cites Nāgārjuna almost three times as often as he cites Dzong-ka-ba whereas Jang-ḡya cites them an equal number of times. For both, however, Dzong-ka-ba is the dominant figure; as Jam-ȳang-shay-ba (*Meditation on Emptiness*, p. 594, adapted slightly) says:

> For an unconfused account with respect to what is uncommon [to the Consequence School I, Jam-ȳang-shay-ba] having taken as valid the good explanations of the three — the great being, the foremost [Dzong-ka-ba who is the] father and his two spiritual sons [Gyel-tsap and Kay-drup], will explain the system of the Consequence School just according to them even though I might not cite them in quotation. For, free from error, they expounded clearly through millions of reasons.

Jang-ḡya is more explicitly concerned with putting Dzong-ka-ba's reasoned interpretations before his audience.

91. This is his *Presentation of Tenets, A Precious Garland* (*grub pa'i mtha'i rnam par bzhag pa rin po che'i phreng ba*), which has been translated by Geshe Lhundup Sopa and Jeffrey Hopkins in *Practice and Theory of Tibetan Buddhism*, (London: Rider, 1976; second edition, London: Wisdom Publications, 1987). This pre-

sentation of the schools of tenets is in a tradition, within Ge-luk-ba, of short presentations by Jay-dzun Chö-gyi-gyel-tsen (*rje btsun chos kyi rgyal mtshan*, 1469-1546), the Second Dalai Lama Ge-dun-gya-tso (*dge 'dun rgya mtsho*, 1476-1542), and Drak-ba-shay-drup (*grags pa bshad sgrub, co ne ba*, 1675-1748); see the bibliography for the book titles.

92. The only other major presentation of tenets within the Ge-luk-ba order was written by Jang-gya's biographer, Tu-gen-lo-sang-chö-gyi-nyi-ma, this being his *Mirror of the Good Explanations Showing the Sources and Assertions of All Systems of Tenets* (*grub mtha' thams cad kyi khungs dang 'dod tshul ston pa legs bshad shel gyi me long*), (Sarnath: Chhos Je Lama, 1963); it presents not only the Indian schools but also the Tibetan schools, though in a rather biased way. These texts owe much to a similar presentation of tenets by the great Sa-gya scholar Dak-tsang-shay-rap-rin-chen (*stag tshang lo tsā ba shes rab rin chen*, born 1405), despite their (especially Jam-yang-shay-ba's) opposition to many of his interpretations. That text is Dak-tsang's *Ocean of Good Explanations, Explanation of "Freedom From Extremes Through Understanding All Tenets"* (*grub mtha' kun shes nas mtha' bral grub pa zhes bya ba'i bstan bcos rnam par bshad pa legs bshad kyi rgya mtsho*), (Thimphu: Kun-bzang-stobs rgyal, 1976). Other examples of the genre are to be found in the *Treasury of Tenets, Illuminating the Meaning of All Vehicles* (*theg pa mtha' dag gi don gsal bar byed pa grub pa'i mtha' rin po che'i mdzod*) and *Precious Treasury of the Supreme Vehicle* (*theg pa'i mchog rin po che'i mdzod*), (Gangtok, Dodrup Chen Rinpoche, 1969[?]) by the great Nying-ma scholar Long-chen-rap-jam (*klong chen rab 'byams/ klong chen dri med 'od zer*, 1308-1363).

93. *dbu ma thal 'gyur pa, prāsaṅgika-mādhyamika*.

94. For a brief description of the four seals, see Sopa and Hopkins, *Practice and Theory of Tibetan Buddhism* (London: Rider and Co., 1976), p. 68.

95. *grub pa'i mtha', siddhānta*.

96. The term "Lesser Vehicle" (*theg dman, hīnayāna*) has its origin in the writings of Great Vehicle (*theg chen, mahāyāna*) authors and was, of course, not used by those to whom it was ascribed. Substitutes such as "non-Mahāyāna", "Nikāya Buddhism", and "Theravādayāna" have been suggested in order to avoid the pejorative sense of "Lesser". However, "Lesser Vehi-

cle" is a convenient term in this particular context for a type of practice that is seen, in the tradition which provides the perspective of this book, to be surpassed — but not negated — by a higher system of practice. The "Lesser Vehicle" is not despised, most of it being incorporated into the "Great Vehicle". The monks' and nuns' vows are Lesser Vehicle, as is much of the course of study in Ge-luk-ba monastic universities — years of study are put into the topics of Epistemology (*tshad ma, pramāṇa*), Manifest Knowledge (*chos mngon pa, abhidharma*), and Discipline (*'dul ba, vinaya*), all of which are mostly Lesser Vehicle in perspective. ("Lesser Vehicle" and "Low Vehicle" are used interchangeably in this book.)

97. The Tibetan and Sanskrit for the four schools of tenets are:

Great Exposition School (*bye brag smra ba, vaibhāṣika*)
Sūtra School (*mdo sde pa, sautrāntika*)
Mind Only School (*sems tsam pa, cittamātra*)
Middle Way School (*dbu ma pa, mādhyamika*)
  Autonomy School (*rang rgyud pa, svātantrika*)
    Sūtra Autonomy School (*mdo sde spyod pa dbu ma rang rgyud pa, sautrāntikasvātantrikamādhyamika*)
    Yogic Autonomy School (*rnal 'byor spyod pa dbu ma rang rgyud pa, yogācārasvātantrikamādhyamika*)
  Consequence School (*thal 'gyur pa, prāsaṅgika*).

98. As cited in Gön-chok-jik-may-wang-bo's (*dkon mchog 'jigs med dbang po*, 1728-91) *Presentation of Tenets*, the *Descent into Laṅkā Sūtra* (*lang kar gshegs pa'i mdo, laṅkāvatārasūtra*) says:

My doctrine has two modes,
Advice and established conclusions.
To children I speak advice
And to yogis, established conclusions.

Gön-chok-jik-may-wang-bo himself says:

The etymology for 'tenet' is: A tenet [literally, an established conclusion] is a meaning which was made firm, decided upon, or established in reliance on scripture and/or reasoning and which, from the perspective of one's mind, will not be forsaken for something else.

The qualification "from the perspective of one's mind" indicates that, for the proponent at this time, the tenet is a decided conclusion; the qualification allows for changing one's mind and switching tenets later. See his *Presentation of Tenets, A Precious Garland* (*grub pa'i mtha'i rnam par bzhag pa rin po che'i phreng ba*), translated by Geshe Lhundup Sopa and Jeffrey Hopkins in *Practice and Theory of Tibetan Buddhism*, p. 53, translation adjusted.

99. *rang rgyud kyi sbyor ba, svatantraprayoga.* Often, the pervasion, or major premise, is not explicitly expressed, as in, "The subject, a pot, is impermanent because of being a product — for example, a sound." Roughly speaking, the pervasion, or major premise, is: whatever is a product is necessarily impermanent. Since it is not explicitly expressed, the above statement is technically not a syllogism but an enthymeme, an argument containing one or more suppressed premises; however, as it is implicit in the above statement and the more formal Buddhist format does include such, the term "syllogism" is used here. See Daniel Perdue, "Practice and Theory of Philosophical Debate in Tibetan Buddhist Education" (Ann Arbor: University Microfilms, 1983), p. 1170; Perdue's massive and important work is forthcoming from Wisdom Publications, London.

100. *thal 'gyur, prasaṅga.*
101. *tsong kha pa*, 1357-1419.
102. *zhi gnas, śamatha.*
103. *tshogs lam, saṃbhāramārga.*
104. See the Fifth Dalai Lama's description of this in my forthcoming *Deity Yoga* (London: Wisdom Publications), chapter one. This is currently available in "Practice of Emptiness", trans. by Jeffrey Hopkins, (Dharmsala: Library of Tibetan Works and Archives, 1974), p. 10. The text itself is Nga-w̄ang-lo-sang-gya-tso (*ngag dbang blo bzang rgya mtsho*, 1617-1682), *Instruction on the Stages of the Path to Enlightenment, Sacred Word of Mañjushrī* (*byang chub lam gyi rim pa'i khrid yig 'jam pa'i dbyangs kyi zhal lung*), (Thimphu, Bhutan: kun bzang stobs rgyal, 1976).

105. *rtse* or *rtsal.*
106. *tshig gsal, prasannapadā;* for editions and translations, see the Bibliography. For the context of this quote, see *Meditation on Emptiness*, p. 526.

107. The bracketed addition is taken from the *Four Interwoven Commentaries on (Dzong-ka-ba's) "Great Exposition of the Stages of*

the Path" (The Lam rim chen mo of the incomparable Tsong-kha-pa, with the interlineal notes of Ba-so Chos-kyi-rgyal-mtshan, Sde-drug Mkhan-chen Ngag-dbang-rab-rtan, 'Jam-dbyangs-bzhad-pa'i-rdo-rje, and Bra-sti Dge-bshes Rin-chen-don-grub, New Delhi: Chos-'phel-legs-ldan, 1972), 592.2. With respect to "who do not know suchness" the Sanskrit (Poussin, 36.1) is merely *tadanabhijña* "who do not know that [or those, which could refer to 'the definitions']" whereas the Tibetan reads *de kho na mi shes pa'i* "who do not know suchness". The *Four Interwoven Commentaries* (592.3) takes it even further: *chos kyi de kho na nyid ma shes pa'i* "who do not know the suchness of phenomena". I have followed the Tibetan as it presumably reflects a reading of *tad* as meaning *tattva* (see Poussin, p. 36, n. 3) by the translators. The "Poussin" references are to: Chandrakīrti, *Mūlamadhyamakakārikās de Nāgārjuna avec la Prasannapadā Commentaire de Candrakīrti* publiée par Louis de la Vallée Poussin, Bibliotheca Buddhica IV, (Osnabrück: Biblio Verlag, 1970).

108. The *Four Hundred (bstan bcos bzhi brgya pa zhes bya ba'i tshig le'ur byas pa, catuḥśatakaśāstrakārikā)*, VIII.19. For the context, see Karen Lang, "Aryadeva on the Bodhisattva's Cultivation of Merit and Knowledge", (Ann Arbor: University Microfilms, 1983), p. 320. See also the *Four Interwoven Commentaries*, 590.2; the passage is cited in *Meditation on Emptiness*, p. 837 n. 458.

109. For the context of this quote, see *Meditation on Emptiness*, p. 525.

110. *dbu ma la 'jug pa'i bshad pa/ dbu ma la 'jug pa'i rang 'grel, madhyamakāvatārabhāṣya*. For editions and translations, see the Bibliography.

111. *Treatise on the Middle Way/ Fundamental Treatise on the Middle Way, Called "Wisdom" (dbu ma'i bstan bcos/ dbu ma rtsa ba'i tshig le'ur byas pa shes rab ces bya ba, madhyamakaśāstra/ prajñānāmamūlamadhyamakakārikā)*. For editions and translations, see the Bibliography.

112. In *dbu ma la 'jug pa (madhaymakāvatāra), 'jug pa (avatāra)* is seen by some Tibetan scholars as meaning "add on" and hence "supplement". The basic meaning of the word is "enter", and thus in such titles other Tibetan scholars and most, if not all, Western scholars take the term to mean "introduction". For detailed discussion of my translation of *madhyamakāvatāra* as *Supplement to the "Treatise on the Middle Way"*, see my *Meditation on Emptiness*, pp. 462-9 and 866-9.

113. *rgyal po la gtam bya ba rin po che'i phreng ba, rājapari-kathāratnāvalī.*

114. *mdo kun las btus pa, sūtrasamuccaya.*

115. See Nāgārjuna's description of the ten grounds in Nāgār-juna and Kaysang Gyatso, *Precious Garland and the Song of the Four Mindfulnesses,* (London: George Allen and Unwin, 1975), pp. 84-7, stanzas 440-461b.

116. *rje btsun chos kyi rgyal mtshan,* 1469-1546. See his *A Good Explanation Adorning the Throats of the Fortunate: A General Meaning Commentary Clarifying Difficult Points in (Dzong-ka-ba's) "Illumination of the Thought: An Explanation of (Chandrakīrti's) 'Supplement to (Nāgārjuna's) "Treatise on the Middle Way" ' "* (*bstan bcos dbu ma la 'jug pa'i rnam bshad dgongs pa rab gsal gyi dka' gnad gsal bar byed pa'i spyi don legs bshad skal bzang mgul rgyan*), Collected Works, (n.p.d. [Se-ra Jay College publication in India in early 1980's]), vol. ma 9a.5-11b.5, especially 11a.2.

117. *byes.*

118. *se rva.*

119. *'jam dbyangs bzhad pa,* 1648-1721. See his *Great Exposi-tion of the Middle Way/ Analysis of (Chandrakīrti's) "Supplement to (Nāgārjuna's) 'Treatise on the Middle Way' ", Treasury of Scripture and Reasoning, Thoroughly Illuminating the Profound Meaning [of Emptiness], Entrance for the Fortunate* (*dbu ma chen mo/ dbu ma 'jug pa'i mtha' dpyod lung rigs gter mdzod zab don kun gsal skal bzang 'jug ngogs*), (Buxaduor: Go-mang, 1967), 6a.1ff.

120. *sgo mang.*

121. *'bras spungs.*

122. *mngon par rtogs pa'i rgyan, abhisamayālaṃkāra.* For this point, see Jam-yang-shay-ba's *Great Exposition of the Middle Way* 7b.5.

123. The two bracketed additions are from Geshe Rabten, *Annotations For the Difficult Points of (Dzong-ka-ba's) "Essence of the Good Explanations", Joyous Festival For The Unbiased With Clear Awareness* (*drang nges rnam 'byed legs bshad snying po dka' gnad rnams mchan bur bkod pa gzur gnas blo gsal dga' ston*), (n.p.d. [edition in India in the early 1970's]), 271.1. For Robert A.F. Thurman's translation of this passage, see his *Essence of True Eloquence* (Princeton: 1984), p. 289. For more context, see the next note.

124. *legs bshad snying po,* (Varanasi, 1973), 140.20; the brack-

eted additions are taken from Geshe Rabten, *Annotations*, 272.5-272.6. With more context, the citation reads:

> [Chandrakīrti] describes his own system as not shared with the commentaries [on Nāgārjuna's thought] by other Proponents of the Middle Way. His *Autocommentary on the "Supplement to (Nāgārjuna's) 'Treatise on the Middle Way'"* says:
>
> > May scholars ascertain that just as, except for Nāgārjuna's *Treatise on the Middle Way*, this doctrine called "emptiness" is not expressed non-erroneously in other treatises, so the system which appears in this [treatise] — set out together with objections and answers to any [other] system — does not exist, in terms of the doctrine of emptiness, in other treatises. Therefore, it should be understood that a certain [scholar's] propounding that just what is propounded as ultimate in the system of the Sūtra School is asserted as conventional by the Proponents of the Middle Way is a proposition [made] only by one who does not know the suchness of Nāgārjuna's *Treatise on the Middle Way*.
>
> At the end of saying this, Chandrakīrti also says with respect to the system of Great Exposition School:
>
> > This is because a supramundane doctrine is not fit to be similar to a mundane doctrine. Scholars should ascertain, "This system is uncommon."

Through the reason of his own system's not being shared with other Proponents of the Middle Way, he posits that one who asserts that what are propounded as ultimate by the two Proponents of [Truly Existent External] Objects [i.e., the Great Exposition School and the Sūtra School] are propounded as conventionalities by the Proponents of the Middle Way does not know the Middle Way suchness. The reason is that in his own system, phenomena that are established by way of their own character are not asserted even conventionally, whereas those [phenomena presented in the two systems propounding truly existent external objects] are only posited in the context of that [establishment of objects by way of their own character].

For Robert Thurman's translation of this passage, see his *Tsong Khapa's Speech of Gold in the Essence of True Eloquence*, (Princeton: Princeton University Press, 1984), pp. 288-9.

125. *kun gzhi rnam shes, ālayavijñāna*.

126. *don dam pa byang chub kyi sems bsgom pa'i rim pa yi ger bris pa, paramārthabodhicittabhāvanākramavarṇasaṃgraha*, P5431, vol. 103 246.5.2. The passage is cited in *Meditation on Emptiness*, pp. 586-7; see also p. 857 n. 504. The Peking edition wrongly reads *stong pa gnyis* instead of *stong pa nyid*. The brackets are from Nga-ŵang-ḃel-den (*ngag dbang dpal ldan*, born 1797), *Annotations for (Jam-ȳang-shay-ḃa's) "Great Exposition of Tenets", Freeing the Knots of the Difficult Points, Precious Jewel of Clear Thought (grub mtha' chen mo'i mchan 'grel dka' gnad mdud grol blo gsal gces nor)*, (Sarnath: Pleasure of Elegant Sayings Press, 1964), dbu 59b.4-7, which confirms the latter reading as does Jang-ġya, 409.10. Nga-ŵang-ḃel-den says that since Buddha's teaching that all phenomena are selfless cannot be defeated by any opponent, his teaching was proclaimed like the great roar of a lion (whose roar no other animal dares to answer).

The Tibetan scholars with whom I have worked have identified Shūra (*dpa' bo*) as Ashvaghoṣha. For references to controversy about this, see D.S. Ruegg's *The Literature of the Madhyamaka School of Philosophy in India* (Wiesbaden: Otto Harrasowitz, 1981), 119-21.

For a very thorough discussion of the usage of the term "Thoroughly Non-Abiding Proponents of the Middle Way School" for Consequentialists and "Reason-Established Illusionists" for the Autonomists, see Appendix One in Elizabeth Napper, "Dependent-Arising and Emptiness: A Tibetan Buddhist Interpretation of Mādhyamika Philosophy Emphasizing the Compatibility of Emptiness and Conventional Phenomena", pp. 576-631.

127. *rgyal tshab dar ma rin chen*, 1364-1432; *mkhas sgrub dge legs dpal bzang po*, 1385-1438.

128. Guy M. Newland is translating the section on the two truths; Jules B. Levinson, on the path; and S. Brian Daley, on the fruits of the path.

129. *blo gnod med la snang ba'i dbang gis bzhag pa ma yin par rang gi thun mong ma yin pa'i sdod lugs kyi ngos nas grub pa.*

130. See pp. 178-191 of the Tibetan.

131. See *Meditation on Emptiness*, pp. 303-304, and Jam-ȳang-shay-ba's *Great Exposition of the Middle Way*, 179b.5ff.

132. This was the speculation of the late Go-mang scholar Geshe Gedün Lodrö, who taught in his later years at the University of Hamburg.

133. *mdo sde spyod pa'i dbu ma rang rgyud pa, sautrāntikasvātantrikamādhyamika.*

134. *rnal 'byor spyod pa'i dbu ma rang rgyud pa, yogācārasvātantrikamādhyamika.*

135. *rang rgyal, pratyekabuddha.*

136. *byang chub sems dpa'i rnal 'byor spyod pa bzhi brgya pa, bodhisattvayogācāracatuḥśataka,* VIII.16. The title is cited this way in Chandrakīrti's *Commentary on (Āryadeva's) "Four Hundred"* (*byang chub sems dpa'i rnal 'byor spyod pa bzhi brgya pa'i rgya cher 'grel pa, bodhisattvayogācāracatuḥśatakaṭīkā*), Vol. 8 (No. 3865) of the *sDe dge Tibetan Tripiṭaka — bsTan ḥgyur preserved at the Faculty of Letters, University of Tokyo*, Tokyo, 1979. For the context, see Karen Lang, "Aryadeva on the Bodhisattva's Cultivation of Merit and Knowledge", (Ann Arbor: University Microfilms, 1983), p. 318.

136a. 35ab. The second line reads either *de srid de las* or *de srid de la;* the first reading is as given in the citation; the second would read:

As long as the aggregates are [mis]conceived,
For that [person] there is [mis]conception of an I.

Both readings are seen as showing that a consciousness conceiving the inherent existence of the aggregates serves as a cause of a consciousness conceiving that a person inherently exists. In stanzas 29-32, Nāgārjuna speaks of the mental and physical aggregates as arising from misconception of I, but this does not contradict the above explanation because in these stanzas he is speaking about the mental and physical aggregates of a lifetime in cyclic existence as being produced from ignorance of the nature of the self, whereas in these two lines he is speaking about the *consciousness conceiving* the inherent existence of the I as being caused by the *consciousness conceiving* of the inherent existence of the aggregates.

137. *shes rab kyi pha rol tu phyin pa, prajñāpāramitā.*

138. The Tibetan word for "true existence" here is *dngos po,* which is usually translated as "thing" but is accepted as meaning *bden par grub pa* in certain contexts. For extended discussion of this, see Elizabeth Napper, "Dependent-Arising and Emptiness: A Tibetan Buddhist Interpretation of Mādhyamika Philosophy Emphasizing the Compatibility of Emptiness and Conventional Phenomena", (Ann Arbor: University Microfilms, 1981), p. 83 and n. 87.

139. *byang chub sems dpa'i spyod pa la 'jug pa, bodhi[sattva]caryāvatāra,* IX. 41cd. This is cited in Dzong-ka-ba's *Illumination of the Thought (dgongs pa rab gsal);* see *Compassion in Tibetan Buddhism,* (London: Rider and Co., 1980), p. 155.

140. *nyon mongs, kleśa.*

141. *stong gzhi.*

142. *chos, dharma.*

143. VI.179. Bracketed material is from Dzong-ka-ba, *Illumination of the Thought, Extensive Explanation of (Chandrakīrti's) "Supplement to (Nāgārjuna's) 'Treatise on the Middle Way' " (dbu ma la 'jug pa'i rgya cher bshad pa dgongs pa rab gsal),* (Dharamsala: Shes rig par khang edition, n.d.), 228.19.

144. This is with the significant exception that, according to Nga-wang-bel-den, even Dzong-ka-ba holds that in inferential realization of emptiness, the subject can still appear. See n. 580 and n. 581 in Elizabeth Napper, "Dependent-Arising and Emptiness: A Tibetan Buddhist Interpretation of Mādhyamika Philosophy Emphasizing the Compatibility of Emptiness and Conventional Phenomena"; in n. 580 Napper refers to:

> ... Nga-wang-bel-den's *Presentation of the Grounds and Paths of Mantra (sngags kyi sa lam),* (rgyud smad par khang edition, no other data), 10.2, where he says, "... it must be asserted that the conceptual reasoning consciousness that realizes emptiness perceives the subject — the basis of emptiness ..." and cites as his reason the fact that such is stated in Dzong-ka-ba's *Ocean of Reasoning, Explanation of (Nāgārjuna's) "Treatise on the Middle Way"* and *Great Exposition of the Stages of the Path.* Nga-wang-bel-den cites those passages from Dzong-ka-ba in his *Presentation of the Two Truths,* 216.5-218.4; the first portion of the passage from the *Great Exposition* is given in the next note.

145. *Fundamental Treatise on the Middle Way Called "Wisdom"* (*dbu ma rtsa ba'i tshig le'ur byas pa shes rab ces bya ba, prajñānāma-mūlamadhyamakakārikā*), XIII.1. This is cited by Chandrakīrti in his *Clear Words* (P5260, Vol. 98 8.1.8); for the Sanskrit, see Chandrakīrti, *Mūlamadhyamakakārikās de Nāgārjuna avec la Prasannapadā Commentaire de Candrakīrti* publiée par Louis de la Vallée Poussin, Bibliotheca Buddhica IV, (Osnabrück: Biblio Verlag, 1970), 42.10.

146. *rang bzhin, svabhāva.*

147. *brtag pa mtha' bzung.*

148. *rang ngos nas grub pa, yul steng nas grub pa, rang gi mtshan nyid kyis grub pa, don dam par grub pa, gdags gzhi'i steng nas grub pa, de kho na nyid du grub pa, yang dag par grub pa, khyod khyod kyi gnas lugs su grub pa, rang gi ngo bos grub pa.*

149. *yod pa* (*sat*) and *grub pa* (*siddhi*).

150. *bden par grub pa, don dam par grub pa, yang dag par grub pa.*

151. *rang bzhin gyis grub pa, rang gi mtshan nyid kyis grub pa, rang gi ngo bos grub pa.*

152. *rang dbang ba'i ngo bo.*

153. *rang rgyud, svatantra.*

154. *rang dbang, svairī;* for the Sanskrit, see Jam-ȳang-shay-ba's *Great Exposition of Tenets*, ca 61a.1.

155. For a description of the three modes of a reason, see chapter two.

156. XIV.23; P5246, vol. 95 139.2.7. Brackets are from Chandrakīrti's commentary, P5266, vol. 98 270.3.6.

157. See previous note; translated in context, the passage, as taken from *Meditation on Emptiness*, p. 632, is:

> Here, that which has its own intrinsic existence, has inherent existence, has its own power, or has no dependence on another would exist by itself; therefore, it would not be a dependent-arising.

158. *blo, buddhi/mati.*

159. *rtog pa, kalpanā.*

160. P5246, vol. 95 136.2.1, VIII.3. Brackets are from Chandrakīrti's commentary (P5266, vol. 98 229.5.3). This is cited by Jam-ȳang-shay-ba in his *Great Exposition of Tenets;* see *Meditation on Emptiness*, p. 627.

161. P5166, vol. 98 229.5.3, commenting on VIII.3. This is cited by Jam-yang-shay-ba in his *Great Exposition of Tenets;* see *Meditation on Emptiness,* p. 627.

162. This issue is addressed by the Fifth Dalai Lama, Nga-wang-lo-sang-gya-tso *(ngag dbang blo bzang rgya mtsho,* 1617-1682), in his *Instruction on the Stages of the Path to Enlightenment, Sacred Word of Mañjushrī (byang chub lam gyi rim pa'i khrid yig 'jam pa'i dbyangs kyi zhal lung)* in terms of how the I is conceived:

Furthermore, consciousnesses innately conceiving I — which conceive an I or self based on the [nominally existent] person — are of three types:

1 A conceptual consciousness [correctly] conceiving I which exists in a person who has generated the Middle Way view in his/her mental continuum. This consciousness [correctly] conceives of an I qualified as being only designated in the context of its basis of designation [mind and body].

2 An actual innate [consciousness mis]conceiving an I qualified as being inherently existent. It is to be overcome through its antidote here on this occasion [of the path of wisdom].

3 A conventional validly cognizing consciousness which establishes [the existence of] I. This consciousness exists [for example] in the continuums of those common beings whose mental continuums have not been affected by systems of tenets and who thus do not differentiate between nominal imputation and inherent existence. In this case, the I is not qualified as being either nominally imputed or inherently existent.

For an English translation, see J. Hopkins, "Practice of Emptiness", (Dharamsala: Library of Tibetan Works and Archives, 1974), p. 10. A revised translation, from which the above quotation is taken, is forthcoming in my *Deity Yoga* (London: Wisdom Publications).

163. *'khrul ba* and *ma 'khrul ba.*

164. *phyin ci log pa* and *phyin ci ma log pa.*

165. Nying-ma *(rnying ma),* Ga-gyu *(bka' rgyud),* Sa-gya *(sa skya),* and Ge-luk *(dge lugs).*

166. *chos nyid kyi klong chen po gcig.*

167. Literally (412.11), "as an illustration of a snake" (*sprul gyi mtshan gzhir*).

168. Literally (412.15), "as an illustration of that I" (*nga de'i mtshan gzhir*).

169. This is reported in the colophon to Chandrakīrti's *Clear Words;* in the Tibetan Publishing House, 1968, edition, see 505.2.

170. *nye ba 'khor gyis zhus pa, upāliparipṛcchā.* This passage is cited in Chandrakīrti's *Clear Words* at the end of the eighth chapter; see Poussin, 191.6.

171. *ting nge 'dzin rgyal po, samādhirāja.*

172. Stanza 99.

173. 114bcd.

174. *las, karma.*

175. *'jig tshogs la lta ba, satkāyadṛṣṭi.*

176. See *Meditation on Emptiness*, pp. 679-680; for more discussion, see *Meditation on Emptiness*, n. 739, pp. 888-890.

177. See *Meditation on Emptiness*, pp. 685.

178. Oral teachings. A translation of his lectures of the three principal aspects of the path can be found in the first part of *Compassion in Tibetan Buddhism* (rpt. Ithaca: Snow Lion, 1985).

179. See the chapter on the Consequence School in Dak-tsang Shay-rap-rin-chen, *Ocean of Good Explanations, Explanation of "Freedom From Extremes Through Understanding All Tenets,"* 277.3ff.

180. *nges don, nītārtha.*

181. *drang don, neyārtha.* The term term *drang* in *drang don* has the same spelling as *drang po*, meaning "honest" or "direct", but it can be seen from the Sanskrit *neya*, which is the gerundive derived from the verbal root *nī* meaning "to lead", that the Tibetan is derived from the verb *'dren*, meaning "to lead", the past form being *drang* or *drangs*. As Jam-ȳang-shay-ba points out (see *Meditation on Emptiness*, p. 600), that which is being led is not trainees but the subject matter of texts — the subject matter requires interpretation.

182. In the Varanasi codex edition, for *thob pa la yang dag* (417.4) read *thob pa la yang gang zag dang chos la bdag med pa'i de kho na nyid nges par rtogs dgos pa sher phyogs kyi mdo'i dgongs pa yin te/ shes rab kyi pha rol tu phyin pa'i lung las dngos po'i 'du shes can la thar pa med par gsungs pa dang dus gsum gyi yang dag* in accordance

with the Nam-gyel edition 458.4.

183. *dngos po, bhāva*. This term usually means "that which is able to perform a function" *(don byed nus pa)* and thus strictly refers to impermanent things, but more loosely it can also refer to any phenomenon, permanent or impermanent. Here, however, it is taken as referring to true existence *(bden par grub pa, satyasiddhi)*. For discussion of these usages, see n. 138.

184. *rigs pa drug cu pa'i tshig le'ur byas pa, yuktiṣaṣṭikākārikā*, 4ab. For the edited Tibetan with Sanskrit fragments and English translation, see Chr. Lindtner in *Nagarjuniana*, Indiske Studier 4, (Copenhagen: Akademisk Forlag, 1982), pp. 100-119.

185. *mngon mtho, abhyudaya*. For discussion of "high status" and "definite goodness", see the first chapter of Nāgārjuna's *Precious Garland*.

186. *nges legs, naiḥśreyasa*.

187. Stanza 35. The text, which gives only the first line and "and so forth" *(sogs)*, has been expanded.

188. *med dgag, prasajyapratiṣedha*. The Tibetan and Sanskrit for "affirming negative" are *ma yin dgag, paryudāsapratiṣedha*. For the various types of these, see *Meditation on Emptiness*, pp. 723-725.

189. Tenzin Gyatso, *The Buddhism of Tibet and The Key to the Middle Way* (London: George Allen and Unwin, 1975), p. 77. This book has been reprinted in a combined volume, which also includes a translation of Nāgārjuna's *Precious Garland*, entitled *The Buddhism of Tibet*, (London: George Allen and Unwin, 1983).

190. *snang yul*.

191. *'jug yul*.

192. There are many interpretations of this dictum among Ge-luk-ba scholars. Some posit that manifest and subliminal mental consciousnesses can occur simultaneously; others posit that mental consciousnesses of different but not opposite modes of apprehension can occur simultaneously. See Nga-wang-bel-den *(ngag dbang dpal ldan*, b.1797), *Stating the Mode of Explanation in the Textbooks on the Middle Way and the Perfection of Wisdom in the Lo-sel-ling and Go-mang Colleges: Festival For Those of Clear Intelligence (blo gsal gling dang bkra shis sgo mang grva tshang gi dbu phar gyi yig cha'i bshad tshul bkod pa blo gsal dga' ston)*, Collected Works, (New Delhi: Gurudeva, 1983), vol. ga, 461.4ff.

193. Geshe Gedun Lodrö treated this topic in some detail during a series of lectures at the University of Virginia in 1979.

194. *lkog gyur, parokṣa*.

195. See Geshe Lhundup Sopa and Jeffrey Hopkins, *Practice and Theory of Tibetan Buddhism* (London: Rider and Co., 1976), p. 38.

196. This is from Chandrakīrti's *Supplement to (Nāgārjuna's) "Treatise on the Middle Way"* (VI.116ab). The stanza goes on to say:

When [the conception of an inherently existent] phenomenon does not exist,
These [extreme conceptions] do not arise, just as there is no fire when there is no fuel.

The bracketed additions are from Dzong-ka-ba's *Illumination of the Thought*, P6143, vol. 154 81.1.5ff.

197. A reason, such as the presence of smoke, can prove a predicate, such as the presence of fire, because the predicate (the presence of fire) pervades the reason (the presence of smoke); thus, the presence of the reason can serve as a sign of the presence of the predicate. The reason is the proof (prover), but the predicate is the pervader.

198. *'phags pa 'jam dpal ram par rol pa'i mdo, āryamañjuśrīvikrīdita*.

199. IX.37.

200. *'phags pa dkon mchog sprin, āryaratnamegha*.

201. *tshangs pas zhus pa, brahmāparipṛcchā*.

202. *dbu ma rtsa ba'i 'grel pa buddha pā li ta, buddhapālitamūlamadhyamakavṛtti*. For an edited Tibetan edition of chapters 1-12, see Max Walleser, Bibliotheca Buddhica XVI, (Osnabrück: Biblio Verlag, 1970). For an English translation of chapter 1, see Judit Fehér, in Louis Ligeti, ed., *Tibetan and Buddhist Studies Commemorating the 200th Anniversary of the Birth of Alexander Csoma de Körös*, Vol. 1, (Budapest: Akadémiai Kiado, 1984), pp. 211-240. For an English translation of chapter 18, see Chr. Lindtner in *Indo-Iranian Journal* 23 (1981), pp. 187-217.

203. VI.118ab.

204. In the Varanasi codex edition (420.18) read *dpang por* for *dbang por* in accordance with the Lokesh Chandra edition (682.2).

205. Stanza 77.

206. See the Dalai Lama's explanation of this in Tenzin Gyat-so, *The Buddhism of Tibet and The Key to the Middle Way* (London: George Allen and Unwin, 1975), pp. 80-82. See also my introduction to *The Kālachakra Tantra: Rite of Initiation for the Stage of Generation*, (London: Wisdom Publications, 1985), p. 21.

207. In the Varanasi codex edition (420.18) read *thos* for *thob* in accordance with the Nam-gyel edition (462.5).

208. In the Varanasi codex edition (420.20) read *phong ba* for *phong pa;* the Nam-gyel edition (462.5) reads *bong ba.*

209. Āryadeva's *Four Hundred*, VIII.5. For the context, see Karen Lang, "Aryadeva on the Bodhisattva's Cultivation of Merit and Knowledge", p. 311.

210. See Lati Rinbochay and Elizabeth Napper, *Mind in Tibetan Buddhism* (London: Rider and Company, 1980), p. 24, 106-109.

211. Colophon of Chandrakīrti's *Clear Words*, stanza 8cd, P5260, Vol. 98 92.1 7 For the Sanskrit see J.W. de Jong's very helpful article on this Colophon, missing in Poussin's edition of Chandrakīrti's *Clear Words*, "La Madhyamakaśāstrastuti de Candrakīrti" in *Oriens Extremus*, Jahrg. 9, 1962, pp. 47-56 (reprinted in *J.W. De Jong Buddhist Studies*, pp. 541-50 [Rep. of China: Asian Humanities Press, 1979]).

212. *bdud 'dul ba'i le'u.*

213. *ma skyes dgra'i mdo, ajātaśatrusūtra;* for a more complete title, see the Bibliography.

214. *mtshams med pa'i las kyi sgrib pa*, literally, "karmic obstruction of immediate [retribution]". These are any of the five deeds of killing one's father, killing one's mother, killing a Foe Destroyer, causing blood to flow from the body of a Buddha with evil intent, and causing dissension in the spiritual community.

215. This is Dzong-ka-ba's *Essence of the Good Explanations*, the section identifying the main reasonings in the Consequence School. For Robert A.F. Thurman's translation, see his *Essence of True Eloquence*, p. 364.

216. *sa bcu pa'i mdo, daśabhūmika*. See chapter six in M. Honda, "An Annotated Translation of the 'Daśabhūmika' ", in D. Sinor, ed, *Studies in Southeast and Central Asia*, Śatapiṭaka Series 74. (New Delhi: 1968), pp. 115-276. For a brief discussion

of the ten samenesses, see *Meditation on Emptiness*, pp. 131-133.

217. This is the first stanza of the first chapter, not counting the expression of worship. Jang-gya gives merely the first line and "et cetera" (*sogs*).

218. VI.8-119.

219. For Robert A.F. Thurman's translation, see his *Essence of True Eloquence*, p. 365.

220. VI.160. The bracketed additions are drawn from Dzong-ka-ba, *Illumination of the Thought, Extensive Explanation of (Chandrakīrti's) "Supplement to (Nāgārjuna's) 'Treatise on the Middle Way' "* (*dbu ma la 'jug pa'i rgya cher bshad pa dgongs pa rab gsal*), (Dharamsala: Shes rig par khang edition, n.d.), 218.14-.19.

221. For Robert A.F. Thurman's translation, see his *Essence of True Eloquence*, p. 366.

222. Chandrakīrti's *Supplement to (Nāgārjuna's) "Treatise on the Middle Way"* VI.115. The bracketed additions are drawn from Dzong-ka-ba's *Illumination of the Thought*, 91.2-.6. Notice that Chandrakīrti speaks of cutting through the nets of *bad* views, not of all views in general.

223. *lam rim chung ngu*, P6002, Vol. 152-3. See "The Middle Transcendent Insight" in *Life and Teachings of Tsong Khapa*, Robert A.F. Thurman, ed. (Dharmsala, Library of Tibetan Works and Archives, 1982), pp. 131-135.

224. The text (424.5) reads "in common" (*thun mong du*) which means that the reasoning of dependent-arising refutes a self of *both* persons and phenomena, and thus it has been translated this way.

225. With respect to the term for "diamond fragments", *rdo rje gzegs ma*, Kensur Lekden (1900-1971), an abbot of the Tantric College of Lower Hla-ša, said that this reasoning is called the "diamond fragments" because each of the four reasons is capable of overcoming a conception of inherent existence just as a piece of a diamond has the hardness and so forth of a diamond. Thus, *gzegs ma* (*kaṇā*) means "piece"; hence my earlier translation as "sliver" is perhaps insufficient because it could suggest a weak, thin piece and not a fully functioning fragment. According to Apte, the Sanskrit term also means "facet"; this would seem to be most appropriate when speaking of diamonds (and more appropriate to the meaning since each of the four reasons alone actually is not capable¯ of refuting inherent existence); however,

none of my Tibetan sources, oral or written, has explained it this way. The oral traditions that I have contacted are by no means always accurate; nevertheless, when put together, the various oral strains are quite full, and no Tibetan scholar to date has given this interpretation (one said that *gzegs ma* refers to the points of a vajra). As mentioned above, a problem with the interpretation as fully functioning fragments is that each the four parts of the reasoning, taken alone, cannot refute inherent existence although it appears that the second of the four can.

226. I.1.

227. This section on positive and negative theses is drawn from *Meditation on Emptiness*, pp. 472-473; the material there is drawn from Jam-yang-shay-ba's *Great Exposition of the Middle Way*, 273b.1-2, and from Dzong-ka-ba's *Great Exposition of the Stages of the Path*, P6001, Vol. 152 156.2.2ff.

228. VI.8c-9b. P5262, vol. 98 101.3.4. For Chandrakīrti's own commentary, see P5263, vol. 98 120.3.4ff. Louis de la Vallée Poussin's translation of the section on production from self is in *Muséon*, n.s., v.11, pp. 280.4.

229. Tenzin Gyatso, *The Buddhism of Tibet and The Key to the Middle Way*, p. 68.

230. In the Varanasi codex edition (425.-4) read *pas myu gu myu gu* for *pas myu gu* in accordance with the Nam-gyel edition (468.1).

231. *rang bzhin, prakṛti*.

232. *rnam rol, līla*. "Sport" or "play" here does not carry the sense that emptiness somehow enjoys its "manifestations".

233. *Practice and Theory of Tibetan Buddhism*, p. 41.

234. For these reasonings, see *Meditation on Emptiness*, pp. 640-643, 58, and 136-139.

235. Chandrakīrti's *Supplement to (Nāgārjuna's) "Treatise on the Middle Way"*, VI.32. Louis de la Vallée Poussin's translation of the section on production from other is in *Muséon*, n.s., v.11, p. 309.

236. Dzong-ka-ba's *Illumination of the Thought*, 113, last line.

237. XX 20cd. This is quoted in Chandrakīrti's *Autocommentary on the "Supplement to (Nāgārjuna's) 'Treatise on the Middle Way'"*, commenting on VI.14ab. For more on the reasonings refuting production from other, see *Meditation on Emptiness*, pp. 643-648, 58, 140-148.

238. Chandrakīrti's *Supplement to (Nāgārjuna's) "Treatise on the Middle Way"*, VI.14. Louis de la Vallée Poussin's translation of the section on production from other is in *Muséon*, n.s., v.11, p. 286ff.

239. VI.19d.

240. In the Varanasi codex edition (427.20) read *phra la don* for *bral don* in accordance with the Nam-gyel edition (470.3).

241. VI.32d.

242. Nāgārjuna's *Precious Garland*, 48a.

243. VI.98ab. Louis de la Vallée Poussin's translation is in *Muséon*, n.s., v.12, p. 256, which misnumbers the two lines as 95ab.

244. For a discussion of the names of this school, etc., see *Meditation on Emptiness*, pp. 327-330.

245. Chandrakīrti's *Supplement to (Nāgārjuna's) "Treatise on the Middle Way"*, VI.99. Louis de la Vallée Poussin's translation is in *Muséon*, n.s., v. 12, p. 239.

246. The text (429.2) gives just the first line and "etc."

247. For a discussion of Jam-ȳang-shay-ba's emphasis on the introductory and concluding remarks, see *Meditation on Emptiness*, p. 461; for a discussion of the general topic, see pp. 441-530.

248. *mtha' bzhi skye 'gog.*

249. *rdo rje gzegs ma.*

250. *yod med skye 'gog.*

251. *mu bzhi skye 'gog.*

252. *snang yul.*

253. *rab tu byed pa lag pa'i tshad kyi tshig le'ur byas pa, hastavā-laprakaraṇakārikā.* For speculation on the title, see *Meditation on Emptiness*, p. 863 n. 519.

254. For discussion of this reasoning, see *Meditation on Emptiness*, pp. 63-64, 155-160, and 653-658.

255. *rkyen*, usually translated as "conditions".

256. See *Meditation on Emptiness*, pp. 61-63, 151-154, and 651-653.

257. *dmigs yul.*

258. *snang yul.*

259. *zhen yul.*

260. For the evidence that Jam-ȳang-shay-ba cites for this claim that Autonomists do indeed assert this, see *Meditation on Emptiness*, pp. 695-696.

261. XXII.1. See *Meditation on Emptiness*, p. 688.
262. *gang zag, pudgala.*
263. See *Meditation on Emptiness*, p. 177.
264. *mu stegs pa, tīrthika.*
265. See n. 138.
265a. VI.151; Poussin's translation is in *Muséon*, n.s. v. 12, p. 316. Brackets are from Dzong-ka-ba's *Illumination of the Thought*, P6143, vol. 154 90.2.4ff. Chandrakīrti's own commentary is P5263, vol. 98 146.4.1ff.
266. Tenzin Gyatso, *The Buddhism of Tibet and The Key to the Middle Way* (London: George Allen and Unwin, 1975), pp. 55-56.
267. *yan lag can.*
268. *yan lag 'dus pa tsam.*
269. VI.158. Louis de la Vallée Poussin's translation is in *Muséon*, n.s., v. 12, p. 320. Dzong-ka-ba's *Illumination of the Thought* is 216, last line.
270. In the Varanasi codex edition (435.2) read *gseb* for *gsed* in accordance with the Nam-gyel edition (478.1).
271. See *Meditation on Emptiness*, pp. 695-696. The "evidence" for Bhāvaviveka's asserting that conventionally phenomena are established by way of their own character is limited to a few rather tenuous indications. I hope elsewhere to go into the tenuousness of the evidence in detail.
272. In commentary prior to VI.160.
273. For Robert Thurman's translation of this passage, see his "The Middle Transcendent Insight" in *Life and Teachings of Tsong Khapa*, p. 129.
274. Still, in order to prove some of the reasons that make up the sevenfold reasoning, it seems that you have to know that *phenomena* are selfless. For example, when you prove that the mere collection of the aggregates is not the person, it seems that you have to understand that this mere collection is not established by way of its own character. That itself means that you understand the selflessness with respect to a phenomenon other than a person since the collection of our own mental and physical aggregates is not us, is not a person.

Some scholars try to get around all of this by saying that to understand the selflessness of phenomena does not mean just to understand the selflessness of any phenomenon, but that you *first* understand the selflessness of persons and then turn your mind to some other phenomenon and understand its selflessness. Thus, although you might first understand the selflessness of some phenomenon other than the person, such as a chariot, this is not called a cognition of an emptiness of a phenomenon since the latter occurs only after the emptiness of persons has been cognized.

275. Nga-w̄ang-l̄o-sang-gya-tso (*ngag dbang blo bzang rgya mtsho*, 1617-1682), Dalai Lama V, *Instruction on the Stages of the Path to Enlightenment, Sacred Word of Mañjushrī* (*byang chub lam gyi rim pa'i khrid yig 'jam pa'i dbyangs kyi zhal lung*), (Thimphu: kun-bzang-stobs-rgyal, 1976), 182.5-210.6. For an English translation, see J. Hopkins, "Practice of Emptiness", (Dharamsala: Library of Tibetan Works and Archives, 1974). For this citation, see p. 17.

276. Stanza 45:

> Having thought a mirage to be
> Water and then having gone there,
> One would just be stupid to surmise
> That [previously existent] water does not exist [now].

See Nāgārjuna and Kaysang Gyatso, *Precious Garland and the Song of the Four Mindfulnesses*, (London: George Allen and Unwin, 1975), p. 25.

277. Cited in Dalai Lama V, *Instruction on the Stages of the Path to Enlightenment, Sacred Word of Mañjushrī* in "Practice of Emptiness", p. 21.

278. XXVII.5.

279. VI.127ab. Louis de la Vallée Poussin's translation is in *Muséon*, n.s., v. 12, p. 292.

280. XVIII.lab.

281. VI.66.

282. *gzugs su rung ba;* see, for instance, Pur-bu-jok (*phur bu lcog byams pa rgya mtsho*, 1825-1901), *Explanation of the Lesser Path of Reasoning (rigs lam chung ngu'i rnam par bshad pa)* in the *Magical Key to the Path of Reasoning, Presentation of the Collected Topics Revealing the Meaning of the Treatises on Valid Cognition (tshad ma'i gzhung don 'byed pa'i bsdus grva'i rnam bzhag rigs lam 'phrul gyi sde mig)*, (Buxa India: n.p., 1965). For an English translation, see Daniel E. Perdue, "Practice and Theory of Philo-

sophical Debate in Tibetan Buddhist Education" (Ann Arbor: University Microfilms, 1983).

283. XVIII.1cd.

284. XXVII.7cd.

285. In the Varanasi codex edition (438.16) read *zhib tu* for *zhig tu* in accordance with the Nam-gyel edition (482.1).

286. See *Meditation on Emptiness*, pp. 545-546.

287. VI.158. Louis de la Vallée Poussin's translation is in *Muséon*, n.s., v. 12, p. 320. Dzong-ka-ba's *Illumination of the Thought* is 216, last line. See chapter fifteen, p. 245.

288. In the Varanasi codex edition (439.19) read *tshabs* for *che pas* in accordance with the Nam-gyel edition (483.3).

289. *Explanation of (Shāntideva's) "Engaging in the Bodhisattva Deeds": Entrance of Conqueror Children (byang chub sems dpa'i spyod pa la 'jug pa'i rnam bshad rgyal sras 'jug ngogs)*, (Varanasi: 1973), at the end of chapter IX, 280.6. This and the other three citations from this text were located by Geshe Thupten Gyatso of the Tibetan Buddhist Learning Center, Washington, New Jersey.

290. Nāgārjuna, Āryadeva, Asaṅga, Vasubandhu, Dignāga and Dharmakīrti.

291. *Explanation of (Shāntideva's) "Engaging in the Bodhisattva Deeds"*, at the end of the book, 295.4.

292. In the Varanasi codex edition (441.10) read *'di* for *bdi* in accordance with the Nam-gyel edition (485.1).

293. *Explanation of (Shāntideva's) "Engaging in the Bodhisattva Deeds"*, at the end of chapter IX, 280.11.

294. In the Varanasi codex edition (441.8) read *go 'phang* for *go 'thang* in accordance with the Nam-gyel edition (485.1).

295. *Explanation of (Shāntideva's) "Engaging in the Bodhisattva Deeds"*, at the end of chapter IX, 280.13.

296. In the Varanasi codex edition (441.17) read *thal 'gyur ba'i* for *thal 'gyur ba'i ba'i* in accordance with the Nam-gyel edition (485.4).

297. XVIII.2ab.

298. For a discussion of differing interpretations of "mine", see *Meditation on Emptiness*, n. 739, pp. 888-890.

299. For Jam-yang-shay-ba's presentation, see *Meditation on Emptiness*, pp. 678-681.

300. *gdags gzhi*.

301. *mtshan gzhi*.

302. See *Meditation on Emptiness*, pp. 680-681.

303. See *Meditation on Emptiness*, p. 679.

304. VI.167. Louis de la Vallée Poussin's translation ends with VI.165.

305. Dzong-ka-ba, as cited in Jam-yang-shay-ba's *Great Exposition of the Middle Way* (477a.1) identifies *chags pa (rakta)* in this context as referring to the mind or person that is desirous of an object — that which is made impassioned by passion, i.e., the impassioned.

306. "Illustration" (*mtshan gzhi*) is *lakṣya* in Sanskrit, which is translated into Tibetan both as *mtshon bya* "definiendum" and *mtshan gzhi* "illustration", the latter being a basis in which the definition illustrates the definiendum. It seems to make no difference here whether the term is translated as "illustration" or "definiendum". I prefer the latter for broader symmetry but have deferred to the Tibetan translation and used "illustration".

307. Stanza 162. See Nāgārjuna and Kaysang Gyatso, *Precious Garland and the Song of the Four Mindfulnesses*, p. 41.

308. *blo gros rgya mtshos zhus pa, sāgaramatiparipṛcchā.*

309. The first stanza of his *Praise of Dependent-Arising (rten 'brel stod pa)*, the longer title being *Praise of the Supramundane Victor Buddha from the Approach of His Teaching the Profound Dependent-Arising, Essence of the Good Explanations (sangs rgyas bcom ldan 'das la zab mo rten cing 'grel bar 'byung ba gsung ba'i sgo nas bstod pa legs par bshad pa'i snying po)*, P6016, vol. 153.

310. In Tenzin Gyatso, *The Buddhism of Tibet and The Key to the Middle Way*, p. 82.

311. As is stated in n. 703, pp. 884-885, in *Meditation on Emptiness:*

> The Tibetan translators adopted a code for handling this three-part discussion of the formation of *pratītyasamutpāda:*
>
> *prati* = *rten cing*
> *i* or *itya* = *'brel bar*
> *samutpāda* = *'byung ba*
>
> Their overriding concern was with having a three-part translation equivalent that, when together, makes sense in Tibetan. As a result, the individual equivalents often

make no sense when associated with these various interpretations.

Some Tibetan scholars claim that *rten cing* and *'brel bar* have different meanings; however, since Chandrakīrti says that *prati* (*rten cing*), which itself means *prāpti* (*phrad pa*), modifies the meaning of *itya* (*'brel ba*) into meaning *prāpti* (*phrad pa*), the two words come to have just one meaning, and thus it seems that the two were separated out in Tibetan merely in order to convey, albeit not very well, this discussion of the meaning of the individual parts. Perhaps a better alternative would have been to transliterate the individual parts into Tibetan rather than attempt a translation.

In Chandrakīrti's interpretation, *pratītya* has just one meaning as a continuative meaning "having depended" which in Tibetan is *rten nas* as in the commonly used *rten nas 'byung ba* or *rten 'byung*. Strictly speaking, therefore, in Prāsaṅgika *rten nas 'byung ba* or *rten 'byung* is the most appropriate general term, with *rten cing 'brel bar 'byung ba* suitable only as a code equivalent for the three-part discussion. *rten 'brel* is a common usage that is neither.

There also is an oral teaching that I have heard only once that *rten byung* refers to the dependent-arising of impermanent things and *rten cing 'brel bar 'byung ba* refers also to the dependent-arising of permanent things. However, it seems to me that the reason for the longer version is only to provide separate syllables to represent each element of the discussion in Sanskrit.

It should be noted that the general translation of the word into Tibetan follows Chandrakīrti's understanding of it.

312. See *Meditation on Emptiness*, p. 666.

313. In modern Tibetan, *dgon pa'i til* would be a better translation of *araṇyetilaka* than *dgon pa'i thig le* since *til* is commonly used for "sesame".

314. The text reads "between having depended and eye" (*brten pa dang mig gi bar du*), which somehow must refer to *pratītya*.

315. Jam-ȳang-shay-ba forms the term in considerable detail in order to show how *pratītya* is formed from the verbal root *i* as an indeclinable continuative. In brief, the continuative ending *ya* is substituted for *tvā*; this, in turn, calls for a *t* infix; with *prati*, this

yields *pratītya.* See *Meditation on Emptiness,* pp. 662-663.
316. P5225, Vol. 95 11.4.1.
317. For the shortcomings of the Tibetan translation of this line, see *Meditation on Emptiness,* n. 708 p. 885.
318. 48ab.
319. In the Varanasi codex edition (445.14) read *'di* for *'da* in accordance with the Nam-gyel edition (489.4).
320. In the Varanasi codex edition (445.17) read *phyir ro* for *phyi ro* in accordance with the Nam-gyel edition (489.5).
321. *rten nas 'byung ba, pratītyasamutpāda; 'phrad nas 'byung ba, prāpyasamutpāda; bltos nas 'byung ba, apekṣayasamutpāda.* See *Meditation on Emptiness,* pp. 166, 659, 674-675.
322. Avalokitavrata, *Commentary on (Bhāvaviveka's) "Lamp for (Nāgārjuna's) 'Wisdom' ",* P5259, vol. 96 170.2.1.
323. The Varanasi codex edition (445.18) and the Nam-gyel edition (489.6) both misread *la yab,* whereas it should read *lyap,* in accordance with the Lokesh Chandra edition, 719.5.
324. In the Varanasi codex edition (445.20) read *prati* for *brati* in accordance with the Nam-gyel edition (489.6).
325. In the Varanasi codex edition (446.12) read *'byung* for *'gyur* in accordance with the Nam-gyel edition (490.4).
326. *dngos po, bhāva.*
327. *grub pa, siddha.*
328. In the Varanasi codex edition (448.4) read *ma thon* for *mthon* in accordance with the Nam-gyel edition (492.2).
329. In the Varanasi codex edition (448.6) read *ma thon* for *mthon* in accordance with the Nam-gyel edition (492.3).
330. *Annotations for (Jam-yang-shay-ba's) "Great Exposition of Tenets", Freeing the Knots of the Difficult Points, Precious Jewel of Clear Thought,* dbu 156.2.
331. For Robert Thurman's translation, see "The Middle Transcendent Insight" in *Life and Teachings of Tsong Khapa,* pp. 144-145.
332. See two notes back.
333. Stanza 48.
334. VIII.12. It is difficult to determine whether the term *karma (las)* means action or object. The eighth chapter of Nāgārjuna's *Treatise on the Middle Way* can be read either way, but Dzong-ka-ba's *Ocean of Reasoning, Explanation of (Nāgārjuna's) "Treatise on the Middle Way"* glosses *las (karma)* with *bya ba* and

at the very end of his commentary on the second chapter he adapts VIII.12 to the examination of going, interpreting *las (karma)* as *'gro ba*, going *(gamanaṃ)*. For the latter, see "Analysis of Going and Coming", trans. J. Hopkins, (Dharamsala: Library of Tibetan Works and Archives, 1976), p. 34.

335. P5266, vol. 98 270.3.6, commenting on XIV.23.

336. *nor bzang rgya mtsho*, 1423-1513.

337. The text reads "The subject, uncompounded space, etc." The full statement of consequence is understood by those familiar with such debate and has thus been added.

338. In the Varanasi codex edition (450.13) read *rang ngor* for *rang dor* in accordance with the Nam-gyel edition (495.1).

339. In the Varanasi codex edition (451.2) read *khyad chos* for *khyad sbyor* in accordance with the Nam-gyel edition (495.4).

340. In the Varanasi codex edition (451.11) read *je zab* for *rje zab* in accordance with the Nam-gyel edition (496.1).

341. Shāntideva's *Engaging in the Bodhisattva Deeds*, IX.4ab; see Shāntideva, *Bodhicaryāvatāra*, ed. by Vidhushekhara Bhattacharya, Bibliotheca Indica Vol. 280, (Calcutta: The Asiatic Society, 1960), p. 185.

342. Dak-tsang Shay-rap-rin-chen, *Ocean of Good Explanations, Explanation of "Freedom From Extremes Through Understanding All Tenets"*, 247.6.

343. Jang-ğya, at the beginning of the section on the Middle Way School (301.4), says:

Dak-tsang divided [the teaching and the training] into the three stages of the non-analytical, slightly analytical, and very analytical and then described a view in which the earlier states are refuted by the later. [This description] is amazing because, instead of needing some other opponent to line up contradictions for one's tenets, he himself appears to destroy the presentation of the two truths that he himself posits.

Just before that, Jang-ğya says:

With the exception of the Jo-nang system and, later, the system of the view of the translator Dak-tsang Shay-rap-rin-chen, the instructions on the view of most of the early scholars and adepts each had an Indian scholar or adept as their source.

The above translations are adapted from Donald S. Lopez, Jr. in "The Svātantrika-Mādhyamika School of Mahāyāna Buddhism", (Ann Arbor: University Microfilms, 1982), pp. 405-406; Lopez's work is forthcoming from Snow Lion Publications.

In setting forth three phases, Dak-tsang (see 255.5) is interpreting such passages as that from Āryadeva's *Four Hundred* (VIII.15) which describes three phases of turning away from the non-meritorious, self, and all views. In Ge-luk, "self" in such a passage is interpreted as a self of persons or a coarse conception of self, and "all views" is interpreted as all *bad* views, the root of which is the conception of inherent existence. Does one eventually overcome all views or just all views of inherent existence? In the Ge-luk-ba interpretation, it is definitely just the view of inherent existence that must be overcome; the view of the emptiness of inherent existence must be gained and is never supplanted.

In any case, Dak-tsang presents refutations of Dzong-ka-ba's interpretation of the Consequence School, and this may be behind Jang-gya's suggestion, despite his otherwise broad-minded acceptance of other Tibetans' teachings, that Dak-tsang's three phase teaching and training is a fabrication. The issue, however, is by no means easy to settle.

344. In the Varanasi codex edition (451.17) read *nges pa'i* for *nge sa pa'i* in accordance with the Nam-gyel edition (496.3).

345. In the Varanasi codex edition (452.6) read *pir gyis* for *pari gyis* in accordance with the Nam-gyel edition (496.6).

346. In the Varanasi codex edition (452.12) read *ri mo'i* for *ri bo'i* in accordance with the Nam-gyel edition (497.2).

347. *gtugs* and *thug* are translated variously as "derive from" and "meet back to".

348. VI.114.

349. VI.158. Dzong-ka-ba's *Illumination of the Thought* is 216, last line.

350. For Robert Thurman's translation of this passage, see his *Tsong Khapa's Speech of Gold in the Essence of True Eloquence*, p. 365.

351. For Robert Thurman's translation of this passage, see his *Tsong Khapa's Speech of Gold in the Essence of True Eloquence*, p. 366.

352. Stanza 13. For commentary by the Dalai Lama, see his *Kindness, Clarity, and Insight* (Ithaca: Snow Lion, 1984), pp.

148-153. See also the Fourth Paṇchen Lama's commentary in Geshe Lhundup Sopa and Jeffrey Hopkins, *Practice and Theory of Tibetan Buddhism*, 1976), p. 43, as well as in Geshe Wangyal, *Door of Liberation* (New York: Lotsawa, 1978), pp. 126-60. For Dzong-ka-ba's text, see Robert Thurman, *Life and Teachings of Tsong Khapa* (Dharmsala, Library of Tibetan Works and Archives, 1982), pp. 57-8.

353. In the Varanasi codex edition (456.15) read *gzhan yang* for *gzhan gang* in accordance with the Nam-gyel edition (501.5).

354. *red mda' ba*, 1349-1412. The Śa-ḡya master Ren-da-wa was Dzong-ka-ba's teacher especially for the view of the Middle Way School.

355. In the Varanasi codex edition (457.5) read *rtogs tshe* for *rtogs cha* in accordance with the Nam-gyel edition (502.2).

356. *mngon sum, pratyakṣa*. For discussion of this, see Geshe Lhundup Sopa and Jeffrey Hopkins, *Practice and Theory of Tibetan Buddhism*, pp. 138-139.

Index

Absence. *See* Inherent existence, absence of; True existence, absence of
Achala, 26, 31
Action. *See* Agent
Affirming negative, 159, 185, 186, 384, 471
Affliction/ Afflictive emotion, 35, 37, 64, 70, 75, 149, 281, 301, 330, 418; true cessation of, 199, 200
Agent, 325, 108, 110, 171, 386; in the context of mere nominality, 98, 101, 157, 247, 326-27, 368, 369, 371, 397; in the context of dependent-arising, 313; in sevenfold reasoning, 225, 231, 276, 394, 402; of negation, 201; sprout as, 177, 178, 388
Aggregates, 62, 75, 76, 211, 300, 365; as the basis of designation of the person, 115, 118, 155, 211, 217, 222, 225, 269, 275, 283, 297, 343, 367-68, 393, 401-2, 423; as the "transitory collection," 112; in contemporary Buddhist meditation systems, 106; in Low Vehicle schools of tenets, 73-74; in the sevenfold reasoning, 213-25, 263-66, 269-

78, 280, 394, 398-403, 477; of the One Gone Thus, 212-213, 391; relationship between apprehension of I and apprehension of, 64-66, 97, 109, 113, 115-19, 126, 127, 149, 371-72, 374-75, 392, 466
Ajātashatru Sūtra, 147, 379, 457
Ajitamitra, 271
Alternatives, four, 154, 160, 193-94, 204-6, 382, 390
Altruism, 29, 35, 57, 121, 134, 142, 145, 260
Altruistic intention to become enlightened, 57, 121, 260
Am-do (*a mdo*) Province, 15, 16, 26, 449
Amban, 19, 20, 23, 27
Amitāyus, 28
Analysis of (Chandrakīrti's) "Supplement to (Nāgārjuna's) 'Treatise on the Middle Way' ", Treasury of Scripture and Reasoning, Thoroughly Illuminating the Profound Meaning [of Emptiness], Entrance for the Fortunate (Jam-ȳang-shay-ba). See *Great Exposition of the Middle Way* (Jam-ȳang-shay-ba)
"Analysis of Going and Coming"

synonym of "autonomous", 89, 366
Self-sufficient person, 53, 62-66, 68-70, 72-74, 109, 117, 125, 235, 250
Selflessness, 86, 137, 148; coarse, 125; meaning of, 76, 82; subtle, 62-63; three factors relating to, 75-76. *See also* Selflessness of persons; Selflessness of phenomena
Selflessness of persons, 37, 62-63, 68, 69, 72-74, 76, 82, 108-9, 148, 151-53, 154, 209, 249, 250, 284, 343, 364, 365, 380-82, 391, 423, 477.
Selflessness of phenomena, 62-63, 68, 69, 71, 74, 82, 140, 148, 150, 151, 153, 154, 249, 250, 364, 365, 377, 380-82, 477
Sense direct perception, 40, 287
Sentient beings, 221; altruisic motivation for the sake of, 29, 31, 56, 142, 144, 145, 254, 256, 378; in cyclic existence, 77, 346, 424; sufferings of, 141
Seven-limbed service, 289-90
Sevenfold reasoning, 205, 208, 338, 381-82, 390, 477; applied to mine, 293-97, 406-7; applied to phenomena other than persons, 407-8, 297-302; applying the example in, 263, 76, 398; background of, 209-23, 392-93; brief explanation of, 151-53; comments on, 249-63; easiest for beginners, 194; example of a chariot in, 224-48, 394-98; meets back to dependent-arising, 339, 343, 421-23; refutation of difference of self and aggregates in, 268-73, 400-401; refutation of last five positions in, 401-4; refutation of oneness of self and aggregates in, 264-68, 398-400
Seventh Dalai Lama, 18, 19, 20, 21, 22, 23, 24, 26, 32

Shakabpa, Tsepon W. D., 449
Shākyamuni Buddha, 26, 36, 213, 449
Shāntarakṣhita, 69, 424
Shāntideva, 34, 75, 101, 124, 137, 249, 288, 290, 334, 365, 369, 373, 376, 405, 419, 458; *Engaging in the Bodhisattva Deeds*, 208, 390, 457, 479, 483
Shi-jay-ba (*zhi byed pa*) School, 18
Shibayama Roshi, 298
Ship For Entering the Ocean of Tenets (Ge-dun-gya-tso), 439, 459
Short (in relation to long), 311, 323, 324, 412, 416
Shūra, 60, 363, 457, 458, 465. *See also* Ashvaghoṣha
Shūraṅgama Sūtra, 28
Signlessness, 133, 140, 375, 377
Sixty Stanzas of Reasoning (Nāgārjuna), 125, 157, 306, 310, 312, 374, 410, 412, 457
Sky-flower (example), 270, 400
Sleep, 132, 136, 195, 285, 376
Slightly hidden objects of comprehension, 139
Slogan (*gtam*), 307
Small Exposition of the Stages of the Path to Enlightenment (Dzong-ka-ba), 154, 155, 289, 320-22, 382, 404, 415, 456, 457
Smith, E. Gene, 17, 33, 448-51, 453
Snake (example), 53, 90, 91, 96-98, 149, 247, 340, 367, 368, 470
Snellgrove, David L., 20, 21, 451
Snow (example), 130, 213, 214, 236, 455, 470, 484
Solitary Realizer, 69, 75, 124, 136, 365, 374
Song of the View (Jang-gya), 27
Sources, true, 199
Space, 103, 110, 185, 371
Special insight, 43, 140, 249, 328, 352, 377, 417, 428
Spiritual community, 36, 199, 200, 473